The Java EE 7 Tutorial
Volume 1

Fifth Edition

The Java EE 7 Tutorial

Volume 1

Fifth Edition

Eric Jendrock
Ricardo Cervera-Navarro
Ian Evans
Kim Haase
William Markito

✦✦ Addison-Wesley

Upper Saddle River, NJ ● Boston ● Indianapolis ● San Francisco
New York ● Toronto ● Montreal ● London ● Munich ● Paris ● Madrid
Capetown ● Sydney ● Tokyo ● Singapore ● Mexico City

For information about buying this title in bulk quantities, or for special sales opportunities (which may include electronic versions; custom cover designs; and content particular to your business, training goals, marketing focus, or branding interests), please contact our corporate sales department at corpsales@pearsoned.com or at (800) 382-3419.

For government sales inquiries, please contact governmentsales@pearsoned.com.

For questions about sales outside the United States, please contact international@pearsoned.com.

Visit us on the Web: informit.com/aw

Library of Congress control Number: 2014933972

ISBN-13: 978-0-321-99492-9
ISBN-10: 0-321-99492-2
Text printed in the United States on recycled paper at Edwards Brothers Malloy in Ann Arbor, Michigan.
First printing, May 2014

Contents

7 JavaServer Faces Technology 87

8 Introduction to Facelets 111

10   Using JavaServer Faces Technology in Web Pages 157

13   Using Ajax with JavaServer Faces Technology 231

14 Composite Components: Advanced Topics and an Example 249

15 Creating Custom UI Components and Other Custom Objects 257

17 Java Servlet Technology 351

24   Running the Basic Contexts and Dependency Injection Examples 479

25 Contexts and Dependency Injection for Java EE: Advanced Topics 493

26 Running the Advanced Contexts and Dependency Injection Examples ... 511

Preface

This tutorial is a guide to developing enterprise applications for the Java Platform, Enterprise Edition 7 (Java EE 7), using GlassFish Server Open Source Edition.

GlassFish Server Open Source Edition is the leading open-source and open-community platform for building and deploying next-generation applications and services. GlassFish Server Open Source Edition, developed by the GlassFish project open-source community at `https://glassfish.java.net/`, is the first compatible implementation of the Java EE 7 platform specification. This lightweight, flexible, and open-source application server enables organizations not only to leverage the new capabilities introduced within the Java EE 7 specification, but also to add to their existing capabilities through a faster and more streamlined development and deployment cycle. GlassFish Server Open Source Edition is hereafter referred to as GlassFish Server.

The following topics are addressed here:

- Audience
- Before You Read This Book
- Related Documentation
- The Oracle Accessibility Program
- Conventions
- Default Paths and File Names
- Acknowledgments

Audience

This tutorial is intended for programmers interested in developing and deploying Java EE 7 applications. It covers the technologies comprising the Java EE platform and describes how to develop Java EE components and deploy them on the Java EE Software Development Kit (SDK).

Before You Read This Book

Before proceeding with this book, you should have a good knowledge of the Java programming language. A good way to get to that point is to work through the Java Tutorials (http://docs.oracle.com/javase/tutorial/).

Related Documentation

The Java EE 7 Tutorial, Volume 2 covers Java EE 7 technologies and topics not included in this volume, including Enterprise JavaBeans, Java Persistence, the Java Message Service, security, and others. The volume concludes with three case studies that incorporate multiple Java EE 7 technologies.

The GlassFish Server documentation set describes deployment planning and system installation. To obtain documentation for GlassFish Server Open Source Edition, go to https://glassfish.java.net/docs/.

The Java EE 7 API specification can be viewed at http://docs.oracle.com/javaee/7/api/ and is also provided in the Java EE 7 SDK.

Additionally, the Java EE Specifications at http://www.oracle.com/technetwork/java/javaee/tech/ might be useful.

For information about creating enterprise applications in the NetBeans Integrated Development Environment (IDE), see https://netbeans.org/kb/.

For information about the Java DB database for use with GlassFish Server, see http://www.oracle.com/technetwork/java/javadb/overview/.

The GlassFish Samples project is a collection of sample applications that demonstrate a broad range of Java EE technologies. The GlassFish Samples are bundled with the Java EE Software Development Kit (SDK) and are also available from the GlassFish Samples project page at https://glassfish-samples.java.net/.

The Oracle Accessibility Program

For information about Oracle's commitment to accessibility, visit the Oracle Accessibility Program website at `http://www.oracle.com/pls/topic/lookup?ctx=acc&id=docacc`.

Conventions

The following table describes the typographic conventions that are used in this book.

Convention	Meaning	Example
Boldface	Boldface type indicates graphical user interface elements associated with an action or terms defined in text.	From the **File** menu, choose **Open Project**. A **cache** is a copy that is stored locally.
`Monospace`	Monospace type indicates the names of files and directories, commands within a paragraph, URLs, code in examples, text that appears on the screen, or text that you enter.	Edit your `.login` file. Use `ls -a` to list all files. `machine_name% you have mail.`
Italic	Italic type indicates book titles, emphasis, or placeholder variables for which you supply particular values.	Read Chapter 6 in the *User's Guide*. Do *not* save the file. The command to remove a file is `rm` *filename*.

Default Paths and File Names

The following table describes the default paths and file names that are used in this book.

Placeholder	Description	Default Value
as-install	Represents the base installation directory for GlassFish Server or the SDK of which GlassFish Server is a part.	Installations on the Solaris operating system, Linux operating system, and Mac operating system: *user's-home-directory*`/glassfish4/glassfish` Windows, all installations: *SystemDrive*`:\glassfish4\glassfish`

Placeholder	Description	Default Value
as-install-parent	Represents the parent of the base installation directory for GlassFish Server.	Installations on the Solaris operating system, Linux operating system, and Mac operating system: *user's-home-directory*/`glassfish4` Windows, all installations: *SystemDrive*:`\glassfish4`
tut-install	Represents the base installation directory for the *Java EE Tutorial* after you install GlassFish Server or the SDK and run the Update Tool.	*as-install-parent*/`docs`/`javaee-tutorial`
domain-dir	Represents the directory in which a domain's configuration is stored.	*as-install*/`domains`/`domain1`

Acknowledgments

The Java EE tutorial team would like to thank the Java EE specification leads: Linda DeMichiel, Bill Shannon, Emmanuel Bernard, Ed Burns, Shing Wai Chan, Kin-Man Chung, Danny Coward, Nigel Deakin, Rod Johnson, Roger Kitain, Jitendra Kotamraju, Anthony Lai, Bob Lee, Ron Monzillo, Rajiv Mordani, Pete Muir, Paul Parkinson, Santiago Pericas-Geertsen, Marek Potociar, Sivakumar Thyagarajan, Marina Vatkina, and Chris Vignola.

We would also like to thank the Java EE 7 SDK team, especially Snjezana Sevo-Zenzerovic, Adam Leftik, Michael Chen, and John Clingan.

The JavaServer Faces technology chapters benefited greatly from suggestions by Manfred Riem as well as by the spec leads.

We would like to thank our manager, Alan Sommerer, for his support and steadying influence.

We also thank Jordan Douglas and Dawn Tyler for developing and updating the illustrations. Edna Elle provided invaluable help with tools. Sheila Cepero helped smooth our path in many ways.

Finally, we would like to express our profound appreciation to Greg Doench, Elizabeth Ryan, Caroline Senay, and the production team at Addison-Wesley for graciously seeing our manuscript to publication.

Part I

Introduction

Part I introduces the platform, the tutorial, and the examples. This part contains the following chapters:

- Chapter 1, "Overview"
- Chapter 2, "Using the Tutorial Examples"

1

Overview

This chapter introduces you to Java EE enterprise application development. Here you will review development basics, learn about the Java EE architecture and APIs, become acquainted with important terms and concepts, and find out how to approach Java EE application programming, assembly, and deployment.

Developers today increasingly recognize the need for distributed, transactional, and portable applications that leverage the speed, security, and reliability of server-side technology. **Enterprise applications** provide the business logic for an enterprise. They are centrally managed and often interact with other enterprise software. In the world of information technology, enterprise applications must be designed, built, and produced for less money, with greater speed, and with fewer resources.

With the Java Platform, Enterprise Edition (Java EE), development of Java enterprise applications has never been easier or faster. The aim of the Java EE platform is to provide developers with a powerful set of APIs while shortening development time, reducing application complexity, and improving application performance.

The Java EE platform is developed through the Java Community Process (JCP), which is responsible for all Java technologies. Expert groups composed of interested parties have created Java Specification Requests (JSRs) to define the various Java EE technologies. The work of the Java Community under the JCP program helps to ensure Java technology's standards of stability and cross-platform compatibility.

The Java EE platform uses a simplified programming model. XML deployment descriptors are optional. Instead, a developer can simply enter the information as an **annotation** directly into a Java source file, and the Java EE server will configure the component at deployment and runtime. These annotations are

3

generally used to embed in a program data that would otherwise be furnished in a deployment descriptor. With annotations, you put the specification information in your code next to the program element affected.

In the Java EE platform, dependency injection can be applied to all resources a component needs, effectively hiding the creation and lookup of resources from application code. Dependency injection can be used in Enterprise JavaBeans (EJB) containers, web containers, and application clients. Dependency injection allows the Java EE container to automatically insert references to other required components or resources, using annotations.

This tutorial uses examples to describe the features available in the Java EE platform for developing enterprise applications. Whether you are a new or experienced enterprise developer, you should find the examples and accompanying text a valuable and accessible knowledge base for creating your own solutions.

The following topics are addressed here:

- Java EE 7 Platform Highlights
- Java EE Application Model
- Distributed Multitiered Applications
- Java EE Containers
- Web Services Support
- Java EE Application Assembly and Deployment
- Development Roles
- Java EE 7 APIs
- Java EE 7 APIs in the Java Platform, Standard Edition 7
- GlassFish Server Tools

1.1 Java EE 7 Platform Highlights

The most important goal of the Java EE 7 platform is to simplify development by providing a common foundation for the various kinds of components in the Java EE platform. Developers benefit from productivity improvements with more annotations and less XML configuration, more Plain Old Java Objects (POJOs), and simplified packaging. The Java EE 7 platform includes the following new features:

- New technologies, including the following:
  - Batch Applications for the Java Platform (see Section 1.8.21)
  - Concurrency Utilities for Java EE (see Section 1.8.20)
  - Java API for JSON Processing (JSON-P) (see Section 1.8.19)
  - Java API for WebSocket (see Section 1.8.18)
- New features for EJB components (see Section 1.8.1, "Enterprise JavaBeans Technology," for details)
- New features for servlets (see Section 1.8.2, "Java Servlet Technology," for details)
- New features for JavaServer Faces components (see Section 1.8.3, "JavaServer Faces Technology," for details)
- New features for the Java Message Service (JMS) (see Section 1.8.13, "Java Message Service API," for details)

1.2 Java EE Application Model

The Java EE application model begins with the Java programming language and the Java virtual machine. The proven portability, security, and developer productivity they provide form the basis of the application model. Java EE is designed to support applications that implement enterprise services for customers, employees, suppliers, partners, and others who make demands on or contributions to the enterprise. Such applications are inherently complex, potentially accessing data from a variety of sources and distributing applications to a variety of clients.

To better control and manage these applications, the business functions to support these various users are conducted in the middle tier. The middle tier represents an environment that is closely controlled by an enterprise's information technology department. The middle tier is typically run on dedicated server hardware and has access to the full services of the enterprise.

The Java EE application model defines an architecture for implementing services as multitier applications that deliver the scalability, accessibility, and manageability needed by enterprise-level applications. This model partitions the work needed to implement a multitier service into the following parts:

- The business and presentation logic to be implemented by the developer

- The standard system services provided by the Java EE platform

The developer can rely on the platform to provide solutions for the hard systems-level problems of developing a multitier service.

1.3 Distributed Multitiered Applications

The Java EE platform uses a distributed multitiered application model for enterprise applications. Application logic is divided into components according to function, and the application components that make up a Java EE application are installed on various machines depending on the tier in the multitiered Java EE environment to which the application component belongs.

Figure 1–1 shows two multitiered Java EE applications divided into the tiers described in the following list. The Java EE application parts shown in Figure 1–1 are presented in Section 1.3.2, "Java EE Components."

- Client-tier components run on the client machine.

- Web-tier components run on the Java EE server.

- Business-tier components run on the Java EE server.

- Enterprise information system (EIS)-tier software runs on the EIS server.

Although a Java EE application can consist of all tiers shown in Figure 1–1, Java EE multitiered applications are generally considered to be three-tiered applications because they are distributed over three locations: client machines, the Java EE server machine, and the database or legacy machines at the back end. Three-tiered applications that run in this way extend the standard two-tiered client-and-server model by placing a multithreaded application server between the client application and back-end storage.

Figure 1–1   Multitiered Applications

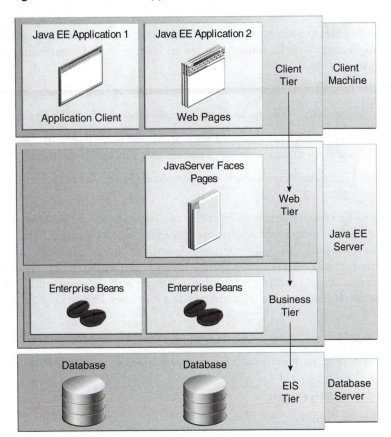

1.3.1 Security

Although other enterprise application models require platform-specific security measures in each application, the Java EE security environment enables security constraints to be defined at deployment time. The Java EE platform makes applications portable to a wide variety of security implementations by shielding application developers from the complexity of implementing security features.

The Java EE platform provides standard declarative access control rules that are defined by the developer and interpreted when the application is deployed on the server. Java EE also provides standard login mechanisms so that application developers do not have to implement these mechanisms in their applications. The same application works in a variety of security environments without changing the source code.

1.3.2 Java EE Components

Java EE applications are made up of components. A **Java EE component** is a self-contained functional software unit that is assembled into a Java EE application with its related classes and files and that communicates with other components.

The Java EE specification defines the following Java EE components:

- Application clients and applets are components that run on the client.

- Java Servlet, JavaServer Faces, and JavaServer Pages (JSP) technology components are web components that run on the server.

- EJB components (enterprise beans) are business components that run on the server.

Java EE components are written in the Java programming language and are compiled in the same way as any program in the language. The differences between Java EE components and "standard" Java classes are that Java EE components are assembled into a Java EE application, they are verified to be well formed and in compliance with the Java EE specification, and they are deployed to production, where they are run and managed by the Java EE server.

1.3.3 Java EE Clients

A Java EE client is usually either a web client or an application client.

1.3.3.1 Web Clients

A **web client** consists of two parts:

- Dynamic web pages containing various types of markup language (HTML, XML, and so on), which are generated by web components running in the web tier

- A web browser, which renders the pages received from the server

A web client is sometimes called a **thin client**. Thin clients usually do not query databases, execute complex business rules, or connect to legacy applications. When you use a thin client, such heavyweight operations are off-loaded to enterprise beans executing on the Java EE server, where they can leverage the security, speed, services, and reliability of Java EE server-side technologies.

1.3.3.2 Application Clients

An **application client** runs on a client machine and provides a way for users to handle tasks that require a richer user interface than can be provided by a markup language. An application client typically has a graphical user interface (GUI) created from the Swing API or the Abstract Window Toolkit (AWT) API, but a command-line interface is certainly possible.

Application clients directly access enterprise beans running in the business tier. However, if application requirements warrant it, an application client can open an HTTP connection to establish communication with a servlet running in the web tier. Application clients written in languages other than Java can interact with Java EE servers, enabling the Java EE platform to interoperate with legacy systems, clients, and non-Java languages.

1.3.3.3 Applets

A web page received from the web tier can include an embedded applet. Written in the Java programming language, an **applet** is a small client application that executes in the Java virtual machine installed in the web browser. However, client systems will likely need the Java Plug-in and possibly a security policy file for the applet to successfully execute in the web browser.

Web components are the preferred API for creating a web client program because no plug-ins or security policy files are needed on the client systems. Also, web components enable cleaner and more modular application design because they provide a way to separate applications programming from web page design. Personnel involved in web page design thus do not need to understand Java programming language syntax to do their jobs.

1.3.3.4 The JavaBeans Component Architecture

The server and client tiers might also include components based on the JavaBeans component architecture (JavaBeans components) to manage the data flow between the following:

- An application client or applet and components running on the Java EE server

- Server components and a database

JavaBeans components are not considered Java EE components by the Java EE specification.

JavaBeans components have properties and have get and set methods for accessing those properties. JavaBeans components used in this way are typically simple in design and implementation but should conform to the naming and design conventions outlined in the JavaBeans component architecture.

1.3.3.5 Java EE Server Communications

Figure 1–2 shows the various elements that can make up the client tier. The client communicates with the business tier running on the Java EE server either directly or, as in the case of a client running in a browser, by going through web pages or servlets running in the web tier.

Figure 1–2   Server Communication

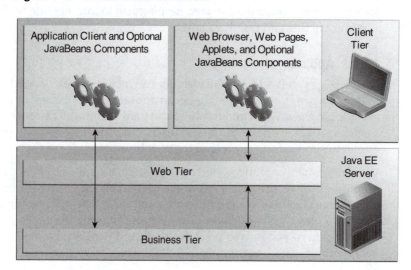

1.3.4 Web Components

Java EE web components are either servlets or web pages created using JavaServer Faces technology and/or JSP technology (JSP pages). **Servlets** are Java programming language classes that dynamically process requests and construct responses. **JSP pages** are text-based documents that execute as servlets but allow a more natural approach to creating static content. **JavaServer Faces technology** builds on servlets and JSP technology and provides a user interface component framework for web applications.

Static HTML pages and applets are bundled with web components during application assembly but are not considered web components by the Java EE specification. Server-side utility classes can also be bundled with web components and, like HTML pages, are not considered web components.

As shown in Figure 1–3, the web tier, like the client tier, might include a JavaBeans component to manage the user input and send that input to enterprise beans running in the business tier for processing.

Figure 1–3   Web Tier and Java EE Applications

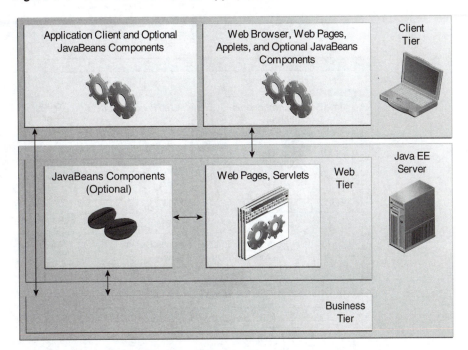

1.3.5 Business Components

Business code, which is logic that solves or meets the needs of a particular business domain such as banking, retail, or finance, is handled by enterprise beans running in either the business tier or the web tier. Figure 1–4 shows how an enterprise bean receives data from client programs, processes it (if necessary), and sends it to the enterprise information system tier for storage. An enterprise bean also retrieves data from storage, processes it (if necessary), and sends it back to the client program.

Figure 1–4   Business and EIS Tiers

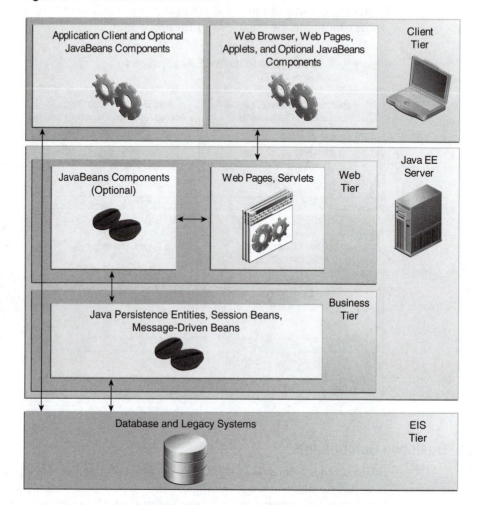

1.3.6 Enterprise Information System Tier

The enterprise information system tier handles EIS software and includes
enterprise infrastructure systems, such as enterprise resource planning (ERP),
mainframe transaction processing, database systems, and other legacy
information systems. For example, Java EE application components might need
access to enterprise information systems for database connectivity.

1.4 Java EE Containers

Normally, thin-client multitiered applications are hard to write because they involve many lines of intricate code to handle transaction and state management, multithreading, resource pooling, and other complex low-level details. The component-based and platform-independent Java EE architecture makes applications easy to write because business logic is organized into reusable components. In addition, the Java EE server provides underlying services in the form of a container for every component type. Because you do not have to develop these services yourself, you are free to concentrate on solving the business problem at hand.

1.4.1 Container Services

Containers are the interface between a component and the low-level, platform-specific functionality that supports the component. Before it can be executed, a web, enterprise bean, or application client component must be assembled into a Java EE module and deployed into its container.

The assembly process involves specifying container settings for each component in the Java EE application and for the Java EE application itself. Container settings customize the underlying support provided by the Java EE server, including such services as security, transaction management, Java Naming and Directory Interface (JNDI) API lookups, and remote connectivity. Here are some of the highlights.

- The Java EE security model lets you configure a web component or enterprise bean so that system resources are accessed only by authorized users.

- The Java EE transaction model lets you specify relationships among methods that make up a single transaction so that all methods in one transaction are treated as a single unit.

- JNDI lookup services provide a unified interface to multiple naming and directory services in the enterprise so that application components can access these services.

- The Java EE remote connectivity model manages low-level communications between clients and enterprise beans. After an enterprise bean is created, a client invokes methods on it as if it were in the same virtual machine.

Because the Java EE architecture provides configurable services, components within the same application can behave differently based on where they are deployed. For example, an enterprise bean can have security settings that allow it a certain level of access to database data in one production environment and another level of database access in another production environment.

The container also manages nonconfigurable services, such as enterprise bean and servlet lifecycles, database connection resource pooling, data persistence, and access to the Java EE platform APIs (see Section 1.8, "Java EE 7 APIs").

1.4.2 Container Types

The **deployment** process installs Java EE application components in the Java EE containers, as illustrated in Figure 1–5.

Figure 1–5   Java EE Server and Containers

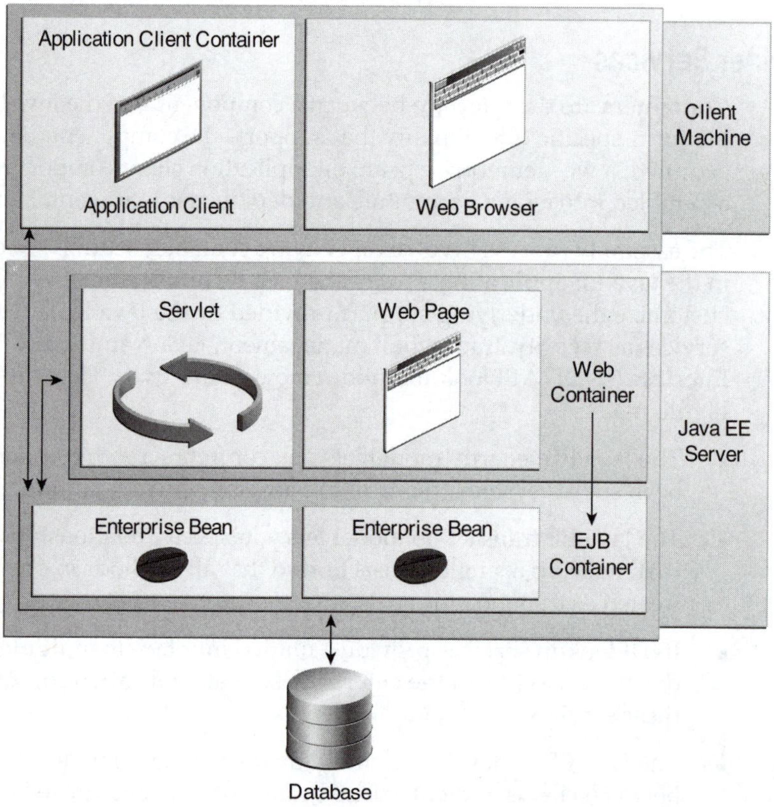

The server and containers are as follows:

- **Java EE server**: The runtime portion of a Java EE product. A Java EE server provides EJB and web containers.

- **EJB container**: Manages the execution of enterprise beans for Java EE applications. Enterprise beans and their container run on the Java EE server.

- **Web container**: Manages the execution of web pages, servlets, and some EJB components for Java EE applications. Web components and their container run on the Java EE server.

- **Application client container**: Manages the execution of application client components. Application clients and their container run on the client.

- **Applet container**: Manages the execution of applets. Consists of a web browser and a Java Plug-in running on the client together.

1.5 Web Services Support

Web services are web-based enterprise applications that use open, XML-based standards and transport protocols to exchange data with calling clients. The Java EE platform provides the XML APIs and tools you need to quickly design, develop, test, and deploy web services and clients that fully interoperate with other web services and clients running on Java-based or non-Java-based platforms.

To write web services and clients with the Java EE XML APIs, all you need to do is pass parameter data to the method calls and process the data returned; for document-oriented web services, you send documents containing the service data back and forth. No low-level programming is needed because the XML API implementations do the work of translating the application data to and from an XML-based data stream that is sent over the standardized XML-based transport protocols. These XML-based standards and protocols are introduced in the following sections.

The translation of data to a standardized XML-based data stream is what makes web services and clients written with the Java EE XML APIs fully interoperable. This does not necessarily mean that the data being transported includes XML tags, because the transported data can itself be plain text, XML data, or any kind of binary data, such as audio, video, maps, program files, computer-aided design (CAD) documents, and the like. The next section introduces XML and explains how parties doing business can use XML tags and schemas to exchange data in a meaningful way.

1.5.1 XML

Extensible Markup Language (XML) is a cross-platform, extensible, text-based standard for representing data. Parties that exchange XML data can create their own tags to describe the data, set up schemas to specify which tags can be used in a particular kind of XML document, and use XML style sheets to manage the display and handling of the data.

For example, a web service can use XML and a schema to produce price lists, and companies that receive the price lists and schema can have their own style sheets to handle the data in a way that best suits their needs. Here are examples.

- One company might put XML pricing information through a program to translate the XML into HTML so that it can post the price lists to its intranet.

- A partner company might put the XML pricing information through a tool to create a marketing presentation.

- Another company might read the XML pricing information into an application for processing.

1.5.2 SOAP Transport Protocol

Client requests and web service responses are transmitted as Simple Object Access Protocol (SOAP) messages over HTTP to enable a completely interoperable exchange between clients and web services, all running on different platforms and at various locations on the Internet. HTTP is a familiar request-and-response standard for sending messages over the Internet, and SOAP is an XML-based protocol that follows the HTTP request-and-response model.

The SOAP portion of a transported message does the following:

- Defines an XML-based envelope to describe what is in the message and explain how to process the message

- Includes XML-based encoding rules to express instances of application-defined data types within the message

- Defines an XML-based convention for representing the request to the remote service and the resulting response

1.5.3 WSDL Standard Format

The Web Services Description Language (WSDL) is a standardized XML format for describing network services. The description includes the name of the service, the location of the service, and ways to communicate with the service. WSDL service descriptions can be published on the Web. GlassFish Server provides a tool for generating the WSDL specification of a web service that uses remote procedure calls to communicate with clients.

1.6 Java EE Application Assembly and Deployment

A Java EE application is packaged into one or more standard units for deployment to any Java EE platform-compliant system. Each unit contains

- A functional component or components, such as an enterprise bean, web page, servlet, or applet

- An optional deployment descriptor that describes its content

Once a Java EE unit has been produced, it is ready to be deployed. Deployment typically involves using a platform's deployment tool to specify location-specific information, such as a list of local users who can access it and the name of the local database. Once deployed on a local platform, the application is ready to run.

1.7 Development Roles

Reusable modules make it possible to divide the application development and deployment process into distinct roles so that different people or companies can perform different parts of the process.

The first two roles, Java EE product provider and tool provider, involve purchasing and installing the Java EE product and tools. After the software is purchased and installed, Java EE components can be developed by application component providers, assembled by application assemblers, and deployed by application deployers. In a large organization, each of these roles might be executed by different individuals or teams. This division of labor works because each of the earlier roles outputs a portable file that is the input for a subsequent role. For example, in the application component development phase, an enterprise bean software developer delivers EJB JAR files. In the application assembly role, another developer may combine these EJB JAR files into a Java EE application and save it in an EAR file. In the application deployment role, a system administrator at the customer site uses the EAR file to install the Java EE application into a Java EE server.

The different roles are not always executed by different people. If you work for a small company, for example, or if you are prototyping a sample application, you might perform tasks in every phase.

1.7.1 Java EE Product Provider

The Java EE product provider is the company that designs and makes available for purchase the Java EE platform APIs and other features defined in the Java EE specification. Product providers are typically application server vendors that implement the Java EE platform according to the Java EE 7 platform specification.

1.7.2 Tool Provider

The tool provider is the company or person who creates development, assembly, and packaging tools used by component providers, assemblers, and deployers.

1.7.3 Application Component Provider

The application component provider is the company or person who creates web components, enterprise beans, applets, or application clients for use in Java EE applications.

1.7.3.1 Enterprise Bean Developer

An enterprise bean developer performs the following tasks to deliver an EJB JAR file that contains one or more enterprise beans:

- Writes and compiles the source code

- Specifies the deployment descriptor (optional)

- Packages the .class files and the deployment descriptor into the EJB JAR file

1.7.3.2 Web Component Developer

A web component developer performs the following tasks to deliver a WAR file containing one or more web components:

- Writes and compiles servlet source code

- Writes JavaServer Faces, JSP, and HTML files

- Specifies the deployment descriptor (optional)

- Packages the .class, .jsp, and .html files and the deployment descriptor into the WAR file

1.7.3.3 Application Client Developer

An application client developer performs the following tasks to deliver a JAR file containing the application client:

- Writes and compiles the source code

- Specifies the deployment descriptor for the client (optional)

- Packages the .class files and the deployment descriptor into the JAR file

1.7.4 Application Assembler

The application assembler is the company or person who receives application modules from component providers and may assemble them into a Java EE application EAR file. The assembler or deployer can edit the deployment descriptor directly or can use tools that correctly add XML tags according to interactive selections.

A software developer performs the following tasks to deliver an EAR file containing the Java EE application:

- Assembles EJB JAR and WAR files created in the previous phases into a Java EE application (EAR) file

- Specifies the deployment descriptor for the Java EE application (optional)

- Verifies that the contents of the EAR file are well formed and comply with the Java EE specification

1.7.5 Application Deployer and Administrator

The application deployer and administrator is the company or person who configures and deploys application clients, web applications, Enterprise JavaBeans components, and Java EE applications; administers the computing and networking infrastructure where Java EE components and applications run; and oversees the runtime environment. Duties include setting transaction controls and security attributes and specifying connections to databases.

During configuration, the deployer follows instructions supplied by the application component provider to resolve external dependencies, specify security settings, and assign transaction attributes. During installation, the deployer moves the application components to the server and generates the container-specific classes and interfaces.

A deployer or system administrator performs the following tasks to install and configure a Java EE application or Java EE components:

- Configures the Java EE application or components for the operational environment

- Verifies that the contents of the EAR, JAR, and/or WAR files are well formed and comply with the Java EE specification

- Deploys (installs) the Java EE application or components into the Java EE server

1.8 Java EE 7 APIs

Figure 1–6 shows the relationships among the Java EE containers.

Figure 1–6   Java EE Containers

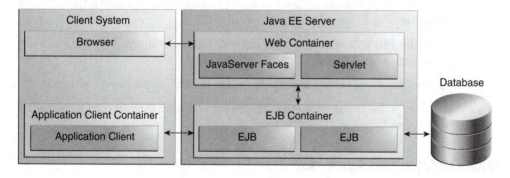

Figure 1–7 shows the availability of the Java EE 7 APIs in the web container.

Figure 1–7   Java EE APIs in the Web Container

Web Container	WebSocket	Java SE
	Concurrency Utilities	
	Batch	
	JSON-P	
	Bean Validation	
	EJB Lite	
	EL	
Servlet	JavaMail	
	JSP	
JavaServer Faces	Connectors	
	Java Persistence	
	JMS	
	Management	
	WS Metadata	
	Web Services	
	JACC	
	JASPIC	
	JAX-RS	
	JAX-WS	
	JSTL	
	JTA	
	CDI	
	Dependency Injection	

New in Java EE 7

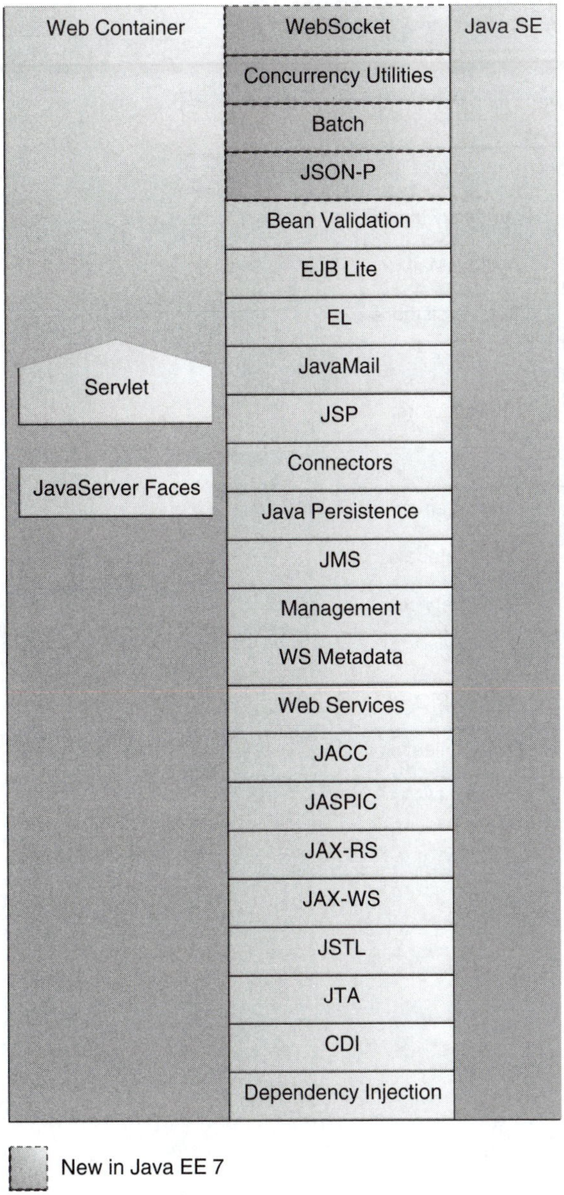

Figure 1–8 shows the availability of the Java EE 7 APIs in the EJB container.

Figure 1–8   Java EE APIs in the EJB Container

New in Java EE 7

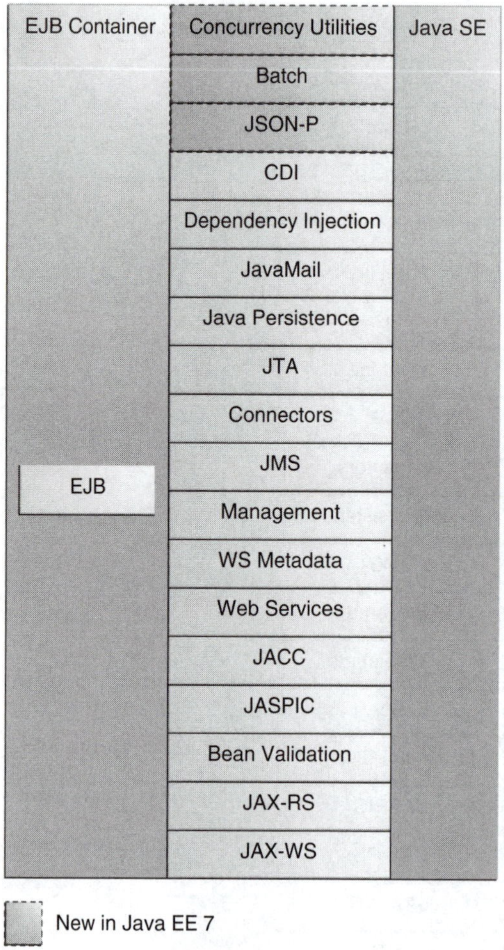

Figure 1–9 shows the availability of the Java EE 7 APIs in the application client container.

Figure 1–9 Java EE APIs in the Application Client Container

Application Client Container	Java Persistence	Java SE
	Management	
	WS Metadata	
	Web Services	
Application Client	JSON-P	
	JMS	
	JAX-WS	
	Bean Validation	
	JavaMail	
	CDI	
	Dependency Injection	

New in Java EE 7

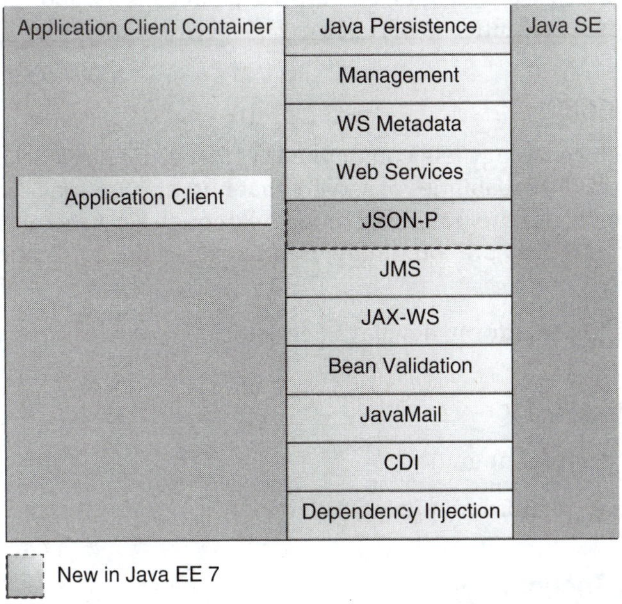

The following sections give a brief summary of the technologies required by the Java EE platform and the APIs used in Java EE applications.

1.8.1 Enterprise JavaBeans Technology

An **Enterprise JavaBeans (EJB) component**, or **enterprise bean**, is a body of code that has fields and methods to implement modules of business logic. You can think of an enterprise bean as a building block that can be used alone or with other enterprise beans to execute business logic on the Java EE server.

Enterprise beans are either session beans or message-driven beans.

- A **session bean** represents a transient conversation with a client. When the client finishes executing, the session bean and its data are gone.

- A **message-driven bean** combines features of a session bean and a message listener, allowing a business component to receive messages asynchronously. Commonly, these are Java Message Service (JMS) messages.

In the Java EE 7 platform, new enterprise bean features include the following:

- Asynchronous local session beans in EJB Lite
- Nonpersistent timers in EJB Lite

The Java EE 7 platform requires Enterprise JavaBeans 3.2 and Interceptors 1.2. The Interceptors specification is part of the EJB specification.

1.8.2 Java Servlet Technology

Java Servlet technology lets you define HTTP-specific servlet classes. A servlet class extends the capabilities of servers that host applications accessed by way of a request-response programming model. Although servlets can respond to any type of request, they are commonly used to extend the applications hosted by web servers.

In the Java EE 7 platform, new Java Servlet technology features include the following:

- Nonblocking I/O
- HTTP protocol upgrade

The Java EE 7 platform requires Servlet 3.1.

1.8.3 JavaServer Faces Technology

JavaServer Faces technology is a user interface framework for building web applications. The main components of JavaServer Faces technology are as follows:

- A GUI component framework.
- A flexible model for rendering components in different kinds of HTML or different markup languages and technologies. A `Renderer` object generates the markup to render the component and converts the data stored in a model object to types that can be represented in a view.
- A standard `RenderKit` for generating HTML 4.01 markup.

The following features support the GUI components:

- Input validation
- Event handling
- Data conversion between model objects and components
- Managed model object creation

- Page navigation configuration

- Expression Language (EL)

All this functionality is available using standard Java APIs and XML-based configuration files.

In the Java EE 7 platform, new features of JavaServer Faces technology include the following:

- HTML5-friendly markup

- Faces Flows

- Resource library contracts

The Java EE 7 platform requires JavaServer Faces 2.2 and Expression Language 3.0.

1.8.4 JavaServer Pages Technology

JavaServer Pages (JSP) technology lets you put snippets of servlet code directly into a text-based document. A JSP page is a text-based document that contains two types of text:

- Static data, which can be expressed in any text-based format, such as HTML or XML

- JSP elements, which determine how the page constructs dynamic content

For information about JSP technology, see the *The Java EE 5 Tutorial* at http://docs.oracle.com/javaee/5/tutorial/doc/.

The Java EE 7 platform requires JavaServer Pages 2.3 for compatibility with earlier releases but recommends the use of Facelets as the display technology in new applications.

1.8.5 JavaServer Pages Standard Tag Library

The JavaServer Pages Standard Tag Library (JSTL) encapsulates core functionality common to many JSP applications. Instead of mixing tags from numerous vendors in your JSP applications, you use a single, standard set of tags. This standardization allows you to deploy your applications on any JSP container that supports JSTL and makes it more likely that the implementation of the tags is optimized.

JSTL has iterator and conditional tags for handling flow control, tags for manipulating XML documents, internationalization tags, tags for accessing databases using SQL, and tags for commonly used functions.

The Java EE 7 platform requires JSTL 1.2.

1.8.6 Java Persistence API

The Java Persistence API (JPA) is a Java standards–based solution for persistence. Persistence uses an object/relational mapping approach to bridge the gap between an object-oriented model and a relational database. The Java Persistence API can also be used in Java SE applications outside of the Java EE environment. Java Persistence consists of the following areas:

- The Java Persistence API
- The query language
- Object/relational mapping metadata

The Java EE 7 platform requires Java Persistence API 2.1.

1.8.7 Java Transaction API

The Java Transaction API (JTA) provides a standard interface for demarcating transactions. The Java EE architecture provides a default auto commit to handle transaction commits and rollbacks. An auto commit means that any other applications that are viewing data will see the updated data after each database read or write operation. However, if your application performs two separate database access operations that depend on each other, you will want to use the JTA API to demarcate where the entire transaction, including both operations, begins, rolls back, and commits.

The Java EE 7 platform requires Java Transaction API 1.2.

1.8.8 Java API for RESTful Web Services

The Java API for RESTful Web Services (JAX-RS) defines APIs for the development of web services built according to the Representational State Transfer (REST) architectural style. A JAX-RS application is a web application that consists of classes packaged as a servlet in a WAR file along with required libraries.

The Java EE 7 platform requires JAX-RS 2.0.

1.8.9 Managed Beans

Managed Beans, lightweight container-managed objects (POJOs) with minimal requirements, support a small set of basic services, such as resource injection, lifecycle callbacks, and interceptors. Managed Beans represent a generalization of the managed beans specified by JavaServer Faces technology and can be used anywhere in a Java EE application, not just in web modules.

The Managed Beans specification is part of the Java EE 7 platform specification (JSR 342). The Java EE 7 platform requires Managed Beans 1.0.

1.8.10 Contexts and Dependency Injection for Java EE

Contexts and Dependency Injection for Java EE (CDI) defines a set of contextual services, provided by Java EE containers, that make it easy for developers to use enterprise beans along with JavaServer Faces technology in web applications. Designed for use with stateful objects, CDI also has many broader uses, allowing developers a great deal of flexibility to integrate different kinds of components in a loosely coupled but typesafe way.

The Java EE 7 platform requires CDI 1.1.

1.8.11 Dependency Injection for Java

Dependency Injection for Java defines a standard set of annotations (and one interface) for use on injectable classes.

In the Java EE platform, CDI provides support for Dependency Injection. Specifically, you can use injection points only in a CDI-enabled application.

The Java EE 7 platform requires Dependency Injection for Java 1.0.

1.8.12 Bean Validation

The Bean Validation specification defines a metadata model and API for validating data in JavaBeans components. Instead of distributing validation of data over several layers, such as the browser and the server side, you can define the validation constraints in one place and share them across the different layers.

The Java EE 7 platform requires Bean Validation 1.1.

1.8.13 Java Message Service API

The Java Message Service (JMS) API is a messaging standard that allows Java EE application components to create, send, receive, and read messages. It enables distributed communication that is loosely coupled, reliable, and asynchronous.

In the platform, new features of JMS include the following:

- A new, simplified API offers a simpler alternative to the previous API. This API includes a `JMSContext` object that combines the functions of a `Connection` and a `Session`.

- All objects with a `close` method implement the `java.lang.Autocloseable` interface so that they can be used in a Java SE 7 `try-with-resources` block.

The Java EE 7 platform requires JMS 2.0.

1.8.14 Java EE Connector Architecture

The Java EE Connector Architecture is used by tools vendors and system integrators to create resource adapters that support access to enterprise information systems that can be plugged in to any Java EE product. A **resource adapter** is a software component that allows Java EE application components to access and interact with the underlying resource manager of the EIS. Because a resource adapter is specific to its resource manager, a different resource adapter typically exists for each type of database or enterprise information system.

The Java EE Connector Architecture also provides a performance-oriented, secure, scalable, and message-based transactional integration of Java EE platform–based web services with existing EISs that can be either synchronous or asynchronous. Existing applications and EISs integrated through the Java EE Connector Architecture into the Java EE platform can be exposed as XML-based web services by using JAX-WS and Java EE component models. Thus JAX-WS and the Java EE Connector Architecture are complementary technologies for enterprise application integration (EAI) and end-to-end business integration.

The Java EE 7 platform requires Java EE Connector Architecture 1.7.

1.8.15 JavaMail API

Java EE applications use the JavaMail API to send email notifications. The JavaMail API has two parts:

- An application-level interface used by the application components to send mail

- A service provider interface

The Java EE platform includes the JavaMail API with a service provider that allows application components to send Internet mail.

The Java EE 7 platform requires JavaMail 1.5.

1.8.16 Java Authorization Contract for Containers

The Java Authorization Contract for Containers (JACC) specification defines a contract between a Java EE application server and an authorization policy provider. All Java EE containers support this contract.

The JACC specification defines `java.security.Permission` classes that satisfy the Java EE authorization model. The specification defines the binding of container-access decisions to operations on instances of these permission classes. It defines the semantics of policy providers that use the new permission classes to address the authorization requirements of the Java EE platform, including the definition and use of roles.

The Java EE 7 platform requires JACC 1.5.

1.8.17 Java Authentication Service Provider Interface for Containers

The Java Authentication Service Provider Interface for Containers (JASPIC) specification defines a service provider interface (SPI) by which authentication providers that implement message authentication mechanisms may be integrated in client or server message-processing containers or runtimes. Authentication providers integrated through this interface operate on network messages provided to them by their calling containers. The authentication providers transform outgoing messages so that the source of each message can be authenticated by the receiving container, and the recipient of the message can be authenticated by the message sender. Authentication providers authenticate each incoming message and return to their calling containers the identity established as a result of the message authentication.

The Java EE 7 platform requires JASPIC 1.1.

1.8.18 Java API for WebSocket

WebSocket is an application protocol that provides full-duplex communications between two peers over TCP. The Java API for WebSocket enables Java EE applications to create endpoints using annotations that specify the configuration parameters of the endpoint and designate its lifecycle callback methods.

The WebSocket API is new to the Java EE 7 platform. The Java EE 7 platform requires Java API for WebSocket 1.0.Clone Git cloud repository

1.8.19 Java API for JSON Processing

JSON is a text-based data exchange format derived from JavaScript that is used in web services and other connected applications. The Java API for JSON Processing

(JSON-P) enables Java EE applications to parse, transform, and query JSON data using the object model or the streaming model.

JSON-P is new to the Java EE 7 platform. The Java EE 7 platform requires JSON-P 1.0.

1.8.20 Concurrency Utilities for Java EE

Concurrency Utilities for Java EE is a standard API for providing asynchronous capabilities to Java EE application components through the following types of objects: managed executor service, managed scheduled executor service, managed thread factory, and context service.

Concurrency Utilities for Java EE is new to the Java EE 7 platform. The Java EE 7 platform requires Concurrency Utilities for Java EE 1.0.

1.8.21 Batch Applications for the Java Platform

Batch jobs are tasks that can be executed without user interaction. The Batch Applications for the Java Platform specification is a batch framework that provides support for creating and running batch jobs in Java applications. The batch framework consists of a batch runtime, a job specification language based on XML, a Java API to interact with the batch runtime, and a Java API to implement batch artifacts.

Batch Applications for the Java Platform is new to the Java EE 7 platform. The Java EE 7 platform requires Batch Applications for the Java Platform 1.0.

1.9 Java EE 7 APIs in the Java Platform, Standard Edition 7

Several APIs that are required by the Java EE 7 platform are included in the Java Platform, Standard Edition 7 (Java SE 7) and are thus available to Java EE applications.

1.9.1 Java Database Connectivity API

The Java Database Connectivity (JDBC) API lets you invoke SQL commands from Java programming language methods. You use the JDBC API in an enterprise bean when you have a session bean access the database. You can also use the JDBC API from a servlet or a JSP page to access the database directly without going through an enterprise bean.

The JDBC API has two parts:

- An application-level interface used by the application components to access a database
- A service provider interface to attach a JDBC driver to the Java EE platform

The Java SE 7 platform requires JDBC 4.1.

1.9.2 Java Naming and Directory Interface API

The Java Naming and Directory Interface (JNDI) API provides naming and directory functionality, enabling applications to access multiple naming and directory services, such as LDAP, DNS, and NIS. The JNDI API provides applications with methods for performing standard directory operations, such as associating attributes with objects and searching for objects using their attributes. Using JNDI, a Java EE application can store and retrieve any type of named Java object, allowing Java EE applications to coexist with many legacy applications and systems.

Java EE naming services provide application clients, enterprise beans, and web components with access to a JNDI naming environment. A **naming environment** allows a component to be customized without the need to access or change the component's source code. A container implements the component's environment and provides it to the component as a JNDI **naming context**.

The naming environment provides four logical namespaces: `java:comp`, `java:module`, `java:app`, and `java:global` for objects available to components, modules, or applications or shared by all deployed applications. A Java EE component can access named system-provided and user-defined objects. The names of some system-provided objects, such as a default JDBC `DataSource` object, a default JMS connection factory, and a JTA `UserTransaction` object, are stored in the `java:comp` namespace. The Java EE platform allows a component to name user-defined objects, such as enterprise beans, environment entries, JDBC `DataSource` objects, and messaging destinations.

A Java EE component can also locate its environment naming context by using JNDI interfaces. A component can create a `javax.naming.InitialContext` object and look up the environment naming context in `InitialContext` under the name `java:comp/env`. A component's naming environment is stored directly in the environment naming context or in any of its direct or indirect subcontexts.

1.9.3 JavaBeans Activation Framework

The JavaBeans Activation Framework (JAF) is used by the JavaMail API. JAF provides standard services to determine the type of an arbitrary piece of data, encapsulate access to it, discover the operations available on it, and create the appropriate JavaBeans component to perform those operations.

1.9.4 Java API for XML Processing

The Java API for XML Processing (JAXP), part of the Java SE platform, supports the processing of XML documents using Document Object Model (DOM), Simple API for XML (SAX), and Extensible Stylesheet Language Transformations (XSLT). JAXP enables applications to parse and transform XML documents independently of a particular XML-processing implementation.

JAXP also provides namespace support, which lets you work with schemas that might otherwise have naming conflicts. Designed to be flexible, JAXP lets you use any XML-compliant parser or XSL processor from within your application and supports the Worldwide Web Consortium (W3C) schema. You can find information on the W3C schema at `http://www.w3.org/XML/Schema`.

1.9.5 Java Architecture for XML Binding

The Java Architecture for XML Binding (JAXB) provides a convenient way to bind an XML schema to a representation in Java language programs. JAXB can be used independently or in combination with JAX-WS, in which case it provides a standard data binding for web service messages. All Java EE application client containers, web containers, and EJB containers support the JAXB API.

The Java EE 7 platform requires JAXB 2.2.

1.9.6 Java API for XML Web Services

The Java API for XML Web Services (JAX-WS) specification provides support for web services that use the JAXB API for binding XML data to Java objects. The JAX-WS specification defines client APIs for accessing web services as well as techniques for implementing web service endpoints. The Implementing Enterprise Web Services specification describes the deployment of JAX-WS-based services and clients. The EJB and Java Servlet specifications also describe aspects of such deployment. JAX-WS-based applications can be deployed using any of these deployment models.

The JAX-WS specification describes the support for message handlers that can process message requests and responses. In general, these message handlers execute in the same container and with the same privileges and execution context as the JAX-WS client or endpoint component with which they are associated. These message handlers have access to the same JNDI namespace as their associated component. Custom serializers and deserializers, if supported, are treated in the same way as message handlers.

The Java EE 7 platform requires JAX-WS 2.2.

1.9.7 SOAP with Attachments API for Java

The SOAP with Attachments API for Java (SAAJ) is a low-level API on which JAX-WS depends. SAAJ enables the production and consumption of messages that conform to the SOAP 1.1 and 1.2 specifications and the SOAP with Attachments note. Most developers do not use the SAAJ API, instead using the higher-level JAX-WS API.

1.9.8 Java Authentication and Authorization Service

The Java Authentication and Authorization Service (JAAS) provides a way for a Java EE application to authenticate and authorize a specific user or group of users to run it.

JAAS is a Java programming language version of the standard Pluggable Authentication Module (PAM) framework, which extends the Java platform security architecture to support user-based authorization.

1.9.9 Common Annotations for the Java Platform

Annotations enable a declarative style of programming in the Java platform.

The Java EE 7 platform requires Common Annotations for the Java Platform 1.2.

1.10 GlassFish Server Tools

GlassFish Server is a compliant implementation of the Java EE 7 platform. In addition to supporting all the APIs described in the previous sections, GlassFish Server includes a number of Java EE tools that are not part of the Java EE 7 platform but are provided as a convenience to the developer.

This section briefly summarizes the tools that make up GlassFish Server. Instructions for starting and stopping GlassFish Server, starting the Administration Console, and starting and stopping the Java DB server are in Chapter 2, "Using the Tutorial Examples."

GlassFish Server contains the tools listed in Table 1–1. Basic usage information for many of the tools appears throughout the tutorial. For detailed information, see the online help in the GUI tools.

Table 1–1   ***GlassFish Server Tools***

Tool	Description
Administration Console	A web-based GUI GlassFish Server administration utility. Used to stop GlassFish Server and to manage users, resources, and applications.
asadmin	A command-line GlassFish Server administration utility. Used to start and stop GlassFish Server and to manage users, resources, and applications.
appclient	A command-line tool that launches the application client container and invokes the client application packaged in the application client JAR file.
capture-schema	A command-line tool to extract schema information from a database, producing a schema file that GlassFish Server can use for container-managed persistence.
package-appclient	A command-line tool to package the application client container libraries and JAR files.
Java DB database	A copy of the Java DB server.
xjc	A command-line tool to transform, or bind, a source XML schema to a set of JAXB content classes in the Java programming language.
schemagen	A command-line tool to create a schema file for each namespace referenced in your Java classes.
wsimport	A command-line tool to generate JAX-WS portable artifacts for a given WSDL file. After generation, these artifacts can be packaged in a WAR file with the WSDL and schema documents, along with the endpoint implementation, and then deployed.
wsgen	A command-line tool to read a web service endpoint class and generate all the required JAX-WS portable artifacts for web service deployment and invocation.

2

Using the Tutorial Examples

This chapter tells you everything you need to know to install, build, and run the examples.

The following topics are addressed here:

- Required Software
- Starting and Stopping GlassFish Server
- Starting the Administration Console
- Starting and Stopping the Java DB Server
- Building the Examples
- Tutorial Example Directory Structure
- Java EE 7 Maven Archetypes in the Tutorial
- Getting the Latest Updates to the Tutorial
- Debugging Java EE Applications

2.1 Required Software

The following software is required to run the examples:

- Java Platform, Standard Edition (see Section 2.1.2)
- Java EE 7 Software Development Kit (see Section 2.1.1)
- Java EE 7 Tutorial Component (see Section 2.1.3)

- NetBeans IDE (see Section 2.1.4)

- Apache Maven (see Section 2.1.5)

2.1.1 Java EE 7 Software Development Kit

GlassFish Server Open Source Edition 4 is targeted as the build and runtime environment for the tutorial examples. To build, deploy, and run the examples, you need a copy of GlassFish Server and, optionally, NetBeans IDE. To obtain GlassFish Server, you must install the Java EE 7 Software Development Kit (SDK), which you can download from `http://www.oracle.com/technetwork/java/javaee/downloads/`. Make sure that you download the Java EE 7 SDK, not the Java EE 7 Web Profile SDK. There are distributions of the Java EE 7 SDK with and without the Java Platform, Standard Edition 7 Development Kit.

2.1.1.1 SDK Installation Tips

Do the following during the installation of the SDK.

- Allow the installer to download and configure the Update Tool. If you access the Internet through a firewall, provide the proxy host and port.

- Configure the GlassFish Server administration user name as `admin`, and specify no password. This is the default setting.

- Accept the default port values for the Admin Port (4848) and the HTTP Port (8080).

- Do not select the check box to create an operating system service for the domain.

You can leave the check box to start the domain after creation selected if you wish, but this is not required.

This tutorial refers to *as-install-parent*, the directory where you install GlassFish Server. For example, the default installation directory on Microsoft Windows is `C:\glassfish4`, so *as-install-parent* is `C:\glassfish4`. GlassFish Server itself is installed in *as-install*, the `glassfish` directory under *as-install-parent*. So on Microsoft Windows, *as-install* is `C:\glassfish4\glassfish`.

After you install GlassFish Server, add the following directories to your PATH to avoid having to specify the full path when you use commands:

```
as-install-parent/bin
as-install/bin
```

2.1.2 Java Platform, Standard Edition

To build, deploy, and run the examples, you need a copy of the Java Platform, Standard Edition 7 Development Kit (JDK 7). Some distributions of the Java EE 7 SDK include JDK 7. You can download JDK 7 software separately from `http://www.oracle.com/technetwork/java/javase/downloads/`.

2.1.3 Java EE 7 Tutorial Component

The tutorial example source is contained in the tutorial component. To obtain the tutorial component, use the Update Tool.

2.1.3.1 To Obtain the Tutorial Component Using the Update Tool

1. Start the Update Tool by performing one of the following actions.

   ■ From the command line, enter the command `updatetool`.

   ■ On a Windows system, from the Start menu, choose **All Programs**, then choose **Java EE 7 SDK**, then choose **Start Update Tool**.

2. Expand the **Java EE 7 SDK** node.

3. Select **Available Updates**.

4. From the list, select the **Java EE 7 Tutorial** check box.

5. Click **Install**.

6. Accept the license agreement.

   After installation, the Java EE 7 Tutorial appears in the list of installed components. The tool is installed in the *as-install-parent*/`docs`/ `javaee-tutorial` directory, which is referred to throughout the tutorial as *tut-install*. This directory contains two subdirectories: `docs` and `examples`. The `examples` directory contains subdirectories for each of the technologies discussed in the tutorial.

Next Steps

Updates to the Java EE 7 Tutorial are published periodically. For details on obtaining these updates, see Section 2.8, "Getting the Latest Updates to the Tutorial."

2.1.4 NetBeans IDE

The NetBeans integrated development environment (IDE) is a free, open-source IDE for developing Java applications, including enterprise applications. NetBeans

IDE supports the Java EE platform. You can build, package, deploy, and run the tutorial examples from within NetBeans IDE.

To run the tutorial examples, you need the latest version of NetBeans IDE. You can download NetBeans IDE from `https://netbeans.org/downloads/`. Make sure that you download the Java EE bundle.

2.1.4.1 To Install NetBeans IDE without GlassFish Server

When you install NetBeans IDE, do not install the version of GlassFish Server that comes with NetBeans IDE. To skip the installation of GlassFish Server, follow these steps.

1. On the first page of the NetBeans IDE Installer wizard, deselect the check box for GlassFish Server and click **OK**.

2. Accept both the License Agreement and the Junit License Agreement.

   A few of the tutorial examples use the Junit library, so you should install it.

3. Continue with the installation of NetBeans IDE.

2.1.4.2 To Add GlassFish Server as a Server Using NetBeans IDE

To run the tutorial examples in NetBeans IDE, you must add your GlassFish Server as a server in NetBeans IDE. Follow these instructions to add GlassFish Server to NetBeans IDE.

1. From the **Tools** menu, choose **Servers**.

2. In the Servers wizard, click **Add Server**.

3. Under **Choose Server**, select **GlassFish Server** and click **Next**.

4. Under **Server Location**, browse to the location of the Java EE 7 SDK and click **Next**.

5. Under **Domain Location**, select **Register Local Domain**.

6. Click **Finish**.

2.1.5 Apache Maven

Maven is a Java technology–based build tool developed by the Apache Software Foundation and is used to build, package, and deploy the tutorial examples. To run the tutorial examples from the command line, you need Maven 3.0 or higher. If you do not already have Maven, you can install it from:

```
http://maven.apache.org
```

Be sure to add the *maven-install*/bin directory to your path.

If you are using NetBeans IDE to build and run the examples, it includes a copy of Maven.

2.2 Starting and Stopping GlassFish Server

You can start and stop GlassFish Server using either NetBeans IDE or the command line.

2.2.1 To Start GlassFish Server Using NetBeans IDE

1. Click the **Services** tab.

2. Expand **Servers**.

3. Right-click the GlassFish Server instance and select **Start**.

2.2.2 To Stop GlassFish Server Using NetBeans IDE

To stop GlassFish Server using NetBeans IDE, right-click the GlassFish Server instance and select **Stop**.

2.2.3 To Start GlassFish Server Using the Command Line

To start GlassFish Server from the command line, open a terminal window or command prompt and execute the following:

```
asadmin start-domain --verbose
```

A **domain** is a set of one or more GlassFish Server instances managed by one administration server. The following elements are associated with a domain.

- **The GlassFish Server port number**: The default is 8080.

- **The administration server's port number**: The default is 4848.

- **An administration user name and password**: The default user name is admin, and by default no password is required.

You specify these values when you install GlassFish Server. The examples in this tutorial assume that you chose the default ports as well as the default user name and lack of password.

With no arguments, the start-domain command initiates the default domain, which is domain1. The --verbose flag causes all logging and debugging output to appear on the terminal window or command prompt. The output also goes into the server log, which is located in *domain-dir*/logs/server.log.

Or, on Windows, from the **Start** menu, choose **All Programs**, then choose **Java EE 7 SDK**, then choose **Start Application Server**.

2.2.4 To Stop GlassFish Server Using the Command Line

To stop GlassFish Server, open a terminal window or command prompt and execute:

```
asadmin stop-domain domain1
```

Or, on Windows, from the **Start** menu, choose **All Programs**, then choose **Java EE 7 SDK**, then choose **Stop Application Server**.

2.3 Starting the Administration Console

To administer GlassFish Server and manage users, resources, and Java EE applications, use the Administration Console tool. GlassFish Server must be running before you invoke the Administration Console. To start the Administration Console, open a browser at http://localhost:4848/.

Or, on Windows, from the **Start** menu, choose **All Programs**, then choose **Java EE 7 SDK**, then choose Administration Console.

2.3.1 To Start the Administration Console Using NetBeans IDE

1. Click the **Services** tab.

2. Expand **Servers**.

3. Right-click the GlassFish Server instance and select **View Domain Admin Console**.

   Note: NetBeans IDE uses your default web browser to open the Administration Console.

2.4 Starting and Stopping the Java DB Server

GlassFish Server includes the Java DB database server.

To start the Java DB server from the command line, open a terminal window or command prompt and execute:

```
asadmin start-database
```

To stop the Java DB server from the command line, open a terminal window or command prompt and execute:

```
asadmin stop-database
```

For information about the Java DB included with GlassFish Server, see `http://www.oracle.com/technetwork/java/javadb/overview/`.

2.4.1 To Start the Database Server Using NetBeans IDE

When you start GlassFish Server using NetBeans IDE, the database server starts automatically. If you ever need to start the server manually, however, follow these steps.

1. Click the **Services** tab.

2. Expand **Databases**.

3. Right-click **Java DB** and select **Start Server**.

Next Steps

To stop the database using NetBeans IDE, right-click **Java DB** and select **Stop Server**.

2.5 Building the Examples

The tutorial examples are distributed with a configuration file for either NetBeans IDE or Maven. Either NetBeans IDE or Maven may be used to build, package, deploy, and run the examples. Directions for building the examples are provided in each chapter.

2.6 Tutorial Example Directory Structure

To facilitate iterative development and keep application source files separate from compiled files, the tutorial examples use the Maven application directory structure.

Each application module has the following structure:

- `pom.xml`: Maven build file

- `src/main/java`: Java source files for the module

- `src/main/resources`: configuration files for the module, with the exception of web applications

- `src/main/webapp`: web pages, style sheets, tag files, and images (web applications only)

- `src/main/webapp/WEB-INF`: configuration files for web applications (web applications only)

When an example has multiple application modules packaged into an EAR file, its submodule directories use the following naming conventions:

- *example-name*-`app-client`: application clients

- *example-name*-`ejb`: enterprise bean JAR files

- *example-name*-`war`: web applications

- *example-name*-`ear`: enterprise applications

- *example-name*-`common`: library JAR containing components, classes, and files used by other modules

The Maven build files (`pom.xml`) distributed with the examples contain goals to compile and assemble the application into the `target` directory and deploy the archive to GlassFish Server.

2.7 Java EE 7 Maven Archetypes in the Tutorial

Some of the chapters have instructions on how to build an example application using Maven archetypes. **Archetypes** are templates for generating a particular Maven project. The Tutorial includes several Maven archetypes for generating Java EE 7 projects.

2.7.1 Installing the Tutorial Archetypes

You must install the included Maven archetypes into your local Maven repository before you can create new projects based on the archetypes. You can install the archetypes using NetBeans IDE or Maven.

2.7.1.1 Installing the Tutorial Archetypes Using NetBeans IDE

1. From the **File** menu, choose **Open Project**.

2. In the Open Project dialog box, navigate to:

   tut-install/examples

3. Select the archetypes folder.

4. Click **Open Project**.

5. In the **Projects** tab, right-click the archetypes project and select **Build**.

2.7.1.2 Installing the Tutorial Archetypes Using Maven

1. In a terminal window, go to:

   tut-install/examples/archetypes/

2. Enter the following command:

   mvn install

2.8 Getting the Latest Updates to the Tutorial

Check for any updates to the tutorial by using the Update Tool included with the Java EE 7 SDK.

2.8.1 To Update the Tutorial Using NetBeans IDE

1. Open the **Services** tab in NetBeans IDE and expand **Servers**.

2. Right-click the GlassFish Server instance and select **View Domain Update Center** to display the Update Tool.

3. Select **Available Updates** in the tree to display a list of updated packages.

4. Look for updates to the Java EE 7 Tutorial (javaee-tutorial) package.

5. If there is an updated version of the Tutorial, select **Java EE 7 Tutorial** (javaee-tutorial) and click **Install**.

2.8.2 To Update the Tutorial Using the Command Line

1. Open a terminal window and enter the following command to display the Update Tool:

   updatetool

2. Select **Available Updates** in the tree to display a list of updated packages.

3. Look for updates to the Java EE 7 Tutorial (javaee-tutorial) package.

4. If there is an updated version of the Tutorial, select **Java EE 7 Tutorial** (javaee-tutorial) and click **Install**.

2.9 Debugging Java EE Applications

This section explains how to determine what is causing an error in your application deployment or execution.

2.9.1 Using the Server Log

One way to debug applications is to look at the server log in *domain-dir*/logs/ server.log. The log contains output from GlassFish Server and your applications. You can log messages from any Java class in your application with System.out.println and the Java Logging APIs (documented at http://docs.oracle.com/javase/7/docs/technotes/guides/ logging/) and from web components with the ServletContext.log method.

If you use NetBeans IDE, logging output appears in the Output window as well as the server log.

If you start GlassFish Server with the --verbose flag, all logging and debugging output will appear on the terminal window or command prompt and the server log. If you start GlassFish Server in the background, debugging information is available only in the log. You can view the server log with a text editor or with the Administration Console log viewer.

2.9.1.1 To Use the Administration Console Log Viewer

1. Select the GlassFish Server node.

2. Click **View Log Files**.

   The log viewer opens and displays the last 40 entries.

3. To display other entries, follow these steps.

   a. Click **Modify Search**.

   b. Specify any constraints on the entries you want to see.

   c. Click **Search** at the top of the log viewer.

2.9.2 Using a Debugger

GlassFish Server supports the Java Platform Debugger Architecture (JPDA). With JPDA, you can configure GlassFish Server to communicate debugging information using a socket.

2.9.2.1 To Debug an Application Using a Debugger

1. Follow these steps to enable debugging in GlassFish Server using the Administration Console:

   a. Expand the **Configurations** node, then expand the **server-config** node.

   b. Select the **JVM Settings** node. The default debug options are set to:

   ```
   -agentlib:jdwp=transport=dt_socket,server=y,suspend=n,address=9009
   ```

   As you can see, the default debugger socket port is 9009. You can change it to a port not in use by GlassFish Server or another service.

   c. Select the **Debug Enabled** check box.

   d. Click **Save**.

2. Stop GlassFish Server and then restart it.

Part II

Platform Basics

Part II introduces platform basics. This part contains the following chapters:

- Chapter 3, "Resource Creation"
- Chapter 4, "Injection"
- Chapter 5, "Packaging"

3

Resource Creation

A resource is a program object that provides connections to such systems as database servers and messaging systems. Java EE components can access a wide variety of resources, including databases, mail sessions, Java Message Service objects, and URLs. The Java EE 7 platform provides mechanisms that allow you to access all these resources in a similar manner. This chapter examines several types of resources and explains how to create them.

The following topics are addressed here:

- Resources and JNDI Naming
- DataSource Objects and Connection Pools
- Creating Resources Administratively

3.1 Resources and JNDI Naming

In a distributed application, components need to access other components and resources, such as databases. For example, a servlet might invoke remote methods on an enterprise bean that retrieves information from a database. In the Java EE platform, the Java Naming and Directory Interface (JNDI) naming service enables components to locate other components and resources.

A **resource** is a program object that provides connections to systems, such as database servers and messaging systems. (A Java Database Connectivity resource is sometimes referred to as a data source.) Each resource object is identified by a unique, people-friendly name, called the JNDI name. For example, the JNDI name of the preconfigured JDBC resource for the Java DB database that is shipped with GlassFish Server is `java:comp/DefaultDataSource`.

An administrator creates resources in a JNDI namespace. In GlassFish Server, you can use either the Administration Console or the asadmin command to create resources. Applications then use annotations to inject the resources. If an application uses resource injection, GlassFish Server invokes the JNDI API, and the application is not required to do so. However, it is also possible for an application to locate resources by making direct calls to the JNDI API.

A resource object and its JNDI name are bound together by the naming and directory service. To create a new resource, a new name/object binding is entered into the JNDI namespace. You inject resources by using the @Resource annotation in an application.

You can use a deployment descriptor to override the resource mapping that you specify in an annotation. Using a deployment descriptor allows you to change an application by repackaging it rather than by both recompiling the source files and repackaging. However, for most applications a deployment descriptor is not necessary.

3.2 DataSource Objects and Connection Pools

To store, organize, and retrieve data, most applications use a relational database. Java EE 7 components may access relational databases through the JDBC API. For information on this API, see http://docs.oracle.com/javase/7/docs/technotes/guides/jdbc/.

In the JDBC API, databases are accessed by using DataSource objects. A DataSource has a set of properties that identify and describe the real-world data source that it represents. These properties include such information as the location of the database server, the name of the database, the network protocol to use to communicate with the server, and so on. In GlassFish Server, a data source is called a JDBC resource.

Applications access a data source by using a connection, and a DataSource object can be thought of as a factory for connections to the particular data source that the DataSource instance represents. In a basic DataSource implementation, a call to the getConnection method returns a connection object that is a physical connection to the data source.

A DataSource object may be registered with a JNDI naming service. If so, an application can use the JNDI API to access that DataSource object, which can then be used to connect to the data source it represents.

DataSource objects that implement connection pooling also produce a connection to the particular data source that the DataSource class represents. The connection object that the getConnection method returns is a handle to a PooledConnection object rather than a physical connection. An application uses the connection object in the same way that it uses a connection. Connection pooling has no effect on application code except that a pooled connection, like all connections, should always be explicitly closed. When an application closes a connection that is pooled, the connection is returned to a pool of reusable connections. The next time getConnection is called, a handle to one of these pooled connections will be returned if one is available. Because connection pooling avoids creating a new physical connection every time one is requested, applications can run significantly faster.

A JDBC connection pool is a group of reusable connections for a particular database. Because creating each new physical connection is time consuming, the server maintains a pool of available connections to increase performance. When it requests a connection, an application obtains one from the pool. When an application closes a connection, the connection is returned to the pool.

Applications that use the Persistence API specify the DataSource object they are using in the jta-data-source element of the persistence.xml file:

```
<jta-data-source>jdbc/MyOrderDB</jta-data-source>
```

This is typically the only reference to a JDBC object for a persistence unit. The application code does not refer to any JDBC objects.

3.3 Creating Resources Administratively

Before you deploy or run some applications, you may need to create resources for them. An application can include a glassfish-resources.xml file that can be used to define resources for that application and others. You can then use the asadmin command, specifying as the argument a file named glassfish-resources.xml, to create the resources administratively, as shown.

```
asadmin add-resources glassfish-resources.xml
```

The glassfish-resources.xml file can be created in any project using NetBeans IDE or by hand. Some of the JMS examples use this approach to resource creation. A file for creating the resources needed for the JMS simple producer example can be found in the jms/simple/producer/src/main/setup directory.

You could also use the asadmin create-jms-resource command to create the resources for this example. When you are done using the resources, you would use the asadmin list-jms-resources command to display their names, and the asadmin delete-jms-resource command to remove them, regardless of the way you created the resources.

4

Injection

This chapter provides an overview of injection in Java EE and describes the two injection mechanisms provided by the platform: resource injection and dependency injection.

Java EE provides injection mechanisms that enable your objects to obtain references to resources and other dependencies without having to instantiate them directly. You declare the required resources and other dependencies in your classes by decorating fields or methods with one of the annotations that mark the field as an injection point. The container then provides the required instances at runtime. Injection simplifies your code and decouples it from the implementations of its dependencies.

The following topics are addressed here:

- Resource Injection
- Dependency Injection
- The Main Differences between Resource Injection and Dependency Injection

4.1 Resource Injection

Resource injection enables you to inject any resource available in the JNDI namespace into any container-managed object, such as a servlet, an enterprise bean, or a managed bean. For example, you can use resource injection to inject data sources, connectors, or custom resources available in the JNDI namespace.

The type you use for the reference to the injected instance is usually an interface, which decouples your code from the implementation of the resource.

For example, the following code injects a DataSource object that provides connections to the default Java DB database shipped with GlassFish Server:

```
public class MyServlet extends HttpServlet {
    @Resource(name="java:comp/DefaultDataSource")
    private javax.sql.DataSource dsc;
    ...
}
```

In addition to field-based injection as in the preceding example, you can inject resources using method-based injection:

```
public class MyServlet extends HttpServlet {
    private javax.sql.DataSource dsc;
    ...
    @Resource(name="java:comp/DefaultDataSource")
    public void setDsc(java.sql.DataSource ds) {
        dsc = ds;
    }
}
```

To use method-based injection, the setter method must follow the JavaBeans conventions for property names: The method name must begin with set, have a void return type, and have only one parameter.

The @Resource annotation is in the javax.annotation package and is defined in JSR 250 (Common Annotations for the Java Platform). Resource injection resolves by name, so it is not typesafe: the type of the resource object is not known at compile time, so you can get runtime errors if the types of the object and its reference do not match.

4.2 Dependency Injection

Dependency injection enables you to turn regular Java classes into managed objects and to inject them into any other managed object. Using dependency injection, your code can declare dependencies on any managed object. The container automatically provides instances of these dependencies at the injection points at runtime, and it also manages the lifecycle of these instances for you.

Dependency injection in Java EE defines scopes, which determine the lifecycle of the objects that the container instantiates and injects. For example, a managed object that is only needed to respond to a single client request (such as a currency converter) has a different scope than a managed object that is needed to process multiple client requests within a session (such as a shopping cart).

You can define managed objects (also called **managed beans**) that you can later inject by assigning a scope to a regular class:

```
@javax.enterprise.context.RequestScoped
public class CurrencyConverter { ... }
```

Use the `javax.inject.Inject` annotation to inject managed beans; for example:

```
public class MyServlet extends HttpServlet {
    @Inject CurrencyConverter cc;
    ...
}
```

As opposed to resource injection, dependency injection is typesafe because it resolves by type. To decouple your code from the implementation of the managed bean, you can reference the injected instances using an interface type and have your managed bean implement that interface.

For more information about dependency injection, see Chapter 23, "Introduction to Contexts and Dependency Injection for Java EE," and JSR 299 (Contexts and Dependency Injection for the Java EE Platform).

4.3 The Main Differences between Resource Injection and Dependency Injection

Table 4–1 lists the main differences between resource injection and dependency injection.

Table 4–1 *Differences between Resource Injection and Dependency Injection*

Injection Mechanism	Can Inject JNDI Resources Directly	Can Inject Regular Classes Directly	Resolves By	Typesafe
Resource Injection	Yes	No	Resource name	No
Dependency Injection	No	Yes	Type	Yes

5

Packaging

This chapter describes packaging. A Java EE application is packaged into one or more standard units for deployment to any Java EE platform–compliant system. Each unit contains a functional component or components, such as an enterprise bean, web page, servlet, or applet, and an optional deployment descriptor that describes its content.

The following topics are addressed here:

- Packaging Applications
- Packaging Enterprise Beans
- Packaging Web Archives
- Packaging Resource Adapter Archives

5.1 Packaging Applications

A Java EE application is delivered in a Java Archive (JAR) file, a Web Archive (WAR) file, or an Enterprise Archive (EAR) file. A WAR or EAR file is a standard JAR (.jar) file with a .war or .ear extension. Using JAR, WAR, and EAR files and modules makes it possible to assemble a number of different Java EE applications using some of the same components. No extra coding is needed; it is only a matter of assembling (or packaging) various Java EE modules into Java EE JAR, WAR, or EAR files.

An EAR file (see Figure 5–1) contains Java EE modules and, optionally, deployment descriptors. A **deployment descriptor**, an XML document with an .xml extension, describes the deployment settings of an application, a module, or a component. Because deployment descriptor information is declarative, it can be changed without the need to modify the source code. At runtime, the Java EE server reads the deployment descriptor and acts upon the application, module, or component accordingly.

Deployment information is most commonly specified in the source code by **annotations**. Deployment descriptors, if present, override what is specified in the source code.

Figure 5–1   EAR File Structure

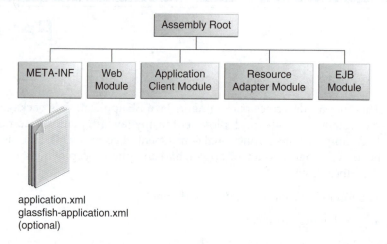

The two types of deployment descriptors are Java EE and runtime. A **Java EE deployment descriptor** is defined by a Java EE specification and can be used to configure deployment settings on any Java EE-compliant implementation. A **runtime deployment descriptor** is used to configure Java EE implementation-specific parameters. For example, the GlassFish Server runtime deployment descriptor contains such information as the context root of a web application as well as GlassFish Server implementation-specific parameters, such as caching directives. The GlassFish Server runtime deployment descriptors are named `glassfish-moduleType.xml` and are located in the same `META-INF` directory as the Java EE deployment descriptor.

A **Java EE module** consists of one or more Java EE components for the same container type and, optionally, one component deployment descriptor of that type. An enterprise bean module deployment descriptor, for example, declares transaction attributes and security authorizations for an enterprise bean. A Java EE module can be deployed as a stand-alone module.

Java EE modules are of the following types:

- EJB modules, which contain class files for enterprise beans and, optionally, an EJB deployment descriptor. EJB modules are packaged as JAR files with a .jar extension.

- Web modules, which contain servlet class files, web files, supporting class files, GIF and HTML files, and, optionally, a web application deployment descriptor. Web modules are packaged as JAR files with a .war (web archive) extension.

- Application client modules, which contain class files and, optionally, an application client deployment descriptor. Application client modules are packaged as JAR files with a .jar extension.

- Resource adapter modules, which contain all Java interfaces, classes, native libraries, and, optionally, a resource adapter deployment descriptor. Together, these implement the Connector architecture (see Section 1.8.14, "Java EE Connector Architecture") for a particular EIS. Resource adapter modules are packaged as JAR files with an .rar (resource adapter archive) extension.

5.2 Packaging Enterprise Beans

This section explains how enterprise beans can be packaged in EJB JAR or WAR modules.

5.2.1 Packaging Enterprise Beans in EJB JAR Modules

An EJB JAR file is portable and can be used for various applications.

To assemble a Java EE application, package one or more modules, such as EJB JAR files, into an EAR file, the archive file that holds the application. When deploying the EAR file that contains the enterprise bean's EJB JAR file, you also deploy the enterprise bean to GlassFish Server. You can also deploy an EJB JAR that is not contained in an EAR file. Figure 5–2 shows the contents of an EJB JAR file.

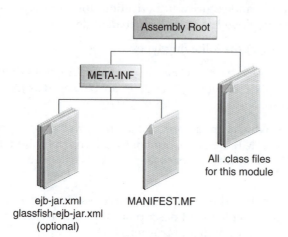

Figure 5–2   Structure of an Enterprise Bean JAR

5.2.2 Packaging Enterprise Beans in WAR Modules

Enterprise beans often provide the business logic of a web application. In these cases, packaging the enterprise bean within the web application's WAR module simplifies deployment and application organization. Enterprise beans may be packaged within a WAR module as Java programming language class files or within a JAR file that is bundled within the WAR module.

To include enterprise bean class files in a WAR module, the class files should be in the WEB-INF/classes directory.

To include a JAR file that contains enterprise beans in a WAR module, add the JAR to the WEB-INF/lib directory of the WAR module.

WAR modules that contain enterprise beans do not require an ejb-jar.xml deployment descriptor. If the application uses ejb-jar.xml, it must be located in the WAR module's WEB-INF directory.

JAR files that contain enterprise bean classes packaged within a WAR module are not considered EJB JAR files, even if the bundled JAR file conforms to the format of an EJB JAR file. The enterprise beans contained within the JAR file are semantically equivalent to enterprise beans located in the WAR module's WEB-INF/classes directory, and the environment namespace of all the enterprise beans are scoped to the WAR module.

For example, suppose that a web application consists of a shopping cart enterprise bean, a credit card–processing enterprise bean, and a Java servlet front end. The shopping cart bean exposes a local, no-interface view and is defined as follows:

```
package com.example.cart;

@Stateless
public class CartBean { ... }
```

The credit card–processing bean is packaged within its own JAR file, cc.jar, exposes a local, no-interface view, and is defined as follows:

```
package com.example.cc;

@Stateless
public class CreditCardBean { ... }
```

The servlet, com.example.web.StoreServlet, handles the web front end and uses both CartBean and CreditCardBean. The WAR module layout for this application is as follows:

```
WEB-INF/classes/com/example/cart/CartBean.class
WEB-INF/classes/com/example/web/StoreServlet
WEB-INF/lib/cc.jar
WEB-INF/ejb-jar.xml
WEB-INF/web.xml
```

5.3 Packaging Web Archives

In the Java EE architecture, a **web module** is the smallest deployable and usable unit of web resources. A web module contains web components and static web content files, such as images, which are called **web resources**. A Java EE web module corresponds to a web application as defined in the Java Servlet specification.

In addition to web components and web resources, a web module can contain other files:

- Server-side utility classes, such as shopping carts
- Client-side classes, such as utility classes

A web module has a specific structure. The top-level directory of a web module is the **document root** of the application. The document root is where XHTML pages, client-side classes and archives, and static web resources, such as images, are stored.

The document root contains a subdirectory named WEB-INF, which can contain the following files and directories:

- classes, a directory that contains server-side classes: servlets, enterprise bean class files, utility classes, and JavaBeans components

- lib, a directory that contains JAR files that contain enterprise beans, and JAR archives of libraries called by server-side classes

- Deployment descriptors, such as web.xml (the web application deployment descriptor) and ejb-jar.xml (an EJB deployment descriptor)

A web module needs a web.xml file if it uses JavaServer Faces technology, if it must specify certain kinds of security information, or if you want to override information specified by web component annotations.

You can also create application-specific subdirectories (that is, package directories) in either the document root or the WEB-INF/classes/ directory.

A web module can be deployed as an unpacked file structure or can be packaged in a JAR file known as a Web Archive (WAR) file. Because the contents and use of WAR files differ from those of JAR files, WAR file names use a .war extension. The web module just described is portable; you can deploy it into any web container that conforms to the Java Servlet specification.

You can provide a runtime deployment descriptor (DD) when you deploy a WAR on GlassFish Server, but it is not required under most circumstances. The runtime DD is an XML file that may contain such information as the **context root** of the web application, the mapping of the portable names of an application's resources to GlassFish Server resources, and the mapping of an application's security roles to users, groups, and principals defined in GlassFish Server. The GlassFish Server web application runtime DD, if used, is named glassfish-web.xml and is located in the WEB-INF directory. The structure of a web module that can be deployed on GlassFish Server is shown in Figure 5–3.

Figure 5–3   Web Module Structure

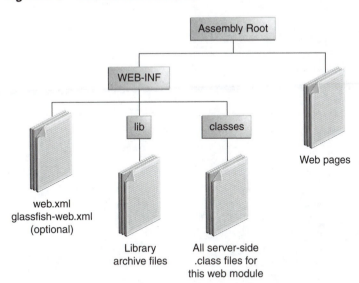

5.4 Packaging Resource Adapter Archives

A Resource Adapter Archive (RAR) file stores XML files, Java classes, and other objects for Java EE Connector Architecture (JCA) applications. A resource adapter can be deployed on any Java EE server, much like a Java EE application. A RAR file can be contained in an Enterprise Archive (EAR) file, or it can exist as a separate file.

The RAR file contains

- A JAR file with the implementation classes of the resource adapter

- An optional META-INF/ directory that can store an ra.xml file and/or an application server–specific deployment descriptor used for configuration purposes

A RAR file can be deployed on the application server as a standalone component or as part of a larger application. In both cases, the adapter is available to all applications using a lookup procedure.

Part III

The Web Tier

Part III explores the technologies in the web tier. This part contains the following chapters:

- Chapter 6, "Getting Started with Web Applications"
- Chapter 7, "JavaServer Faces Technology"
- Chapter 8, "Introduction to Facelets"
- Chapter 9, "Expression Language"
- Chapter 10, "Using JavaServer Faces Technology in Web Pages"
- Chapter 11, "Using Converters, Listeners, and Validators"
- Chapter 12, "Developing with JavaServer Faces Technology"
- Chapter 13, "Using Ajax with JavaServer Faces Technology"
- Chapter 14, "Composite Components: Advanced Topics and an Example"
- Chapter 15, "Creating Custom UI Components and Other Custom Objects"
- Chapter 16, "Configuring JavaServer Faces Applications"
- Chapter 17, "Java Servlet Technology"
- Chapter 18, "Java API for WebSocket"
- Chapter 19, "JSON Processing"
- Chapter 20, "Internationalizing and Localizing Web Applications"

6

Getting Started with Web Applications

This chapter introduces web applications, which typically use JavaServer Faces technology and/or Java Servlet technology. A **web application** is a dynamic extension of a web or application server. Web applications are of the following types:

- **Presentation-oriented**: A **presentation-oriented web application** generates interactive web pages containing various types of markup language (HTML, XHTML, XML, and so on) and dynamic content in response to requests. Development of presentation-oriented web applications is covered in Chapter 7, "JavaServer Faces Technology," through Chapter 20, "Internationalizing and Localizing Web Applications."

- **Service-oriented**: A **service-oriented web application** implements the endpoint of a web service. Presentation-oriented applications are often clients of service-oriented web applications. Development of service-oriented web applications is covered in Chapter 28, "Building Web Services with JAX-WS," through Chapter 31, "JAX-RS: Advanced Topics and an Example," in Part VI, "Web Services."

The following topics are addressed here:

- Web Applications
- Web Application Lifecycle
- A Web Module That Uses JavaServer Faces Technology: The hello1 Example
- A Web Module That Uses Java Servlet Technology: The hello2 Example
- Configuring Web Applications
- Further Information about Web Applications

6.1 Web Applications

In the Java EE platform, **web components** provide the dynamic extension capabilities for a web server. Web components can be Java servlets, web pages implemented with JavaServer Faces technology, web service endpoints, or JSP pages. Figure 6–1 illustrates the interaction between a web client and a web application that uses a servlet. The client sends an HTTP request to the web server. A web server that implements Java Servlet and JavaServer Pages technology converts the request into an HTTPServletRequest object. This object is delivered to a web component, which can interact with JavaBeans components or a database to generate dynamic content. The web component can then generate an HTTPServletResponse or can pass the request to another web component. A web component eventually generates a HTTPServletResponse object. The web server converts this object to an HTTP response and returns it to the client.

Figure 6–1   Java Web Application Request Handling

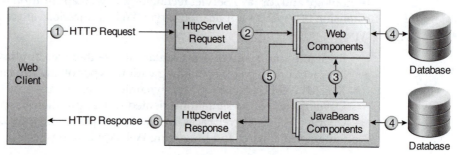

Servlets are Java programming language classes that dynamically process requests and construct responses. Java technologies, such as JavaServer Faces and Facelets, are used for building interactive web applications. (Frameworks can also be used for this purpose.) Although servlets and JavaServer Faces and Facelets pages can be used to accomplish similar things, each has its own strengths. Servlets are best suited for service-oriented applications (web service endpoints can be implemented as servlets) and the control functions of a presentation-oriented application, such as dispatching requests and handling nontextual data. JavaServer Faces and Facelets pages are more appropriate for generating text-based markup, such as XHTML, and are generally used for presentation-oriented applications.

Web components are supported by the services of a runtime platform called a **web container**. A web container provides such services as request dispatching, security, concurrency, and lifecycle management. A web container also gives web components access to such APIs as naming, transactions, and email.

Certain aspects of web application behavior can be configured when the application is installed, or *deployed*, to the web container. The configuration information can be specified using Java EE annotations or can be maintained in a text file in XML format called a web application deployment descriptor (DD). A web application DD must conform to the schema described in the Java Servlet specification.

This chapter gives a brief overview of the activities involved in developing web applications. First, it summarizes the web application lifecycle and explains how to package and deploy very simple web applications on GlassFish Server. The chapter then moves on to configuring web applications and discusses how to specify the most commonly used configuration parameters.

6.2 Web Application Lifecycle

A web application consists of web components; static resource files, such as images and cascading style sheets (CSS); and helper classes and libraries. The web container provides many supporting services that enhance the capabilities of web components and make them easier to develop. However, because a web application must take these services into account, the process for creating and running a web application is different from that of traditional stand-alone Java classes.

The process for creating, deploying, and executing a web application can be summarized as follows:

1. Develop the web component code.
2. Develop the web application deployment descriptor, if necessary.
3. Compile the web application components and helper classes referenced by the components.
4. Optionally, package the application into a deployable unit.
5. Deploy the application into a web container.
6. Access a URL that references the web application.

Developing web component code is covered in the later chapters. Steps 2 through 4 are expanded on in the following sections and illustrated with a Hello, World–style, presentation-oriented application. This application allows a user to enter a name into an HTML form and then displays a greeting after the name is submitted.

The Hello application contains two web components that generate the greeting and the response. This chapter discusses the following simple applications:

- hello1, a JavaServer Faces technology–based application that uses two XHTML pages and a managed bean

- hello2, a servlet-based web application in which the components are implemented by two servlet classes

The applications are used to illustrate tasks involved in packaging, deploying, configuring, and running an application that contains web components.

6.3 A Web Module That Uses JavaServer Faces Technology: The hello1 Example

The hello1 application is a web module that uses JavaServer Faces technology to display a greeting and response. You can use a text editor to view the application files, or you can use NetBeans IDE.

The source code for this application is in the *tut-install*/examples/web/jsf/hello1/ directory.

6.3.1 To View the hello1 Web Module Using NetBeans IDE

1. From the **File** menu, choose **Open Project**.

2. In the Open Project dialog box, navigate to:

   tut-install/examples/web/jsf

3. Select the hello1 folder and click **Open Project**.

4. Expand the **Web Pages** node and double-click the index.xhtml file to view it in the editor.

   The index.xhtml file is the default landing page for a Facelets application. In a typical Facelets application, web pages are created in XHTML. For this application, the page uses simple tag markup to display a form with a graphic image, a header, a field, and two command buttons:

```
<!DOCTYPE html PUBLIC "-//W3C//DTD XHTML 1.0 Transitional//EN"
    "http://www.w3.org/TR/xhtml1/DTD/xhtml1-transitional.dtd">
<html lang="en"
    xmlns="http://www.w3.org/1999/xhtml"
    xmlns:h="http://xmlns.jcp.org/jsf/html">
    <h:head>
        <title>Facelets Hello Greeting</title>
```

```
    </h:head>
    <h:body>
        <h:form>
            <h:graphicImage url="#{resource['images:duke.waving.gif']}"
                             alt="Duke waving his hand"/>
            <h2>Hello, my name is Duke. What's yours?</h2>
            <h:inputText id="username"
                         title="My name is: "
                         value="#{hello.name}"
                         required="true"
                         requiredMessage="Error: A name is required."
                         maxlength="25" />
            <p></p>
            <h:commandButton id="submit" value="Submit"
                             action="response" />
            <h:commandButton id="reset" value="Reset" type="reset" />
        </h:form>
        ...
    </h:body>
</html>
```

The most complex element on the page is the inputText field. The maxlength attribute specifies the maximum length of the field. The required attribute specifies that the field must be filled out; the requiredMessage attribute provides the error message to be displayed if the field is left empty. The title attribute provides the text to be used by screen readers for the visually disabled. Finally, the value attribute contains an expression that will be provided by the Hello managed bean.

The web page connects to the Hello managed bean through the Expression Language (EL) value expression #{hello.name}, which retrieves the value of the name property from the managed bean. Note the use of hello to reference the managed bean Hello. If no name is specified in the @Named annotation of the managed bean, the managed bean is always accessed with the first letter of the class name in lowercase.

The Submit commandButton element specifies the action as response, meaning that when the button is clicked, the response.xhtml page is displayed.

5. Double-click the response.xhtml file to view it.

The response page appears. Even simpler than the greeting page, the response page contains a graphic image, a header that displays the expression provided by the managed bean, and a single button whose `action` element transfers you back to the `index.xhtml` page:

```
<!DOCTYPE html PUBLIC "-//W3C//DTD XHTML 1.0 Transitional//EN"
    "http://www.w3.org/TR/xhtml1/DTD/xhtml1-transitional.dtd">
<html lang="en"
      xmlns="http://www.w3.org/1999/xhtml"
      xmlns:h="http://xmlns.jcp.org/jsf/html">
    <h:head>
        <title>Facelets Hello Response</title>
    </h:head>
    <h:body>
        <h:form>
            <h:graphicImage url="#{resource['images:duke.waving.gif']}"
                            alt="Duke waving his hand"/>
            <h2>Hello, #{hello.name}!</h2>
            <p></p>
            <h:commandButton id="back" value="Back" action="index" />
        </h:form>
    </h:body>
</html>
```

6. Expand the **Source Packages** node, then the `javaeetutorial.hello1` node.

7. Double-click the `Hello.java` file to view it.

   The `Hello` class, called a managed bean class, provides getter and setter methods for the name property used in the Facelets page expressions. By default, the expression language refers to the class name, with the first letter in lowercase (`hello.name`).

```
package javaeetutorial.hello1;

import javax.enterprise.context.RequestScoped;
import javax.inject.Named;

@Named
@RequestScoped
public class Hello {
    private String name;

    public Hello() {
    }

    public String getName() {
        return name;
    }
```

```
public void setName(String user_name) {
    this.name = user_name;
}
}
```

If you use the default name for the bean class, you can specify @Model as the annotation instead of having to specify both @Named and @RequestScoped. The @Model annotation is called a **stereotype**, a term for an annotation that encapsulates other annotations. It is described later in Section 25.8, "Using Stereotypes in CDI Applications." Some examples will use @Model where it is appropriate.

8. Under the **Web Pages** node, expand the **WEB-INF** node and double-click the web.xml file to view it.

The web.xml file contains several elements that are required for a Facelets application. All of the following are created automatically when you use NetBeans IDE to create an application.

- A context parameter specifying the project stage:

```
<context-param>
    <param-name>javax.faces.PROJECT_STAGE</param-name>
    <param-value>Development</param-value>
</context-param>
```

A context parameter provides configuration information needed by a web application. An application can define its own context parameters. In addition, JavaServer Faces technology and Java Servlet technology define context parameters that an application can use.

- A servlet element and its servlet-mapping element specifying the FacesServlet. All files with the .xhtml suffix will be matched:

```
<servlet>
    <servlet-name>Faces Servlet</servlet-name>
    <servlet-class>
        javax.faces.webapp.FacesServlet
    </servlet-class>
    <load-on-startup>1</load-on-startup>
</servlet>
<servlet-mapping>
    <servlet-name>Faces Servlet</servlet-name>
    <url-pattern>*.xhtml</url-pattern>
</servlet-mapping>
```

- A welcome-file-list element specifying the location of the landing page:

```
<welcome-file-list>
    <welcome-file>index.xhtml</welcome-file>
</welcome-file-list>
```

6.3.1.1 Introduction to Scopes

In the Hello.java class, the annotations javax.inject.Named and javax.enterprise.context.RequestScoped identify the class as a managed bean using request scope. Scope defines how application data persists and is shared.

The most commonly used scopes in JavaServer Faces applications are the following:

- **Request** (@RequestScoped): Request scope persists during a single HTTP request in a web application. In an application like hello1, in which the application consists of a single request and response, the bean uses request scope.

- **Session** (@SessionScoped): Session scope persists across multiple HTTP requests in a web application. When an application consists of multiple requests and responses where data needs to be maintained, beans use session scope.

- **Application** (@ApplicationScoped): Application scope persists across all users' interactions with a web application.

For more information on scopes in JavaServer Faces technology, see Section 16.1.1, "Using Managed Bean Scopes."

6.3.2 Packaging and Deploying the hello1 Web Module

A web module must be packaged into a WAR in certain deployment scenarios and whenever you want to distribute the web module. You can package a web module into a WAR file by using Maven or by using the IDE tool of your choice. This tutorial shows you how to use NetBeans IDE or Maven to build, package, and deploy the hello1 sample application.

You can deploy a WAR file to GlassFish Server by:

- Using NetBeans IDE

- Using the asadmin command

- Using the Administration Console

- Copying the WAR file into the *domain-dir*/autodeploy/ directory

Throughout the tutorial, you will use NetBeans IDE or Maven for packaging and deploying.

6.3.2.1 To Build and Package the hello1 Web Module Using NetBeans IDE

1. Start GlassFish Server as described in Section 2.2.1, "To Start GlassFish Server Using NetBeans IDE," if you have not already done so.

2. From the **File** menu, choose **Open Project**.

3. In the Open Project dialog box, navigate to:

    tut-install/examples/web/jsf

4. Select the hello1 folder.

5. Click **Open Project**.

6. In the **Projects** tab, right-click the hello1 project and select **Build**. This command deploys the project to the server.

6.3.2.2 To Build and Package the hello1 Web Module Using Maven

1. Start GlassFish Server as described in Section 2.2.3, "To Start GlassFish Server Using the Command Line," if you have not already done so.

2. In a terminal window, go to:

    tut-install/examples/web/jsf/hello1/

3. Enter the following command:

    ```
    mvn install
    ```

    This command spawns any necessary compilations and creates the WAR file in *tut-install*/examples/web/jsf/hello1/target/. It then deploys the project to the server.

6.3.3 Viewing Deployed Web Modules

GlassFish Server provides two ways to view the deployed web modules: the Administration Console and the asadmin command. You can also use NetBeans IDE to view deployed modules.

6.3.3.1 To View Deployed Web Modules Using the Administration Console

1. Open the URL http://localhost:4848/ in a browser.

2. Select the **Applications** node.

The deployed web modules appear in the **Deployed Applications** table.

6.3.3.2 To View Deployed Web Modules Using the asadmin Command

Enter the following command:

```
asadmin list-applications
```

6.3.3.3 To View Deployed Web Modules Using NetBeans IDE

1. In the **Services** tab, expand the **Servers** node, then expand the GlassFish Server node.

2. Expand the **Applications** node to view the deployed modules.

6.3.4 Running the Deployed hello1 Web Module

Now that the web module is deployed, you can view it by opening the application in a web browser. By default, the application is deployed to host `localhost` on port 8080. The context root of the web application is `hello1`.

1. Open a web browser.

2. Enter the following URL:

```
http://localhost:8080/hello1/
```

3. In the field, enter your name and click **Submit**.

   The response page displays the name you submitted. Click **Back** to try again.

6.3.4.1 Dynamic Reloading of Deployed Modules

If dynamic reloading is enabled, you do not have to redeploy an application or module when you change its code or deployment descriptors. All you have to do is copy the changed pages or class files into the deployment directory for the application or module. The deployment directory for a web module named *context-root* is *domain-dir*/applications/*context-root*. The server checks for changes periodically and redeploys the application, automatically and dynamically, with the changes.

This capability is useful in a development environment because it allows code changes to be tested quickly. Dynamic reloading is not recommended for a production environment, however, because it may degrade performance. In addition, whenever a reload takes place, the sessions at that time become invalid, and the client must restart the session.

In GlassFish Server, dynamic reloading is enabled by default.

6.3.5 Undeploying the hello1 Web Module

You can undeploy web modules and other types of enterprise applications by using either NetBeans IDE or the `asadmin` command.

6.3.5.1 To Undeploy the hello1 Web Module Using NetBeans IDE

1. In the **Services** tab, expand the **Servers** node, then expand the GlassFish Server node.

2. Expand the **Applications** node.

3. Right-click the `hello1` module and select **Undeploy**.

4. To delete the class files and other build artifacts, go back to the **Projects** tab, right-click the project, and select **Clean**.

6.3.5.2 To Undeploy the hello1 Web Module Using the asadmin Command

1. In a terminal window, go to:

   `tut-install/examples/web/jsf/hello1/`

2. Enter the following command:

   `mvn cargo:undeploy`

3. To delete the class files and other build artifacts, enter the following command:

   `mvn clean`

6.4 A Web Module That Uses Java Servlet Technology: The hello2 Example

The `hello2` application is a web module that uses Java Servlet technology to display a greeting and response. You can use a text editor to view the application files, or you can use NetBeans IDE.

The source code for this application is in the *tut-install*/`examples/web/servlet/hello2/` directory.

6.4.1 Mapping URLs to Web Components

When it receives a request, the web container must determine which web component should handle the request. The web container does so by mapping the

URL path contained in the request to a web application and a web component. A URL path contains the context root and, optionally, a URL pattern:

```
http://host:port/context-root[/url-pattern]
```

You set the URL pattern for a servlet by using the @WebServlet annotation in the servlet source file. For example, the GreetingServlet.java file in the hello2 application contains the following annotation, specifying the URL pattern as /greeting:

```
@WebServlet("/greeting")
public class GreetingServlet extends HttpServlet {
    ...
```

This annotation indicates that the URL pattern /greeting follows the context root. Therefore, when the servlet is deployed locally, it is accessed with the following URL:

```
http://localhost:8080/hello2/greeting
```

To access the servlet by using only the context root, specify "/" as the URL pattern.

6.4.2 Examining the hello2 Web Module

The hello2 application behaves almost identically to the hello1 application, but it is implemented using Java Servlet technology instead of JavaServer Faces technology. You can use a text editor to view the application files, or you can use NetBeans IDE.

6.4.2.1 To View the hello2 Web Module Using NetBeans IDE

1. From the **File** menu, choose **Open Project**.

2. In the Open Project dialog box, navigate to:

   tut-install/examples/web/servlet

3. Select the hello2 folder and click **Open Project**.

4. Expand the **Source Packages** node, then expand the javaeetutorial.hello2 node.

5. Double-click the GreetingServlet.java file to view it.

   This servlet overrides the doGet method, implementing the GET method of HTTP. The servlet displays a simple HTML greeting form whose **Submit** button, like that of hello1, specifies a response page for its action. The following excerpt begins with the @WebServlet annotation, which specifies the URL pattern relative to the context root:

```java
@WebServlet("/greeting")
public class GreetingServlet extends HttpServlet {

    @Override
    public void doGet(HttpServletRequest request,
            HttpServletResponse response)
            throws ServletException, IOException {

        response.setContentType("text/html");
        response.setBufferSize(8192);
        try (PrintWriter out = response.getWriter()) {
            out.println("<html lang=\"en\">"
                    + "<head><title>Servlet Hello</title></head>");

            // then write the data of the response
            out.println("<body  bgcolor=\"#ffffff\">"
                + "<img src=\"duke.waving.gif\" "
                + "alt=\"Duke waving his hand\">"
                + "<form method=\"get\">"
                + "<h2>Hello, my name is Duke. What's yours?</h2>"
                + "<input title=\"My name is: \"type=\"text\" "
                + "name=\"username\" size=\"25\">"
                + "<p></p>"
                + "<input type=\"submit\" value=\"Submit\">"
                + "<input type=\"reset\" value=\"Reset\">"
                + "</form>");

            String username = request.getParameter("username");
            if (username != null && username.length()> 0) {
                RequestDispatcher dispatcher =
                    getServletContext().getRequestDispatcher("/response");

                if (dispatcher != null) {
                    dispatcher.include(request, response);
                }
            }
            out.println("</body></html>");
        }
    }
    ...
```

6. Double-click the ResponseServlet.java file to view it.

This servlet also overrides the doGet method, displaying only the response. The following excerpt begins with the @WebServlet annotation, which specifies the URL pattern relative to the context root:

```
@WebServlet("/response")
public class ResponseServlet extends HttpServlet {

    @Override
    public void doGet(HttpServletRequest request,
            HttpServletResponse response)
            throws ServletException, IOException {
        try (PrintWriter out = response.getWriter()) {

            // then write the data of the response
            String username = request.getParameter("username");
            if (username != null && username.length()> 0) {
                out.println("<h2>Hello, " + username + "!</h2>");
            }
        }
    }
}
...
```

6.4.3 Running the hello2 Example

You can use either NetBeans IDE or Maven to build, package, deploy, and run the hello2 example.

6.4.3.1 To Run the hello2 Example Using NetBeans IDE

1. Start GlassFish Server as described in Section 2.2.1, "To Start GlassFish Server Using NetBeans IDE," if you have not already done so.

2. From the **File** menu, choose **Open Project**.

3. In the Open Project dialog box, navigate to:

    tut-install/examples/web/servlet

4. Select the hello2 folder.

5. Click **Open Project**.

6. In the **Projects** tab, right-click the hello2 project and select **Build** to package and deploy the project.

7. In a web browser, open the following URL:

    http://localhost:8080/hello2/greeting

The URL specifies the context root, followed by the URL pattern.

The application looks much like the `hello1` application. The major difference is that after you click **Submit** the response appears below the greeting, not on a separate page.

6.4.3.2 To Run the hello2 Example Using Maven

1. Start GlassFish Server as described in Section 2.2.3, "To Start GlassFish Server Using the Command Line," if you have not already done so.

2. In a terminal window, go to:

    tut-install/examples/web/servlet/hello2/

3. Enter the following command:

    ```
    mvn install
    ```

    This target builds the WAR file, copies it to the *tut-install*/examples/web/hello2/target/ directory, and deploys it.

4. In a web browser, open the following URL:

    ```
    http://localhost:8080/hello2/greeting
    ```

    The URL specifies the context root, followed by the URL pattern.

    The application looks much like the `hello1` application. The major difference is that after you click **Submit** the response appears below the greeting, not on a separate page.

6.5 Configuring Web Applications

This section describes the following tasks involved with configuring web applications:

- Setting context parameters
- Declaring welcome files
- Mapping errors to error screens
- Declaring resource references

6.5.1 Setting Context Parameters

The web components in a web module share an object that represents their application context. You can pass context parameters to the context, or you can pass initialization parameters to a servlet. Context parameters are available to the entire application. For information on initialization parameters, see Section 17.4, "Creating and Initializing a Servlet."

6.5.1.1 To Add a Context Parameter Using NetBeans IDE

These steps apply generally to web applications but do not apply specifically to the examples in this chapter.

1. Open the project.

2. Expand the project's node in the **Projects** tree.

3. Expand the **Web Pages** node and then the **WEB-INF** node.

4. Double-click web.xml.

   If the project does not have a web.xml file, create one by following the steps in Section 6.5.1.2, "To Create a web.xml File Using NetBeans IDE."

5. Click **General** at the top of the editor window.

6. Expand the **Context Parameters** node.

7. Click **Add**.

8. In the Add Context Parameter dialog box, in the **Parameter Name** field, enter the name that specifies the context object.

9. In the **Parameter Value** field, enter the parameter to pass to the context object.

10. Click **OK**.

6.5.1.2 To Create a web.xml File Using NetBeans IDE

1. From the **File** menu, choose **New File**.

2. In the New File wizard, select the **Web** category, then select **Standard Deployment Descriptor** under **File Types**.

3. Click **Next**.

4. Click **Finish**.

   A basic web.xml file appears in web/WEB-INF/.

6.5.2 Declaring Welcome Files

The **welcome files** mechanism allows you to specify a list of files that the web container can append to a request for a URL (called a valid partial request) that is not mapped to a web component. For example, suppose that you define a welcome file `welcome.html`. When a client requests a URL such as *host:port/webapp/directory*, where *directory* is not mapped to a servlet or XHTML page, the file *host:port/webapp/directory/*`welcome.html` is returned to the client.

If a web container receives a valid partial request, the web container examines the welcome file list, appends to the partial request each welcome file in the order specified, and checks whether a static resource or servlet in the WAR is mapped to that request URL. The web container then sends the request to the first resource that matches in the WAR.

If no welcome file is specified, GlassFish Server will use a file named `index.html` as the default welcome file. If there is no welcome file and no file named `index.html`, GlassFish Server returns a directory listing.

You specify welcome files in the `web.xml` file. The welcome file specification for the `hello1` example looks like this:

```
<welcome-file-list>
    <welcome-file>index.xhtml</welcome-file>
</welcome-file-list>
```

A specified welcome file must not have a leading or trailing slash (/).

The `hello2` example does not specify a welcome file, because the URL request is mapped to the `GreetingServlet` web component through the URL pattern `/greeting`.

6.5.3 Mapping Errors to Error Screens

When an error occurs during execution of a web application, you can have the application display a specific error screen according to the type of error. In particular, you can specify a mapping between the status code returned in an HTTP response or a Java programming language exception returned by any web component and any type of error screen.

You can have multiple `error-page` elements in your deployment descriptor. Each element identifies a different error that causes an error page to open. This error page can be the same for any number of `error-page` elements.

6.5.3.1 To Set Up Error Mapping Using NetBeans IDE

These steps apply generally to web applications but do not apply specifically to the examples in this chapter.

1. Open the project.

2. Expand the project's node in the **Projects** tab.

3. Expand the **Web Pages** node and then the **WEB-INF** node.

4. Double-click web.xml.

   If the project does not have a web.xml file, create one by following the steps in Section 6.5.1.2, "To Create a web.xml File Using NetBeans IDE."

5. Click **Pages** at the top of the editor window.

6. Expand the **Error Pages** node.

7. Click **Add**.

8. In the Add Error Page dialog box, click **Browse** to locate the page that you want to act as the error page.

9. Specify either an error code or an exception type.

   ▪ To specify an error code, in the **Error Code** field enter the HTTP status code that will cause the error page to be opened, or leave the field blank to include all error codes.

   ▪ To specify an exception type, in the **Exception Type** field enter the exception that will cause the error page to load. To specify all throwable errors and exceptions, enter java.lang.Throwable.

10. Click **OK**.

6.5.4 Declaring Resource References

If your web component uses such objects as enterprise beans, data sources, or web services, you use Java EE annotations to inject these resources into your application. Annotations eliminate a lot of the boilerplate lookup code and configuration elements that previous versions of Java EE required.

Although resource injection using annotations can be more convenient for the developer, there are some restrictions on using it in web applications. First, you can inject resources only into container-managed objects, because a container must have control over the creation of a component so that it can perform the injection into a component. As a result, you cannot inject resources into such objects as simple JavaBeans components. However, managed beans are managed by the container; therefore, they can accept resource injections.

Components that can accept resource injections are listed in Table 6–1.

This section explains how to use a couple of the annotations supported by a web container to inject resources. Chapter 9, "Running the Persistence Examples," in *The Java EE 7 Tutorial, Volume 2*, explains how web applications use annotations supported by the Java Persistence API. Chapter 19, "Getting Started Securing Web

Applications," in *The Java EE 7 Tutorial, Volume 2*, explains how to use annotations to specify information about securing web applications. See Chapter 23, "Resource Adapters and Contracts," in *The Java EE 7 Tutorial, Volume 2*, for more information on resources.

Table 6–1   Web Components That Accept Resource Injections

Component	Interface/Class
Servlets	`javax.servlet.Servlet`
Servlet filters	`javax.servlet.ServletFilter`
Event listeners	`javax.servlet.ServletContextListener`
	`javax.servlet.ServletContextAttributeListener`
	`javax.servlet.ServletRequestListener`
	`javax.servlet.ServletRequestAttributeListener`
	`javax.servlet.http.HttpSessionListener`
	`javax.servlet.http.HttpSessionAttributeListener`
	`javax.servlet.http.HttpSessionBindingListener`
Managed beans	Plain Old Java Objects

6.5.4.1 Declaring a Reference to a Resource

The `@Resource` annotation is used to declare a reference to a resource, such as a data source, an enterprise bean, or an environment entry.

The `@Resource` annotation is specified on a class, a method, or a field. The container is responsible for injecting references to resources declared by the `@Resource` annotation and mapping it to the proper JNDI resources.

In the following example, the `@Resource` annotation is used to inject a data source into a component that needs to make a connection to the data source, as is done when using JDBC technology to access a relational database:

```
@Resource javax.sql.DataSource catalogDS;
public getProductsByCategory() {
    // get a connection and execute the query
    Connection conn = catalogDS.getConnection();
    ...
}
```

The container injects this data source prior to the component's being made available to the application. The data source JNDI mapping is inferred from the field name, `catalogDS`, and the type, `javax.sql.DataSource`.

If you have multiple resources that you need to inject into one component, you need to use the @Resources annotation to contain them, as shown by the following example:

```
@Resources ({
    @Resource(name="myDB" type=javax.sql.DataSource.class),
    @Resource(name="myMQ" type=javax.jms.ConnectionFactory.class)
})
```

The web application examples in this tutorial use the Java Persistence API to access relational databases. This API does not require you to explicitly create a connection to a data source. Therefore, the examples do not use the @Resource annotation to inject a data source. However, this API supports the @PersistenceUnit and @PersistenceContext annotations for injecting EntityManagerFactory and EntityManager instances, respectively. Chapter 9, "Running the Persistence Examples," in *The Java EE 7 Tutorial, Volume 2*, describes these annotations and the use of the Java Persistence API in web applications.

6.5.4.2 Declaring a Reference to a Web Service

The @WebServiceRef annotation provides a reference to a web service. The following example shows uses the @WebServiceRef annotation to declare a reference to a web service. WebServiceRef uses the wsdlLocation element to specify the URI of the deployed service's WSDL file:

```
...
import javax.xml.ws.WebServiceRef;
...
public class ResponseServlet extends HTTPServlet {
@WebServiceRef(wsdlLocation="http://localhost:8080/helloservice/hello?wsdl")
static HelloService service;
```

6.6 Further Information about Web Applications

For more information on web applications, see

- JavaServer Faces 2.2 specification:

  http://jcp.org/en/jsr/detail?id=344

- Java Servlet 3.1 specification:

  http://jcp.org/en/jsr/detail?id=340

7

JavaServer Faces Technology

JavaServer Faces technology is a server-side component framework for building Java technology–based web applications.

JavaServer Faces technology consists of the following:

- An API for representing components and managing their state; handling events, server-side validation, and data conversion; defining page navigation; supporting internationalization and accessibility; and providing extensibility for all these features

- Tag libraries for adding components to web pages and for connecting components to server-side objects

JavaServer Faces technology provides a well-defined programming model and various tag libraries. The tag libraries contain tag handlers that implement the component tags. These features significantly ease the burden of building and maintaining web applications with server-side user interfaces (UIs). With minimal effort, you can complete the following tasks.

- Create a web page.

- Drop components onto a web page by adding component tags.

- Bind components on a page to server-side data.

- Wire component-generated events to server-side application code.

- Save and restore application state beyond the life of server requests.

- Reuse and extend components through customization.

This chapter provides an overview of JavaServer Faces technology. After explaining what a JavaServer Faces application is and reviewing some of the primary benefits of using JavaServer Faces technology, this chapter describes the process of creating a simple JavaServer Faces application. This chapter also introduces the JavaServer Faces lifecycle by describing the example JavaServer Faces application and its progression through the lifecycle stages.

The following topics are addressed here:

- What Is a JavaServer Faces Application?
- JavaServer Faces Technology Benefits
- A Simple JavaServer Faces Application
- User Interface Component Model
- Navigation Model
- The Lifecycle of a JavaServer Faces Application
- Partial Processing and Partial Rendering
- Further Information about JavaServer Faces Technology

7.1 What Is a JavaServer Faces Application?

The functionality provided by a JavaServer Faces application is similar to that of any other Java web application. A typical JavaServer Faces application includes the following parts.

- A set of web pages in which components are laid out.
- A set of tags to add components to the web page.
- A set of **managed beans**, which are lightweight, container-managed objects (POJOs). In a JavaServer Faces application, managed beans serve as backing beans, which define properties and functions for UI components on a page.
- A web deployment descriptor (web.xml file).
- Optionally, one or more **application configuration resource files**, such as a faces-config.xml file, which can be used to define page navigation rules and configure beans and other custom objects, such as custom components.
- Optionally, a set of custom objects, which can include custom components, validators, converters, or listeners, created by the application developer.
- Optionally, a set of custom tags for representing custom objects on the page.

Figure 7–1 shows the interaction between client and server in a typical JavaServer Faces application. In response to a client request, a web page is rendered by the web container that implements JavaServer Faces technology.

Figure 7–1   Responding to a Client Request for a JavaServer Faces Page

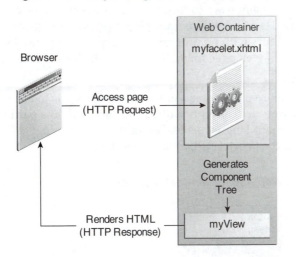

The web page, `myfacelet.xhtml`, is built using JavaServer Faces component tags. Component tags are used to add components to the `view` (represented by `myView` in the diagram), which is the server-side representation of the page. In addition to components, the web page can also reference objects, such as the following:

- Any event listeners, validators, and converters that are registered on the components

- The JavaBeans components that capture the data and process the application-specific functionality of the components

On request from the client, the view is rendered as a response. Rendering is the process whereby, based on the server-side view, the web container generates output, such as HTML or XHTML, that can be read by the client, such as a browser.

7.2 JavaServer Faces Technology Benefits

One of the greatest advantages of JavaServer Faces technology is that it offers a clean separation between behavior and presentation for web applications. A JavaServer Faces application can map HTTP requests to component-specific event handling and manage components as stateful objects on the server. JavaServer Faces technology allows you to build web applications that implement the finer-grained separation of behavior and presentation that is traditionally offered by client-side UI architectures.

The separation of logic from presentation also allows each member of a web application development team to focus on a single piece of the development process and provides a simple programming model to link the pieces. For example, page authors with no programming expertise can use JavaServer Faces technology tags in a web page to link to server-side objects without writing any scripts.

Another important goal of JavaServer Faces technology is to leverage familiar component and web-tier concepts without limiting you to a particular scripting technology or markup language. JavaServer Faces technology APIs are layered directly on top of the Servlet API, as shown in Figure 7–2.

Figure 7–2   Java Web Application Technologies

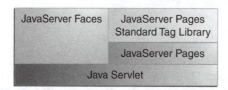

This layering of APIs enables several important application use cases, such as using different presentation technologies, creating your own custom components directly from the component classes, and generating output for various client devices.

Facelets technology, available as part of JavaServer Faces technology, is the preferred presentation technology for building JavaServer Faces technology–based web applications. For more information on Facelets technology features, see Chapter 8, "Introduction to Facelets."

Facelets technology offers several advantages.

- Code can be reused and extended for components through the templating and composite component features.

- You can use annotations to automatically register the managed bean as a resource available for JavaServer Faces applications. In addition, implicit navigation rules allow developers to quickly configure page navigation (see Section 7.5, "Navigation Model," for details). These features reduce the manual configuration process for applications.

- Most important, JavaServer Faces technology provides a rich architecture for managing component state, processing component data, validating user input, and handling events.

7.3 A Simple JavaServer Faces Application

JavaServer Faces technology provides an easy and user-friendly process for creating web applications. Developing a simple JavaServer Faces application typically requires the following tasks, which have already been described in Section 6.3, "A Web Module That Uses JavaServer Faces Technology: The hello1 Example":

- Creating web pages using component tags

- Developing managed beans

- Mapping the `FacesServlet` instance

The `hello1` example includes a managed bean and two Facelets web pages. When accessed by a client, the first web page asks the user for his or her name, and the second page responds by providing a greeting.

For details on Facelets technology, see Chapter 8, "Introduction to Facelets." For details on using EL expressions, see Chapter 9, "Expression Language." For details on the JavaServer Faces programming model and building web pages using JavaServer Faces technology, see Chapter 10, "Using JavaServer Faces Technology in Web Pages."

Every web application has a lifecycle. Common tasks, such as handling incoming requests, decoding parameters, modifying and saving state, and rendering web pages to the browser, are all performed during a web application lifecycle. Some web application frameworks hide the details of the lifecycle from you, whereas others require you to manage them manually.

By default, JavaServer Faces automatically handles most of the lifecycle actions for you. However, it also exposes the various stages of the request lifecycle so that you can modify or perform different actions if your application requirements warrant it.

The lifecycle of a JavaServer Faces application starts and ends with the following activity: The client makes a request for the web page, and the server responds with the page. The lifecycle consists of two main phases: Execute and Render.

During the **Execute** phase, several actions can take place.

- The application view is built or restored.

- The request parameter values are applied.

- Conversions and validations are performed for component values.

- Managed beans are updated with component values.

- Application logic is invoked.

For a first (initial) request, only the view is built. For subsequent (postback) requests, some or all of the other actions can take place.

In the **Render** phase, the requested view is rendered as a response to the client. Rendering is typically the process of generating output, such as HTML or XHTML, that can be read by the client, usually a browser.

The following short description of the example JavaServer Faces application passing through its lifecycle summarizes the activity that takes place behind the scenes.

The hello1 example application goes through the following stages when it is deployed on GlassFish Server.

1. When the hello1 application is built and deployed on GlassFish Server, the application is in an uninitiated state.

2. When a client makes an initial request for the index.xhtml web page, the hello1 Facelets application is compiled.

3. The compiled Facelets application is executed, and a new component tree is constructed for the hello1 application and placed in a FacesContext.

4. The component tree is populated with the component and the managed bean property associated with it, represented by the EL expression hello.name.

5. A new view is built, based on the component tree.

6. The view is rendered to the requesting client as a response.

7. The component tree is destroyed automatically.

8. On subsequent (postback) requests, the component tree is rebuilt, and the saved state is applied.

For full details on the lifecycle, see Section 7.6, "The Lifecycle of a JavaServer Faces Application."

7.4 User Interface Component Model

In addition to the lifecycle description, an overview of JavaServer Faces architecture provides better understanding of the technology.

JavaServer Faces components are the building blocks of a JavaServer Faces view. A component can be a user interface (UI) component or a non-UI component.

JavaServer Faces UI components are configurable, reusable elements that compose the user interfaces of JavaServer Faces applications. A component can be simple, such as a button, or can be compound, such as a table composed of multiple components.

JavaServer Faces technology provides a rich, flexible component architecture that includes the following:

- A set of `javax.faces.component.UIComponent` classes for specifying the state and behavior of UI components

- A rendering model that defines how to render the components in various ways

- A conversion model that defines how to register data converters onto a component

- An event and listener model that defines how to handle component events

- A validation model that defines how to register validators onto a component

This section briefly describes each of these pieces of the component architecture.

7.4.1 User Interface Component Classes

JavaServer Faces technology provides a set of UI component classes and associated behavioral interfaces that specify all the UI component functionality, such as holding component state, maintaining a reference to objects, and driving event handling and rendering for a set of standard components.

The component classes are completely extensible, allowing component writers to create their own custom components. See Chapter 15, "Creating Custom UI Components and Other Custom Objects," for more information.

The abstract base class for all components is `javax.faces.component.UIComponent`. JavaServer Faces UI component classes extend the `UIComponentBase` class (a subclass of `UIComponent`), which defines the default state and behavior of a component. The following set of component classes is included with JavaServer Faces technology.

- `UIColumn`: Represents a single column of data in a `UIData` component.

- `UICommand`: Represents a control that fires actions when activated.

- `UIData`: Represents a data binding to a collection of data represented by a `javax.faces.model.DataModel` instance.

- `UIForm`: Represents an input form to be presented to the user. Its child components represent (among other things) the input fields to be included when the form is submitted. This component is analogous to the `form` tag in HTML.

- `UIGraphic`: Displays an image.

- `UIInput`: Takes data input from a user. This class is a subclass of `UIOutput`.

- `UIMessage`: Displays a localized error message.

- `UIMessages`: Displays a set of localized error messages.

- `UIOutcomeTarget`: Displays a link in the form of a link or a button.

- `UIOutput`: Displays data output on a page.

- `UIPanel`: Manages the layout of its child components.

- `UIParameter`: Represents substitution parameters.

- `UISelectBoolean`: Allows a user to set a `boolean` value on a control by selecting or deselecting it. This class is a subclass of the `UIInput` class.

- `UISelectItem`: Represents a single item in a set of items.

- `UISelectItems`: Represents an entire set of items.

- `UISelectMany`: Allows a user to select multiple items from a group of items. This class is a subclass of the `UIInput` class.

- `UISelectOne`: Allows a user to select one item from a group of items. This class is a subclass of the `UIInput` class.

- `UIViewParameter`: Represents the query parameters in a request. This class is a subclass of the `UIInput` class.

- `UIViewRoot`: Represents the root of the component tree.

In addition to extending `UIComponentBase`, the component classes also implement one or more **behavioral interfaces**, each of which defines certain behavior for a set of components whose classes implement the interface.

These behavioral interfaces, all defined in the `javax.faces.component` package unless otherwise stated, are as follows.

- `ActionSource`: Indicates that the component can fire an action event. This interface is intended for use with components based on JavaServer Faces technology 1.1_01 and earlier versions. This interface is deprecated in JavaServer Faces 2.

- `ActionSource2`: Extends `ActionSource` and therefore provides the same functionality. However, it allows components to use the Expression Language (EL) when they are referencing methods that handle action events.

- `EditableValueHolder`: Extends `ValueHolder` and specifies additional features for editable components, such as validation and emitting value-change events.

- `NamingContainer`: Mandates that each component rooted at this component have a unique ID.

- `StateHolder`: Denotes that a component has state that must be saved between requests.

- `ValueHolder`: Indicates that the component maintains a local value as well as the option of accessing data in the model tier.

- `javax.faces.event.SystemEventListenerHolder`: Maintains a list of `javax.faces.event.SystemEventListener` instances for each type of `javax.faces.event.SystemEvent` defined by that class.

- `javax.faces.component.behavior.ClientBehaviorHolder`: Adds the ability to attach `javax.faces.component.behavior.ClientBehavior` instances, such as a reusable script.

`UICommand` implements `ActionSource2` and `StateHolder`. `UIOutput` and component classes that extend `UIOutput` implement `StateHolder` and `ValueHolder`. `UIInput` and component classes that extend `UIInput` implement `EditableValueHolder`, `StateHolder`, and `ValueHolder`. `UIComponentBase` implements `StateHolder`.

Only component writers will need to use the component classes and behavioral interfaces directly. Page authors and application developers will use a standard component by including a tag that represents it on a page. Most of the components can be rendered in different ways on a page. For example, a `UICommand` component can be rendered as a button or a link.

The next section explains how the rendering model works and how page authors can choose to render the components by selecting the appropriate tags.

7.4.2 Component Rendering Model

The JavaServer Faces component architecture is designed such that the functionality of the components is defined by the component classes, whereas the component rendering can be defined by a separate renderer class. This design has several benefits, including the following.

- Component writers can define the behavior of a component once but create multiple renderers, each of which defines a different way to render the component to the same client or to different clients.

- Page authors and application developers can change the appearance of a component on the page by selecting the tag that represents the appropriate combination of component and renderer.

A **render kit** defines how component classes map to component tags that are appropriate for a particular client. The JavaServer Faces implementation includes a standard HTML render kit for rendering to an HTML client.

The render kit defines a set of javax.faces.render.Renderer classes for each component that it supports. Each Renderer class defines a different way to render the particular component to the output defined by the render kit. For example, a UISelectOne component has three different renderers. One of them renders the component as a group of options. Another renders the component as a combo box. The third one renders the component as a list box. Similarly, a UICommand component can be rendered as a button or a link, using the h:commandButton or h:commandLink tag. The command part of each tag corresponds to the UICommand class, specifying the functionality, which is to fire an action. The Button or Link part of each tag corresponds to a separate Renderer class that defines how the component appears on the page.

Each custom tag defined in the standard HTML render kit is composed of the component functionality (defined in the UIComponent class) and the rendering attributes (defined by the Renderer class).

Section 10.2, "Adding Components to a Page Using HTML Tag Library Tags," lists all supported component tags and illustrates how to use the tags in an example.

The JavaServer Faces implementation provides a custom tag library for rendering components in HTML.

7.4.3 Conversion Model

A JavaServer Faces application can optionally associate a component with server-side object data. This object is a JavaBeans component, such as a managed bean. An application gets and sets the object data for a component by calling the appropriate object properties for that component.

When a component is bound to an object, the application has two views of the component's data.

- The model view, in which data is represented as data types, such as int or long.

- The presentation view, in which data is represented in a manner that can be read or modified by the user. For example, a java.util.Date might be represented as a text string in the format mm/dd/yy or as a set of three text strings.

The JavaServer Faces implementation automatically converts component data between these two views when the bean property associated with the component is of one of the types supported by the component's data. For example, if a UISelectBoolean component is associated with a bean property of type java.lang.Boolean, the JavaServer Faces implementation will automatically convert the component's data from String to Boolean. In addition, some component data must be bound to properties of a particular type. For example, a UISelectBoolean component must be bound to a property of type boolean or java.lang.Boolean.

Sometimes you might want to convert a component's data to a type other than a standard type, or you might want to convert the format of the data. To facilitate this, JavaServer Faces technology allows you to register a javax.faces.convert.Converter implementation on UIOutput components and components whose classes subclass UIOutput. If you register the Converter implementation on a component, the Converter implementation converts the component's data between the two views.

You can either use the standard converters supplied with the JavaServer Faces implementation or create your own custom converter. Custom converter creation is covered in Chapter 15, "Creating Custom UI Components and Other Custom Objects."

7.4.4 Event and Listener Model

The JavaServer Faces event and listener model is similar to the JavaBeans event model in that it has strongly typed event classes and listener interfaces that an application can use to handle events generated by components.

The JavaServer Faces specification defines three types of events: application events, system events, and data-model events.

Application events are tied to a particular application and are generated by a UIComponent. They represent the standard events available in previous versions of JavaServer Faces technology.

An event object identifies the component that generated the event and stores information about the event. To be notified of an event, an application must provide an implementation of the listener class and must register it on the component that generates the event. When the user activates a component, such as by clicking a button, an event is fired. This causes the JavaServer Faces implementation to invoke the listener method that processes the event.

JavaServer Faces supports two kinds of application events: action events and value-change events.

An **action event** (class `javax.faces.event.ActionEvent`) occurs when the user activates a component that implements `ActionSource`. These components include buttons and links.

A **value-change event** (class `javax.faces.event.ValueChangeEvent`) occurs when the user changes the value of a component represented by `UIInput` or one of its subclasses. An example is selecting a check box, an action that results in the component's value changing to `true`. The component types that can generate these types of events are the `UIInput`, `UISelectOne`, `UISelectMany`, and `UISelectBoolean` components. Value-change events are fired only if no validation errors are detected.

Depending on the value of the `immediate` property (see Section 10.2.1.2, "The immediate Attribute") of the component emitting the event, action events can be processed during the Invoke Application phase or the Apply Request Values phase, and value-change events can be processed during the Process Validations phase or the Apply Request Values phase.

System events are generated by an `Object` rather than a `UIComponent`. They are generated during the execution of an application at predefined times. They are applicable to the entire application rather than to a specific component.

A **data-model event** occurs when a new row of a `UIData` component is selected.

There are two ways to cause your application to react to action events or value-change events that are emitted by a standard component:

- Implement an event listener class to handle the event, and register the listener on the component by nesting either an `f:valueChangeListener` tag or an `f:actionListener` tag inside the component tag.

- Implement a method of a managed bean to handle the event, and refer to the method with a method expression from the appropriate attribute of the component's tag.

See Section 15.6, "Implementing an Event Listener," for information on how to implement an event listener. See Section 11.2, "Registering Listeners on Components," for information on how to register the listener on a component.

See Section 12.3.2, "Writing a Method to Handle an Action Event," and Section 12.3.4, "Writing a Method to Handle a Value-Change Event," for information on how to implement managed bean methods that handle these events.

See Section 11.4, "Referencing a Managed Bean Method," for information on how to refer to the managed bean method from the component tag.

When emitting events from custom components, you must implement the appropriate event class and manually queue the event on the component in addition to implementing an event listener class or a managed bean method that handles the event. Section 15.7, "Handling Events for Custom Components," explains how to do this.

7.4.5 Validation Model

JavaServer Faces technology supports a mechanism for validating the local data of editable components (such as text fields). This validation occurs before the corresponding model data is updated to match the local value.

Like the conversion model, the validation model defines a set of standard classes for performing common data validation checks. The JavaServer Faces core tag library also defines a set of tags that correspond to the standard `javax.faces.validator.Validator` implementations. See Section 11.3, "Using the Standard Validators," for a list of all the standard validation classes and corresponding tags.

Most of the tags have a set of attributes for configuring the validator's properties, such as the minimum and maximum allowable values for the component's data. The page author registers the validator on a component by nesting the validator's tag within the component's tag.

In addition to validators that are registered on the component, you can declare a default validator that is registered on all `UIInput` components in the application. For more information on default validators, see Section 16.6, "Using Default Validators."

The validation model also allows you to create your own custom validator and corresponding tag to perform custom validation. The validation model provides two ways to implement custom validation.

■ Implement a `Validator` interface that performs the validation.

■ Implement a managed bean method that performs the validation.

If you are implementing a `Validator` interface, you must also do the following.

■ Register the `Validator` implementation with the application.

■ Create a custom tag or use an `f:validator` tag to register the validator on the component.

In the previously described standard validation model, the validator is defined for each input component on a page. The Bean Validation model allows the validator to be applied to all fields in a page. See Chapter 21, "Introduction to Bean Validation," and Chapter 22, "Bean Validation: Advanced Topics," for more information on Bean Validation.

7.5 Navigation Model

The JavaServer Faces navigation model makes it easy to define page navigation and to handle any additional processing that is needed to choose the sequence in which pages are loaded.

In JavaServer Faces technology, **navigation** is a set of rules for choosing the next page or view to be displayed after an application action, such as when a button or link is clicked.

Navigation can be implicit or user-defined. **Implicit navigation** comes into play when user-defined navigation rules are not configured in the application configuration resource files.

When you add a component such as a commandButton to a Facelets page, and assign another page as the value for its action property, the default navigation handler will try to match a suitable page within the application implicitly. In the following example, the default navigation handler will try to locate a page named response.xhtml within the application and navigate to it:

```
<h:commandButton value="submit" action="response">
```

User-defined navigation rules are declared in zero or more application configuration resource files, such as faces-config.xml, by using a set of XML elements. The default structure of a navigation rule is as follows.

```
<navigation-rule>
    <description></description>
    <from-view-id></from-view-id>
    <navigation-case>
        <from-action></from-action>
        <from-outcome></from-outcome>
        <if></if>
        <to-view-id></to-view-id>
    </navigation-case>
</navigation-rule>
```

User-defined navigation is handled as follows.

- Define the rules in the application configuration resource file.

- Refer to an outcome String from the button or link component's action attribute. This outcome String is used by the JavaServer Faces implementation to select the navigation rule.

Here is an example navigation rule:

```
<navigation-rule>
    <from-view-id>/greeting.xhtml</from-view-id>
    <navigation-case>
        <from-outcome>success</from-outcome>
        <to-view-id>/response.xhtml</to-view-id>
    </navigation-case>
</navigation-rule>
```

This rule states that when a command component (such as an h:commandButton or an h:commandLink) on greeting.xhtml is activated, the application will navigate from the greeting.xhtml page to the response.xhtml page if the outcome referenced by the button component's tag is success. Here is an h:commandButton tag from greeting.xhtml that would specify a logical outcome of success:

```
<h:commandButton id="submit" value="Submit" action="success"/>
```

As the example demonstrates, each navigation-rule element defines how to get from one page (specified in the from-view-id element) to the other pages of the application. The navigation-rule elements can contain any number of navigation-case elements, each of which defines the page to open next (defined by to-view-id) based on a logical outcome (defined by from-outcome).

In more complicated applications, the logical outcome can also come from the return value of an **action method** in a managed bean. This method performs some processing to determine the outcome. For example, the method can check whether the password the user entered on the page matches the one on file. If it does, the method might return success; otherwise, it might return failure. An outcome of failure might result in the logon page being reloaded. An outcome of success might cause the page displaying the user's credit card activity to open. If you want the outcome to be returned by a method on a bean, you must refer to the method using a method expression with the action attribute, as shown by this example:

```
<h:commandButton id="submit" value="Submit"
                 action="#{cashierBean.submit}" />
```

When the user clicks the button represented by this tag, the corresponding component generates an action event. This event is handled by the default `javax.faces.event.ActionListener` instance, which calls the action method referenced by the component that triggered the event. The action method returns a logical outcome to the action listener.

The listener passes the logical outcome and a reference to the action method that produced the outcome to the default `javax.faces.application.NavigationHandler`. The `NavigationHandler` selects the page to display next by matching the outcome or the action method reference against the navigation rules in the application configuration resource file by the following process.

1. The `NavigationHandler` selects the navigation rule that matches the page currently displayed.

2. It matches the outcome or the action method reference that it received from the default `javax.faces.event.ActionListener` with those defined by the navigation cases.

3. It tries to match both the method reference and the outcome against the same navigation case.

4. If the previous step fails, the navigation handler attempts to match the outcome.

5. Finally, the navigation handler attempts to match the action method reference if the previous two attempts failed.

6. If no navigation case is matched, it displays the same view again.

When the `NavigationHandler` achieves a match, the Render Response phase begins. During this phase, the page selected by the `NavigationHandler` will be rendered.

The Duke's Tutoring case study example application uses navigation rules in the business methods that handle creating, editing, and deleting the users of the application. (See Chapter 29, "Duke's Tutoring Case Study Example," in *The Java EE 7 Tutorial, Volume* 2.) For example, the form for creating a student has the following h:commandButton tag:

```
<h:commandButton id="submit"
            action="#{adminBean.createStudent(studentManager.newStudent)}"
            value="#{bundle['action.submit']}"/>
```

The action event calls the `dukestutoring.ejb.AdminBean.createStudent` method:

```
public String createStudent(Student student) {
    em.persist(student);
    return "createdStudent";
}
```

The return value of `createdStudent` has a corresponding navigation case in the `faces-config.xml` configuration file:

```
<navigation-rule>
    <from-view-id>/admin/student/createStudent.xhtml</from-view-id>
    <navigation-case>
        <from-outcome>createdStudent</from-outcome>
        <to-view-id>/admin/index.xhtml</to-view-id>
    </navigation-case>
</navigation-rule>
```

After the student is created, the user is returned to the Administration index page.

For more information on how to define navigation rules, see Section 16.9, "Configuring Navigation Rules."

For more information on how to implement action methods to handle navigation, see Section 12.3.2, "Writing a Method to Handle an Action Event."

For more information on how to reference outcomes or action methods from component tags, see Section 11.4.1, "Referencing a Method That Performs Navigation."

7.6 The Lifecycle of a JavaServer Faces Application

The lifecycle of an application refers to the various stages of processing of that application, from its initiation to its conclusion. All applications have lifecycles. During a web application lifecycle, common tasks are performed, including the following.

- Handling incoming requests
- Decoding parameters
- Modifying and saving state
- Rendering web pages to the browser

The JavaServer Faces web application framework manages lifecycle phases automatically for simple applications or allows you to manage them manually for more complex applications as required.

JavaServer Faces applications that use advanced features may require interaction with the lifecycle at certain phases. For example, Ajax applications use partial processing features of the lifecycle (see Section 7.7, "Partial Processing and Partial Rendering"). A clearer understanding of the lifecycle phases is key to creating well-designed components.

A simplified view of the JavaServer faces lifecycle, consisting of the two main phases of a JavaServer Faces web application, is introduced in Section 7.3, "A Simple JavaServer Faces Application." This section examines the JavaServer Faces lifecycle in more detail.

7.6.1 Overview of the JavaServer Faces Lifecycle

The lifecycle of a JavaServer Faces application begins when the client makes an HTTP request for a page and ends when the server responds with the page, translated to HTML.

The lifecycle can be divided into two main phases: **Execute** and **Render**. The Execute phase is further divided into subphases to support the sophisticated component tree. This structure requires that component data be converted and validated, component events be handled, and component data be propagated to beans in an orderly fashion.

A JavaServer Faces page is represented by a tree of components, called a **view**. During the lifecycle, the JavaServer Faces implementation must build the view while considering the state saved from a previous submission of the page. When the client requests a page, the JavaServer Faces implementation performs several tasks, such as validating the data input of components in the view and converting input data to types specified on the server side.

The JavaServer Faces implementation performs all these tasks as a series of steps in the JavaServer Faces request-response lifecycle. Figure 7–3 illustrates these steps.

Figure 7–3   JavaServer Faces Standard Request-Response Lifecycle

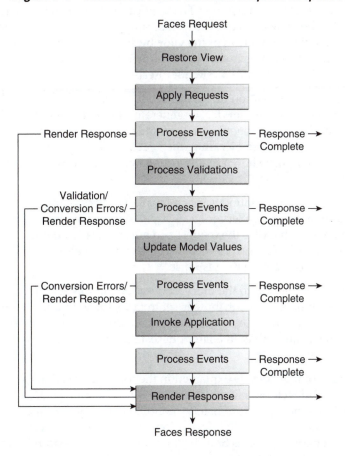

The request-response lifecycle handles two kinds of requests: initial requests and postbacks. An **initial request** occurs when a user makes a request for a page for the first time. A **postback request** occurs when a user submits the form contained on a page that was previously loaded into the browser as a result of executing an initial request.

When the lifecycle handles an initial request, it executes only the Restore View and Render Response phases, because there is no user input or action to process. Conversely, when the lifecycle handles a postback, it executes all of the phases.

Usually, the first request for a JavaServer Faces page comes in from a client, as a result of clicking a link or button component on a JavaServer Faces page. To render a response that is another JavaServer Faces page, the application creates a new view and stores it in the `javax.faces.context.FacesContext` instance, which represents all of the information associated with processing an incoming request and creating a response. The application then acquires object references needed by the view and calls the `FacesContext.renderResponse` method, which forces immediate rendering of the view by skipping to the Render Response phase of the lifecycle, as is shown by the arrows labelled Render Response in Figure 7–3. (See Section 7.6.7, "Render Response Phase.")

Sometimes, an application might need to redirect to a different web application resource, such as a web service, or generate a response that does not contain JavaServer Faces components. In these situations, the developer must skip the Render Response phase by calling the `FacesContext.responseComplete` method. This situation is also shown in Figure 7–3, with the arrows labelled Response Complete.

The most common situation is that a JavaServer Faces component submits a request for another JavaServer Faces page. In this case, the JavaServer Faces implementation handles the request and automatically goes through the phases in the lifecycle to perform any necessary conversions, validations, and model updates and to generate the response.

There is one exception to the lifecycle described in this section. When a component's `immediate` attribute is set to `true`, the validation, conversion, and events associated with these components are processed during the Apply Request Values phase rather than in a later phase. (See Section 7.6.3, "Apply Request Values Phase.")

The details of the lifecycle explained in the following sections are primarily intended for developers who need to know information such as when validations, conversions, and events are usually handled and ways to change how and when they are handled. For more information on each of the lifecycle phases, download the latest JavaServer Faces Specification documentation from `http://jcp.org/en/jsr/detail?id=344`.

The JavaServer Faces application lifecycle Execute phase contains the following subphases:

- Restore View Phase

- Apply Request Values Phase

- Process Validations Phase

- Update Model Values Phase

- Invoke Application Phase

- Render Response Phase

7.6.2 Restore View Phase

When a request for a JavaServer Faces page is made, usually by an action, such as when a link or a button component is clicked, the JavaServer Faces implementation begins the Restore View phase.

During this phase, the JavaServer Faces implementation builds the view of the page, wires event handlers and validators to components in the view, and saves the view in the `FacesContext` instance, which contains all the information needed to process a single request. All the application's components, event handlers, converters, and validators have access to the `FacesContext` instance.

If the request for the page is an initial request, the JavaServer Faces implementation creates an empty view during this phase and the lifecycle advances to the Render Response phase, during which the empty view is populated with the components referenced by the tags in the page.

If the request for the page is a postback, a view corresponding to this page already exists in the `FacesContext` instance. During this phase, the JavaServer Faces implementation restores the view by using the state information saved on the client or the server.

7.6.3 Apply Request Values Phase

After the component tree is restored during a postback request, each component in the tree extracts its new value from the request parameters by using its `decode` (`processDecodes()`) method. The value is then stored locally on each component.

If any `decode` methods or event listeners have called the `renderResponse` method on the current `FacesContext` instance, the JavaServer Faces implementation skips to the Render Response phase.

If any events have been queued during this phase, the JavaServer Faces implementation broadcasts the events to interested listeners.

If some components on the page have their `immediate` attributes (see Section 10.2.1.2, "The immediate Attribute") set to `true`, then the validations, conversions, and events associated with these components will be processed during this phase. If any conversion fails, an error message associated with the component is generated and queued on `FacesContext`. This message will be displayed during the Render Response phase, along with any validation errors resulting from the Process Validations phase.

At this point, if the application needs to redirect to a different web application resource or generate a response that does not contain any JavaServer Faces components, it can call the `FacesContext.responseComplete` method.

At the end of this phase, the components are set to their new values, and messages and events have been queued.

If the current request is identified as a partial request, the partial context is retrieved from the FacesContext, and the partial processing method is applied.

7.6.4 Process Validations Phase

During this phase, the JavaServer Faces implementation processes all validators registered on the components in the tree by using its validate (processValidators) method. It examines the component attributes that specify the rules for the validation and compares these rules to the local value stored for the component. The JavaServer Faces implementation also completes conversions for input components that do not have the immediate attribute set to true.

If the local value is invalid, or if any conversion fails, the JavaServer Faces implementation adds an error message to the FacesContext instance, and the lifecycle advances directly to the Render Response phase so that the page is rendered again with the error messages displayed. If there were conversion errors from the Apply Request Values phase, the messages for these errors are also displayed.

If any validate methods or event listeners have called the renderResponse method on the current FacesContext, the JavaServer Faces implementation skips to the Render Response phase.

At this point, if the application needs to redirect to a different web application resource or generate a response that does not contain any JavaServer Faces components, it can call the FacesContext.responseComplete method.

If events have been queued during this phase, the JavaServer Faces implementation broadcasts them to interested listeners.

If the current request is identified as a partial request, the partial context is retrieved from the FacesContext, and the partial processing method is applied.

7.6.5 Update Model Values Phase

After the JavaServer Faces implementation determines that the data is valid, it traverses the component tree and sets the corresponding server-side object properties to the components' local values. The JavaServer Faces implementation updates only the bean properties pointed at by an input component's value attribute. If the local data cannot be converted to the types specified by the bean properties, the lifecycle advances directly to the Render Response phase so that the page is re-rendered with errors displayed. This is similar to what happens with validation errors.

If any `updateModels` methods or any listeners have called the `renderResponse` method on the current `FacesContext` instance, the JavaServer Faces implementation skips to the Render Response phase.

At this point, if the application needs to redirect to a different web application resource or generate a response that does not contain any JavaServer Faces components, it can call the `FacesContext.responseComplete` method.

If any events have been queued during this phase, the JavaServer Faces implementation broadcasts them to interested listeners.

If the current request is identified as a partial request, the partial context is retrieved from the `FacesContext`, and the partial processing method is applied.

7.6.6 Invoke Application Phase

During this phase, the JavaServer Faces implementation handles any application-level events, such as submitting a form or linking to another page.

At this point, if the application needs to redirect to a different web application resource or generate a response that does not contain any JavaServer Faces components, it can call the `FacesContext.responseComplete` method.

If the view being processed was reconstructed from state information from a previous request and if a component has fired an event, these events are broadcast to interested listeners.

Finally, the JavaServer Faces implementation transfers control to the Render Response phase.

7.6.7 Render Response Phase

During this phase, JavaServer Faces builds the view and delegates authority to the appropriate resource for rendering the pages.

If this is an initial request, the components that are represented on the page will be added to the component tree. If this is not an initial request, the components are already added to the tree and need not be added again.

If the request is a postback and errors were encountered during the Apply Request Values phase, Process Validations phase, or Update Model Values phase, the original page is rendered again during this phase. If the pages contain `h:message` or `h:messages` tags, any queued error messages are displayed on the page.

After the content of the view is rendered, the state of the response is saved so that subsequent requests can access it. The saved state is available to the Restore View phase.

7.7 Partial Processing and Partial Rendering

The JavaServer Faces lifecycle spans all of the execute and render processes of an application. It is also possible to process and render only parts of an application, such as a single component. For example, the JavaServer Faces Ajax framework can generate requests containing information on which particular component may be processed and which particular component may be rendered back to the client.

Once such a partial request enters the JavaServer Faces lifecycle, the information is identified and processed by a javax.faces.context.PartialViewContext object. The JavaServer Faces lifecycle is still aware of such Ajax requests and modifies the component tree accordingly.

The execute and render attributes of the f:ajax tag are used to identify which components may be executed and rendered. For more information on these attributes, see Chapter 13, "Using Ajax with JavaServer Faces Technology."

7.8 Further Information about JavaServer Faces Technology

For more information on JavaServer Faces technology, see

- JavaServer Faces 2.2 specification:

    http://jcp.org/en/jsr/detail?id=344

- JavaServer Faces project website:

    https://javaserverfaces.java.net/

8

Introduction to Facelets

The term **Facelets** refers to the view declaration language for JavaServer Faces technology. Facelets is a part of the JavaServer Faces specification and also the preferred presentation technology for building JavaServer Faces technology–based applications. JavaServer Pages (JSP) technology, previously used as the presentation technology for JavaServer Faces, does not support all the new features available in JavaServer Faces in the Java EE 7 platform. JSP technology is considered to be a deprecated presentation technology for JavaServer Faces.

The following topics are addressed here:

- What Is Facelets?
- The Lifecycle of a Facelets Application
- Developing a Simple Facelets Application: The guessnumber-jsf Example Application
- Using Facelets Templates
- Composite Components
- Web Resources
- Relocatable Resources
- Resource Library Contracts
- HTML5-Friendly Markup

8.1 What Is Facelets?

Facelets is a powerful but lightweight page declaration language that is used to build JavaServer Faces views using HTML style templates and to build component trees. Facelets features include the following:

- Use of XHTML for creating web pages
- Support for Facelets tag libraries in addition to JavaServer Faces and JSTL tag libraries
- Support for the Expression Language (EL)
- Templating for components and pages

The advantages of Facelets for large-scale development projects include the following:

- Support for code reuse through templating and composite components
- Functional extensibility of components and other server-side objects through customization
- Faster compilation time
- Compile-time EL validation
- High-performance rendering

In short, the use of Facelets reduces the time and effort that needs to be spent on development and deployment.

Facelets views are usually created as XHTML pages. JavaServer Faces implementations support XHTML pages created in conformance with the XHTML Transitional Document Type Definition (DTD), as listed at `http://www.w3.org/TR/xhtml1/#a_dtd_XHTML-1.0-Transitional`. By convention, web pages built with XHTML have an `.xhtml` extension.

JavaServer Faces technology supports various tag libraries to add components to a web page. To support the JavaServer Faces tag library mechanism, Facelets uses XML namespace declarations. Table 8–1 lists the tag libraries supported by Facelets.

Table 8–1 *Tag Libraries Supported by Facelets*

Tag Library	URI	Prefix	Example	Contents
JavaServer Faces Facelets Tag Library	`http://xmlns.jcp.org/jsf/facelets`	`ui:`	`ui:component` `ui:insert`	Tags for templating

JavaServer Faces HTML Tag Library	`http://xmlns.jcp.org/jsf/html`	`h:`	`h:head`
			`h:body`
			`h:outputText`
			`h:inputText`
				JavaServer Faces component tags for all `UIComponent` objects

JavaServer Faces Core Tag Library	`http://xmlns.jcp.org/jsf/core`	`f:`	`f:actionListener` `f:attribute`	Tags for JavaServer Faces custom actions that are independent of any particular render kit
Pass-through Elements Tag Library	`http://xmlns.jcp.org/jsf`	`jsf:`	`jsf:id`	Tags to support HTML5-friendly markup
Pass-through Attributes Tag Library	`http://xmlns.jcp.org/jsf/passthrough`	`p:`	`p:type`	Tags to support HTML5-friendly markup
Composite Component Tag Library	`http://xmlns.jcp.org/jsf/composite`	`cc:`	`cc:interface`	Tags to support composite components
JSTL Core Tag Library	`http://xmlns.jcp.org/jsp/jstl/core`	`c:`	`c:forEach` `c:catch`	JSTL 1.2 Core Tags
JSTL Functions Tag Library	`http://xmlns.jcp.org/jsp/jstl/functions`	`fn:`	`fn:toUpperCase` `fn:toLowerCase`	JSTL 1.2 Functions Tags

Facelets provides two namespaces to support HTML5-friendly markup. For details, see Section 8.9, "HTML5-Friendly Markup."

Facelets supports tags for composite components, for which you can declare custom prefixes. For more information on composite components, see Section 8.5, "Composite Components."

The namespace prefixes shown in the table are conventional, not mandatory. As is always the case when you declare an XML namespace, you can specify any prefix in your Facelets page. For example, you can declare the prefix for the composite component tag library as

```
xmlns:composite="http://java.sun.com/jsf/composite"
```

instead of as

```
xmlns:cc="http://java.sun.com/jsf/composite"
```

Based on the JavaServer Faces support for Expression Language (EL) syntax, Facelets uses EL expressions to reference properties and methods of managed beans. EL expressions can be used to bind component objects or values to methods or properties of managed beans that are used as backing beans. For more information on using EL expressions, see Chapter 9, "Expression Language," and Section 12.1.2, "Using the EL to Reference Managed Beans."

8.2 The Lifecycle of a Facelets Application

The JavaServer Faces specification defines the lifecycle of a JavaServer Faces application. For more information on this lifecycle, see Section 7.6, "The Lifecycle of a JavaServer Faces Application." The following steps describe that process as applied to a Facelets-based application.

1. When a client, such as a browser, makes a new request to a page that is created using Facelets, a new component tree or `javax.faces.component.UIViewRoot` is created and placed in the `FacesContext`.

2. The `UIViewRoot` is applied to the Facelets, and the view is populated with components for rendering.

3. The newly built view is rendered back as a response to the client.

4. On rendering, the state of this view is stored for the next request. The state of input components and form data is stored.

5. The client may interact with the view and request another view or change from the JavaServer Faces application. At this time, the saved view is restored from the stored state.

6. The restored view is once again passed through the JavaServer Faces lifecycle, which eventually will either generate a new view or re-render the current view if there were no validation problems and no action was triggered.

7. If the same view is requested, the stored view is rendered once again.

8. If a new view is requested, then the process described in Step 2 is continued.

9. The new view is then rendered back as a response to the client.

8.3 Developing a Simple Facelets Application: The guessnumber-jsf Example Application

This section describes the general steps involved in developing a JavaServer Faces application. The following tasks are usually required:

- Developing the managed beans

- Creating the pages using the component tags

- Defining page navigation

- Mapping the FacesServlet instance

- Adding managed bean declarations

8.3.1 Creating a Facelets Application

The example used in this tutorial is the guessnumber-jsf application. The application presents you with a page that asks you to guess a number from 0 to 10, validates your input against a random number, and responds with another page that informs you whether you guessed the number correctly or incorrectly.

The source code for this application is in the *tut-install*/examples/web/jsf/ guessnumber-jsf/ directory.

8.3.1.1 Developing a Managed Bean

In a typical JavaServer Faces application, each page of the application connects to a managed bean that serves as a backing bean. The backing bean defines the methods and properties that are associated with the components. In this example, both pages use the same backing bean.

The following managed bean class, UserNumberBean.java, generates a random number from 0 to 10 inclusive:

```
package javaeetutorial.guessnumber;

import java.io.Serializable;
import java.util.Random;
import javax.enterprise.context.SessionScoped;
import javax.inject.Named;

@Named
```

```java
@SessionScoped
public class UserNumberBean implements Serializable {

    private static final long serialVersionUID = 5443351151396868724L;
    Integer randomInt = null;
    Integer userNumber = null;
    String response = null;
    private int maximum = 10;
    private int minimum = 0;

    public UserNumberBean() {
        Random randomGR = new Random();
        randomInt = new Integer(randomGR.nextInt(maximum + 1));
        // Print number to server log
        System.out.println("Duke's number: " + randomInt);
    }

    public void setUserNumber(Integer user_number) {
        userNumber = user_number;
    }

    public Integer getUserNumber() {
        return userNumber;
    }

    public String getResponse() {
        if ((userNumber == null) || (userNumber.compareTo(randomInt) !=0 )) {
            return "Sorry, " + userNumber + " is incorrect.";
        } else {
            return "Yay! You got it!";
        }
    }

    public int getMaximum() {
        return (this.maximum);
    }
    public void setMaximum(int maximum) {
        this.maximum = maximum;
    }

    public int getMinimum() {
        return (this.minimum);
    }

    public void setMinimum(int minimum) {
        this.minimum = minimum;
    }
```

```
}
```

Note the use of the @Named annotation, which makes the managed bean accessible through the EL. The @SessionScoped annotation registers the bean scope as session to enable you to make multiple guesses as you run the application.

8.3.1.2 Creating Facelets Views

To create a page or view, you add components to the pages, wire the components to backing bean values and properties, and register converters, validators, or listeners on the components.

For the example application, XHTML web pages serve as the front end. The first page of the example application is a page called greeting.xhtml. A closer look at various sections of this web page provides more information.

The first section of the web page declares the content type for the page, which is XHTML:

```
<!DOCTYPE html PUBLIC "-//W3C//DTD XHTML 1.0 Transitional//EN"
  "http://www.w3.org/TR/xhtml1/DTD/xhtml1-transitional.dtd">
```

The next section specifies the language of the XHTML page and then declares the XML namespace for the tag libraries that are used in the web page:

```
<html lang="en"
      xmlns="http://www.w3.org/1999/xhtml"
      xmlns:h="http://xmlns.jcp.org/jsf/html"
      xmlns:f="http://xmlns.jcp.org/jsf/core">
```

The next section uses various tags to insert components into the web page:

```
<h:head>
    <h:outputStylesheet library="css" name="default.css"/>
    <title>Guess Number Facelets Application</title>
</h:head>
<h:body>
    <h:form>
        <h:graphicImage value="#{resource['images:wave.med.gif']}"
                        alt="Duke waving his hand"/>
        <h2>
            Hi, my name is Duke. I am thinking of a number from
            #{userNumberBean.minimum} to #{userNumberBean.maximum}.
            Can you guess it?
        </h2>
        <p><h:inputText id="userNo"
                        title="Enter a number from 0 to 10:"
                        value="#{userNumberBean.userNumber}">
```

```
                        <f:validateLongRange minimum="#{userNumberBean.minimum}"
                                             maximum="#{userNumberBean.maximum}"/>
                    </h:inputText>
                    <h:commandButton id="submit" value="Submit"
                                     action="response"/>
                </p>
                <h:message showSummary="true" showDetail="false"
                        style="color: #d20005;
                        font-family: 'New Century Schoolbook', serif;
                        font-style: oblique;
                        text-decoration: overline"
                        id="errors1"
                        for="userNo"/>
        </h:form>
    </h:body>
```

Note the use of the following tags:

- Facelets HTML tags (those beginning with h:) to add components

- The Facelets core tag f:validateLongRange to validate the user input

An h:inputText tag accepts user input and sets the value of the managed bean property userNumber through the EL expression #{userNumberBean.userNumber}. The input value is validated for value range by the JavaServer Faces standard validator tag f:validateLongRange.

The image file, wave.med.gif, is added to the page as a resource, as is the style sheet. For more details about the resources facility, see Section 8.6, "Web Resources."

An h:commandButton tag with the ID submit starts validation of the input data when a user clicks the button. Using implicit navigation, the tag redirects the client to another page, response.xhtml, which shows the response to your input. The page specifies only response, which by default causes the server to look for response.xhtml.

You can now create the second page, response.xhtml, with the following content:

```
<!DOCTYPE html PUBLIC "-//W3C//DTD XHTML 1.0 Transitional//EN"
    "http://www.w3.org/TR/xhtml1/DTD/xhtml1-transitional.dtd">

<html lang="en"
     xmlns="http://www.w3.org/1999/xhtml"
     xmlns:h="http://xmlns.jcp.org/jsf/html">

    <h:head>
        <h:outputStylesheet library="css" name="default.css"/>
```

```
        <title>Guess Number Facelets Application</title>
    </h:head>
    <h:body>
        <h:form>
            <h:graphicImage value="#{resource['images:wave.med.gif']}"
                            alt="Duke waving his hand"/>
            <h2>
                <h:outputText id="result" value="#{userNumberBean.response}"/>
            </h2>
            <h:commandButton id="back" value="Back" action="greeting"/>
        </h:form>
    </h:body>
</html>
```

This page also uses implicit navigation, setting the action attribute for the **Back** button to send the user to the greeting.xhtml page.

8.3.2 Configuring the Application

Configuring a JavaServer Faces application involves mapping the Faces Servlet in the web deployment descriptor file, such as a web.xml file, and possibly adding managed bean declarations, navigation rules, and resource bundle declarations to the application configuration resource file, faces-config.xml.

If you are using NetBeans IDE, a web deployment descriptor file is automatically created for you. In such an IDE-created web.xml file, change the default greeting page, which is index.xhtml, to greeting.xhtml. Here is an example web.xml file, showing this change in **bold**.

```
<?xml version="1.0" encoding="UTF-8"?>
<web-app version="3.1" xmlns="http://xmlns.jcp.org/xml/ns/javaee"
  xmlns:xsi="http://www.w3.org/2001/XMLSchema-instance"
  xsi:schemaLocation="http://xmlns.jcp.org/xml/ns/javaee
  http://xmlns.jcp.org/xml/ns/javaee/web-app_3_1.xsd">
    <context-param>
        <param-name>javax.faces.PROJECT_STAGE</param-name>
        <param-value>Development</param-value>
    </context-param>
    <servlet>
        <servlet-name>Faces Servlet</servlet-name>
        <servlet-class>javax.faces.webapp.FacesServlet</servlet-class>
        <load-on-startup>1</load-on-startup>
    </servlet>
    <servlet-mapping>
        <servlet-name>Faces Servlet</servlet-name>
        <url-pattern>*.xhtml</url-pattern>
```

```
    </servlet-mapping>
    <session-config>
        <session-timeout>
            30
        </session-timeout>
    </session-config>
    <welcome-file-list>
        <welcome-file>greeting.xhtml</welcome-file>
    </welcome-file-list>
</web-app>
```

Note the use of the context parameter PROJECT_STAGE. This parameter identifies the status of a JavaServer Faces application in the software lifecycle.

The stage of an application can affect the behavior of the application. For example, if the project stage is defined as Development, debugging information is automatically generated for the user. If not defined by the user, the default project stage is Production.

8.3.3 Running the guessnumber-jsf Facelets Example

You can use either NetBeans IDE or Maven to build, package, deploy, and run the guessnumber-jsf example.

8.3.3.1 To Build, Package, and Deploy the guessnumber-jsf Example Using NetBeans IDE

1. Make sure that GlassFish Server has been started (see Section 2.2, "Starting and Stopping GlassFish Server").

2. From the **File** menu, choose **Open Project**.

3. In the Open Project dialog box, navigate to:

   tut-install/examples/web/jsf

4. Select the guessnumber-jsf folder.

5. Click **Open Project**.

6. In the **Projects** tab, right-click the guessnumber-jsf project and select **Build**.

   This option builds the example application and deploys it to your GlassFish Server instance.

8.3.3.2 To Build, Package, and Deploy the guessnumber-jsf Example Using Maven

1. Make sure that GlassFish Server has been started (see Section 2.2, "Starting and Stopping GlassFish Server").

2. In a terminal window, go to:

   `tut-install/examples/web/jsf/guessnumber-jsf/`

3. Enter the following command:

   `mvn install`

   This command builds and packages the application into a WAR file, `guessnumber-jsf.war`, that is located in the `target` directory. It then deploys it to the server.

8.3.3.3 To Run the guessnumber-jsf Example

1. Open a web browser.

2. Enter the following URL in your web browser:

   `http://localhost:8080/guessnumber-jsf`

3. In the field, enter a number from 0 to 10 and click **Submit**.

   Another page appears, reporting whether your guess is correct or incorrect.

4. If you guessed incorrectly, click **Back** to return to the main page.

   You can continue to guess until you get the correct answer, or you can look in the server log, where the `UserNumberBean` constructor displays the correct answer.

8.4 Using Facelets Templates

JavaServer Faces technology provides the tools to implement user interfaces that are easy to extend and reuse. Templating is a useful Facelets feature that allows you to create a page that will act as the base, or **template**, for the other pages in an application. By using templates, you can reuse code and avoid recreating similarly constructed pages. Templating also helps in maintaining a standard look and feel in an application with a large number of pages.

Table 8–2 lists Facelets tags that are used for templating and their respective functionality.

Table 8–2   Facelets Templating Tags

Tag	Function
ui:component	Defines a component that is created and added to the component tree.
ui:composition	Defines a page composition that optionally uses a template. Content outside of this tag is ignored.
ui:debug	Defines a debug component that is created and added to the component tree.
ui:decorate	Similar to the composition tag but does not disregard content outside this tag.
ui:define	Defines content that is inserted into a page by a template.
ui:fragment	Similar to the component tag but does not disregard content outside this tag.
ui:include	Encapsulates and reuses content for multiple pages.
ui:insert	Inserts content into a template.
ui:param	Used to pass parameters to an included file.
ui:repeat	Used as an alternative for loop tags, such as c:forEach or h:dataTable.
ui:remove	Removes content from a page.

For more information on Facelets templating tags, see the documentation at http://docs.oracle.com/javaee/7/javaserverfaces/2.2/vdldocs/facelets/.

The Facelets tag library includes the main templating tag ui:insert. A template page that is created with this tag allows you to define a default structure for a page. A template page is used as a template for other pages, usually referred to as client pages.

Here is an example of a template saved as template.xhtml:

```
<!DOCTYPE html PUBLIC "-//W3C//DTD XHTML 1.0 Transitional//EN"
     "http://www.w3.org/TR/xhtml1/DTD/xhtml1-transitional.dtd">
<html xmlns="http://www.w3.org/1999/xhtml"
     xmlns:ui="http://xmlns.jcp.org/jsf/facelets"
     xmlns:h="http://xmlns.jcp.org/jsf/html">
   <h:head>
      <meta http-equiv="Content-Type"
            content="text/html; charset=UTF-8" />
      <h:outputStylesheet library="css" name="default.css"/>
      <h:outputStylesheet library="css" name="cssLayout.css"/>
```

```
            <title>Facelets Template</title>
        </h:head>

        <h:body>
            <div id="top" class="top">
                <ui:insert name="top">Top Section</ui:insert>
            </div>
            <div>
            <div id="left">
                <ui:insert name="left">Left Section</ui:insert>
            </div>
            <div id="content" class="left_content">
                <ui:insert name="content">Main Content</ui:insert>
            </div>
            </div>
        </h:body>
</html>
```

The example page defines an XHTML page that is divided into three sections: a top section, a left section, and a main section. The sections have style sheets associated with them. The same structure can be reused for the other pages of the application.

The client page invokes the template by using the ui:composition tag. In the following example, a client page named templateclient.xhtml invokes the template page named template.xhtml from the preceding example. A client page allows content to be inserted with the help of the ui:define tag.

```
<!DOCTYPE html PUBLIC "-//W3C//DTD XHTML 1.0 Transitional//EN"
    "http://www.w3.org/TR/xhtml1/DTD/xhtml1-transitional.dtd">
<html xmlns="http://www.w3.org/1999/xhtml"
      xmlns:ui="http://xmlns.jcp.org/jsf/facelets"
      xmlns:h="http://xmlns.jcp.org/jsf/html">

    <h:body>
        <ui:composition template="./template.xhtml">
            <ui:define name="top">
                Welcome to Template Client Page
            </ui:define>

            <ui:define name="left">
                <h:outputLabel value="You are in the Left Section"/>
            </ui:define>

            <ui:define name="content">
                <h:graphicImage value="#{resource['images:wave.med.gif']}"/>
                <h:outputText value="You are in the Main Content Section"/>
```

```
        </ui:define>
      </ui:composition>
    </h:body>
  </html>
```

You can use NetBeans IDE to create Facelets template and client pages. For more information on creating these pages, see `https://netbeans.org/kb/docs/web/jsf20-intro.html`.

8.5 Composite Components

JavaServer Faces technology offers the concept of composite components with Facelets. A **composite component** is a special type of template that acts as a component.

Any component is essentially a piece of reusable code that behaves in a particular way. For example, an input component accepts user input. A component can also have validators, converters, and listeners attached to it to perform certain defined actions.

A composite component consists of a collection of markup tags and other existing components. This reusable, user-created component has a customized, defined functionality and can have validators, converters, and listeners attached to it like any other component.

With Facelets, any XHTML page that contains markup tags and other components can be converted into a composite component. Using the resources facility, the composite component can be stored in a library that is available to the application from the defined resources location.

Table 8–3 lists the most commonly used composite tags and their functions.

Table 8–3   Composite Component Tags

Tag	Function
composite:interface	Declares the usage contract for a composite component. The composite component can be used as a single component whose feature set is the union of the features declared in the usage contract.
composite:implementation	Defines the implementation of the composite component. If a composite:interface element appears, there must be a corresponding composite:implementation.

Table 8–3 (Cont.) Composite Component Tags

Tag	Function
composite:attribute	Declares an attribute that may be given to an instance of the composite component in which this tag is declared.
composite:insertChildren	Any child components or template text within the composite component tag in the using page will be reparented into the composite component at the point indicated by this tag's placement within the composite:implementation section.
composite:valueHolder	Declares that the composite component whose contract is declared by the composite:interface in which this element is nested exposes an implementation of ValueHolder suitable for use as the target of attached objects in the using page.
composite:editableValueHolder	Declares that the composite component whose contract is declared by the composite:interface in which this element is nested exposes an implementation of EditableValueHolder suitable for use as the target of attached objects in the using page.
composite:actionSource	Declares that the composite component whose contract is declared by the composite:interface in which this element is nested exposes an implementation of ActionSource2 suitable for use as the target of attached objects in the using page.

For more information and a complete list of Facelets composite tags, see the documentation at http://docs.oracle.com/javaee/7/javaserverfaces/2.2/vdldocs/facelets/.

The following example shows a composite component that accepts an email address as input:

```
<!DOCTYPE html PUBLIC "-//W3C//DTD XHTML 1.0 Transitional//EN"
  "http://www.w3.org/TR/xhtml1/DTD/xhtml1-transitional.dtd">
<html xmlns="http://www.w3.org/1999/xhtml"
  xmlns:composite="http://xmlns.jcp.org/jsf/composite"
  xmlns:h="http://xmlns.jcp.org/jsf/html">

  <h:head>
    <title>This content will not be displayed</title>
  </h:head>
  <h:body>
    <composite:interface>
```

```
                <composite:attribute name="value" required="false"/>
            </composite:interface>

            <composite:implementation>
                <h:outputLabel value="Email id: "></h:outputLabel>
                <h:inputText value="#{cc.attrs.value}"></h:inputText>
            </composite:implementation>
        </h:body>
</html>
```

Note the use of cc.attrs.value when defining the value of the inputText component. The word cc in JavaServer Faces is a reserved word for composite components. The #{cc.attrs.*attribute-name*} expression is used to access the attributes defined for the composite component's interface, which in this case happens to be value.

The preceding example content is stored as a file named email.xhtml in a folder named resources/emcomp, under the application web root directory. This directory is considered a library by JavaServer Faces, and a component can be accessed from such a library. For more information on resources, see Section 8.6, "Web Resources."

The web page that uses this composite component is generally called a **using page**. The using page includes a reference to the composite component, in the xml namespace declarations:

```
<!DOCTYPE html PUBLIC "-//W3C//DTD XHTML 1.0 Transitional//EN"
    "http://www.w3.org/TR/xhtml1/DTD/xhtml1-transitional.dtd">
<html xmlns="http://www.w3.org/1999/xhtml"
    xmlns:h="http://xmlns.jcp.org/jsf/html"
    xmlns:em="http://xmlns.jcp.org/jsf/composite/emcomp">

    <h:head>
        <title>Using a sample composite component</title>
    </h:head>

    <body>
        <h:form>
            <em:email value="Enter your email id" />
        </h:form>
    </body>
</html>
```

The local composite component library is defined in the xmlns namespace with the declaration xmlns:em="http://xmlns.jcp.org/jsf/composite/emcomp". The component itself is accessed through the em:email tag. The preceding example content can be stored as a web page named `emuserpage.xhtml` under the web root directory. When compiled and deployed on a server, it can be accessed with the following URL:

```
http://localhost:8080/application-name/emuserpage.xhtml
```

See Chapter 14, "Composite Components: Advanced Topics and an Example," for more information and an example.

8.6 Web Resources

Web resources are any software artifacts that the web application requires for proper rendering, including images, script files, and any user-created component libraries. Resources must be collected in a standard location, which can be one of the following.

- A resource packaged in the web application root must be in a subdirectory of a `resources` directory at the web application root: `resources/resource-identifier`.

- A resource packaged in the web application's classpath must be in a subdirectory of the `META-INF/resources` directory within a web application: `META-INF/resources/resource-identifier`. You can use this file structure to package resources in a JAR file bundled in the web application.

The JavaServer Faces runtime will look for the resources in the preceding listed locations, in that order.

Resource identifiers are unique strings that conform to the following format (all on one line):

```
[locale-prefix/][library-name/][library-version/]resource-name
[/resource-version]
```

Elements of the resource identifier in brackets (`[]`) are optional, indicating that only a *resource-name*, which is usually a file name, is a required element. For example, the most common way to specify a style sheet, image, or script is to use the `library` and `name` attributes, as in the following tag from the `guessnumber-jsf` example:

```
<h:outputStylesheet library="css" name="default.css"/>
```

This tag specifies that the `default.css` style sheet is in the directory `web/resources/css`.

You can also specify the location of an image using the following syntax, also from the `guessnumber-jsf` example:

```
<h:graphicImage value="#{resource['images:wave.med.gif']}"/>
```

This tag specifies that the image named `wave.med.gif` is in the directory `web/resources/images`.

Resources can be considered as a library location. Any artifact, such as a composite component or a template that is stored in the `resources` directory, becomes accessible to the other application components, which can use it to create a resource instance.

8.7 Relocatable Resources

You can place a resource tag in one part of a page and specify that it be rendered in another part of the page. To do this, you use the `target` attribute of a tag that specifies a resource. Acceptable values for this attribute are as follows.

- `"head"` renders the resource in the `head` element.
- `"body"` renders the resource in the `body` element.
- `"form"` renders the resource in the `form` element.

For example, the following `h:outputScript` tag is placed within an `h:form` element, but it renders the JavaScript in the `head` element:

```
<h:form>
    <h:outputScript name="myscript.js" library="mylibrary" target="head"/>
</h:form>
```

The `h:outputStylesheet` tag also supports resource relocation, in a similar way.

Relocatable resources are essential for composite components that use stylesheets and can also be useful for composite components that use JavaScript. See Section 14.4, "The compositecomponentexample Example Application," for an example.

8.8 Resource Library Contracts

Resource library contracts allow you to define a different look and feel for different parts of one or more applications, instead of either having to use the same look and feel for all or having to specify a different look on a page-by-page basis.

To do this, you create a `contracts` section of your web application. Within the `contracts` section, you can specify any number of named areas, each of which is called a contract. Within each contract you can specify resources such as template files, stylesheets, JavaScript files, and images.

For example, you could specify two contracts named c1 and c2, each of which uses a template and other files:

```
src/main/webapp
    WEB-INF/
    contracts
        c1
            template.xhtml
            style.css
            myImg.gif
            myJS.js
        c2
            template.xhtml
            style2.css
            img2.gif
            JS2.js
    index.xhtml
    ...
```

One part of the application can use c1, while another can use c2.

Another way to use contracts is to specify a single contract that contains multiple templates:

```
src/main/webapp
    contracts
        myContract
            template1.xhtml
            template2.xhtml
            style.css
            img.png
            img2.png
```

You can package a resource library contract in a JAR file for reuse in different applications. If you do so, the contracts must be located under `META-INF/contracts`. You can then place the JAR file in the `WEB-INF/lib` directory of an application. This means that the application would be organized as follows:

```
src/main/webapp/
    WEB-INF/lib/myContract.jar
    ...
```

You can specify the contract usage within an application's `faces-config.xml` file, under the `resource-library-contracts` element. You need to use this element only if your application uses more than one contract, however.

8.8.1 The hello1-rlc Example Application

The `hello1-rlc` example modifies the simple `hello1` example from Section 6.3, "A Web Module That Uses JavaServer Faces Technology: The hello1 Example," to use two resource library contracts. Each of the two pages in the application uses a different contract.

The managed bean for `hello1-rlc`, `Hello.java`, is identical to the one for `hello1` (except that it replaces the `@Named` and `@RequestScoped` annotations with `@Model`).

The source code for this application is in the *tut-install*/examples/web/jsf/hello1-rlc/ directory.

8.8.1.1 Configuring the hello1-rlc Example

The `faces-config.xml` file for the `hello1-rlc` example contains the following elements:

```
<resource-library-contracts>
    <contract-mapping>
        <url-pattern>/reply/*</url-pattern>
        <contracts>reply</contracts>
    </contract-mapping>
    <contract-mapping>
        <url-pattern>*</url-pattern>
        <contracts>hello</contracts>
    </contract-mapping>
</resource-library-contracts>
```

The `contract-mapping` elements within the `resource-library-contracts` element map each contract to a different set of pages within the application. One contract, named `reply`, is used for all pages under the `reply` area of the application (`/reply/*`). The other contract, `hello`, is used for all other pages in the application (`*`).

The application is organized as follows:

```
hello1-rlc
    pom.xml
    src/main/java/javaeetutorial/hello1rlc/Hello.java
    src/main/webapp
        WEB-INF
            faces-config.xml
```

```
        web.xml
    contracts
        hello
            default.css
            duke.handsOnHips.gif
            template.xhtml
        reply
            default.css
            duke.thumbsup.gif
            template.xhtml
    reply
        response.xhtml
    greeting.xhtml
```

The web.xml file specifies the welcome-file as greeting.xhtml. Because it is not located under src/main/webapp/reply, this Facelets page uses the hello contract, whereas src/main/webapp/reply/response.xhtml uses the reply contract.

8.8.1.2 The Facelets Pages for the hello1-rlc Example

The greeting.xhtml and response.xhtml pages have identical code calling in their templates:

```
<ui:composition template="/template.xhtml">
```

The template.xhtml files in the hello and reply contracts differ only in two respects: the placeholder text for the title element ("Hello Template" and "Reply Template") and the graphic that each specifies.

The default.css stylesheets in the two contracts differ in only one respect: the background color specified for the body element.

8.8.1.3 To Build, Package, and Deploy the hello1-rlc Example Using NetBeans IDE

1. Make sure that GlassFish Server has been started (see Section 2.2, "Starting and Stopping GlassFish Server").

2. From the **File** menu, choose **Open Project**.

3. In the Open Project dialog box, navigate to:

   tut-install/examples/web/jsf

4. Select the hello1-rlc folder.

5. Click **Open Project**.

6. In the **Projects** tab, right-click the `hello1-rlc` project and select **Build**.

   This option builds the example application and deploys it to your GlassFish Server instance.

8.8.1.4 To Build, Package, and Deploy the hello1-rlc Example Using Maven

1. Make sure that GlassFish Server has been started (see Section 2.2, "Starting and Stopping GlassFish Server").

2. In a terminal window, go to:

   `tut-install/examples/web/jsf/hello1-rlc/`

3. Enter the following command:

   ```
   mvn install
   ```

   This command builds and packages the application into a WAR file, `hello1-rlc.war`, that is located in the `target` directory. It then deploys it to your GlassFish Server instance.

8.8.1.5 To Run the hello1-rlc Example

1. Enter the following URL in your web browser:

   `http://localhost:8080/hello1-rlc`

2. The `greeting.xhtml` page looks just like the one from `hello1` except for its background color and graphic.

3. In the text field, enter your name and click **Submit**.

4. The response page also looks just like the one from `hello1` except for its background color and graphic.

   The page displays the name you submitted. Click **Back** to return to the `greeting.xhtml` page.

8.9 HTML5-Friendly Markup

When you want to produce user interface features for which HTML does not have its own elements, you can create a custom JavaServer Faces component and insert it in your Facelets page. This mechanism can cause a simple element to create complex web code. However, creating such a component is a significant task (see Chapter 15, "Creating Custom UI Components and Other Custom Objects").

HTML5 offers new elements and attributes that can make it unnecessary to write your own components. It also provides many new capabilities for existing components. JavaServer Faces technology supports HTML5 not by introducing new UI components that imitate HTML5 ones but by allowing you to use HTML5 markup directly. It also allows you to use JavaServer Faces attributes within HTML5 elements. JavaServer Faces technology support for HTML5 falls into two categories:

- Pass-through elements
- Pass-through attributes

The effect of the HTML5-friendly markup feature is to offer the Facelets page author almost complete control over the rendered page output, rather than having to pass this control off to component authors. You can mix and match JavaServer Faces and HTML5 components and elements as you see fit.

8.9.1 Using Pass-Through Elements

Pass-through elements allow you to use HTML5 tags and attributes but to treat them as equivalent to JavaServer Faces components associated with a server-side `UIComponent` instance.

To make an element that is not a JavaServer Faces element a pass-through element, specify at least one of its attributes using the `http://xmlns.jcp.org/jsf` namespace. For example, the following code declares the namespace with the short name `jsf`:

```
<html ... xmlns:jsf="http://xmlns.jcp.org/jsf"
...
    <input type="email" jsf:id="email" name="email"
           value="#{reservationBean.email}" required="required"/>
```

Here, the `jsf` prefix is placed on the `id` attribute so that the HTML5 input tag's attributes are treated as part of the Facelets page. This means that, for example, you can use EL expressions to retrieve managed bean properties.

Table 8–4 shows how pass-through elements are rendered as Facelets tags. The JSF implementation uses the element name and the identifying attribute to determine the corresponding Facelets tag that will be used in the server-side processing. The browser, however, interprets the markup that the page author has written.

Table 8–4 How Facelets Renders HTML5 Elements

HTML5 Element Name	Identifying Attribute	Facelets Tag
a	jsf:action	h:commandLink
a	jsf:actionListener	h:commandLink
a	jsf:value	h:outputLink
a	jsf:outcome	h:link
body		h:body
button		h:commandButton
button	jsf:outcome	h:button
form		h:form
head		h:head
img		h:graphicImage
input	type="button"	h:commandButton
input	type="checkbox"	h:selectBooleanCheckbox
input	type="color"	h:inputText
input	type="date"	h:inputText
input	type="datetime"	h:inputText
input	type="datetime-local"	h:inputText
input	type="email"	h:inputText
input	type="month"	h:inputText
input	type="number"	h:inputText
input	type="range"	h:inputText
input	type="search"	h:inputText
input	type="time"	h:inputText
input	type="url"	h:inputText
input	type="week"	h:inputText
input	type="file"	h:inputFile
input	type="hidden"	h:inputHidden
input	type="password"	h:inputSecret
input	type="reset"	h:commandButton

Table 8–4   (Cont.) How Facelets Renders HTML5 Elements

HTML5 Element Name	Identifying Attribute	Facelets Tag
input	type="submit"	h:commandButton
input	type="*"	h:inputText
label		h:outputLabel
link		h:outputStylesheet
script		h:outputScript
select	multiple="*"	h:selectManyListbox
select		h:selectOneListbox
textarea		h:inputTextarea

8.9.2 Using Pass-Through Attributes

Pass-through attributes are the converse of pass-through elements. They allow you to pass attributes that are not JavaServer Faces attributes through to the browser without interpretation. If you specify a pass-through attribute in a JavaServer Faces UIComponent, the attribute name and value are passed straight through to the browser without being interpreted by JavaServer Faces components or renderers. There are several ways to specify pass-through attributes.

- Use the JavaServer Faces namespace for pass-through attributes to prefix the attribute names within a JavaServer Faces component. For example, the following code declares the namespace with the short name p, then passes the type, min, max, required, and title attributes through to the HTML5 input component:

```
<html ... xmlns:p="http://xmlns.jcp.org/jsf/passthrough"
...

<h:form prependId="false">
<h:inputText id="nights" p:type="number" value="#{bean.nights}"
          p:min="1" p:max="30" p:required="required"
          p:title="Enter a number between 1 and 30 inclusive.">
    ...
```

This will cause the following markup to be rendered (assuming that bean.nights has a default value set to 1):

```
<input id="nights" type="number" value="1" min="1" max="30"
      required="required"
```

```
                    title="Enter a number between 1 and 30 inclusive.">
```

- To pass a single attribute, nest the `f:passThroughAttribute` tag within a component tag. For example:

```
<h:inputText value="#{user.email}">
    <f:passThroughAttribute name="type" value="email" />
</h:inputText>
```

This code would be rendered similarly to the following:

```
<input value="me@me.com" type="email" />
```

- To pass a group of attributes, nest the `f:passThroughAttributes` tag within a component tag, specifying an EL value that must evaluate to a `Map<String, Object>`. For example:

```
<h:inputText value="#{bean.nights}">
    <f:passThroughAttributes value="#{bean.nameValuePairs}" />
</h:inputText>
```

If the bean used the following `Map` declaration and initialized the map in the constructor as follows, the markup would be similar to the output of the code that uses the pass-through attribute namespace:

```
private Map<String, Object> nameValuePairs;
...
public Bean() {
    this.nameValuePairs = new HashMap<>();
    this.nameValuePairs.put("type", "number");
    this.nameValuePairs.put("min", "1");
    this.nameValuePairs.put("max", "30");
    this.nameValuePairs.put("required", "required");
    this.nameValuePairs.put("title",
            "Enter a number between 1 and 4 inclusive.");
}
```

8.9.3 The reservation Example Application

The `reservation` example application provides a set of HTML5 input elements of various types to simulate purchasing tickets for a theatrical event. It consists of two Facelets pages, `reservation.xhtml` and `confirmation.xhtml`, and a backing bean, `ReservationBean.java`. The pages use both pass-through attributes and pass-through elements.

The source code for this application is in the *tut-install*/examples/web/jsf/reservation/ directory.

8.9.3.1 The Facelets Pages for the reservation Application

The first important feature of the Facelets pages for the reservation application is the DOCTYPE header. Most Facelets pages in JavaServer Faces applications refer to the XHTML DTD. The facelets pages for this application begin simply with the following DOCTYPE header, which indicates an HTML5 page:

```
<!DOCTYPE html>
```

The namespace declarations in the html element of the reservation.xhtml page specify both the jsf and the passthrough namespaces:

```
<html lang="en"
      xmlns="http://www.w3.org/1999/xhtml"
      xmlns:f="http://xmlns.jcp.org/jsf/core"
      xmlns:h="http://xmlns.jcp.org/jsf/html"
      xmlns:p="http://xmlns.jcp.org/jsf/passthrough"
      xmlns:jsf="http://xmlns.jcp.org/jsf">
```

Next, an empty h:head tag followed by an h:outputStylesheet tag within the h:body tag illustrates the use of a relocatable resource (as described in Section 8.7, "Relocatable Resources"):

```
<h:head>
</h:head>
<h:body>
    <h:outputStylesheet name="css/stylesheet.css" target="head"/>
```

The reservation.xhtml page uses pass-through elements for most of the form fields on the page. This allows it to use some HTML5-specific input element types, such as date and email. For example, the following element renders both a date format and a calendar from which you can choose a date. The jsf prefix on the id attribute makes the element a pass-through one:

```
<input type="date" jsf:id="date" name="date"
       value="#{reservationBean.date}" required="required"
       title="Enter or choose a date."/>
```

The field for the number of tickets, however, uses the h:passThroughAttributes tag to pass a Map defined in the managed bean. It also recalculates the total in response to a change in the field:

```
<h:inputText id="tickets" value="#{reservationBean.tickets}">
    <f:passThroughAttributes value="#{reservationBean.ticketAttrs}"/>
    <f:ajax event="change" render="total"
            listener="#{reservationBean.calculateTotal}"/>
</h:inputText>
```

The field for the price specifies the `number` type as a pass-through attribute of the `h:inputText` element, offering a range of four ticket prices. Here, the p prefix on the HTML5 attributes passes them through to the browser uninterpreted by the JavaServer Faces input component:

```
<h:inputText id="price" p:type="number"
             value="#{reservationBean.price}"
             p:min="80" p:max="120"
             p:step="20" p:required="required"
             p:title="Enter a price: 80, 100, 120, or 140.">
    <f:ajax event="change" render="total"
            listener="#{reservationBean.calculateTotal}"/>
</h:inputText>
```

The output of the `calculateTotal` method that is specified as the listener for the Ajax event is rendered in the output element whose `id` and `name` value is `total`. See Chapter 13, "Using Ajax with JavaServer Faces Technology," for more information.

The second Facelets page, `confirmation.xhtml`, uses a pass-through `output` element to display the values entered by the user and provides a Facelets `h:commandButton` tag to allow the user to return to the `reservation.xhtml` page.

8.9.3.2 The Managed Bean for the reservation Application

The session-scoped managed bean for the reservation application, `ReservationBean.java`, contains properties for all the elements on the Facelets pages. It also contains two methods, `calculateTotal` and `clear`, that act as listeners for Ajax events on the `reservation.xhtml` page.

8.9.3.3 To Build, Package, and Deploy the reservation Example Using NetBeans IDE

1. Make sure that GlassFish Server has been started (see Section 2.2, "Starting and Stopping GlassFish Server").

2. From the **File** menu, choose **Open Project**.

3. In the Open Project dialog box, navigate to:

    tut-install/examples/web/jsf

4. Select the `reservation` folder.

5. Click **Open Project**.

6. In the **Projects** tab, right-click the `reservation` project and select **Build**.

This option builds the example application and deploys it to your GlassFish Server instance.

8.9.3.4 To Build, Package, and Deploy the reservation Example Using Maven

1. Make sure that GlassFish Server has been started (see Section 2.2, "Starting and Stopping GlassFish Server").

2. In a terminal window, go to:

   tut-install/examples/web/jsf/reservation/

3. Enter the following command:

   ```
   mvn install
   ```

   This command builds and packages the application into a WAR file, reservation.war, that is located in the target directory. It then deploys the WAR file to your GlassFish Server instance.

8.9.3.5 To Run the reservation Example

At the time of the publication of this tutorial, the browser that most fully implements HTML5 is Google Chrome, and it is recommended that you use it to run this example. Other browsers are catching up, however, and may work equally well by the time you read this.

1. Enter the following URL in your web browser:

   ```
   http://localhost:8080/reservation
   ```

2. Enter information in the fields of the reservation.xhtml page.

   The **Performance Date** field has a date field with up and down arrows that allow you to increment and decrement the month, day, and year as well as a larger down arrow that brings up a date editor in calendar form.

   The **Number of Tickets** and **Ticket Price** fields also have up and down arrows that allow you to increment and decrement the values within the allowed range and steps. The Estimated Total changes when you change either of these two fields.

   Email addresses and dates are checked for format, but not for validity (you can make a reservation for a past date, for instance).

3. Click **Make Reservation** to complete the reservation or **Clear** to restore the fields to their default values.

4. If you click **Make Reservation**, the confirmation.xhtml page appears, displaying the submitted values.

   Click **Back** to return to the reservation.xhtml page.

9

Expression Language

This chapter introduces the Expression Language (also referred to as the EL), which provides an important mechanism for enabling the presentation layer (web pages) to communicate with the application logic (managed beans). The EL is used by several JavaEE technologies, such as JavaServer Faces technology, JavaServer Pages (JSP) technology, and Contexts and Dependency Injection for Java EE (CDI). The EL can also be used in stand-alone environments. This chapter only covers the use of the EL in Java EE containers.

The following topics are addressed here:

- Overview of the EL

- Immediate and Deferred Evaluation Syntax

- Value and Method Expressions

- Operations on Collection Objects

- Operators

- Reserved Words

- Examples of EL Expressions

- Further Information about the Expression Language

9.1 Overview of the EL

The EL allows page authors to use simple expressions to dynamically access data from JavaBeans components. For example, the `test` attribute of the following conditional tag is supplied with an EL expression that compares 0 with the number of items in the session-scoped bean named `cart`.

```
<c:if test="${sessionScope.cart.numberOfItems > 0}">
  ...
</c:if>
```

See Section 12.1.2, "Using the EL to Reference Managed Beans," for more information on how to use the EL in JavaServer Faces applications.

To summarize, the EL provides a way to use simple expressions to perform the following tasks:

- Dynamically read application data stored in JavaBeans components, various data structures, and implicit objects

- Dynamically write data, such as user input into forms, to JavaBeans components

- Invoke arbitrary static and public methods

- Dynamically perform arithmetic, boolean, and string operations

- Dynamically construct collection objects and perform operations on collections

In a JavaServer Faces page, an EL expression can be used either in static text or in the attribute of a custom tag or standard action.

Finally, the EL provides a pluggable API for resolving expressions so that custom resolvers that can handle expressions not already supported by the EL can be implemented.

9.2 Immediate and Deferred Evaluation Syntax

The EL supports both immediate and deferred evaluation of expressions. **Immediate evaluation** means that the expression is evaluated and the result returned as soon as the page is first rendered. **Deferred evaluation** means that the technology using the expression language can use its own machinery to evaluate the expression sometime later during the page's lifecycle, whenever it is appropriate to do so.

Those expressions that are evaluated immediately use the ${} syntax. Expressions whose evaluation is deferred use the #{} syntax.

Because of its multiphase lifecycle, JavaServer Faces technology uses mostly deferred evaluation expressions. During the lifecycle, component events are handled, data is validated, and other tasks are performed in a particular order. Therefore, a JavaServer Faces implementation must defer evaluation of expressions until the appropriate point in the lifecycle.

Other technologies using the EL might have different reasons for using deferred expressions.

9.2.1 Immediate Evaluation

All expressions using the `${}` syntax are evaluated immediately. These expressions can appear as part of a template (static) text or as the value of a tag attribute that can accept runtime expressions.

The following example shows a tag whose `value` attribute references an immediate evaluation expression that updates the quantity of books retrieved from the backing bean named `catalog`:

```
<h:outputText value="${catalog.bookQuantity}" />
```

The JavaServer Faces implementation evaluates the expression `${catalog.bookQuantity}`, converts it, and passes the returned value to the tag handler. The value is updated on the page.

9.2.2 Deferred Evaluation

Deferred evaluation expressions take the form `#{expr}` and can be evaluated at other phases of a page lifecycle as defined by whatever technology is using the expression. In the case of JavaServer Faces technology, its controller can evaluate the expression at different phases of the lifecycle, depending on how the expression is being used in the page.

The following example shows a JavaServer Faces `h:inputText` tag, which represents a field component into which a user enters a value. The `h:inputText` tag's `value` attribute references a deferred evaluation expression that points to the `name` property of the `customer` bean:

```
<h:inputText id="name" value="#{customer.name}" />
```

For an initial request of the page containing this tag, the JavaServer Faces implementation evaluates the `#{customer.name}` expression during the render-response phase of the lifecycle. During this phase, the expression merely accesses the value of `name` from the `customer` bean, as is done in immediate evaluation.

For a postback request, the JavaServer Faces implementation evaluates the expression at different phases of the lifecycle, during which the value is retrieved from the request, validated, and propagated to the `customer` bean.

As shown in this example, deferred evaluation expressions can be

- Value expressions that can be used to both read and write data
- Method expressions

Value expressions (both immediate and deferred) and method expressions are explained in the next section.

9.3 Value and Method Expressions

The EL defines two kinds of expressions: value expressions and method expressions. **Value expressions** can be evaluated to yield a value, and **method expressions** are used to reference a method.

9.3.1 Value Expressions

Value expressions can be further categorized into **rvalue** and **lvalue** expressions. An lvalue expression can specify a target, such as an object, a bean property, or elements of a collection, that can be assigned a value. An rvalue expression cannot specify such a target.

All expressions that are evaluated immediately use the `${}` delimiters, and although the expression can be an lvalue expression, no assignments will ever happen. Expressions whose evaluation can be deferred use the `#{}` delimiters and can act as both rvalue and lvalue expressions; if the expression is an lvalue expression, it can be assigned a new value. Consider the following two value expressions:

```
${customer.name}
```

```
#{customer.name}
```

The former uses immediate evaluation syntax, whereas the latter uses deferred evaluation syntax. The first expression accesses the name property, gets its value, and passes the value to the tag handler. With the second expression, the tag handler can defer the expression evaluation to a later time in the page lifecycle if the technology using this tag allows.

In the case of JavaServer Faces technology, the latter tag's expression is evaluated immediately during an initial request for the page. During a postback request, this expression can be used to set the value of the name property with user input.

9.3.1.1 Referencing Objects

A top-level identifier (such as `customer` in the expression `customer.name`) can refer to the following objects:

- Lambda parameters

- EL variables

- Managed beans

- Implicit objects

- Classes of static fields and methods

To refer to these objects, you write an expression using a variable that is the name of the object. The following expression references a managed bean called `customer`:

```
${customer}
```

You can use a custom EL resolver to alter the way variables are resolved. For instance, you can provide an EL resolver that intercepts objects with the name `customer`, so that `${customer}` returns a value in the EL resolver instead. (JavaServer Faces technology uses an EL resolver to handle managed beans.)

An `enum` constant is a special case of a static field, and you can reference such a constant directly. For example, consider this `enum` class:

```
public enum Suit {hearts, spades, diamonds, clubs}
```

In the following expression, in which `mySuit` is an instance of `Suit`, you can compare `suit.hearts` to the instance:

```
${mySuit == suit.hearts}
```

9.3.1.2 Referencing Object Properties or Collection Elements

To refer to properties of a bean, static fields or methods of a class, or items of a collection, you use the `.` or `[]` notation. The same syntax can be used for attributes of an implicit object, because attributes are placed in a map.

To reference the `name` property of the `customer` bean, use either the expression `${customer.name}` or the expression `${customer["name"]}`. Here, the part inside the brackets is a `String` literal that is the name of the property to reference. The `[]` syntax is more general than the `.` syntax, because the part inside the brackets can be any `String` expression, not just literals.

You can use double or single quotes for the `String` literal. You can also combine the [] and . notations, as shown here:

```
${customer.address["street"]}
```

You can reference a static field or method using the syntax *classname.field*, as in the following example:

```
Boolean.FALSE
```

The *classname* is the name of the class without the package name. By default, all the `java.lang` packages are imported. You can import other packages, classes, and static fields as needed.

If you are accessing an item in an array or list, you must use the [] notation and specify an index in the array or list. The index is an expression that can be converted to `int`. The following example references the first of the customer orders, assuming that `customer.orders` is a `List`:

```
${customer.orders[1]}
```

If you are accessing an item in a `Map`, you must specify the key for the `Map`. If the key is a `String` literal, the dot (.) notation can be used. Assuming that `customer.orders` is a `Map` with a `String` key, the following examples reference the item with the key `"socks"`:

```
${customer.orders["socks"]}
```

```
${customer.orders.socks}
```

9.3.1.3 Referencing Literals

The EL defines the following literals:

- **Boolean**: `true` and `false`
- **Integer**: As in Java
- **Floating-point**: As in Java
- **String**: With single and double quotes; " is escaped as \", ' is escaped as \', and \ is escaped as \\
- **Null**: `null`

Here are some examples:

- `${"literal"}`

- `${true}`

- `${57}`

9.3.1.4 Parameterized Method Calls

The EL offers support for parameterized method calls.

Both the `.` and `[]` operators can be used for invoking method calls with parameters, as shown in the following expression syntax:

- *expr-a* [*expr-b*] (*parameters*)

- *expr-a* . *identifier-b* (*parameters*)

In the first expression syntax, *expr-a* is evaluated to represent a bean object. The expression *expr-b* is evaluated and cast to a string that represents a method in the bean represented by *expr-a*. In the second expression syntax, *expr-a* is evaluated to represent a bean object, and *identifier-b* is a string that represents a method in the bean object. The *parameters* in parentheses are the arguments for the method invocation. Parameters can be zero or more values of expressions, separated by commas.

Parameters are supported for both value expressions and method expressions. In the following example, which is a modified tag from the guessnumber application, a random number is provided as an argument rather than from user input to the method call:

```
<h:inputText value="#{userNumberBean.userNumber('5')}">
```

The preceding example uses a value expression.

Consider the following example of a JavaServer Faces component tag that uses a method expression:

```
<h:commandButton action="#{trader.buy}" value="buy"/>
```

The EL expression `trader.buy` calls the `trader` bean's `buy` method. You can modify the tag to pass on a parameter. Here is the revised tag in which a parameter is passed:

```
<h:commandButton action="#{trader.buy('SOMESTOCK')}" value="buy"/>
```

In the preceding example, you are passing the string `'SOMESTOCK'` (a stock symbol) as a parameter to the `buy` method.

9.3.1.5 Where Value Expressions Can Be Used

Value expressions using the ${} delimiters can be used

- In static text

- In any standard or custom tag attribute that can accept an expression

The value of an expression in static text is computed and inserted into the current output. Here is an example of an expression embedded in static text:

```
<some:tag>
    some text ${expr} some text
</some:tag>
```

A tag attribute can be set in the following ways.

- With a single expression construct:

  ```
  <some:tag value="${expr}"/>
  ```

  ```
  <another:tag value="#{expr}"/>
  ```

  These expressions are evaluated, and the result is converted to the attribute's expected type.

- With one or more expressions separated or surrounded by text:

  ```
  <some:tag value="some${expr}${expr}text${expr}"/>
  ```

  ```
  <another:tag value="some#{expr}#{expr}text#{expr}"/>
  ```

  These kinds of expression, called **composite expressions**, are evaluated from left to right. Each expression embedded in the composite expression is converted to a String and then concatenated with any intervening text. The resulting String is then converted to the attribute's expected type.

- With text only:

  ```
  <some:tag value="sometext"/>
  ```

  The attribute's String value is converted to the attribute's expected type.

You can use the string concatenation operator += to create a single expression from what would otherwise be a composite expression. For example, you could change the composite expression

```
<some:tag value="sometext ${expr} moretext"/>
```

to the following:

```
<some:tag value="${sometext += expr += moretext}"/>
```

All expressions used to set attribute values are evaluated in the context of an expected type. If the result of the expression evaluation does not match the expected type exactly, a type conversion will be performed. For example, the expression ${1.2E4} provided as the value of an attribute of type float will result in the following conversion:

```
Float.valueOf("1.2E4").floatValue()
```

9.3.2 Method Expressions

Another feature of the EL is its support of deferred method expressions. A method expression is used to refer to a public method of a bean and has the same syntax as an lvalue expression.

In JavaServer Faces technology, a component tag represents a component on a page. The component tag uses method expressions to specify methods that can be invoked to perform some processing for the component. These methods are necessary for handling events that the components generate and for validating component data, as shown in this example:

```
<h:form>
    <h:inputText id="name"
                 value="#{customer.name}"
                 validator="#{customer.validateName}"/>
    <h:commandButton id="submit"
                     action="#{customer.submit}" />
</h:form>
```

The h:inputText tag displays as a field. The validator attribute of this h:inputText tag references a method, called validateName, in the bean, called customer.

Because a method can be invoked during different phases of the lifecycle, method expressions must always use the deferred evaluation syntax.

Like lvalue expressions, method expressions can use the . and the [] operators. For example, #{object.method} is equivalent to #{object["method"]}. The literal inside the [] is converted to String and is used to find the name of the method that matches it.

Method expressions can be used only in tag attributes and only in the following ways:

- With a single expression construct, where *bean* refers to a JavaBeans component and *method* refers to a method of the JavaBeans component:

```
<some:tag value="#{bean.method}"/>
```

The expression is evaluated to a method expression, which is passed to the tag handler. The method represented by the method expression can then be invoked later.

- With text only:

```
<some:tag value="sometext"/>
```

Method expressions support literals primarily to support `action` attributes in JavaServer Faces technology. When the method referenced by this method expression is invoked, the method returns the `String` literal, which is then converted to the expected return type, as defined in the tag's tag library descriptor.

9.3.3 Lambda Expressions

A lambda expression is a value expression with parameters. The syntax is similar to that of the lambda expression in the Java programming language, except that in the EL, the body of the lambda expression is an EL expression.

For basic information on lambda expressions, see `http://docs.oracle.com/javase/tutorial/java/javaOO/lambdaexpressions.html`.

Note: Lambda expressions are part of Java SE 8, but you can use them in EL expressions with Java SE 7, the Java version associated with the Java EE 7 platform.

A lambda expression uses the arrow token (`->`) operator. The identifiers to the left of the operator are called lambda parameters. The body, to the right of the operator, must be an EL expression. The lambda parameters are enclosed in parentheses; the parentheses can be omitted if there is only one parameter. Here are some examples:

```
x -> x+1
(x, y) -> x + y
() -> 64
```

A lambda expression behaves like a function. It can be invoked immediately. For example, the following invocation evaluates to 7:

```
((x, y) -> x + y)(3, 4)
```

You can use a lambda expression in conjunction with the assignment and semicolon operators. For example, the following code assigns the previous lambda expression to a variable and then invokes it. The result is again 7:

```
v = (x, y) -> x + y; v(3, 4)
```

A lambda expression can also be passed as an argument to a method and be invoked in the method. It can also be nested in another lambda expression.

9.4 Operations on Collection Objects

The EL supports operations on collection objects: sets, lists, and maps. It allows the dynamic creation of collection objects, which can then be operated on using streams and pipelines.

> **Note:** Like lambda expressions, operations on collection objects are part of Java SE 8, but you can use them in EL expressions with Java SE 7, the Java version associated with the Java EE 7 platform.

For example, you can construct a set as follows:

```
{1,2,3}
```

You can construct a list as follows; a list can contain various types of items:

```
[1,2,3]
[1, "two", [three,four]]
```

You can construct a map by using a colon to define the entries, as follows:

```
{"one":1, "two":2, "three":3}
```

You operate on collection objects using method calls to the stream of elements derived from the collection. Some operations return another stream, which allows additional operations. Therefore, you can chain these operations together in a pipeline.

A stream pipeline consists of the following:

- A source (the `Stream` object)

- Any number of intermediate operations that return a stream (for example, `filter` and `map`)

- A terminal operation that does not return a stream (for example, `toList()`)

The `stream` method obtains a `Stream` from a `java.util.Collection` or a Java array. The stream operations do not modify the original collection object.

For example, you might generate a list of titles of history books as follows:

```
books.stream().filter(b->b.category == 'history')
              .map(b->b.title)
              .toList()
```

The following simpler example returns a sorted version of the original list:

```
[1,3,5,2].stream().sorted().toList()
```

Streams and stream operations are documented in the Java SE 8 API documentation, available at `http://docs.oracle.com/javase/8/docs/api/`. The following subset of operations is supported by the EL:

```
allMatch
anyMatch
average
count
distinct
filter
findFirst
flatMap
forEach
iterator
limit
map
max
min
noneMatch
peek
reduce
sorted
substream
sum
```

```
toArray
toList
```

See the EL specification at `http://www.jcp.org/en/jsr/detail?id=341`
for details on these operations.

9.5 Operators

In addition to the `.` and `[]` operators discussed in Section 9.3, "Value and Method
Expressions," the EL provides the following operators, which can be used in
rvalue expressions only.

- **Arithmetic**: `+, -` (binary), `*, /` and `div`, `%` and `mod`, `-` (unary).

- **String concatenation**: `+=`.

- **Logical**: `and, &&, or, ||, not, !`.

- **Relational**: `==, eq, !=, ne, <, lt, >, gt, <=, ge, >=, le`. Comparisons can be made
  against other values or against Boolean, string, integer, or floating-point
  literals.

- **Empty**: The `empty` operator is a prefix operation that can be used to determine
  whether a value is `null` or empty.

- **Conditional**: `A ? B : C`. Evaluate `B` or `C`, depending on the result of the
  evaluation of `A`.

- **Lambda expression**: `->`, the arrow token.

- **Assignment**: `=`.

- **Semicolon**: `;`.

The precedence of operators, highest to lowest, left to right, is as follows:

- `[]` `.`

- `()` (used to change the precedence of operators)

- `-` (unary) `not` `!` `empty`

- `*` `/` `div` `%` `mod`

- `+` `-` (binary)

- `+=`

- `<> <= >= lt gt le ge`

- `== != eq ne`

- `&& and`
- `|| or`
- `? :`
- `->`
- `=`
- `;`

9.6 Reserved Words

The following words are reserved for the EL and should not be used as identifiers:

```
and
or
not
eq
ne
lt
gt
le
ge
true
false
null
instanceof
empty
div
mod
```

9.7 Examples of EL Expressions

Table 9–1 contains example EL expressions and the result of evaluating them.

Table 9–1   Example EL Expressions

EL Expression	Result
`${1> (4/2)}`	false
`${4.0>= 3}`	true
`${100.0 == 100}`	true
`${(10*10) ne 100}`	false

Table 9–1   (Cont.) Example EL Expressions

EL Expression	Result
`${'a' > 'b'}`	`false`
`${'hip' lt 'hit'}`	`true`
`${4> 3}`	`true`
`${1.2E4 + 1.4}`	`12001.4`
`${3 div 4}`	`0.75`
`${10 mod 4}`	`2`
`${((x, y) -> x + y)(3, 5.5)}`	`8.5`
`[1,2,3,4].stream().sum()`	`10`
`[1,3,5,2].stream().sorted().toList()`	`[1, 2, 3, 5]`
`${!empty param.Add}`	`False` if the request parameter named `Add` is `null` or an empty string
`${pageContext.request.contextPath}`	The context path
`${sessionScope.cart.numberOfItems}`	The value of the `numberOfItems` property of the session-scoped attribute named `cart`
`${param['mycom.productId']}`	The value of the request parameter named `mycom.productId`
`${header["host"]}`	The host
`${departments[deptName]}`	The value of the entry named `deptName` in the `departments` map
`${requestScope['javax.servlet.forward.servlet_path']}`	The value of the request-scoped attribute named `javax.servlet.forward.servlet_path`
`#{customer.lName}`	Gets the value of the property `lName` from the `customer` bean during an initial request; sets the value of `lName` during a postback
`#{customer.calcTotal}`	The return value of the method `calcTotal` of the `customer` bean

9.8 Further Information about the Expression Language

For more information about the EL, see

■   The Expression Language 3.0 specification:

   `http://www.jcp.org/en/jsr/detail?id=341`

- The EL specification website:

  `https://java.net/projects/el-spec/`

10

Using JavaServer Faces Technology in Web Pages

Web pages (Facelets pages, in most cases) represent the presentation layer for web applications. The process of creating web pages for a JavaServer Faces application includes using component tags to add components to the page and wire them to backing beans, validators, listeners, converters, and other server-side objects that are associated with the page.

This chapter explains how to create web pages using various types of component and core tags. In the next chapter, you will learn about adding converters, validators, and listeners to component tags to provide additional functionality to components.

Many of the examples in this chapter are taken from Chapter 28, "Duke's Bookstore Case Study Example," in *The Java EE 7 Tutorial, Volume 2*.

The following topics are addressed here:

- Setting Up a Page
- Adding Components to a Page Using HTML Tag Library Tags
- Using Core Tags

10.1 Setting Up a Page

A typical JavaServer Faces web page includes the following elements:

- A set of namespace declarations that declare the JavaServer Faces tag libraries

- Optionally, the HTML head (h:head) and body (h:body) tags

- A form tag (h:form) that represents the user input components

To add the JavaServer Faces components to your web page, you need to provide the page access to the two standard tag libraries: the JavaServer Faces HTML render kit tag library and the JavaServer Faces core tag library. The JavaServer Faces standard HTML tag library defines tags that represent common HTML user interface components. This library is linked to the HTML render kit at `http://docs.oracle.com/javaee/7/javaserverfaces/2.2/renderkitdocs/`. The JavaServer Faces core tag library defines tags that perform core actions and are independent of a particular render kit.

For a complete list of JavaServer Faces Facelets tags and their attributes, refer to the documentation at `http://docs.oracle.com/javaee/7/javaserverfaces/2.2/vdldocs/facelets/`.

To use any of the JavaServer Faces tags, you need to include appropriate directives at the top of each page specifying the tag libraries.

For Facelets applications, the XML namespace directives uniquely identify the tag library URI and the tag prefix.

For example, when you create a Facelets XHTML page, include namespace directives as follows:

```
<html xmlns="http://www.w3.org/1999/xhtml"
      xmlns:h="http://xmlns.jcp.org/jsf/html"
      xmlns:f="http://xmlns.jcp.org/jsf/core">
```

The XML namespace URI identifies the tag library location, and the prefix value is used to distinguish the tags belonging to that specific tag library. You can also use other prefixes instead of the standard h or f. However, when including the tag in the page you must use the prefix that you have chosen for the tag library. For example, in the following web page the form tag must be referenced using the h prefix because the preceding tag library directive uses the h prefix to distinguish the tags defined in the HTML tag library:

```
<h:form ...>
```

Section 10.2, "Adding Components to a Page Using HTML Tag Library Tags," and Section 10.3, "Using Core Tags," describe how to use the component tags from the

JavaServer Faces standard HTML tag library and the core tags from the JavaServer Faces core tag library.

10.2 Adding Components to a Page Using HTML Tag Library Tags

The tags defined by the JavaServer Faces standard HTML tag library represent HTML form components and other basic HTML elements. These components display data or accept data from the user. This data is collected as part of a form and is submitted to the server, usually when the user clicks a button. This section explains how to use each of the component tags shown in Table 10–1.

Table 10–1   The Component Tags

Tag	Functions	Rendered As	Appearance
h:column	Represents a column of data in a data component	A column of data in an HTML table	A column in a table
h:commandButton	Submits a form to the application	An HTML `<input type=value>` element for which the `type` value can be `"submit"`, `"reset"`, or `"image"`	A button
h:commandLink	Links to another page or location on a page	An HTML `<a href>` element	A link
h:dataTable	Represents a data wrapper	An HTML `<table>` element	A table that can be updated dynamically
h:form	Represents an input form (inner tags of the form receive the data that will be submitted with the form)	An HTML `<form>` element	No appearance
h:graphicImage	Displays an image	An HTML `<img>` element	An image
h:inputFile	Allows a user to upload a file	An HTML `<input type="file">` element	A field with a **Browse...** button
h:inputHidden	Allows a page author to include a hidden variable in a page	An HTML `<input type="hidden">` element	No appearance
h:inputSecret	Allows a user to input a string without the actual string appearing in the field	An HTML `<input type="password">` element	A field that displays a row of characters instead of the actual string entered
h:inputText	Allows a user to input a string	An HTML `<input type="text">` element	A field

Table 10–1   (Cont.) The Component Tags

Tag	Functions	Rendered As	Appearance
h:inputTextarea	Allows a user to enter a multiline string	An HTML `<textarea>` element	A multirow field
h:message	Displays a localized message	An HTML `<span>` tag if styles are used	A text string
h:messages	Displays localized messages	A set of HTML `<span>` tags if styles are used	A text string
h:outputFormat	Displays a formatted message	Plain text	Plain text
h:outputLabel	Displays a nested component as a label for a specified input field	An HTML `<label>` element	Plain text
h:outputLink	Links to another page or location on a page without generating an action event	An HTML `<a>` element	A link
h:outputText	Displays a line of text	Plain text	Plain text
h:panelGrid	Displays a table	An HTML `<table>` element with `<tr>` and `<td>` elements	A table
h:panelGroup	Groups a set of components under one parent	A HTML `<div>` or `<span>` element	A row in a table
h:selectBooleanCheckbox	Allows a user to change the value of a Boolean choice	An HTML `<input type="checkbox">` element	A check box
h:selectManyCheckbox	Displays a set of check boxes from which the user can select multiple values	A set of HTML `<input>` elements of type `checkbox`	A group of check boxes
h:selectManyListbox	Allows a user to select multiple items from a set of items all displayed at once	An HTML `<select>` element	A box
h:selectManyMenu	Allows a user to select multiple items from a set of items	An HTML `<select>` element	A menu
h:selectOneListbox	Allows a user to select one item from a set of items all displayed at once	An HTML `<select>` element	A box

Table 10–1   (Cont.) The Component Tags

Tag	Functions	Rendered As	Appearance
h:selectOneMenu	Allows a user to select one item from a set of items	An HTML `<select>` element	A menu
h:selectOneRadio	Allows a user to select one item from a set of items	An HTML `<input type="radio">` element	A group of options

The tags correspond to components in the `javax.faces.component` package. The components are discussed in more detail in Chapter 12, "Developing with JavaServer Faces Technology."

The next section explains the important attributes that are common to most component tags. For each of the components discussed in the following sections, Section 12.2, "Writing Bean Properties," explains how to write a bean property bound to that particular component or its value.

For reference information about the tags and their attributes, see the API documentation for the Facelets tag library at `http://docs.oracle.com/javaee/7/javaserverfaces/2.2/vdldocs/facelets/`.

10.2.1 Common Component Tag Attributes

Most of the component tags support the attributes shown in Table 10–2.

Table 10–2   Common Component Tag Attributes

Attribute	Description
binding	Identifies a bean property and binds the component instance to it.
id	Uniquely identifies the component.
immediate	If set to `true`, indicates that any events, validation, and conversion associated with the component should happen when request parameter values are applied.
rendered	Specifies a condition under which the component should be rendered. If the condition is not satisfied, the component is not rendered.
style	Specifies a Cascading Style Sheet (CSS) style for the tag.
styleClass	Specifies a CSS class that contains definitions of the styles.
value	Specifies the value of the component in the form of a value expression.

All the tag attributes except `id` can accept expressions, as defined by the EL, described in Chapter 9, "Expression Language."

An attribute such as `rendered` or `value` can be set on the page and then modified in the backing bean for the page.

10.2.1.1 The id Attribute

The `id` attribute is not usually required for a component tag but is used when another component or a server-side class must refer to the component. If you don't include an `id` attribute, the JavaServer Faces implementation automatically generates a component ID. Unlike most other JavaServer Faces tag attributes, the `id` attribute takes expressions using only the evaluation syntax described in Section 9.2.1, "Immediate Evaluation," which uses the `${}` delimiters. For more information on expression syntax, see Section 9.3.1, "Value Expressions."

10.2.1.2 The immediate Attribute

Input components and command components (those that implement the `ActionSource` interface, such as buttons and links) can set the `immediate` attribute to `true` to force events, validations, and conversions to be processed when request parameter values are applied.

You need to carefully consider how the combination of an input component's `immediate` value and a command component's `immediate` value determines what happens when the command component is activated.

Suppose that you have a page with a button and a field for entering the quantity of a book in a shopping cart. If the `immediate` attributes of both the button and the field are set to `true`, the new value entered in the field will be available for any processing associated with the event that is generated when the button is clicked. The event associated with the button as well as the events, validation, and conversion associated with the field are all handled when request parameter values are applied.

If the button's `immediate` attribute is set to `true` but the field's `immediate` attribute is set to `false`, the event associated with the button is processed without updating the field's local value to the model layer. The reason is that any events, conversion, and validation associated with the field occur *after* request parameter values are applied.

The `bookshowcart.xhtml` page of the Duke's Bookstore case study has examples of components using the `immediate` attribute to control which component's data is updated when certain buttons are clicked. The `quantity` field for each book does not set the `immediate` attribute, so the value is `false` (the default).

```
<h:inputText id="quantity"
             size="4"
             value="#{item.quantity}"
             title="#{bundle.ItemQuantity}">
    <f:validateLongRange minimum="0"/>
    ...
</h:inputText>
```

The immediate attribute of the **Continue Shopping** hyperlink is set to true, while the immediate attribute of the **Update Quantities** hyperlink is set to false:

```
<h:commandLink id="continue"
               action="bookcatalog"
               immediate="true">
    <h:outputText value="#{bundle.ContinueShopping}"/>
</h:commandLink>
...
<h:commandLink id="update"
               action="#{showcart.update}"
               immediate="false">
    <h:outputText value="#{bundle.UpdateQuantities}"/>
</h:commandLink>
```

If you click the **Continue Shopping** hyperlink, none of the changes entered into the quantity input fields will be processed. If you click the **Update Quantities** hyperlink, the values in the quantity fields will be updated in the shopping cart.

10.2.1.3 The rendered Attribute

A component tag uses a Boolean EL expression along with the rendered attribute to determine whether the component will be rendered. For example, the commandLink component in the following section of a page is not rendered if the cart contains no items:

```
<h:commandLink id="check"
    ...
    rendered="#{cart.numberOfItems > 0}">
    <h:outputText
        value="#{bundle.CartCheck}"/>
</h:commandLink>
```

Unlike nearly every other JavaServer Faces tag attribute, the rendered attribute is restricted to using rvalue expressions. As explained in Section 9.3, "Value and Method Expressions," these rvalue expressions can only read data; they cannot write the data back to the data source. Therefore, expressions used with rendered attributes can use the arithmetic operators and literals that rvalue expressions can use but lvalue expressions cannot use. For example, the expression in the preceding example uses the > operator.

Note: In this example and others, bundle refers to a java.util.ResourceBundle file that contains locale-specific strings to be displayed. Resource bundles are discussed in Chapter 20, "Internationalizing and Localizing Web Applications."

10.2.1.4 The style and styleClass Attributes

The style and styleClass attributes allow you to specify CSS styles for the rendered output of your tags. Section 10.2.13, "Displaying Error Messages with the h:message and h:messages Tags," describes an example of using the style attribute to specify styles directly in the attribute. A component tag can instead refer to a CSS class.

The following example shows the use of a dataTable tag that references the style class list-background:

```
<h:dataTable id="items"
             ...
             styleClass="list-background"
             value="#{cart.items}"
             var="book">
```

The style sheet that defines this class is stylesheet.css, which will be included in the application. For more information on defining styles, see the Cascading Style Sheets specifications and drafts at http://www.w3.org/Style/CSS/.

10.2.1.5 The value and binding Attributes

A tag representing an output component uses the value and binding attributes to bind its component's value or instance, respectively, to a data object. The value attribute is used more commonly than the binding attribute, and examples appear throughout this chapter. For more information on these attributes, see Section 12.1.1, "Creating a Managed Bean"; Section 12.2.1, "Writing Properties Bound to Component Values"; and Section 12.2.2, "Writing Properties Bound to Component Instances."

10.2.2 Adding HTML Head and Body Tags

The HTML head (h:head) and body (h:body) tags add HTML page structure to JavaServer Faces web pages.

- The h:head tag represents the head element of an HTML page.

- The h:body tag represents the body element of an HTML page.

The following is an example of an XHTML page using the usual head and body markup tags:

```
<!DOCTYPE html PUBLIC "-//W3C//DTD XHTML 1.0 Transitional//EN"
  "http://www.w3.org/TR/xhtml1/DTD/xhtml1-transitional.dtd">
<html xmlns="http://www.w3.org/1999/xhtml">
    <head>
        <title>Add a title</title>
    </head>
    <body>
        Add Content
    </body>
</html>
```

The following is an example of an XHTML page using h:head and h:body tags:

```
<!DOCTYPE html PUBLIC "-//W3C//DTD XHTML 1.0 Transitional//EN"
  "http://www.w3.org/TR/xhtml1/DTD/xhtml1-transitional.dtd">
<html xmlns="http://www.w3.org/1999/xhtml"
      xmlns:h="http://xmlns.jcp.org/jsf/html">
    <h:head>
        Add a title
    </h:head>
    <h:body>
        Add Content
    </h:body>
</html>
```

Both of the preceding example code segments render the same HTML elements. The head and body tags are useful mainly for resource relocation. For more information on resource relocation, see Section 10.2.17, "Resource Relocation Using h:outputScript and h:outputStylesheet Tags."

10.2.3 Adding a Form Component

An h:form tag represents an input form, which includes child components that can contain data that is either presented to the user or submitted with the form.

Figure 10–1 shows a typical login form in which a user enters a user name and password, then submits the form by clicking the **Login** button.

Figure 10–1   A Typical Form

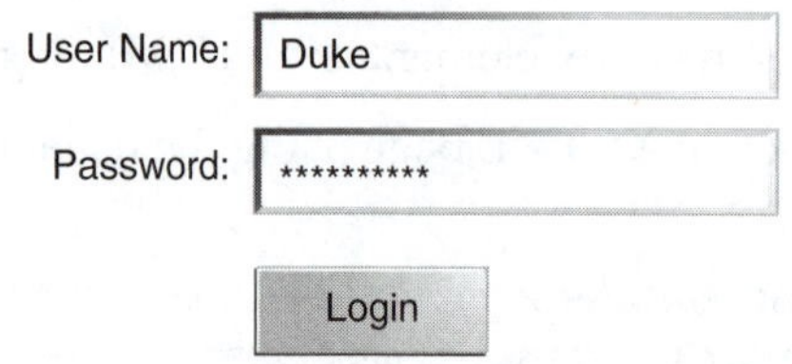

User Name: | Duke

Password: | **********

[Login]

The h:form tag represents the form on the page and encloses all the components that display or collect data from the user, as shown here:

```
<h:form>
... other JavaServer Faces tags and other content...
</h:form>
```

The h:form tag can also include HTML markup to lay out the components on the page. Note that the h:form tag itself does not perform any layout; its purpose is to collect data and to declare attributes that can be used by other components in the form.

A page can include multiple h:form tags, but only the values from the form submitted by the user will be included in the postback request.

10.2.4 Using Text Components

Text components allow users to view and edit text in web applications. The basic types of text components are as follows:

- Label, which displays read-only text

- Field, which allows users to enter text (on one or more lines), often to be submitted as part of a form

- Password field, which is a type of field that displays a set of characters, such as asterisks, instead of the password text that the user enters

Figure 10–2 shows examples of these text components.

Figure 10–2 **Example Text Components**

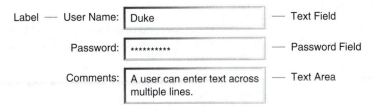

Text components can be categorized as either input or output. A JavaServer Faces output component, such as a label, is rendered as read-only text. A JavaServer Faces input component, such as a field, is rendered as editable text.

The input and output components can each be rendered in various ways to display more specialized text.

Table 10–3 lists the tags that represent the input components.

Table 10–3 **Input Tags**

Tag	Function
h:inputHidden	Allows a page author to include a hidden variable in a page
h:inputSecret	The standard password field: accepts one line of text with no spaces and displays it as a set of asterisks as it is entered
h:inputText	The standard field: accepts a one-line text string
h:inputTextarea	The standard multiline field: accepts multiple lines of text

The input tags support the tag attributes shown in Table 10–4 in addition to those described in Section 10.2.1, "Common Component Tag Attributes." Note that this table does not include all the attributes supported by the input tags but just those that are used most often. For the complete list of attributes, refer to the documentation at http://docs.oracle.com/javaee/7/ javaserverfaces/2.2/vdldocs/facelets/.

Table 10–4 **Input Tag Attributes**

Attribute	Description
converter	Identifies a converter that will be used to convert the component's local data. See Section 11.1, "Using the Standard Converters," for more information on how to use this attribute.
converterMessage	Specifies an error message to display when the converter registered on the component fails.

Table 10–4 (Cont.) Input Tag Attributes

Attribute	Description
dir	Specifies the direction of the text displayed by this component. Acceptable values are ltr, meaning left to right, and rtl, meaning right to left.
label	Specifies a name that can be used to identify this component in error messages.
lang	Specifies the code for the language used in the rendered markup, such as en or pt-BR.
required	Takes a boolean value that indicates whether the user must enter a value in this component.
requiredMessage	Specifies an error message to display when the user does not enter a value into the component.
validator	Identifies a method expression pointing to a managed bean method that performs validation on the component's data. See Section 11.4.3, "Referencing a Method That Performs Validation," for an example of using the f:validator tag.
validatorMessage	Specifies an error message to display when the validator registered on the component fails to validate the component's local value.
valueChangeListener	Identifies a method expression that points to a managed bean method that handles the event of entering a value in this component. See Section 11.4.4, "Referencing a Method That Handles a Value-Change Event," for an example of using valueChangeListener.

Table 10–5 lists the tags that represent the output components.

Table 10–5 Output Tags

Tag	Function
h:outputFormat	Displays a formatted message
h:outputLabel	The standard read-only label: displays a component as a label for a specified input field
h:outputLink	Displays an <a href> tag that links to another page without generating an action event
h:outputText	Displays a one-line text string

The output tags support the converter tag attribute in addition to those listed in Section 10.2.1, "Common Component Tag Attributes."

The rest of this section explains how to use some of the tags listed in Table 10–3 and Table 10–5. The other tags are written in a similar way.

10.2.4.1 Rendering a Field with the h:inputText Tag

The h:inputText tag is used to display a field. A similar tag, the h:outputText tag, displays a read-only, single-line string. This section shows you how to use the h:inputText tag. The h:outputText tag is written in a similar way.

Here is an example of an h:inputText tag:

```
<h:inputText id="name"
             label="Customer Name"
             size="30"
             value="#{cashierBean.name}"
             required="true"
             requiredMessage="#{bundle.ReqCustomerName}">
    <f:valueChangeListener
        type="javaeetutorial.dukesbookstore.listeners.NameChanged" />
 </h:inputText>
```

The label attribute specifies a user-friendly name that will be used in the substitution parameters of error messages displayed for this component.

The value attribute refers to the name property of a managed bean named CashierBean. This property holds the data for the name component. After the user submits the form, the value of the name property in CashierBean will be set to the text entered in the field corresponding to this tag.

The required attribute causes the page to reload, displaying errors, if the user does not enter a value in the name field. The JavaServer Faces implementation checks whether the value of the component is null or is an empty string.

If your component must have a non-null value or a String value at least one character in length, you should add a required attribute to your tag and set its value to true. If your tag has a required attribute that is set to true and the value is null or a zero-length string, no other validators that are registered on the tag are called. If your tag does not have a required attribute set to true, other validators that are registered on the tag are called, but those validators must handle the possibility of a null or zero-length string. See Section 21.2, "Validating Null and Empty Strings," for more information.

10.2.4.2 Rendering a Password Field with the h:inputSecret Tag

The h:inputSecret tag renders an <input type="password"> HTML tag. When the user types a string into this field, a row of asterisks is displayed instead of the text entered by the user. Here is an example:

```
<h:inputSecret redisplay="false"
               value="#{loginBean.password}" />
```

In this example, the redisplay attribute is set to false. This will prevent the password from being displayed in a query string or in the source file of the resulting HTML page.

10.2.4.3 Rendering a Label with the h:outputLabel Tag

The h:outputLabel tag is used to attach a label to a specified input field for the purpose of making it accessible. The following page uses an h:outputLabel tag to render the label of a check box:

```
<h:selectBooleanCheckbox id="fanClub"
                         rendered="false"
                         binding="#{cashierBean.specialOffer}" />
<h:outputLabel for="fanClub"
               rendered="false"
               binding="#{cashierBean.specialOfferText}">
    <h:outputText id="fanClubLabel"
                  value="#{bundle.DukeFanClub}" />
</h:outputLabel>
...
```

The h:selectBooleanCheckbox tag and the h:outputLabel tag have rendered attributes that are set to false on the page but are set to true in the CashierBean under certain circumstances. The for attribute of the h:outputLabel tag maps to the id of the input field to which the label is attached. The h:outputText tag nested inside the h:outputLabel tag represents the label component. The value attribute on the h:outputText tag indicates the text that is displayed next to the input field.

Instead of using an h:outputText tag for the text displayed as a label, you can simply use the h:outputLabel tag's value attribute. The following code snippet shows what the previous code snippet would look like if it used the value attribute of the h:outputLabel tag to specify the text of the label:

```
<h:selectBooleanCheckbox id="fanClub"
                         rendered="false"
                         binding="#{cashierBean.specialOffer}" />
```

```
<h:outputLabel for="fanClub"
               rendered="false"
               binding="#{cashierBean.specialOfferText}"
               value="#{bundle.DukeFanClub}" />
</h:outputLabel>
...
```

10.2.4.4 Rendering a Link with the h:outputLink Tag

The h:outputLink tag is used to render a link that, when clicked, loads another page but does not generate an action event. You should use this tag instead of the h:commandLink tag if you always want the URL specified by the h:outputLink tag's value attribute to open and do not want any processing to be performed when the user clicks the link. Here is an example:

```
<h:outputLink value="javadocs">
    Documentation for this demo
</h:outputLink>
```

The text in the body of the h:outputLink tag identifies the text that the user clicks to get to the next page.

10.2.4.5 Displaying a Formatted Message with the h:outputFormat Tag

The h:outputFormat tag allows display of concatenated messages as a MessageFormat pattern, as described in the API documentation for java.text.MessageFormat. Here is an example of an h:outputFormat tag:

```
<h:outputFormat value="Hello, {0}!">
    <f:param value="#{hello.name}"/>
</h:outputFormat>
```

The value attribute specifies the MessageFormat pattern. The f:param tag specifies the substitution parameters for the message. The value of the parameter replaces the {0} in the sentence. If the value of "#{hello.name}" is "Bill", the message displayed in the page is as follows:

```
Hello, Bill!
```

An h:outputFormat tag can include more than one f:param tag for those messages that have more than one parameter that must be concatenated into the message. If you have more than one parameter for one message, make sure that you put the f:param tags in the proper order so that the data is inserted in the correct place in the message. Here is the preceding example modified with an additional parameter:

```
<h:outputFormat value="Hello, {0}! You are visitor number {1} to the page.">
    <f:param value="#{hello.name}" />
    <f:param value="#{bean.numVisitor}"/>
</h:outputFormat>
```

The value of {1} is replaced by the second parameter. The parameter is an EL expression, bean.numVisitor, in which the property numVisitor of the managed bean bean keeps track of visitors to the page. This is an example of a value-expression-enabled tag attribute accepting an EL expression. The message displayed in the page is now as follows:

```
Hello, Bill! You are visitor number 10 to the page.
```

10.2.5 Using Command Component Tags for Performing Actions and Navigation

In JavaServer Faces applications, the button and link component tags are used to perform actions, such as submitting a form, and for navigating to another page. These tags are called command component tags because they perform an action when activated.

The h:commandButton tag is rendered as a button. The h:commandLink tag is rendered as a link.

In addition to the tag attributes listed in Section 10.2.1, "Common Component Tag Attributes," the h:commandButton and h:commandLink tags can use the following attributes.

- action, which is either a logical outcome String or a method expression pointing to a bean method that returns a logical outcome String. In either case, the logical outcome String is used to determine what page to access when the command component tag is activated.

- actionListener, which is a method expression pointing to a bean method that processes an action event fired by the command component tag.

See Section 11.4.1, "Referencing a Method That Performs Navigation," for more information on using the action attribute. See Section 11.4.2, "Referencing a Method That Handles an Action Event," for details on using the actionListener attribute.

10.2.5.1 Rendering a Button with the h:commandButton Tag

If you are using an h:commandButton component tag, the data from the current page is processed when a user clicks the button, and the next page is opened. Here is an example of the h:commandButton tag:

```
<h:commandButton value="Submit"
                 action="#{cashierBean.submit}"/>
```

Clicking the button will cause the submit method of CashierBean to be invoked because the action attribute references this method. The submit method performs some processing and returns a logical outcome.

The value attribute of the example h:commandButton tag references the button's label. For information on how to use the action attribute, see Section 11.4.1, "Referencing a Method That Performs Navigation."

10.2.5.2 Rendering a Link with the h:commandLink Tag

The h:commandLink tag represents an HTML link and is rendered as an HTML <a> element.

An h:commandLink tag must include a nested h:outputText tag, which represents the text that the user clicks to generate the event. Here is an example:

```
<h:commandLink id="Duke" action="bookstore">
    <f:actionListener
        type="javaeetutorial.dukesbookstore.listeners.LinkBookChangeListener"
/>
    <h:outputText value="#{bundle.Book201}"/>
/h:commandLink>
```

This tag will render HTML that looks something like the following:

```
<a id="_idt16:Duke" href="#"
    onclick="mojarra.jsfcljs(document.getElementById('j_idt16'),
    {'j_idt16:Duke':'j_idt16:Duke'},'');
    return false;">My Early Years: Growing Up on Star7, by Duke</a>
```

> **Note:** The h:commandLink tag will render JavaScript scripting language. If you use this tag, make sure that your browser is enabled for JavaScript technology.

10.2.6 Adding Graphics and Images with the h:graphicImage Tag

In a JavaServer Faces application, use the h:graphicImage tag to render an image on a page:

```
<h:graphicImage id="mapImage" url="/resources/images/book_all.jpg"/>
```

In this example, the url attribute specifies the path to the image. The URL of the example tag begins with a slash (/), which adds the relative context path of the web application to the beginning of the path to the image.

Alternatively, you can use the facility described in Section 8.6, "Web Resources," to point to the image location. Here are two examples:

```
<h:graphicImage id="mapImage"
                name="book_all.jpg"
                library="images"
                alt="#{bundle.ChooseBook}"
                usemap="#bookMap" />


<h:graphicImage value="#{resource['images:wave.med.gif']}"/>
```

You can use similar syntax to refer to an image in a style sheet. The following syntax in a style sheet specifies that the image is to be found at resources/img/top-background.jpg:

```
header {
    position: relative;
    height: 150px;
    background: #fff url(#{resource['img:top-background.jpg']}) repeat-x;
    ...
```

10.2.7 Laying Out Components with the h:panelGrid and h:panelGroup Tags

In a JavaServer Faces application, you use a panel as a layout container for a set of other components. A panel is rendered as an HTML table. Table 10–6 lists the tags used to create panels.

Table 10–6   Panel Component Tags

Tag	Attributes	Function
h:panelGrid	columns, columnClasses, footerClass, headerClass, panelClass, rowClasses, role	Displays a table
h:panelGroup	layout	Groups a set of components under one parent

The h:panelGrid tag is used to represent an entire table. The h:panelGroup tag is used to represent rows in a table. Other tags are used to represent individual cells in the rows.

The columns attribute defines how to group the data in the table and therefore is required if you want your table to have more than one column. The h:panelGrid tag also has a set of optional attributes that specify CSS classes: columnClasses, footerClass, headerClass, panelClass, and rowClasses. The role attribute can have the value "presentation" to indicate that the purpose of the table is to format the display rather than to show data.

If the headerClass attribute value is specified, the h:panelGrid tag must have a header as its first child. Similarly, if a footerClass attribute value is specified, the h:panelGrid tag must have a footer as its last child.

Here is an example:

```
<h:panelGrid columns="2"
             headerClass="list-header"
             styleClass="list-background"
             rowClasses="list-row-even, list-row-odd"
             summary="#{bundle.CustomerInfo}"
             title="#{bundle.Checkout}"
             role="presentation">
    <f:facet name="header">
        <h:outputText value="#{bundle.Checkout}"/>
    </f:facet>

    <h:outputLabel for="name" value="#{bundle.Name}" />
    <h:inputText id="name" size="30"
                value="#{cashierBean.name}"
                required="true"
                requiredMessage="#{bundle.ReqCustomerName}">
        <f:valueChangeListener
            type="javaeetutorial.dukesbookstore.listeners.NameChanged" />
    </h:inputText>
    <h:message styleClass="error-message" for="name"/>

    <h:outputLabel for="ccno" value="#{bundle.CCNumber}"/>
    <h:inputText id="ccno"
                size="19"
                converterMessage="#{bundle.CreditMessage}"
                required="true"
                requiredMessage="#{bundle.ReqCreditCard}">
    <f:converter converterId="ccno"/>
    <f:validateRegex
        pattern="\d{16}|\d{4} \d{4} \d{4} \d{4}|\d{4}-\d{4}-\d{4}-\d{4}" />
```

```
            </h:inputText>
            <h:message styleClass="error-message"  for="ccno"/>
            . . .
</h:panelGrid>
```

The preceding h:panelGrid tag is rendered as a table that contains components in which a customer inputs personal information. This h:panelGrid tag uses style sheet classes to format the table. The following code shows the list-header definition:

```
.list-header {
    background-color: #ffffff;
    color: #000000;
    text-align: center;
}
```

Because the h:panelGrid tag specifies a headerClass, the h:panelGrid tag must contain a header. The example h:panelGrid tag uses an f:facet tag for the header. Facets can have only one child, so an h:panelGroup tag is needed if you want to group more than one component within an f:facet. The example h:panelGrid tag has only one cell of data, so an h:panelGroup tag is not needed. (For more information about facets, see Section 10.2.12, "Using Data-Bound Table Components."

The h:panelGroup tag has an attribute, layout, in addition to those listed in Section 10.2.1, "Common Component Tag Attributes." If the layout attribute has the value block, an HTML div element is rendered to enclose the row; otherwise, an HTML span element is rendered to enclose the row. If you are specifying styles for the h:panelGroup tag, you should set the layout attribute to block in order for the styles to be applied to the components within the h:panelGroup tag. You should do this because styles, such as those that set width and height, are not applied to inline elements, which is how content enclosed by the span element is defined.

An h:panelGroup tag can also be used to encapsulate a nested tree of components so that the tree of components appears as a single component to the parent component.

Data, represented by the nested tags, is grouped into rows according to the value of the columns attribute of the h:panelGrid tag. The columns attribute in the example is set to 2, and therefore the table will have two columns. The column in which each component is displayed is determined by the order in which the component is listed on the page modulo 2. So, if a component is the fifth one in the list of components, that component will be in the 5 modulo 2 column, or column 1.

10.2.8 Displaying Components for Selecting One Value

Another commonly used component is one that allows a user to select one value, whether it is the only value available or one of a set of choices. The most common tags for this kind of component are as follows:

- An h:selectBooleanCheckbox tag, displayed as a check box, which represents a Boolean state

- An h:selectOneRadio tag, displayed as a set of options

- An h:selectOneMenu tag, displayed as a scrollable list

- An h:selectOneListbox tag, displayed as an unscrollable list

Figure 10–3 shows examples of these components.

Figure 10–3   Example Components for Selecting One Item

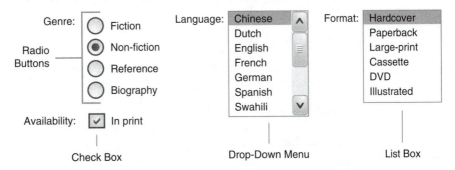

10.2.8.1 Displaying a Check Box Using the h:selectBooleanCheckbox Tag

The h:selectBooleanCheckbox tag is the only tag that JavaServer Faces technology provides for representing a Boolean state.

Here is an example that shows how to use the h:selectBooleanCheckbox tag:

```
<h:selectBooleanCheckbox id="fanClub"
                         rendered="false"
                         binding="#{cashierBean.specialOffer}" />
<h:outputLabel for="fanClub"
               rendered="false"
               binding="#{cashierBean.specialOfferText}"
               value="#{bundle.DukeFanClub}" />
```

The h:selectBooleanCheckbox tag and the h:outputLabel tag have rendered attributes that are set to false on the page but are set to true in the CashierBean under certain circumstances. When the h:selectBooleanCheckbox tag is rendered, it displays a check box to allow users to indicate whether they want to join the Duke Fan Club. When the h:outputLabel tag is rendered, it displays the label for the check box. The label text is represented by the value attribute.

10.2.8.2 Displaying a Menu Using the h:selectOneMenu Tag

A component that allows the user to select one value from a set of values can be rendered as a box or a set of options. This section describes the h:selectOneMenu tag. The h:selectOneRadio and h:selectOneListbox tags are used in a similar way. The h:selectOneListbox tag is similar to the h:selectOneMenu tag except that h:selectOneListbox defines a size attribute that determines how many of the items are displayed at once.

The h:selectOneMenu tag represents a component that contains a list of items from which a user can select one item. This menu component is sometimes known as a drop-down list or a combo box. The following code snippet shows how the h:selectOneMenu tag is used to allow the user to select a shipping method:

```
<h:selectOneMenu id="shippingOption"
                 required="true"
                 value="#{cashierBean.shippingOption}">
   <f:selectItem itemValue="2"
                 itemLabel="#{bundle.QuickShip}"/>
   <f:selectItem itemValue="5"
                 itemLabel="#{bundle.NormalShip}"/>
   <f:selectItem itemValue="7"
                 itemLabel="#{bundle.SaverShip}"/>
</h:selectOneMenu>
```

The value attribute of the h:selectOneMenu tag maps to the property that holds the currently selected item's value. In this case, the value is set by the backing bean. You are not required to provide a value for the currently selected item. If you don't provide a value, the browser determines which one is selected.

Like the h:selectOneRadio tag, the h:selectOneMenu tag must contain either an f:selectItems tag or a set of f:selectItem tags for representing the items in the list. Section 10.2.10, "Using the f:selectItem and f:selectItems Tags," describes these tags.

10.2.9 Displaying Components for Selecting Multiple Values

In some cases, you need to allow your users to select multiple values rather than just one value from a list of choices. You can do this using one of the following component tags:

- An h:selectManyCheckbox tag, displayed as a set of check boxes

- An h:selectManyMenu tag, displayed as a menu

- An h:selectManyListbox tag, displayed as a box

Figure 10–4 shows examples of these components.

Figure 10–4   Example Components for Selecting Multiple Values

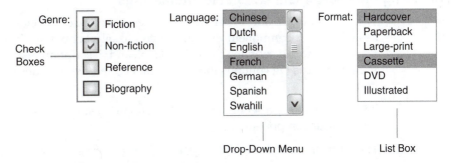

These tags allow the user to select zero or more values from a set of values. This section explains the h:selectManyCheckbox tag. The h:selectManyListbox and h:selectManyMenu tags are used in a similar way.

Unlike a menu, a list displays a subset of items in a box; a menu displays only one item at a time when the user is not selecting the menu. The size attribute of the h:selectManyListbox tag determines the number of items displayed at one time. The box includes a scroll bar for scrolling through any remaining items in the list.

The h:selectManyCheckbox tag renders a group of check boxes, with each check box representing one value that can be selected:

```
<h:selectManyCheckbox id="newslettercheckbox"
                      layout="pageDirection"
                      value="#{cashierBean.newsletters}">
    <f:selectItems value="#{cashierBean.newsletterItems}"/>
</h:selectManyCheckbox>
```

The value attribute of the h:selectManyCheckbox tag identifies the newsletters property of the CashierBean managed bean. This property holds the values of the currently selected items from the set of check boxes. You are not required to provide a value for the currently selected items. If you don't provide a value, the first item in the list is selected by default. In the CashierBean managed bean, this value is instantiated to 0, so no items are selected by default.

The layout attribute indicates how the set of check boxes is arranged on the page. Because layout is set to pageDirection, the check boxes are arranged vertically. The default is lineDirection, which aligns the check boxes horizontally.

The h:selectManyCheckbox tag must also contain a tag or set of tags representing the set of check boxes. To represent a set of items, you use the f:selectItems tag. To represent each item individually, you use the f:selectItem tag. The following section explains these tags in more detail.

10.2.10 Using the f:selectItem and f:selectItems Tags

The f:selectItem and f:selectItems tags represent components that can be nested inside a component that allows you to select one or multiple items. An f:selectItem tag contains the value, label, and description of a single item. An f:selectItems tag contains the values, labels, and descriptions of the entire list of items.

You can use either a set of f:selectItem tags or a single f:selectItems tag within your component tag.

The advantages of using the f:selectItems tag are as follows.

- Items can be represented by using different data structures, including Array, Map, and Collection. The value of the f:selectItems tag can represent even a generic collection of POJOs.

- Different lists can be concatenated into a single component, and the lists can be grouped within the component.

- Values can be generated dynamically at runtime.

The advantages of using f:selectItem are as follows.

- Items in the list can be defined from the page.

- Less code is needed in the backing bean for the f:selectItem properties.

The rest of this section shows you how to use the f:selectItems and f:selectItem tags.

10.2.10.1 Using the f:selectItems Tag

The following example from Section 10.2.9, "Displaying Components for Selecting Multiple Values," shows how to use the h:selectManyCheckbox tag:

```
<h:selectManyCheckbox id="newslettercheckbox"
                      layout="pageDirection"
                      value="#{cashierBean.newsletters}">
    <f:selectItems value="#{cashierBean.newsletterItems}"/>
</h:selectManyCheckbox>
```

The value attribute of the f:selectItems tag is bound to the managed bean property cashierBean.newsletterItems. The individual SelectItem objects are created programmatically in the managed bean.

See Section 12.2.1.7, "UISelectItems Properties," for information on how to write a managed bean property for one of these tags.

10.2.10.2 Using the f:selectItem Tag

The f:selectItem tag represents a single item in a list of items. Here is the example from Section 10.2.8.2, "Displaying a Menu Using the h:selectOneMenu Tag," once again:

```
<h:selectOneMenu id="shippingOption"
                 required="true"
                 value="#{cashierBean.shippingOption}">
    <f:selectItem itemValue="2"
                  itemLabel="#{bundle.QuickShip}"/>
    <f:selectItem itemValue="5"
                  itemLabel="#{bundle.NormalShip}"/>
    <f:selectItem itemValue="7"
                  itemLabel="#{bundle.SaverShip}"/>
</h:selectOneMenu>
```

The itemValue attribute represents the value for the f:selectItem tag. The itemLabel attribute represents the String that appears in the list component on the page.

The itemValue and itemLabel attributes are value-binding enabled, meaning that they can use value-binding expressions to refer to values in external objects. These attributes can also define literal values, as shown in the example h:selectOneMenu tag.

10.2.11 Displaying the Results from Selection Components

If you display components that allow a user to select values, you may also want to display the result of the selection.

For example, you might want to thank a user who selected the checkbox to join the Duke Fan Club, as described in Section 10.2.8.1, "Displaying a Check Box Using the h:selectBooleanCheckbox Tag." Because the checkbox is bound to the specialOffer property of CashierBean, a UISelectBoolean value, you can call the isSelected method of the property to determine whether to render a thank-you message:

```
<h:outputText value="#{bundle.DukeFanClubThanks}"
              rendered="#{cashierBean.specialOffer.isSelected()}"/>
```

Similarly, you might want to acknowledge that a user subscribed to newsletters using the h:selectManyCheckbox tag, as described in Section 10.2.9, "Displaying Components for Selecting Multiple Values." To do so, you can retrieve the value of the newsletters property, the String array that holds the selected items:

```
<h:outputText value="#{bundle.NewsletterThanks}"
              rendered="#{!empty cashierBean.newsletters}"/>
<ul>
    <ui:repeat value="#{cashierBean.newsletters}" var="nli">
        <li><h:outputText value="#{nli}" /></li>
    </ui:repeat>
</ul>
```

An introductory thank-you message is displayed only if the newsletters array is not empty. Then a ui:repeat tag, a simple way to show values in a loop, displays the contents of the selected items in an itemized list. (This tag is listed in Table 8–2 on page 122.)

10.2.12 Using Data-Bound Table Components

Data-bound table components display relational data in a tabular format. In a JavaServer Faces application, the h:dataTable component tag supports binding to a collection of data objects and displays the data as an HTML table. The h:column tag represents a column of data within the table, iterating over each record in the data source, which is displayed as a row. Here is an example:

```
<h:dataTable id="items"
             captionClass="list-caption
             columnClasses="list-column-center, list-column-left,
             list-column-right, list-column-center"
             footerClass="list-footer"
             headerClass="list-header"
```

```
                    rowClasses="list-row-even, list-row-odd"
                    styleClass="list-background"
                    summary="#{bundle.ShoppingCart}"
                    value="#{cart.items}"
                    border="1"
                    var="item">
    <h:column>
        <f:facet name="header">
            <h:outputText value="#{bundle.ItemQuantity}"/>
        </f:facet>
        <h:inputText id="quantity"
                    size="4"
                    value="#{item.quantity}"
                    title="#{bundle.ItemQuantity}">
            <f:validateLongRange minimum="0"/>
            <f:valueChangeListener
                type="javaeetutorial.dukesbookstore.listeners.QuantityChanged"/>
        </h:inputText>
    </h:column>
    <h:column>
        <f:facet name="header">
            <h:outputText value="#{bundle.ItemTitle}"/>
        </f:facet>
        <h:commandLink action="#{showcart.details}">
            <h:outputText value="#{item.item.title}"/>
        </h:commandLink>
    </h:column>
    ...
    <f:facet name="footer">
        <h:panelGroup>
            <h:outputText value="#{bundle.Subtotal}"/>
            <h:outputText value="#{cart.total}" />
                <f:convertNumber currencySymbol="$" type="currency"/>
            </h:outputText>
        </h:panelGroup>
    </f:facet>
    <f:facet name="caption">
        <h:outputText value="#{bundle.Caption}"/>
    </f:facet>
</h:dataTable>
```

The example h:dataTable tag displays the books in the shopping cart as well as
the quantity of each book in the shopping cart, the prices, and a set of buttons the
user can click to remove books from the shopping cart.

The h:column tags represent columns of data in a data component. While the data component is iterating over the rows of data, it processes the column component associated with each h:column tag for each row in the table.

The h:dataTable tag shown in the preceding code example iterates through the list of books (cart.items) in the shopping cart and displays their titles, authors, and prices. Each time the h:dataTable tag iterates through the list of books, it renders one cell in each column.

The h:dataTable and h:column tags use facets to represent parts of the table that are not repeated or updated. These parts include headers, footers, and captions.

In the preceding example, h:column tags include f:facet tags for representing column headers or footers. The h:column tag allows you to control the styles of these headers and footers by supporting the headerClass and footerClass attributes. These attributes accept space-separated lists of CSS classes, which will be applied to the header and footer cells of the corresponding column in the rendered table.

Facets can have only one child, so an h:panelGroup tag is needed if you want to group more than one component within an f:facet. Because the facet tag representing the footer includes more than one tag, the h:panelGroup tag is needed to group those tags. Finally, this h:dataTable tag includes an f:facet tag with its name attribute set to caption, causing a table caption to be rendered above the table.

This table is a classic use case for a data component because the number of books might not be known to the application developer or the page author when that application is developed. The data component can dynamically adjust the number of rows of the table to accommodate the underlying data.

The value attribute of an h:dataTable tag references the data to be included in the table. This data can take the form of any of the following:

- A list of beans
- An array of beans
- A single bean
- A javax.faces.model.DataModel object
- A java.sql.ResultSet object
- A javax.servlet.jsp.jstl.sql.Result object
- A javax.sql.RowSet object

All data sources for data components have a DataModel wrapper. Unless you explicitly construct a DataModel wrapper, the JavaServer Faces implementation will create one around data of any of the other acceptable types. See Section 12.2, "Writing Bean Properties," for more information on how to write properties for use with a data component.

The var attribute specifies a name that is used by the components within the h:dataTable tag as an alias to the data referenced in the value attribute of h:dataTable.

In the example h:dataTable tag, the value attribute points to a list of books. The var attribute points to a single book in that list. As the h:dataTable tag iterates through the list, each reference to item points to the current book in the list.

The h:dataTable tag also has the ability to display only a subset of the underlying data. This feature is not shown in the preceding example. To display a subset of the data, you use the optional first and rows attributes.

The first attribute specifies the first row to be displayed. The rows attribute specifies the number of rows, starting with the first row, to be displayed. For example, if you wanted to display records 2 through 10 of the underlying data, you would set first to 2 and rows to 9. When you display a subset of the data in your pages, you might want to consider including a link or button that causes subsequent rows to display when clicked. By default, both first and rows are set to zero, and this causes all the rows of the underlying data to display.

Table 10–7 shows the optional attributes for the h:dataTable tag.

Table 10–7   Optional Attributes for the h:dataTable Tag

Attribute	Defines Styles For
captionClass	Table caption
columnClasses	All the columns
footerClass	Footer
headerClass	Header
rowClasses	Rows
styleClass	The entire table

Each of the attributes in Table 10–7 can specify more than one style. If columnClasses or rowClasses specifies more than one style, the styles are applied to the columns or rows in the order that the styles are listed in the attribute. For example, if columnClasses specifies styles list-column-center and list-column-right, and if the table has two columns, the first column will have style list-column-center, and the second column will have style list-column-right.

If the style attribute specifies more styles than there are columns or rows, the remaining styles will be assigned to columns or rows starting from the first column or row. Similarly, if the style attribute specifies fewer styles than there are columns or rows, the remaining columns or rows will be assigned styles starting from the first style.

10.2.13 Displaying Error Messages with the h:message and h:messages Tags

The h:message and h:messages tags are used to display error messages when conversion or validation fails. The h:message tag displays error messages related to a specific input component, whereas the h:messages tag displays the error messages for the entire page.

Here is an example h:message tag from the guessnumber-jsf application:

```
<p>
    <h:inputText id="userNo"
                 title="Type a number from 0 to 10:"
                 value="#{userNumberBean.userNumber}">
        <f:validateLongRange minimum="#{userNumberBean.minimum}"
                             maximum="#{userNumberBean.maximum}"/>
    </h:inputText>
    <h:commandButton id="submit" value="Submit"
                     action="response"/>
</p>
<h:message showSummary="true" showDetail="false"
           style="color: #d20005;
           font-family: 'New Century Schoolbook', serif;
           font-style: oblique;
           text-decoration: overline"
           id="errors1"
           for="userNo"/>
```

The for attribute refers to the ID of the component that generated the error message. The error message is displayed at the same location that the h:message tag appears in the page. In this case, the error message will appear below the **Submit** button.

The style attribute allows you to specify the style of the text of the message. In the example in this section, the text will be a shade of red, New Century Schoolbook, serif font family, and oblique style, and a line will appear over the text. The message and messages tags support many other attributes for defining styles. For more information on these attributes, refer to the documentation at http://docs.oracle.com/javaee/7/javaserverfaces/2.2/vdldocs/facelets/.

Another attribute supported by the h:messages tag is the layout attribute. Its default value is list, which indicates that the messages are displayed in a bullet list using the HTML ul and li elements. If you set the attribute value to table, the messages will be rendered in a table using the HTML table element.

The preceding example shows a standard validator that is registered on the input component. The message tag displays the error message that is associated with this validator when the validator cannot validate the input component's value. In general, when you register a converter or validator on a component, you are queueing the error messages associated with the converter or validator on the component. The h:message and h:messages tags display the appropriate error messages that are queued on the component when the validators or converters registered on that component fail to convert or validate the component's value.

Standard error messages are provided with standard converters and standard validators. An application architect can override these standard messages and supply error messages for custom converters and validators by registering custom error messages with the application.

10.2.14 Creating Bookmarkable URLs with the h:button and h:link Tags

The ability to create bookmarkable URLs refers to the ability to generate links based on a specified navigation outcome and on component parameters.

In HTTP, most browsers by default send GET requests for URL retrieval and POST requests for data processing. The GET requests can have query parameters and can be cached, which is not advised for POST requests, which send data to servers for processing. The other JavaServer Faces tags capable of generating links use either simple GET requests, as in the case of h:outputLink, or POST requests, as in the case of h:commandLink or h:commandButton tags. GET requests with query parameters provide finer granularity to URL strings. These URLs are created with one or more name=value parameters appended to the simple URL after a ? character and separated by either &; or & strings.

To create a bookmarkable URL, use an h:link or h:button tag. Both of these tags can generate a link based on the outcome attribute of the component. For example:

```
<h:link outcome="somepage" value="Message" />
```

The h:link tag will generate a URL link that points to the somepage.xhtml file on the same server. The following sample HTML is generated from the preceding tag, assuming that the application name is simplebookmark:

```
<a href="/simplebookmark/somepage.xhtml>Message</a>
```

This is a simple GET request that cannot pass any data from page to page. To create more complex GET requests and utilize the complete functionality of the h:link tag, use view parameters.

10.2.15 Using View Parameters to Configure Bookmarkable URLs

To pass a parameter from one page to another, use the includeViewParams attribute in your h:link tag and, in addition, use an f:param tag to specify the name and value to be passed. Here the h:link tag specifies the outcome page as personal.xhtml and provides a parameter named Result whose value is a managed bean property:

```
<h:body>
    <h:form>
        <h:graphicImage url="#{resource['images:duke.waving.gif']}"
                        alt="Duke waving his hand"/>
        <h2>Hello, #{hello.name}!</h2>
        <p>I've made your
            <h:link outcome="personal" value="personal greeting page!"
                    includeViewParams="true">
                <f:param name="Result" value="#{hello.name}"/>
            </h:link>
        </p>
        <h:commandButton id="back" value="Back" action="index" />
    </h:form>
</h:body>
```

If the includeViewParams attribute is set on the component, the view parameters are added to the hyperlink. Therefore, the resulting URL will look something like this if the value of hello.name is Timmy:

```
http://localhost:8080/bookmarks/personal.xhtml?Result=Timmy
```

On the outcome page, specify the core tags f:metadata and f:viewparam as the source of parameters for configuring the URLs. View parameters are declared as part of f:metadata for a page, as shown in the following example:

```
<f:metadata>
    <f:viewParam name="Result" value="#{hello.name}"/>
</f:metadata>
```

This allows you to specify the bean property value on the page:

```
<h:outputText value="Howdy, #{hello.name}!" />
```

As a view parameter, the name also appears in the page's URL. If you edit the URL, you change the output on the page.

Because the URL can be the result of various parameter values, the order of the URL creation has been predefined. The order in which the various parameter values are read is as follows:

1. Component

2. Navigation-case parameters

3. View parameters

10.2.16 The bookmarks Example Application

The bookmarks example application modifies the hello1 application described in Section 6.3, "A Web Module That Uses JavaServer Faces Technology: The hello1 Example," to use a bookmarkable URL that uses view parameters.

Like hello1, the application includes the Hello.java managed bean, an index.xhtml page, and a response.xhtml page. In addition, it includes a personal.xhtml page, to which a bookmarkable URL and view parameters are passed from the response.xhtml page, as described in Section 10.2.15, "Using View Parameters to Configure Bookmarkable URLs."

You can use either NetBeans IDE or Maven to build, package, deploy, and run the bookmarks example. The source code for this example is in the *tut-install*/ examples/web/jsf/bookmarks/ directory.

10.2.16.1 To Build, Package, and Deploy the bookmarks Example Using NetBeans IDE

1. Make sure that GlassFish Server has been started (see Section 2.2, "Starting and Stopping GlassFish Server").

2. From the **File** menu, choose **Open Project**.

3. In the Open Project dialog box, navigate to:

   tut-install/examples/web/jsf

4. Select the bookmarks folder.

5. Click **Open Project**.

6. In the **Projects** tab, right-click the bookmarks project and select **Build**.

   This option builds the example application and deploys it to your GlassFish Server instance.

10.2.16.2 To Build, Package, and Deploy the bookmarks Example Using Maven

1. Make sure that GlassFish Server has been started (see Section 2.2, "Starting and Stopping GlassFish Server").

2. In a terminal window, go to:

   tut-install/examples/web/jsf/bookmarks/

3. Enter the following command:

   `mvn install`

   This command builds and packages the application into a WAR file, `bookmarks.war`, that is located in the `target` directory. It then deploys the WAR file to your GlassFish Server instance.

10.2.16.3 To Run the bookmarks Example

1. Enter the following URL in your web browser:

   `http://localhost:8080/bookmarks`

2. In the text field, enter a name and click **Submit**.

3. On the response page, move your mouse over the "personal greeting page" link to view the URL with the view parameter, then click the link.

   The `personal.xhtml` page opens, displaying a greeting to the name you typed.

4. In the **URL** field, modify the **Result** parameter value and press **Return**.

   The name in the greeting changes to what you typed.

10.2.17 Resource Relocation Using h:outputScript and h:outputStylesheet Tags

Resource relocation refers to the ability of a JavaServer Faces application to specify the location where a resource can be rendered. Resource relocation can be defined with the following HTML tags:

- `h:outputScript`

- `h:outputStylesheet`

These tags have `name` and `target` attributes, which can be used to define the render location. For a complete list of attributes for these tags, see the documentation at `http://docs.oracle.com/javaee/7/javaserverfaces/2.2/vdldocs/facelets/`.

For the h:outputScript tag, the name and target attributes define where the output of a resource may appear. Here is an example:

```
<html xmlns="http://www.w3.org/1999/xhtml"
    xmlns:h="http://xmlns.jcp.org/jsf/html">
    <h:head id="head">
        <title>Resource Relocation</title>
    </h:head>
    <h:body id="body">
        <h:form id="form">
            <h:outputScript name="hello.js"/>
            <h:outputStylesheet name="hello.css"/>
        </h:form>
    </h:body>
</html>
```

Because the target attribute is not defined in the tags, the style sheet hello.css is rendered in the head element of the page, and the hello.js script is rendered in the body of the page.

Here is the HTML generated by the preceding code:

```
<html xmlns="http://www.w3.org/1999/xhtml">
    <head>
        <title>Resource Relocation</title>
        <link type="text/css" rel="stylesheet"
            href="/context-root/javax.faces.resource/hello.css"/>
    </head>
    <body>
        <form id="form" name="form" method="post"
            action="..." enctype="...">
            <script type="text/javascript"
                src="/context-root/javax.faces.resource/hello.js">
            </script>
        </form>
    </body>
</html>
```

If you set the target attribute for the h:outputScript tag, the incoming GET request provides the location parameter. Here is an example:

```
<html xmlns="http://www.w3.org/1999/xhtml"
    xmlns:h="http://xmlns.jcp.org/jsf/html">
    <h:head id="head">
        <title>Resource Relocation</title>
    </h:head>
    <h:body id="body">
        <h:form id="form">
```

```
                    <h:outputScript name="hello.js" target="#{param.location}"/>
                    <h:outputStylesheet name="hello.css"/>
            </h:form>
        </h:body>
</html>
```

In this case, if the incoming request does not provide a location parameter, the default locations will still apply: The style sheet is rendered in the head, and the script is rendered inline. However, if the incoming request specifies the location parameter as the head, both the style sheet and the script will be rendered in the head element.

The HTML generated by the preceding code is as follows:

```
<html xmlns="http://www.w3.org/1999/xhtml">
    <head>
        <title>Resource Relocation</title>
        <link type="text/css" rel="stylesheet"
                href="/context-root/javax.faces.resource/hello.css"/>
        <script type="text/javascript"
                src="/context-root/javax.faces.resource/hello.js">
          </script>
    </head>
    <body>
        <form id="form" name="form" method="post"
                action="..." enctype="...">
        </form>
    </body>
</html>
```

Similarly, if the incoming request provides the location parameter as the body, the script will be rendered in the body element.

The preceding section describes simple uses for resource relocation. That feature can add even more functionality for the components and pages. A page author does not have to know the location of a resource or its placement.

By using a @ResourceDependency annotation for the components, component authors can define the resources for the component, such as a style sheet and script. This allows the page authors freedom from defining resource locations.

10.3 Using Core Tags

The tags included in the JavaServer Faces core tag library are used to perform core actions that are not performed by HTML tags.

Table 10–8 lists the event-handling core tags.

Table 10–8   Event-Handling Core Tags

Tag	Function
f:actionListener	Adds an action listener to a parent component
f:phaseListener	Adds a PhaseListener to a page
f:setPropertyActionListener	Registers a special action listener whose sole purpose is to push a value into a managed bean when a form is submitted
f:valueChangeListener	Adds a value-change listener to a parent component

Table 10–9 lists the data-conversion core tags.

Table 10–9   Data-Conversion Core Tags

Tag	Function
f:converter	Adds an arbitrary converter to the parent component
f:convertDateTime	Adds a DateTimeConverter instance to the parent component
f:convertNumber	Adds a NumberConverter instance to the parent component

Table 10–10 lists the facet core tags.

Table 10–10   Facet Core Tags

Tag	Function
f:facet	Adds a nested component that has a special relationship to its enclosing tag
f:metadata	Registers a facet on a parent component

Table 10–11 lists the core tags that represent items in a list.

Table 10–11   Core Tags That Represent Items in a List

Tag	Function
f:selectItem	Represents one item in a list of items
f:selectItems	Represents a set of items

Table 10–12 lists the validator core tags.

Table 10–12   Validator Core Tags

Tag	Function
f:validateDoubleRange	Adds a DoubleRangeValidator to a component
f:validateLength	Adds a LengthValidator to a component
f:validateLongRange	Adds a LongRangeValidator to a component
f:validator	Adds a custom validator to a component
f:validateRegEx	Adds a RegExValidator to a component
f:validateBean	Delegates the validation of a local value to a BeanValidator
f:validateRequired	Enforces the presence of a value in a component

Table 10–13 lists the core tags that fall into other categories.

Table 10–13   Miscellaneous Core Tags

Tag Category	Tag	Function
Attribute configuration	f:attribute	Adds configurable attributes to a parent component
Localization	f:loadBundle	Specifies a ResourceBundle that is exposed as a Map
Parameter substitution	f:param	Substitutes parameters into a MessageFormat instance and adds query string name-value pairs to a URL
Ajax	f:ajax	Associates an Ajax action with a single component or a group of components based on placement
Event	f:event	Allows installing a ComponentSystemEventListener on a component

These tags, which are used in conjunction with component tags, are explained in other sections of this tutorial.

Table 10–14 lists the sections that explain how to use specific core tags.

Table 10–14   **Where the Core Tags Are Explained**

Tags	Where Explained
Event-handling tags	Section 11.2, "Registering Listeners on Components"
Data-conversion tags	Section 11.1, "Using the Standard Converters"
f:facet	Section 10.2.12, "Using Data-Bound Table Components," and Section 10.2.7, "Laying Out Components with the h:panelGrid and h:panelGroup Tags"
f:loadBundle	Section 20.2.2, "Setting the Resource Bundle"
f:metadata	Section 10.2.15, "Using View Parameters to Configure Bookmarkable URLs"
f:param	Section 10.2.4.5, "Displaying a Formatted Message with the h:outputFormat Tag"
f:selectItem and f:selectItems	Section 10.2.10, "Using the f:selectItem and f:selectItems Tags"
Validator tags	Section 11.3, "Using the Standard Validators"
f:ajax	Chapter 13, "Using Ajax with JavaServer Faces Technology"

11

Using Converters, Listeners, and Validators

The previous chapter described components and explained how to add them to a web page. This chapter provides information on adding more functionality to the components through converters, listeners, and validators.

- Converters are used to convert data that is received from the input components. Converters allow an application to bring the strongly typed features of the Java programming language into the String-based world of HTTP servlet programming.

- Listeners are used to listen to the events happening in the page and perform actions as defined.

- Validators are used to validate the data that is received from the input components. Validators allow an application to express constraints on form input data to ensure that the necessary requirements are met before the input data is processed.

The following topics are addressed here:

- Using the Standard Converters
- Registering Listeners on Components
- Using the Standard Validators
- Referencing a Managed Bean Method

11.1 Using the Standard Converters

The JavaServer Faces implementation provides a set of `Converter` implementations that you can use to convert component data. The purpose of conversion is to take the `String`-based data coming in from the Servlet API and convert it to strongly typed Java objects suitable for the business domain. For more information on the conceptual details of the conversion model, see Section 7.4.3, "Conversion Model."

The standard `Converter` implementations are located in the `javax.faces.convert` package. Normally, converters are implicitly assigned based on the type of the EL expression pointed to by the value of the component. However, these converters can also be accessed by a converter ID. Table 11–1 shows the converter classes and their associated converter IDs.

Table 11–1   Converter Classes and Converter IDs

Class in the javax.faces.convert Package	Converter ID
BigDecimalConverter	javax.faces.BigDecimal
BigIntegerConverter	javax.faces.BigInteger
BooleanConverter	javax.faces.Boolean
ByteConverter	javax.faces.Byte
CharacterConverter	javax.faces.Character
DateTimeConverter	javax.faces.DateTime
DoubleConverter	javax.faces.Double
EnumConverter	javax.faces.Enum
FloatConverter	javax.faces.Float
IntegerConverter	javax.faces.Integer
LongConverter	javax.faces.Long
NumberConverter	javax.faces.Number
ShortConverter	javax.faces.Short

A standard error message is associated with each of these converters. If you have registered one of these converters onto a component on your page and the converter is not able to convert the component's value, the converter's error message will display on the page. For example, the following error message appears if `BigIntegerConverter` fails to convert a value:

```
{0} must be a number consisting of one or more digits
```

In this case, the {0} substitution parameter will be replaced with the name of the input component on which the converter is registered.

Two of the standard converters (DateTimeConverter and NumberConverter) have their own tags, which allow you to configure the format of the component data using the tag attributes. For more information about using DateTimeConverter, see Section 11.1.2, "Using DateTimeConverter." For more information about using NumberConverter, see Section 11.1.3, "Using NumberConverter." The following section explains how to convert a component's value, including how to register other standard converters with a component.

11.1.1 Converting a Component's Value

To use a particular converter to convert a component's value, you need to register the converter onto the component. You can register any of the standard converters in one of the following ways.

- Nest one of the standard converter tags inside the component's tag. These tags are f:convertDateTime and f:convertNumber, which are described in Section 11.1.2, "Using DateTimeConverter," and Section 11.1.3, "Using NumberConverter," respectively.

- Bind the value of the component to a managed bean property of the same type as the converter. This is the most common technique.

- Refer to the converter from the component tag's converter attribute, specifying the ID of the converter class.

- Nest an f:converter tag inside of the component tag, and use either the f:converter tag's converterId attribute or its binding attribute to refer to the converter.

As an example of the second technique, if you want a component's data to be converted to an Integer, you can simply bind the component's value to a managed bean property. Here is an example:

```
Integer age = 0;
public Integer getAge(){ return age;}
public void setAge(Integer age) {this.age = age;}
```

The data from the h:inputText tag in the this example will be converted to a java.lang.Integer value. The Integer type is a supported type of NumberConverter. If you don't need to specify any formatting instructions using the f:convertNumber tag attributes, and if one of the standard converters will suffice, you can simply reference that converter by using the component tag's converter attribute.

You can also nest an f:converter tag within the component tag and use either the converter tag's converterId attribute or its binding attribute to reference the converter.

The converterId attribute must reference the converter's ID. Here is an example that uses one of the converter IDs listed in Table 11–1:

```
<h:inputText value="#{loginBean.age}">
    <f:converter converterId="javax.faces.Integer" />
</h:inputText>
```

Instead of using the converterId attribute, the f:converter tag can use the binding attribute. The binding attribute must resolve to a bean property that accepts and returns an appropriate Converter instance.

You can also create custom converters and register them on components using the f:converter tag. For details, see Section 15.10, "Creating and Using a Custom Converter."

11.1.2 Using DateTimeConverter

You can convert a component's data to a java.util.Date by nesting the convertDateTime tag inside the component tag. The convertDateTime tag has several attributes that allow you to specify the format and type of the data. Table 11–2 lists the attributes.

Here is a simple example of a convertDateTime tag:

```
<h:outputText value="#{cashierBean.shipDate}">
    <f:convertDateTime type="date" dateStyle="full" />
</h:outputText>
```

When binding the DateTimeConverter to a component, ensure that the managed bean property to which the component is bound is of type java.util.Date. In the preceding example, cashierBean.shipDate must be of type java.util.Date.

The example tag can display the following output:

```
Saturday, September 21, 2013
```

You can also display the same date and time by using the following tag in which the date format is specified:

```
<h:outputText value="#{cashierBean.shipDate}">
    <f:convertDateTime pattern="EEEEEEE, MMM dd, yyyy" />
</h:outputText>
```

If you want to display the example date in Spanish, you can use the locale attribute:

```
<h:outputText value="#{cashierBean.shipDate}">
    <f:convertDateTime dateStyle="full"
                       locale="es"
                       timeStyle="long" type="both" />
</h:outputText>
```

This tag would display the following output:

```
jueves 24 de octubre de 2013 15:07:04 GMT
```

Refer to the "Customizing Formats" lesson of the *Java Tutorial* at http://docs.oracle.com/javase/tutorial/i18n/format/simpleDateFormat.html for more information on how to format the output using the pattern attribute of the convertDateTime tag.

Table 11–2   Attributes for the f:convertDateTime Tag

Attribute	Type	Description
binding	DateTimeConverter	Used to bind a converter to a managed bean property.
dateStyle	String	Defines the format, as specified by java.text.DateFormat, of a date or the date part of a date string. Applied only if type is date or both and if pattern is not defined. Valid values: default, short, medium, long, and full. If no value is specified, default is used.
for	String	Used with composite components. Refers to one of the objects within the composite component inside which this tag is nested.
locale	String or Locale	Locale whose predefined styles for dates and times are used during formatting or parsing. If not specified, the Locale returned by FacesContext.getLocale will be used.
pattern	String	Custom formatting pattern that determines how the date/time string should be formatted and parsed. If this attribute is specified, dateStyle, timeStyle, and type attributes are ignored.
timeStyle	String	Defines the format, as specified by java.text.DateFormat, of a time or the time part of a date string. Applied only if type is time and pattern is not defined. Valid values: default, short, medium, long, and full. If no value is specified, default is used.

Table 11–2   (Cont.) Attributes for the f:convertDateTime Tag

Attribute	Type	Description
timeZone	String or TimeZone	Time zone in which to interpret any time information in the date string.
type	String	Specifies whether the string value will contain a date, a time, or both. Valid values are date, time, or both. If no value is specified, date is used.

11.1.3 Using NumberConverter

You can convert a component's data to a java.lang.Number by nesting the convertNumber tag inside the component tag. The convertNumber tag has several attributes that allow you to specify the format and type of the data. Table 11–3 lists the attributes.

The following example uses a convertNumber tag to display the total prices of the contents of a shopping cart:

```
<h:outputText value="#{cart.total}">
    <f:convertNumber currencySymbol="$" type="currency"/>
</h:outputText>
```

When binding the NumberConverter to a component, ensure that the managed bean property to which the component is bound is of a primitive type or has a type of java.lang.Number. In the preceding example, cart.total is of type double.

Here is an example of a number that this tag can display:

$934

This result can also be displayed by using the following tag in which the currency pattern is specified:

```
<h:outputText id="cartTotal" value="#{cart.total}">
    <f:convertNumber pattern="$####" />
</h:outputText>
```

See the "Customizing Formats" lesson of the *Java Tutorial* at http://docs.oracle.com/javase/tutorial/i18n/format/decimalFormat.html for more information on how to format the output by using the pattern attribute of the convertNumber tag.

Table 11–3   Attributes for the f:convertNumber Tag

Attribute	Type	Description
binding	NumberConverter	Used to bind a converter to a managed bean property.
currencyCode	String	ISO 4217 currency code, used only when formatting currencies.
currencySymbol	String	Currency symbol, applied only when formatting currencies.
for	String	Used with composite components. Refers to one of the objects within the composite component inside which this tag is nested.
groupingUsed	Boolean	Specifies whether formatted output contains grouping separators.
integerOnly	Boolean	Specifies whether only the integer part of the value will be parsed.
locale	String or Locale	Locale whose number styles are used to format or parse data.
maxFractionDigits	int	Maximum number of digits formatted in the fractional part of the output.
maxIntegerDigits	int	Maximum number of digits formatted in the integer part of the output.
minFractionDigits	int	Minimum number of digits formatted in the fractional part of the output.
minIntegerDigits	int	Minimum number of digits formatted in the integer part of the output.
pattern	String	Custom formatting pattern that determines how the number string is formatted and parsed.
type	String	Specifies whether the string value is parsed and formatted as a number, currency, or percentage. If not specified, number is used.

11.2 Registering Listeners on Components

An application developer can implement listeners as classes or as managed bean methods. If a listener is a managed bean method, the page author references the method from either the component's valueChangeListener attribute or its actionListener attribute. If the listener is a class, the page author can reference the listener from either an f:valueChangeListener tag or an f:actionListener tag and nest the tag inside the component tag to register the listener on the component.

Section 11.4.2, "Referencing a Method That Handles an Action Event," and Section 11.4.4, "Referencing a Method That Handles a Value-Change Event," explain how a page author uses the valueChangeListener and actionListener attributes to reference managed bean methods that handle events.

This section explains how to register a NameChanged value-change listener and a BookChange action listener implementation on components. The Duke's Bookstore case study includes both of these listeners. (See Chapter 28, "Duke's Bookstore Case Study Example," in *The Java EE 7 Tutorial, Volume 2*, for details.)

11.2.1 Registering a Value-Change Listener on a Component

A page author can register a ValueChangeListener implementation on a component that implements EditableValueHolder by nesting an f:valueChangeListener tag within the component's tag on the page. The f:valueChangeListener tag supports the attributes shown in Table 11–4, one of which must be used.

Table 11–4   *Attributes for the f:valueChangeListener Tag*

Attribute	Description
type	References the fully qualified class name of a ValueChangeListener implementation. Can accept a literal or a value expression.
binding	References an object that implements ValueChangeListener. Can accept only a value expression, which must point to a managed bean property that accepts and returns a ValueChangeListener implementation.

The following example shows a value-change listener registered on a component:

```
<h:inputText id="name"
             size="30"
             value="#{cashierBean.name}"
             required="true"
             requiredMessage="#{bundle.ReqCustomerName}">
    <f:valueChangeListener
        type="javaeetutorial.dukesbookstore.listeners.NameChanged" />
</h:inputText>
```

In the example, the core tag type attribute specifies the custom NameChanged listener as the ValueChangeListener implementation registered on the name component.

After this component tag is processed and local values have been validated, its corresponding component instance will queue the ValueChangeEvent associated with the specified ValueChangeListener to the component.

The binding attribute is used to bind a ValueChangeListener implementation to a managed bean property. This attribute works in a similar way to the binding attribute supported by the standard converter tags. See Section 15.12, "Binding Component Values and Instances to Managed Bean Properties," for more information.

11.2.2 Registering an Action Listener on a Component

A page author can register an ActionListener implementation on a command component by nesting an f:actionListener tag within the component's tag on the page. Similarly to the f:valueChangeListener tag, the f:actionListener tag supports both the type and binding attributes. One of these attributes must be used to reference the action listener.

Here is an example of an h:commandLink tag that references an ActionListener implementation:

```
<h:commandLink id="Duke" action="bookstore">
    <f:actionListener
    type="javaeetutorial.dukesbookstore.listeners.LinkBookChangeListener" />
    <h:outputText value="#{bundle.Book201}"/>
</h:commandLink>
```

The type attribute of the f:actionListener tag specifies the fully qualified class name of the ActionListener implementation. Similarly to the f:valueChangeListener tag, the f:actionListener tag also supports the binding attribute. See Section 15.13, "Binding Converters, Listeners, and Validators to Managed Bean Properties," for more information about binding listeners to managed bean properties.

In addition to the actionListener tag that allows you register a custom listener onto a component, the core tag library includes the f:setPropertyActionListener tag. You use this tag to register a special action listener onto the ActionSource instance associated with a component. When the component is activated, the listener will store the object referenced by the tag's value attribute into the object referenced by the tag's target attribute.

The bookcatalog.xhtml page of the Duke's Bookstore application uses f:setPropertyActionListener with two components: the h:commandLink component used to link to the bookdetails.xhtml page and the h:commandButton component used to add a book to the cart:

```
<h:dataTable id="books"
    value="#{store.books}"
    var="book"
    headerClass="list-header"
    styleClass="list-background"
    rowClasses="list-row-even, list-row-odd"
    border="1"
    summary="#{bundle.BookCatalog}" >
    ...
    <h:column>
        <f:facet name="header">
            <h:outputText value="#{bundle.ItemTitle}"/>
        </f:facet>
        <h:commandLink action="#{catalog.details}"
                    value="#{book.title}">
            <f:setPropertyActionListener target="#{requestScope.book}"
                                        value="#{book}"/>
        </h:commandLink>
    </h:column>
    ...
    <h:column>
        <f:facet name="header">
            <h:outputText value="#{bundle.CartAdd}"/>
        </f:facet>
        <h:commandButton id="add"
                        action="#{catalog.add}"
                        value="#{bundle.CartAdd}">
            <f:setPropertyActionListener target="#{requestScope.book}"
                                        value="#{book}"/>
        </h:commandButton>
    </h:column>
```

The h:commandLink and h:commandButton tags are within an h:dataTable tag, which iterates over the list of books. The var attribute refers to a single book in the list of books.

The object referenced by the var attribute of an h:dataTable tag is in page scope. However, in this case you need to put this object into request scope so that when the user activates the commandLink component to go to bookdetails.xhtml or activates the commandButton component to go to bookcatalog.xhtml, the book data is available to those pages. Therefore, the f:setPropertyActionListener tag is used to set the current book object into request scope when the commandLink or commandButton component is activated.

In the preceding example, the f:setPropertyActionListener tag's value attribute references the book object. The f:setPropertyActionListener tag's target attribute references the value expression requestScope.book, which is where the book object referenced by the value attribute is stored when the commandLink or the commandButton component is activated.

11.3 Using the Standard Validators

JavaServer Faces technology provides a set of standard classes and associated tags that page authors and application developers can use to validate a component's data. Table 11–5 lists all the standard validator classes and the tags that allow you to use the validators from the page.

Table 11–5   The Validator Classes

Validator Class	Tag	Function
BeanValidator	validateBean	Registers a bean validator for the component.
DoubleRangeValidator	validateDoubleRange	Checks whether the local value of a component is within a certain range. The value must be floating-point or convertible to floating-point.
LengthValidator	validateLength	Checks whether the length of a component's local value is within a certain range. The value must be a java.lang.String.
LongRangeValidator	validateLongRange	Checks whether the local value of a component is within a certain range. The value must be any numeric type or String that can be converted to a long.
RegexValidator	validateRegex	Checks whether the local value of a component is a match against a regular expression from the java.util.regex package.
RequiredValidator	validateRequired	Ensures that the local value is not empty on an EditableValueHolder component.

All of these validator classes implement the Validator interface. Component writers and application developers can also implement this interface to define their own set of constraints for a component's value.

Similar to the standard converters, each of these validators has one or more standard error messages associated with it. If you have registered one of these validators onto a component on your page and the validator is unable to validate the component's value, the validator's error message will display on the page. For example, the error message that displays when the component's value exceeds the maximum value allowed by LongRangeValidator is as follows:

```
{1}: Validation Error: Value is greater than allowable maximum of "{0}"
```

In this case, the {1} substitution parameter is replaced by the component's label or id, and the {0} substitution parameter is replaced with the maximum value allowed by the validator.

See Section 10.2.13, "Displaying Error Messages with the h:message and h:messages Tags," for information on how to display validation error messages on the page when validation fails.

Instead of using the standard validators, you can use Bean Validation to validate data. If you specify bean validation constraints on your managed bean properties, the constraints are automatically placed on the corresponding fields on your application's web pages. See Chapter 21, "Introduction to Bean Validation," for more information. You do not need to specify the validateBean tag to use Bean Validation, but the tag allows you to use more advanced Bean Validation features. For example, you can use the validationGroups attribute of the tag to specify constraint groups.

11.3.1 Validating a Component's Value

To validate a component's value using a particular validator, you need to register that validator on the component. You can do this in one of the following ways.

- Nest the validator's corresponding tag (shown in Table 11–5) inside the component's tag. Section 11.3.2, "Using Validator Tags," explains how to use the validateLongRange tag. You can use the other standard tags in the same way.

- Refer to a method that performs the validation from the component tag's validator attribute.

- Nest a validator tag inside the component tag, and use either the validator tag's validatorId attribute or its binding attribute to refer to the validator.

See Section 11.4.3, "Referencing a Method That Performs Validation," for more information on using the validator attribute.

The validatorId attribute works similarly to the converterId attribute of the converter tag, as described in Section 11.1.1, "Converting a Component's Value."

Keep in mind that validation can be performed only on components that implement `EditableValueHolder`, because these components accept values that can be validated.

11.3.2 Using Validator Tags

The following example shows how to use the `f:validateLongRange` validator tag on an input component named `quantity`:

```
<h:inputText id="quantity" size="4" value="#{item.quantity}">
    <f:validateLongRange minimum="1"/>
</h:inputText>
<h:message for="quantity"/>
```

This tag requires the user to enter a number that is at least 1. The `validateLongRange` tag also has a `maximum` attribute, which sets a maximum value for the input.

The attributes of all the standard validator tags accept EL value expressions. This means that the attributes can reference managed bean properties rather than specify literal values. For example, the `f:validateLongRange` tag in the preceding example can reference managed bean properties called `minimum` and `maximum` to get the minimum and maximum values acceptable to the validator implementation, as shown in this snippet from the `guessnumber-jsf` example:

```
<h:inputText id="userNo"
             title="Type a number from 0 to 10:"
             value="#{userNumberBean.userNumber}">
    <f:validateLongRange minimum="#{userNumberBean.minimum}"
                         maximum="#{userNumberBean.maximum}"/>
</h:inputText>
```

The following `f:validateRegex` tag shows how you might ensure that a password is from 4 to 10 characters long and contains at least one digit, at least one lowercase letter, and at least one uppercase letter:

```
<f:validateRegex pattern="((?=.*\d)(?=.*[a-z])(?=.*[A-Z]).{4,10})"
                 for="passwordVal"/>
```

11.4 Referencing a Managed Bean Method

A component tag has a set of attributes for referencing managed bean methods that can perform certain functions for the component associated with the tag. These attributes are summarized in Table 11–6.

Table 11–6   Component Tag Attributes That Reference Managed Bean Methods

Attribute	Function
action	Refers to a managed bean method that performs navigation processing for the component and returns a logical outcome String
actionListener	Refers to a managed bean method that handles action events
validator	Refers to a managed bean method that performs validation on the component's value
valueChangeListener	Refers to a managed bean method that handles value-change events

Only components that implement ActionSource can use the action and actionListener attributes. Only components that implement EditableValueHolder can use the validator or valueChangeListener attributes.

The component tag refers to a managed bean method using a method expression as a value of one of the attributes. The method referenced by an attribute must follow a particular signature, which is defined by the tag attribute's definition in the documentation at http://docs.oracle.com/javaee/7/ javaserverfaces/2.2/vldocs/facelets/. For example, the definition of the validator attribute of the inputText tag is the following:

```
void validate(javax.faces.context.FacesContext,
              javax.faces.component.UIComponent, java.lang.Object)
```

The following sections give examples of how to use the attributes.

11.4.1 Referencing a Method That Performs Navigation

If your page includes a component, such as a button or a link, that causes the application to navigate to another page when the component is activated, the tag corresponding to this component must include an action attribute. This attribute does one of the following:

- Specifies a logical outcome String that tells the application which page to access next

- References a managed bean method that performs some processing and returns a logical outcome String

The following example shows how to reference a navigation method:

```
<h:commandButton value="#{bundle.Submit}"
                 action="#{cashierBean.submit}" />
```

See Section 12.3.1, "Writing a Method to Handle Navigation," for information on how to write such a method.

11.4.2 Referencing a Method That Handles an Action Event

If a component on your page generates an action event, and if that event is handled by a managed bean method, you refer to the method by using the component's `actionListener` attribute.

The following example shows how such a method could be referenced:

```
<h:commandLink id="Duke" action="bookstore"
               actionListener="#{actionBean.chooseBookFromLink}">
```

The `actionListener` attribute of this component tag references the `chooseBookFromLink` method using a method expression. The `chooseBookFromLink` method handles the event when the user clicks the link rendered by this component. See Section 12.3.2, "Writing a Method to Handle an Action Event," for information on how to write such a method.

11.4.3 Referencing a Method That Performs Validation

If the input of one of the components on your page is validated by a managed bean method, refer to the method from the component's tag by using the `validator` attribute.

The following simplified example from Section 24.2, "The guessnumber-cdi CDI Example," shows how to reference a method that performs validation on `inputGuess`, an input component:

```
<h:inputText id="inputGuess"
    value="#{userNumberBean.userNumber}"
    required="true" size="3"
    disabled="#{userNumberBean.number eq userNumberBean.userNumber ...}"
    validator="#{userNumberBean.validateNumberRange}">
</h:inputText>
```

The managed bean method `validateNumberRange` verifies that the input value is within the valid range, which changes each time another guess is made. See Section 12.3.3, "Writing a Method to Perform Validation," for information on how to write such a method.

11.4.4 Referencing a Method That Handles a Value-Change Event

If you want a component on your page to generate a value-change event and you want that event to be handled by a managed bean method instead of a

ValueChangeListener implementation, you refer to the method by using the component's valueChangeListener attribute:

```
<h:inputText id="name"
             size="30"
             value="#{cashierBean.name}"
             required="true"
             valueChangeListener="#{cashierBean.processValueChange}" />
</h:inputText>
```

The valueChangeListener attribute of this component tag references the processValueChange method of CashierBean by using a method expression. The processValueChange method handles the event of a user entering a name in the input field rendered by this component.

Section 12.3.4, "Writing a Method to Handle a Value-Change Event," describes how to implement a method that handles a ValueChangeEvent.

12

Developing with JavaServer Faces Technology

This chapter provides an overview of managed beans and explains how to write methods and properties of managed beans that are used by a JavaServer Faces application. This chapter also introduces the Bean Validation feature.

Chapter 10, "Using JavaServer Faces Technology in Web Pages," and Chapter 11, "Using Converters, Listeners, and Validators," show how to add components to a page and connect them to server-side objects by using component tags and core tags. These chapters also show how to provide additional functionality to the components through converters, listeners, and validators. Developing a JavaServer Faces application also involves the task of programming the server-side objects: managed beans, converters, event handlers, and validators.

The following topics are addressed here:

- Managed Beans in JavaServer Faces Technology
- Writing Bean Properties
- Writing Managed Bean Methods

12.1 Managed Beans in JavaServer Faces Technology

A typical JavaServer Faces application includes one or more managed beans, each of which can be associated with the components used in a particular page. This section introduces the basic concepts of creating, configuring, and using managed beans in an application.

12.1.1 Creating a Managed Bean

A managed bean is created with a constructor with no arguments, a set of properties, and a set of methods that perform functions for a component. Each of the managed bean properties can be bound to one of the following:

- A component value
- A component instance
- A converter instance
- A listener instance
- A validator instance

The most common functions that managed bean methods perform include the following:

- Validating a component's data
- Handling an event fired by a component
- Performing processing to determine the next page to which the application must navigate

As with all JavaBeans components, a property consists of a private data field and a set of accessor methods, as shown by this code:

```
private Integer userNumber = null;
...
public void setUserNumber(Integer user_number) {
    userNumber = user_number;
}
public Integer getUserNumber() {
    return userNumber;
}
```

When bound to a component's value, a bean property can be any of the basic primitive and numeric types or any Java object type for which the application has access to an appropriate converter. For example, a property can be of type java.util.Date if the application has access to a converter that can convert the Date type to a String and back again. See Section 12.2, "Writing Bean Properties," for information on which types are accepted by which component tags.

When a bean property is bound to a component instance, the property's type must be the same as the component object. For example, if a javax.faces.component.UISelectBoolean component is bound to the property, the property must accept and return a UISelectBoolean object. Likewise, if the property is bound to a converter, validator, or listener instance, the property must be of the appropriate converter, validator, or listener type.

For more information on writing beans and their properties, see Section 12.2, "Writing Bean Properties."

12.1.2 Using the EL to Reference Managed Beans

To bind component values and objects to managed bean properties or to reference managed bean methods from component tags, page authors use the Expression Language syntax. As explained in Section 9.1, "Overview of the EL," the following are some of the features that the EL offers:

- Deferred evaluation of expressions

- The ability to use a value expression to both read and write data

- Method expressions

Deferred evaluation of expressions is important because the JavaServer Faces lifecycle is split into several phases in which component event handling, data conversion and validation, and data propagation to external objects are all performed in an orderly fashion. The implementation must be able to delay the evaluation of expressions until the proper phase of the lifecycle has been reached. Therefore, the implementation's tag attributes always use deferred-evaluation syntax, which is distinguished by the #{} delimiter.

To store data in external objects, almost all JavaServer Faces tag attributes use lvalue expressions, which are expressions that allow both getting and setting data on external objects.

Finally, some component tag attributes accept method expressions that reference methods that handle component events or validate or convert component data.

To illustrate a JavaServer Faces tag using the EL, the following tag references a method that validates user input:

```
<h:inputText id="inputGuess"
        value="#{userNumberBean.userNumber}"
        required="true" size="3"
        disabled="#{userNumberBean.number eq userNumberBean.userNumber ...}"
        validator="#{userNumberBean.validateNumberRange}" />
```

This tag binds the inputGuess component's value to the UserNumberBean.userNumber managed bean property by using an lvalue expression. The tag uses a method expression to refer to the UserNumberBean.validateNumberRange method, which performs validation of the component's local value. The local value is whatever the user types into the field corresponding to this tag. This method is invoked when the expression is evaluated.

Nearly all JavaServer Faces tag attributes accept value expressions. In addition to referencing bean properties, value expressions can reference lists, maps, arrays, implicit objects, and resource bundles.

Another use of value expressions is to bind a component instance to a managed bean property. A page author does this by referencing the property from the `binding` attribute:

```
<h:outputLabel for="fanClub"
               rendered="false"
               binding="#{cashierBean.specialOfferText}">
               value="#{bundle.DukeFanClub}"/>
</h:outputLabel>
```

In addition to using expressions with the standard component tags, you can configure your custom component properties to accept expressions by creating `javax.el.ValueExpression` or `javax.el.MethodExpression` instances for them.

For information on the EL, see Chapter 9, "Expression Language."

For information on referencing managed bean methods from component tags, see Section 11.4, "Referencing a Managed Bean Method."

12.2 Writing Bean Properties

As explained in Section 12.1, "Managed Beans in JavaServer Faces Technology," a managed bean property can be bound to one of the following items:

- A component value

- A component instance

- A converter implementation

- A listener implementation

- A validator implementation

These properties follow the conventions of JavaBeans components (also called beans). For more information on JavaBeans components, see the *JavaBeans Tutorial* at `http://docs.oracle.com/javase/tutorial/javabeans/`.

The component's tag binds the component's value to a managed bean property by using its `value` attribute and binds the component's instance to a managed bean property by using its `binding` attribute. Likewise, all the converter, listener, and validator tags use their `binding` attributes to bind their associated implementations to managed bean properties. For more information, see Section 15.12, "Binding Component Values and Instances to Managed Bean Properties," and Section 15.13, "Binding Converters, Listeners, and Validators to Managed Bean Properties."

To bind a component's value to a managed bean property, the type of the property must match the type of the component's value to which it is bound. For example, if a managed bean property is bound to a `UISelectBoolean` component's value, the property should accept and return a `boolean` value or a `Boolean` wrapper `Object` instance.

To bind a component instance to a managed bean property, the property must match the type of component. For example, if a managed bean property is bound to a `UISelectBoolean` instance, the property should accept and return a `UISelectBoolean` value.

Similarly, to bind a converter, listener, or validator implementation to a managed bean property, the property must accept and return the same type of converter, listener, or validator object. For example, if you are using the `convertDateTime` tag to bind a `javax.faces.convert.DateTimeConverter` to a property, that property must accept and return a `DateTimeConverter` instance.

The rest of this section explains how to write properties that can be bound to component values, to component instances for the component objects described in Section 10.2, "Adding Components to a Page Using HTML Tag Library Tags," and to converter, listener, and validator implementations.

12.2.1 Writing Properties Bound to Component Values

To write a managed bean property that is bound to a component's value, you must match the property type to the component's value.

Table 12–1 lists the `javax.faces.component` classes and the acceptable types of their values.

Table 12–1   Acceptable Types of Component Values

Component Class	Acceptable Types of Component Values
`UIInput`, `UIOutput`, `UISelectItem`, `UISelectOne`	Any of the basic primitive and numeric types or any Java programming language object type for which an appropriate `javax.faces.convert.Converter` implementation is available
`UIData`	array of beans, `List` of beans, single bean, `java.sql.ResultSet`, `javax.servlet.jsp.jstl.sql.Result`, `javax.sql.RowSet`

Table 12–1   (Cont.) Acceptable Types of Component Values

Component Class	Acceptable Types of Component Values
UISelectBoolean	boolean or Boolean
UISelectItems	java.lang.String, Collection, Array, Map
UISelectMany	array or List, although elements of the array or List can be any of the standard types

When they bind components to properties by using the value attributes of the component tags, page authors need to ensure that the corresponding properties match the types of the components' values.

12.2.1.1 UIInput and UIOutput Properties

The UIInput and UIOutput component classes are represented by the component tags that begin with h:input and h:output, respectively (for example, h:inputText and h:outputText).

In the following example, an h:inputText tag binds the name component to the name property of a managed bean called CashierBean.

```
<h:inputText id="name"
             size="30"
             value="#{cashierBean.name}"/>
```

The following code snippet from the managed bean CashierBean shows the bean property type bound by the preceding component tag:

```
protected String name = null;

public void setName(String name) {
    this.name = name;
}
public String getName() {
    return this.name;
}
```

As described in Section 11.1, "Using the Standard Converters," to convert the value of an input or output component you can either apply a converter or create the bean property bound to the component with the matching type. Here is the example tag, from Section 11.1.2, "Using DateTimeConverter," that displays the date on which items will be shipped.

```
<h:outputText value="#{cashierBean.shipDate}">
    <f:convertDateTime type="date" dateStyle="full"/>
</h:outputText>
```

The bean property represented by this tag must have a type of java.util.Date. The following code snippet shows the shipDate property, from the managed bean CashierBean, that is bound by the tag's value in the preceding example:

```
private Date shipDate;

public Date getShipDate() {
    return this.shipDate;
}
public void setShipDate(Date shipDate) {
    this.shipDate = shipDate;
}
```

12.2.1.2 UIData Properties

The UIData component class is represented by the h:dataTable component tag.

UIData components must be bound to one of the managed bean property types listed in Table 12–1. Data components are discussed in Section 10.2.12, "Using Data-Bound Table Components." Here is part of the start tag of dataTable from that section:

```
<h:dataTable id="items"
    ...
    value="#{cart.items}"
    ...
    var="item">
```

The value expression points to the items property of a shopping cart bean named cart. The cart bean maintains a map of ShoppingCartItem beans.

The getItems method from the cart bean populates a List with ShoppingCartItem instances that are saved in the items map when the customer adds books to the cart, as shown in the following code segment:

```
public synchronized List<ShoppingCartItem> getItems() {
    List<ShoppingCartItem> results = new ArrayList<ShoppingCartItem>();
    results.addAll(this.items.values());
    return results;
}
```

All the components contained in the UIData component are bound to the properties of the cart bean that is bound to the entire UIData component. For example, here is the h:outputText tag that displays the book title in the table:

```
<h:commandLink action="#{showcart.details}">
    <h:outputText value="#{item.item.title}"/>
</h:commandLink>
```

The title is actually a link to the bookdetails.xhtml page. The h:outputText tag uses the value expression #{item.item.title} to bind its UIOutput component to the title property of the Book entity. The first item in the expression is the ShoppingCartItem instance that the h:dataTable tag is referencing while rendering the current row. The second item in expression refers to the item property of ShoppingCartItem, which returns an Object (in this case, a Book). The title part of the expression refers to the title property of Book. The value of the UIOutput component corresponding to this tag is bound to the title property of the Book entity:

```
private String title;
...
public String getTitle() {
    return title;
}
public void setTitle(String title) {
    this.title = title;
}
```

12.2.1.3 UISelectBoolean Properties

The UISelectBoolean component class is represented by the component tag h:selectBooleanCheckbox.

Managed bean properties that hold a UISelectBoolean component's data must be of boolean or Boolean type. The example selectBooleanCheckbox tag from Section 10.2.8, "Displaying Components for Selecting One Value," binds a component to a property. The following example shows a tag that binds a component value to a boolean property:

```
<h:selectBooleanCheckbox title="#{bundle.receiveEmails}"
                         value="#{custFormBean.receiveEmails}">
</h:selectBooleanCheckbox>
<h:outputText value="#{bundle.receiveEmails}">
```

Here is an example property that can be bound to the component represented by the example tag:

```
private boolean receiveEmails = false;
...
public void setReceiveEmails(boolean receiveEmails) {
    this.receiveEmails = receiveEmails;
}
public boolean getReceiveEmails() {
    return receiveEmails;
}
```

12.2.1.4 UISelectMany Properties

The UISelectMany component class is represented by the component tags that begin with h:selectMany (for example, h:selectManyCheckbox and h:selectManyListbox).

Because a UISelectMany component allows a user to select one or more items from a list of items, this component must map to a bean property of type List or array. This bean property represents the set of currently selected items from the list of available items.

The following example of the selectManyCheckbox tag comes from Section 10.2.9, "Displaying Components for Selecting Multiple Values":

```
<h:selectManyCheckbox id="newslettercheckbox"
                      layout="pageDirection"
                      value="#{cashierBean.newsletters}">
    <f:selectItems value="#{cashierBean.newsletterItems}"/>
</h:selectManyCheckbox>
```

Here is the bean property that maps to the value of the selectManyCheckbox tag from the preceding example:

```
private String[] newsletters;

public void setNewsletters(String[] newsletters) {
    this.newsletters = newsletters;
}
public String[] getNewsletters() {
    return this.newsletters;
}
```

The UISelectItem and UISelectItems components are used to represent all the values in a UISelectMany component. See Section 12.2.1.6, "UISelectItem Properties," and Section 12.2.1.7, "UISelectItems Properties," for information on writing the bean properties for the `UISelectItem` and `UISelectItems` components.

12.2.1.5 UISelectOne Properties

The `UISelectOne` component class is represented by the component tags that begin with `h:selectOne` (for example, `h:selectOneRadio` and `h:selectOneListbox`).

`UISelectOne` properties accept the same types as `UIInput` and `UIOutput` properties, because a `UISelectOne` component represents the single selected item from a set of items. This item can be any of the primitive types and anything else for which you can apply a converter.

Here is an example of the `h:selectOneMenu` tag from Section 10.2.8.2, "Displaying a Menu Using the h:selectOneMenu Tag":

```
<h:selectOneMenu id="shippingOption"
                 required="true"
                 value="#{cashierBean.shippingOption}">
    <f:selectItem itemValue="2"
                  itemLabel="#{bundle.QuickShip}"/>
    <f:selectItem itemValue="5"
                  itemLabel="#{bundle.NormalShip}"/>
    <f:selectItem itemValue="7"
                  itemLabel="#{bundle.SaverShip}"/>
 </h:selectOneMenu>
```

Here is the bean property corresponding to this tag:

```
private String shippingOption = "2";

public void setShippingOption(String shippingOption) {
    this.shippingOption = shippingOption;
}
public String getShippingOption() {
    return this.shippingOption;
}
```

Note that `shippingOption` represents the currently selected item from the list of items in the `UISelectOne` component.

The `UISelectItem` and `UISelectItems` components are used to represent all the values in a `UISelectOne` component. This is explained in Section 10.2.8.2, "Displaying a Menu Using the h:selectOneMenu Tag."

For information on how to write the managed bean properties for the UISelectItem and UISelectItems components, see Section 12.2.1.6, "UISelectItem Properties," and Section 12.2.1.7, "UISelectItems Properties."

12.2.1.6 UISelectItem Properties

A UISelectItem component represents a single value in a set of values in a UISelectMany or a UISelectOne component. A UISelectItem component must be bound to a managed bean property of type javax.faces.model.SelectItem. A SelectItem object is composed of an Object representing the value along with two Strings representing the label and the description of the UISelectItem object.

The example selectOneMenu tag from Section 12.2.1.5, "UISelectOne Properties," contains selectItem tags that set the values of the list of items in the page. Here is an example of a bean property that can set the values for this list in the bean:

```
SelectItem itemOne = null;

SelectItem getItemOne(){
    return itemOne;
}
void setItemOne(SelectItem item) {
    itemOne = item;
}
```

12.2.1.7 UISelectItems Properties

UISelectItems components are children of UISelectMany and UISelectOne components. Each UISelectItems component is composed of a set of either UISelectItem instances or any collection of objects, such as an array, a list, or even POJOs.

The following code snippet from CashierBean shows how to write the properties for selectItems tags containing SelectItem instances.

```
private String[] newsletters;
private static final SelectItem[] newsletterItems = {
    new SelectItem("Duke's Quarterly"),
    new SelectItem("Innovator's Almanac"),
    new SelectItem("Duke's Diet and Exercise Journal"),
    new SelectItem("Random Ramblings")
};
...
public void setNewsletters(String[] newsletters) {
    this.newsletters = newsletters;
}
```

```
public String[] getNewsletters() {
    return this.newsletters;
}

public SelectItem[] getNewsletterItems() {
    return newsletterItems;
}
```

Here, the newsletters property represents the SelectItems object, whereas the newsletterItems property represents a static array of SelectItem objects. The SelectItem class has several constructors; in this example, the first argument is an Object representing the value of the item, whereas the second argument is a String representing the label that appears in the UISelectMany component on the page.

12.2.2 Writing Properties Bound to Component Instances

A property bound to a component instance returns and accepts a component instance rather than a component value. The following components bind a component instance to a managed bean property:

```
<h:selectBooleanCheckbox id="fanClub"
                         rendered="false"
                         binding="#{cashierBean.specialOffer}" />
<h:outputLabel for="fanClub"
               rendered="false"
               binding="#{cashierBean.specialOfferText}"
               value="#{bundle.DukeFanClub}" />
</h:outputLabel>
```

The selectBooleanCheckbox tag renders a check box and binds the fanClub UISelectBoolean component to the specialOffer property of CashierBean. The outputLabel tag binds the value of the value attribute, which represents the check box's label, to the specialOfferText property of CashierBean. If the user orders more than $100 worth of books and clicks the **Submit** button, the submit method of CashierBean sets both components' rendered properties to true, causing the check box and label to display when the page is re-rendered.

Because the components corresponding to the example tags are bound to the managed bean properties, these properties must match the components' types. This means that the specialOfferText property must be of type UIOutput, and the specialOffer property must be of type UISelectBoolean:

```
UIOutput specialOfferText = null;
UISelectBoolean specialOffer = null;
```

```
public UIOutput getSpecialOfferText() {
    return this.specialOfferText;
}
public void setSpecialOfferText(UIOutput specialOfferText) {
    this.specialOfferText = specialOfferText;
}

public UISelectBoolean getSpecialOffer() {
    return this.specialOffer;
}
public void setSpecialOffer(UISelectBoolean specialOffer) {
    this.specialOffer = specialOffer;
}
```

For more general information on component binding, see Section 12.1, "Managed Beans in JavaServer Faces Technology."

For information on how to reference a managed bean method that performs navigation when a button is clicked, see Section 11.4.1, "Referencing a Method That Performs Navigation."

For more information on writing managed bean methods that handle navigation, see Section 12.3.1, "Writing a Method to Handle Navigation."

12.2.3 Writing Properties Bound to Converters, Listeners, or Validators

All the standard converter, listener, and validator tags included with JavaServer Faces technology support binding attributes that allow you to bind converter, listener, or validator implementations to managed bean properties.

The following example shows a standard convertDateTime tag using a value expression with its binding attribute to bind the javax.faces.convert.DateTimeConverter instance to the convertDate property of LoginBean:

```
<h:inputText value="#{loginBean.birthDate}">
    <f:convertDateTime binding="#{loginBean.convertDate}" />
</h:inputText>
```

The convertDate property must therefore accept and return a DateTimeConverter object, as shown here:

```
private DateTimeConverter convertDate;
public DateTimeConverter getConvertDate() {
        ...
    return convertDate;
}
```

```
public void setConvertDate(DateTimeConverter convertDate) {
    convertDate.setPattern("EEEEEEEE, MMM dd, yyyy");
    this.convertDate = convertDate;
}
```

Because the converter is bound to a managed bean property, the managed bean property can modify the attributes of the converter or add new functionality to it. In the case of the preceding example, the property sets the date pattern that the converter uses to parse the user's input into a Date object.

The managed bean properties that are bound to validator or listener implementations are written in the same way and have the same general purpose.

12.3 Writing Managed Bean Methods

Methods of a managed bean can perform several application-specific functions for components on the page. These functions include

- Performing processing associated with navigation

- Handling action events

- Performing validation on the component's value

- Handling value-change events

By using a managed bean to perform these functions, you eliminate the need to implement the javax.faces.validator.Validator interface to handle the validation or one of the listener interfaces to handle events. Also, by using a managed bean instead of a Validator implementation to perform validation, you eliminate the need to create a custom tag for the Validator implementation.

In general, it is good practice to include these methods in the same managed bean that defines the properties for the components referencing these methods. The reason for doing so is that the methods might need to access the component's data to determine how to handle the event or to perform the validation associated with the component.

The following sections explain how to write various types of managed bean methods.

12.3.1 Writing a Method to Handle Navigation

An **action method**, a managed bean method that handles navigation processing, must be a public method that takes no parameters and returns an Object, which is the logical outcome that the navigation system uses to determine the page to display next. This method is referenced using the component tag's action attribute.

The following action method is from the managed bean CashierBean, which is invoked when a user clicks the **Submit** button on the page. If the user has ordered more than $100 worth of books, this method sets the rendered properties of the fanClub and specialOffer components to true, causing them to be displayed on the page the next time that page is rendered.

After setting the components' rendered properties to true, this method returns the logical outcome null. This causes the JavaServer Faces implementation to re-render the page without creating a new view of the page, retaining the customer's input. If this method were to return purchase, which is the logical outcome to use to advance to a payment page, the page would re-render without retaining the customer's input. In this case, you want to re-render the page without clearing the data.

If the user does not purchase more than $100 worth of books or if the thankYou component has already been rendered, the method returns bookreceipt. The JavaServer Faces implementation loads the bookreceipt.xhtml page after this method returns:

```java
public String submit() {
    ...
    if ((cart().getTotal() > 100.00) && !specialOffer.isRendered()) {
        specialOfferText.setRendered(true);
        specialOffer.setRendered(true);
        return null;
    } else if (specialOffer.isRendered() && !thankYou.isRendered()) {
        thankYou.setRendered(true);
        return null;
    } else {
        ...
        cart.clear();
        return ("bookreceipt");
    }
}
```

Typically, an action method will return a String outcome, as shown in the preceding example. Alternatively, you can define an Enum class that encapsulates all possible outcome strings and then make an action method return an enum constant, which represents a particular String outcome defined by the Enum class.

The following example uses an `Enum` class to encapsulate all logical outcomes:

```
public enum Navigation {
    main, accountHist, accountList, atm, atmAck, transferFunds,
    transferAck, error
}
```

When it returns an outcome, an action method uses the dot notation to reference the outcome from the `Enum` class:

```
public Object submit(){
    ...
    return Navigation.accountHist;
}
```

Section 11.4.1, "Referencing a Method That Performs Navigation," explains how a component tag references this method. Section 12.2.2, "Writing Properties Bound to Component Instances," explains how to write the bean properties to which the components are bound.

12.3.2 Writing a Method to Handle an Action Event

A managed bean method that handles an action event must be a public method that accepts an action event and returns `void`. This method is referenced using the component tag's `actionListener` attribute. Only components that implement `javax.faces.component.ActionSource` can refer to this method.

In the following example, a method from a managed bean named `ActionBean` processes the event of a user clicking one of the links on the page:

```
public void chooseBookFromLink(ActionEvent event) {
    String current = event.getComponent().getId();
    FacesContext context = FacesContext.getCurrentInstance();
    String bookId = books.get(current);
    context.getExternalContext().getSessionMap().put("bookId", bookId);
}
```

This method gets the component that generated the event from the event object; then it gets the component's ID, which is a code for the book. The method matches the code against a `HashMap` object that contains the book codes and corresponding book ID values. Finally, the method sets the book ID by using the selected value from the `HashMap` object.

Section 11.4.2, "Referencing a Method That Handles an Action Event," explains how a component tag references this method.

12.3.3 Writing a Method to Perform Validation

Instead of implementing the `javax.faces.validator.Validator` interface to perform validation for a component, you can include a method in a managed bean to take care of validating input for the component. A managed bean method that performs validation must accept a `javax.faces.context.FacesContext`, the component whose data must be validated, and the data to be validated, just as the `validate` method of the `Validator` interface does. A component refers to the managed bean method by using its `validator` attribute. Only values of `UIInput` components or values of components that extend `UIInput` can be validated.

Here is an example of a managed bean method that validates user input, from Section 24.2, "The guessnumber-cdi CDI Example":

```
public void validateNumberRange(FacesContext context,
                                UIComponent toValidate,
                                Object value) {
    if (remainingGuesses <= 0) {
        ((UIInput) toValidate).setValid(false);
        FacesMessage message = new FacesMessage("No guesses left!");
        context.addMessage(toValidate.getClientId(context), message);
        return;
    }

    int input = (Integer) value;
    if (input < minimum || input> maximum) {
        ((UIInput) toValidate).setValid(false);
        FacesMessage message = new FacesMessage("Invalid guess");
        context.addMessage(toValidate.getClientId(context), message);
    }
}
```

The `validateNumberRange` method performs two different validations.

- If the user has run out of guesses, the method sets the `valid` property of the `UIInput` component to `false`. Then it queues a message onto the `FacesContext` instance, associating the message with the component ID, and returns.

- If the user has some remaining guesses, the method then retrieves the local value of the component. If the input value is outside the allowable range, the method again sets the `valid` property of the `UIInput` component to `false`, queues a different message on the `FacesContext` instance, and returns.

See Section 11.4.3, "Referencing a Method That Performs Validation," for information on how a component tag references this method.

12.3.4 Writing a Method to Handle a Value-Change Event

A managed bean that handles a value-change event must use a public method that accepts a value-change event and returns void. This method is referenced using the component's valueChangeListener attribute. This section explains how to write a managed bean method to replace the javax.faces.event.ValueChangeListener implementation.

The following example tag comes from Section 11.2.1, "Registering a Value-Change Listener on a Component," where the h:inputText tag with the id of name has a ValueChangeListener instance registered on it. This ValueChangeListener instance handles the event of entering a value in the field corresponding to the component. When the user enters a value, a value-change event is generated, and the processValueChange(ValueChangeEvent) method of the ValueChangeListener class is invoked:

```
<h:inputText id="name"
             size="30"
             value="#{cashierBean.name}"
             required="true"
             requiredMessage="#{bundle.ReqCustomerName}">
    <f:valueChangeListener
        type="javaeetutorial.dukesbookstore.listeners.NameChanged" />
</h:inputText>
```

Instead of implementing ValueChangeListener, you can write a managed bean method to handle this event. To do this, you move the processValueChange(ValueChangeEvent) method from the ValueChangeListener class, called NameChanged, to your managed bean.

Here is the managed bean method that processes the event of entering a value in the name field on the page:

```
public void processValueChange(ValueChangeEvent event)
        throws AbortProcessingException {
    if (null != event.getNewValue()) {
        FacesContext.getCurrentInstance().getExternalContext().
                getSessionMap().put("name", event.getNewValue());
    }
}
```

To make this method handle the ValueChangeEvent generated by an input component, reference this method from the component tag's valueChangeListener attribute. See Section 11.4.4, "Referencing a Method That Handles a Value-Change Event," for more information.

13

Using Ajax with JavaServer Faces Technology

Ajax is an acronym for Asynchronous JavaScript and XML, a group of web technologies that enable creation of dynamic and highly responsive web applications. Using Ajax, web applications can retrieve content from the server without interfering with the display on the client. In the Java EE 7 platform, JavaServer Faces technology provides built-in support for Ajax.

Early web applications were created mostly as static web pages. When a static web page is updated by a client, the entire page has to reload to reflect the update. In effect, every update needs a page reload to reflect the change. Repetitive page reloads can result in excessive network access and can impact application performance. Technologies such as Ajax were created to overcome these deficiencies.

This chapter describes using Ajax functionality in JavaServer Faces web applications.

The following topics are addressed here:

- Overview of Ajax
- Using Ajax Functionality with JavaServer Faces Technology
- Using Ajax with Facelets
- Sending an Ajax Request
- Monitoring Events on the Client
- Handling Errors
- Receiving an Ajax Response

- Ajax Request Lifecycle
- Grouping of Components
- Loading JavaScript as a Resource
- The ajaxguessnumber Example Application
- Further Information about Ajax in JavaServer Faces Technology

13.1 Overview of Ajax

Ajax refers to JavaScript and XML, technologies that are widely used for creating dynamic and asynchronous web content. While Ajax is not limited to JavaScript and XML technologies, more often than not they are used together by web applications. The focus of this tutorial is on using JavaScript based Ajax functionality in JavaServer Faces web applications.

JavaScript is a dynamic scripting language for web applications. It allows users to add enhanced functionality to user interfaces and allows web pages to interact with clients asynchronously. JavaScript runs mainly on the client side (as in a browser) and thereby reduces server access by clients.

When a JavaScript function sends an asynchronous request from the client to the server, the server sends back a response that is used to update the page's Document Object Model (DOM). This response is often in the format of an XML document. The term *Ajax* refers to this interaction between the client and server.

The server response need not be in XML only; it can also be in other formats, such as JSON (see Section 19.1, "Introduction to JSON," and `http://www.json.org/`). This tutorial does not focus on the response formats.

Ajax enables asynchronous and partial updating of web applications. Such functionality allows for highly responsive web pages that are rendered in near real time. Ajax-based web applications can access server and process information and can also retrieve data without interfering with the display and rendering of the current web page on a client (such as a browser).

Some of the advantages of using Ajax are as follows:

- Form data validation in real time, eliminating the need to submit the form for verification
- Enhanced functionality for web pages, such as user name and password prompts
- Partial update of the web content, avoiding complete page reloads

13.2 Using Ajax Functionality with JavaServer Faces Technology

Ajax functionality can be added to a JavaServer Faces application in one of the following ways:

- Adding the required JavaScript code to an application

- Using the built-in Ajax resource library

In earlier releases of the Java EE platform, JavaServer Faces applications provided Ajax functionality by adding the necessary JavaScript to the web page. In the Java EE 7 platform, standard Ajax support is provided by a built-in JavaScript resource library.

With the support of this JavaScript resource library, JavaServer Faces standard UI components, such as buttons, labels, or text fields, can be enabled for Ajax functionality. You can also load this resource library and use its methods directly from within the managed bean code. The next sections of the tutorial describe the use of the built-in Ajax resource library.

In addition, because the JavaServer Faces technology component model can be extended, custom components can be created with Ajax functionality.

The tutorial examples include an Ajax version of the guessnumber application, ajaxguessnumber. See Section 13.11, "The ajaxguessnumber Example Application," for more information.

The Ajax specific f:ajax tag and its attributes are explained in the next sections.

13.3 Using Ajax with Facelets

As mentioned in the previous section, JavaServer Faces technology supports Ajax by using a built-in JavaScript resource library that is provided as part of the JavaServer Faces core libraries. This built-in Ajax resource can be used in JavaServer Faces web applications in one of the following ways.

- By using the f:ajax tag along with another standard component in a Facelets application. This method adds Ajax functionality to any UI component without additional coding and configuration.

- By using the JavaScript API method jsf.ajax.request() directly within the Facelets application. This method provides direct access to Ajax methods and allows customized control of component behavior.

13.3.1 Using the f:ajax Tag

The f:ajax tag is a JavaServer Faces core tag that provides Ajax functionality to any regular UI component when used in conjunction with that component. In the following example, Ajax behavior is added to an input component by including the f:ajax core tag:

```
<h:inputText value="#{bean.message}">
    <f:ajax />
</h:inputText>
```

In this example, although Ajax is enabled, the other attributes of the f:ajax tag are not defined. If an event is not defined, the default action for the component is performed. For the inputText component, when no event attribute is specified, the default event is valueChange. Table 13–1 lists the attributes of the f:ajax tag and their default actions.

Table 13–1 Attributes of the f:ajax Tag

Name	Type	Description
disabled	javax.el.ValueExpression that evaluates to a Boolean	A Boolean value that identifies the tag status. A value of true indicates that the Ajax behavior should not be rendered. A value of false indicates that the Ajax behavior should be rendered. The default value is false.
event	javax.el.ValueExpression that evaluates to a String	A String that identifies the type of event to which the Ajax action will apply. If specified, it must be one of the events supported by the component. If not specified, the default event (the event that triggers the Ajax request) is determined for the component. The default event is action for javax.faces.component.ActionSource components and valueChange for javax.faces.component.EditableValueHolder components.
execute	javax.el.ValueExpression that evaluates to an Object	A Collection that identifies a list of components to be executed on the server. If a literal is specified, it must be a space-delimited String of component identifiers and/or one of the keywords. If a ValueExpression is specified, it must refer to a property that returns a Collection of String objects. If not specified, the default value is @this.

Table 13–1   (Cont.) Attributes of the f:ajax Tag

Name	Type	Description
immediate	javax.el.ValueExpression that evaluates to a Boolean	A Boolean value that indicates whether inputs are to be processed early in the lifecycle. If true, behavior events generated from this behavior are broadcast during the Apply Request Values phase. Otherwise, the events will be broadcast during the Invoke Application phase.
listener	javax.el.MethodExpression	The name of the listener method that is called when a javax.faces.event.AjaxBehaviorEvent has been broadcast for the listener.
onevent	javax.el.ValueExpression that evaluates to a String	The name of the JavaScript function that handles UI events.
onerror	javax.el.ValueExpression that evaluates to a String	The name of the JavaScript function that handles errors.
render	javax.el.ValueExpression that evaluates to an Object	A Collection that identifies a list of components to be rendered on the client. If a literal is specified, it must be a space-delimited String of component identifiers and/or one of the keywords. If a ValueExpression is specified, it must refer to a property that returns a Collection of String objects. If not specified, the default value is @none.

The keywords listed in Table 13–2 can be used with the execute and render attributes of the f:ajax tag.

Table 13–2   Execute and Render Keywords

Keyword	Description
@all	All component identifiers
@form	The form that encloses the component
@none	No component identifiers
@this	The element that triggered the request

Note that when you use the f:ajax tag in a Facelets page, the JavaScript resource library is loaded implicitly. This resource library can also be loaded explicitly as described in Section 13.10, "Loading JavaScript as a Resource."

13.4 Sending an Ajax Request

To activate Ajax functionality, the web application must create an Ajax request and send it to the server. The server then processes the request.

The application uses the attributes of the f:ajax tag listed in Table 13–1 to create the Ajax request. The following sections explain the process of creating and sending an Ajax request using some of these attributes.

> **Note:** Behind the scenes, the jsf.ajax.request() method of the JavaScript resource library collects the data provided by the f:ajax tag and posts the request to the JavaServer Faces lifecycle.

13.4.1 Using the event Attribute

The event attribute defines the event that triggers the Ajax action. Some of the possible values for this attribute are click, keyup, mouseover, focus, and blur.

If not specified, a default event based on the parent component will be applied. The default event is action for javax.faces.component.ActionSource components, such as a commandButton, and valueChange for javax.faces.component.EditableValueHolder components, such as inputText. In the following example, an Ajax tag is associated with the button component, and the event that triggers the Ajax action is a mouse click:

```
<h:commandButton id="submit" value="Submit">
    <f:ajax event="click" />
</h:commandButton>
<h:outputText id="result" value="#{userNumberBean.response}" />
```

> **Note:** You may have noticed that the listed events are very similar to JavaScript events. In fact, they are based on JavaScript events, but do not have the on prefix.

For a command button, the default event is click, so you do not actually need to specify event="click" to obtain the desired behavior.

13.4.2 Using the execute Attribute

The execute attribute defines the component or components to be executed on the server. The component is identified by its id attribute. You can specify more than one executable component. If more than one component is to be executed, specify a space-delimited list of components.

When a component is executed, it participates in all phases of the request-processing lifecycle except the Render Response phase.

The `execute` attribute value can also be a keyword, such as `@all`, `@none`, `@this`, or `@form`. The default value is `@this`, which refers to the component within which the `f:ajax` tag is nested.

The following code specifies that the `h:inputText` component with the `id` value of `userNo` should be executed when the button is clicked:

```
<h:inputText id="userNo"
             title="Type a number from 0 to 10:"
             value="#{userNumberBean.userNumber}">
    ...
</h:inputText>
<h:commandButton id="submit" value="Submit">
    <f:ajax event="click" execute="userNo" />
</h:commandButton>
```

13.4.3 Using the immediate Attribute

The `immediate` attribute indicates whether user inputs are to be processed early in the application lifecycle or later. If the attribute is set to `true`, events generated from this component are broadcast during the Apply Request Values phase. Otherwise, the events will be broadcast during the Invoke Application phase.

If not defined, the default value of this attribute is `false`.

13.4.4 Using the listener Attribute

The `listener` attribute refers to a method expression that is executed on the server side in response to an Ajax action on the client. The listener's `javax.faces.event.AjaxBehaviorListener.processAjaxBehavior` method is called once during the Invoke Application phase of the lifecycle. In the following code from the `reservation` example application (see Section 8.9.3, "The reservation Example Application"), a `listener` attribute is defined by an `f:ajax` tag, which refers to a method from the bean:

```
<f:ajax event="change" render="total"
        listener="#{reservationBean.calculateTotal}"/>
```

Whenever either the price or the number of tickets ordered changes, the `calculateTotal` method of `ReservationBean` recalculates the total cost of the tickets and displays it in the output component named `total`.

13.5 Monitoring Events on the Client

To monitor ongoing Ajax requests, use the onevent attribute of the f:ajax tag. The value of this attribute is the name of a JavaScript function. JavaServer Faces calls the onevent function at each stage of the processing of an Ajax request: begin, complete, and success.

When calling the JavaScript function assigned to the onevent property, JavaServer Faces passes a data object to it. The data object contains the properties listed in Table 13–3.

Table 13–3   Properties of the onevent Data Object

Property	Description
responseXML	The response to the Ajax call in XML format
responseText	The response to the Ajax call in text format
responseCode	The response to the Ajax call in numeric code
source	The source of the current Ajax event: the DOM element
status	The status of the current Ajax call: begin, complete, or success
type	The type of the Ajax call: event

By using the status property of the data object, you can identify the current status of the Ajax request and monitor its progress. In the following example, monitormyajaxevent is a JavaScript function that monitors the Ajax request sent by the event:

```
<f:ajax event="click" render="statusmessage" onevent="monitormyajaxevent"/>
```

13.6 Handling Errors

JavaServer Faces handles Ajax errors through use of the onerror attribute of the f:ajax tag. The value of this attribute is the name of a JavaScript function.

When there is an error in processing a Ajax request, JavaServer Faces calls the defined onerror JavaScript function and passes a data object to it. The data object contains all the properties available for the onevent attribute and, in addition, the following properties:

- description
- errorName
- errorMessage

The `type` is `error`. The `status` property of the data object contains one of the valid error values listed in Table 13–4.

Table 13–4   Valid Error Values for the Data Object status Property

Values	Description
emptyResponse	No Ajax response from server.
httpError	One of the valid HTTP errors: `request.status==null` or `request.status==undefined` or `request.status<200` or `request.status>=300`.
malformedXML	The Ajax response is not well formed.
serverError	The Ajax response contains an `error` element.

In the following example, any errors that occurred in processing the Ajax request are handled by the `handlemyajaxerror` JavaScript function:

```
<f:ajax event="click" render="errormessage" onerror="handlemyajaxerror"/>
```

13.7 Receiving an Ajax Response

After the application sends an Ajax request, it is processed on the server side, and a response is sent back to the client. As described earlier, Ajax allows for partial updating of web pages. To enable such partial updating, JavaServer Faces technology allows for partial processing of the view. The handling of the response is defined by the `render` attribute of the `f:ajax` tag.

Similar to the `execute` attribute, the `render` attribute defines which sections of the page will be updated. The value of a `render` attribute can be one or more component `id` values, one of the keywords `@this`, `@all`, `@none`, or `@form`, or an EL expression. In the following example, the `render` attribute identifies an output component to be displayed when the button component is clicked (the default event for a command button):

```
<h:commandButton id="submit" value="Submit">
    <f:ajax execute="userNo" render="result" />
</h:commandButton>
<h:outputText id="result" value="#{userNumberBean.response}" />
```

> **Note:** Behind the scenes, once again the `jsf.ajax.request()` method handles the response. It registers a response-handling callback when the original request is created. When the response is sent back to the client, the callback is invoked. This callback automatically updates the client-side DOM to reflect the rendered response.

13.8 Ajax Request Lifecycle

An Ajax request varies from other typical JavaServer Faces requests, and its processing is also handled differently by the JavaServer Faces lifecycle.

As described in Section 7.7, "Partial Processing and Partial Rendering," when an Ajax request is received, the state associated with that request is captured by the `javax.faces.context.PartialViewContext`. This object provides access to information such as which components are targeted for processing/rendering. The `processPartial` method of `PartialViewContext` uses this information to perform partial component tree processing and rendering.

The `execute` attribute of the `f:ajax` tag identifies which segments of the server-side component tree should be processed. Because components can be uniquely identified in the JavaServer Faces component tree, it is easy to identify and process a single component, a few components, or a whole tree. This is made possible by the `visitTree` method of the `UIComponent` class. The identified components then run through the JavaServer Faces request lifecycle phases.

Similar to the `execute` attribute, the `render` attribute identifies which segments of the JavaServer Faces component tree need to be rendered during the render response phase.

During the render response phase, the `render` attribute is examined. The identified components are found and asked to render themselves and their children. The components are then packaged up and sent back to the client as a response.

13.9 Grouping of Components

The previous sections describe how to associate a single UI component with Ajax functionality. You can also associate Ajax with more than one component at a time by grouping them together on a page. The following example shows how a number of components can be grouped by using the `f:ajax` tag:

```
<f:ajax>
    <h:form>
```

```
        <h:inputText id="input1" value="#{user.name}"/>
        <h:commandButton id="Submit"/>
    </h:form>
</f:ajax>
```

In the example, neither component is associated with any Ajax event or render attributes yet. Therefore, no action will take place in case of user input. You can associate the above components with an event and a render attribute as follows:

```
<f:ajax event="click" render="@all">
    <h:form>
        <h:inputText id="input1" value="#{user.name}"/>
        <h:commandButton id="Submit"/>
    </h:form>
</f:ajax>
```

In the updated example, when the user clicks either component, the updated results will be displayed for all components. You can further fine-tune the Ajax action by adding specific events to each of the components, in which case Ajax functionality becomes cumulative. Consider the following example:

```
<f:ajax event="click" render="@all">
    ...
    <h:commandButton id="Submit">
        <f:ajax event="mouseover"/>
    </h:commandButton>
    ...
</f:ajax>
```

Now the button component will fire an Ajax action in case of a mouseover event as well as a mouse-click event.

13.10 Loading JavaScript as a Resource

The JavaScript resource file bundled with JavaServer Faces technology is named jsf.js and is available in the javax.faces library. This resource library supports Ajax functionality in JavaServer Faces applications.

If you use the f:ajax tag on a page, the jsf.js resource is automatically delivered to the client. It is not necessary to use the h:outputScript tag to specify this resource. You may want to use the h:outputScript tag to specify other JavaScript libraries.

In order to use a JavaScript resource directly with a UIComponent, you must explicitly load the resource in either of the following ways:

- By using the h:outputScript tag directly in a Facelets page

- By using the javax.faces.application.ResourceDependency annotation on a UIComponent Java class

13.10.1 Using JavaScript API in a Facelets Application

To use the bundled JavaScript resource API directly in a web application, such as a Facelets page, you need to first identify the default JavaScript resource for the page with the help of the h:outputScript tag. For example, consider the following section of a Facelets page:

```
<h:form>
    <h:outputScript name="jsf.js" library="javax.faces" target="head"/>
</h:form>
```

Specifying the target as head causes the script resource to be rendered within the head element on the HTML page.

In the next step, identify the component to which you would like to attach the Ajax functionality. Add the Ajax functionality to the component by using the JavaScript API. For example, consider the following:

```
<h:form>
    <h:outputScript name="jsf.js" library="javax.faces" target="head">
    <h:inputText id="inputname" value="#{userBean.name}"/>
    <h:outputText id="outputname" value="#{userBean.name}"/>
    <h:commandButton id="submit" value="Submit"
                    onclick="jsf.ajax.request(this, event,
                              {execute:'inputname',render:'outputname'});
                              return false;" />
</h:form>
```

The jsf.ajax.request method takes up to three parameters that specify source, event, and options. The source parameter identifies the DOM element that triggered the Ajax request, typically this. The optional event parameter identifies the DOM event that triggered this request. The optional options parameter contains a set of name/value pairs from Table 13–5.

Table 13–5   Possible Values for the Options Parameter

Name	Value
execute	A space-delimited list of client identifiers or one of the keywords listed in Table 13–2. The identifiers reference the components that will be processed during the Execute phase of the lifecycle.
render	A space-delimited list of client identifiers or one of the keywords listed in Table 13–2. The identifiers reference the components that will be processed during the Render phase of the lifecycle.
onevent	A String that is the name of the JavaScript function to call when an event occurs.
onerror	A String that is the name of the JavaScript function to call when an error occurs.
params	An object that may include additional parameters to include in the request.

If no identifier is specified, the default assumed keyword for the execute attribute is @this, and for the render attribute it is @none.

You can also place the JavaScript method in a file and include it as a resource.

13.10.2 Using the @ResourceDependency Annotation in a Bean Class

Use the javax.faces.application.ResourceDependency annotation to cause the bean class to load the default jsf.js library.

To load the Ajax resource from the server side, use the jsf.ajax.request method within the bean class. This method is usually used when creating a custom component or a custom renderer for a component.

The following example shows how the resource is loaded in a bean class:

```
@ResourceDependency(name="jsf.js" library="javax.faces" target="head")
```

13.11 The ajaxguessnumber Example Application

To demonstrate the advantages of using Ajax, revisit the guessnumber example from Chapter 8, "Introduction to Facelets." If you modify this example to use Ajax, the response need not be displayed on the response.xhtml page. Instead, an asynchronous call is made to the bean on the server side, and the response is displayed on the originating page by executing just the input component rather than by form submission.

The source code for this application is in the *tut-install*/examples/web/jsf/ajaxguessnumber/ directory.

13.11.1 The ajaxguessnumber Source Files

The changes to the guessnumber application occur in two source files.

13.11.1.1 The ajaxgreeting.xhtml Facelets Page

The Facelets page for ajaxguessnumber, ajaxgreeting.xhtml, is almost the same as the greeting.xhtml page for the guessnumber application:

```
<h:head>
    <h:outputStylesheet library="css" name="default.css"/>
    <title>Ajax Guess Number Facelets Application</title>
</h:head>
<h:body>
    <h:form id="AjaxGuess">
        <h:graphicImage value="#{resource['images:wave.med.gif']}"
                        alt="Duke waving his hand"/>
        <h2>
            Hi, my name is Duke. I am thinking of a number from
            #{dukesNumberBean.minimum} to #{dukesNumberBean.maximum}.
            Can you guess it?
        </h2>
        <p>
            <h:inputText id="userNo"
                         title="Enter a number from 0 to 10:"
                         value="#{userNumberBean.userNumber}">
                <f:validateLongRange minimum="#{dukesNumberBean.minimum}"
                                     maximum="#{dukesNumberBean.maximum}"/>
            </h:inputText>

            <h:commandButton id="submit" value="Submit">
                <f:ajax execute="userNo" render="outputGroup" />
            </h:commandButton>
        </p>
        <p>
            <h:panelGroup layout="block" id="outputGroup">
                <h:outputText id="result" style="color:blue"
                              value="#{userNumberBean.response}"
                              rendered="#{!facesContext.validationFailed}"/>
                <h:message id="errors1"
                           showSummary="true"
                           showDetail="false"
                           style="color: #d20005;
                           font-family: 'New Century Schoolbook', serif;
                           font-style: oblique;
                           text-decoration: overline"
                           for="userNo"/>
```

```
        </h:panelGroup>
      </p>
    </h:form>
</h:body>
```

The most important change is in the h:commandButton tag. The action attribute is removed from the tag, and an f:ajax tag is added.

The f:ajax tag specifies that when the button is clicked the h:inputText component with the id value userNo is executed. The components within the outputGroup panel group are then rendered. If a validation error occurs, the managed bean is not executed, and the validation error message is displayed in the message pane. Otherwise, the result of the guess is rendered in the result component.

13.11.1.2 The UserNumberBean Backing Bean

A small change is also made in the UserNumberBean code so that the output component does not display any message for the default (null) value of the property response. Here is the modified bean code:

```
public String getResponse() {
    if ((userNumber != null)
            && (userNumber.compareTo(dukesNumberBean.getRandomInt()) == 0)) {
        return "Yay! You got it!";
    }
    if (userNumber == null) {
        return null;
    } else {
        return "Sorry, " + userNumber + " is incorrect.";
    }
}
```

13.11.1.3 The DukesNumberBean CDI Managed Bean

The DukesNumberBean session-scoped CDI managed bean stores the range of guessable numbers and the randomly chosen number from that range. It is injected into UserNumberBean with the CDI @Inject annotation so that the value of the random number can be compared to the number the user submitted:

```
@Inject
DukesNumberBean dukesNumberBean;
```

You will learn more about CDI in Chapter 23, "Introduction to Contexts and Dependency Injection for Java EE."

13.11.2 Running the ajaxguessnumber Example

You can use either NetBeans IDE or Maven to build, package, deploy, and run the
ajaxguessnumber application.

13.11.2.1 To Build, Package, and Deploy the ajaxguessnumber Example Using NetBeans IDE

1. Make sure that GlassFish Server has been started (see Section 2.2, "Starting and Stopping GlassFish Server").

2. From the **File** menu, choose **Open Project**.

3. In the Open Project dialog box, navigate to:

   tut-install/examples/web/jsf

4. Select the ajaxguessnumber folder.

5. Click **Open Project**.

6. In the **Projects** tab, right-click the ajaxguessnumber project and select **Build**.

   This command builds and packages the application into a WAR file,
   ajaxguessnumber.war, located in the target directory. It then deploys the
   application.

13.11.2.2 To Build, Package, and Deploy the ajaxguessnumber Example Using Maven

1. Make sure that GlassFish Server has been started (see Section 2.2, "Starting and Stopping GlassFish Server").

2. In a terminal window, go to:

   tut-install/examples/web/jsf/ajaxguessnumber/

3. Enter the following command:

   ```
   mvn install
   ```

   This command builds and packages the application into a WAR file,
   ajaxguessnumber.war, located in the target directory. It then deploys the
   application.

13.11.2.3 To Run the ajaxguessnumber Example

1. In a web browser, enter the following URL:

   ```
   http://localhost:8080/ajaxguessnumber
   ```

2. Enter a value in the field and click **Submit**.

   If the value is in the range of 0 to 10, a message states whether the guess is correct or incorrect. If the value is outside that range or if the value is not a number, an error message appears in red.

13.12 Further Information about Ajax in JavaServer Faces Technology

For more information on Ajax in JavaServer Faces Technology, see

- JavaServer Faces project website:

  ```
  https://javaserverfaces.java.net/
  ```

- JavaServer Faces JavaScript Library APIs:

  ```
  http://docs.oracle.com/javaee/7/javaserverfaces/2.2/
  jsdocs/symbols/jsf.ajax.html
  ```

14

Composite Components: Advanced Topics and an Example

This chapter describes the advanced features of composite components in JavaServer Faces technology.

A composite component is a special type of JavaServer Faces template that acts as a component. If you are new to composite components, see Section 8.5, "Composite Components," before you proceed with this chapter.

The following topics are addressed here:

- Attributes of a Composite Component
- Invoking a Managed Bean
- Validating Composite Component Values
- The compositecomponentexample Example Application

14.1 Attributes of a Composite Component

You define an attribute of a composite component by using the `composite:attribute` tag. Table 14–1 lists the commonly used attributes of this tag.

Table 14–1   Commonly Used Attributes of the composite:attribute Tag

Attribute	Description
name	Specifies the name of the composite component attribute to be used in the using page. Alternatively, the name attribute can specify standard event handlers such as action, actionListener, and managed bean.
default	Specifies the default value of the composite component attribute.
required	Specifies whether it is mandatory to provide a value for the attribute.
method-signature	Specifies a subclass of java.lang.Object as the type of the composite component's attribute. The method-signature element declares that the composite component attribute is a method expression. The type attribute and the method-signature attribute are mutually exclusive. If you specify both, method-signature is ignored. The default type of an attribute is java.lang.Object. **Note:** Method expressions are similar to value expressions, but rather than supporting the dynamic retrieval and setting of properties, method expressions support the invocation of a method of an arbitrary object, passing a specified set of parameters and returning the result from the called method (if any).
type	Specifies a fully qualified class name as the type of the attribute. The type attribute and the method-signature attribute are mutually exclusive. If you specify both, method-signature is ignored. The default type of an attribute is java.lang.Object.

The following code snippet defines a composite component attribute and assigns it a default value:

```
<composite:attribute name="username" default="admin"/>
```

The following code snippet uses the method-signature element:

```
<composite:attribute name="myaction"
               method-signature="java.lang.String action()"/>
```

The following code snippet uses the type element:

```
<composite:attribute name="dateofjoining" type="java.util.Date"/>
```

14.2 Invoking a Managed Bean

To enable a composite component to handle server-side data, you can invoke a managed bean in one of the following ways.

- Pass the reference of the managed bean to the composite component.

- Directly use the properties of the managed bean.

The example application described in Section 14.4, "The compositecomponentexample Example Application," shows how to use a managed bean with a composite component by passing the reference of the managed bean to the component.

14.3 Validating Composite Component Values

JavaServer Faces provides the following tags for validating values of input components. These tags can be used with the `composite:valueHolder` or the `composite:editableValueHolder` tag.

Table 14–2 lists commonly used validator tags. See Section 11.3, "Using the Standard Validators," for details and a complete list.

Table 14–2   Validator Tags

Tag Name	Description
f:validateBean	Delegates the validation of the local value to the Bean Validation API.
f:validateRegex	Uses the `pattern` attribute to validate the wrapping component. The entire pattern is matched against the `String` value of the component. If it matches, it is valid.
f:validateRequired	Enforces the presence of a value. Has the same effect as setting the `required` element of a composite component's attribute to `true`.

14.4 The compositecomponentexample Example Application

The `compositecomponentexample` application creates a composite component that accepts a name (or any other string). The component interacts with a managed bean that calculates whether the letters in the name, if converted to numeric values, add up to a prime number. The component displays the sum of the letter values and reports whether it is or is not prime.

The `compositecomponentexample` application has a composite component file, a using page, and a managed bean.

The source code for this application is in the *tut-install*/examples/web/jsf/ compositecomponentexample/ directory.

14.4.1 The Composite Component File

The composite component file is an XHTML file, /web/resources/ezcomp/ PrimePanel.xhtml. It has a composite:interface section that declares the labels for the name and a command button. It also declares a managed bean, which defines properties for the name.

```
<composite:interface>
    <composite:attribute name="namePrompt"
                         default="Name, word, or phrase: "/>
    <composite:attribute name="calcButtonText" default="Calculate"/>
    <composite:attribute name="calcAction"
                         method-signature="java.lang.String action()"/>
    <composite:attribute name="primeBean"/>
    <composite:editableValueHolder name="nameVal" targets="form:name"/>
</composite:interface>
```

The composite component implementation accepts the input value for the name property of the managed bean. The h:outputStylesheet tag specifies the stylesheet as a relocatable resource. The implementation then specifies the format of the output, using properties of the managed bean, as well as the format of error messages. The sum value is rendered only after it has been calculated, and the report of whether the sum is prime or not is rendered only if the input value is validated.

```
<composite:implementation>
    <h:form id="form">
        <h:outputStylesheet library="css" name="default.css"
                           target="head"/>
        <h:panelGrid columns="2" role="presentation">
            <h:outputLabel for="name"
                          value="#{cc.attrs.namePrompt}"/>
            <h:inputText id="name"
                        size="45"
                        value="#{cc.attrs.primeBean.name}"
                        required="true"/>
        </h:panelGrid>
        <p>
            <h:commandButton id="calcButton"
                            value="#{cc.attrs.calcButtonText}"
                            action="#{cc.attrs.calcAction}">
                <f:ajax execute="name" render="outputGroup"/>
            </h:commandButton>
```

```
        </p>

        <h:panelGroup id="outputGroup" layout="block">
            <p>
                <h:outputText id="result" style="color:blue"
                            rendered="#{cc.attrs.primeBean.totalSum gt 0}"
                            value="Sum is #{cc.attrs.primeBean.totalSum}" />
            </p>
            <p>
                <h:outputText id="response" style="color:blue"
                            value="#{cc.attrs.primeBean.response}"
                            rendered="#{!facesContext.validationFailed}"/>
                <h:message id="errors1"
                            showSummary="true"
                            showDetail="false"
                            style="color: #d20005;
                            font-family: 'New Century Schoolbook', serif;
                            font-style: oblique;
                            text-decoration: overline"
                            for="name"/>
            </p>
        </h:panelGroup>
    </h:form>
</composite:implementation>
```

14.4.2 The Using Page

The using page in this example application, web/index.xhtml, is an XHTML file that invokes the PrimePanel.xhtml composite component file along with the managed bean. It validates the user's input.

```
<div id="compositecomponent">
    <ez:PrimePanel primeBean="#{primeBean}"
                calcAction="#{primeBean.calculate}">
    </ez:PrimePanel>
</div>
```

14.4.3 The Managed Bean

The managed bean, PrimeBean.java, defines a method called calculate, which performs the calculations on the input string and sets properties accordingly. The bean first creates an array of prime numbers. It calculates the sum of the letters in the string, with 'a' equal to 1 and 'z' equal to 26, and determines whether the value can be found in the array of primes. An uppercase letter in the input string has the same value as its lowercase equivalent.

The bean specifies the minimum and maximum size of the name string, which is enforced by the Bean Validation @Size constraint. The bean uses the @Model annotation, a shortcut for @Named and @RequestScoped, as described in Step 7 of Section 6.3.1, "To View the hello1 Web Module Using NetBeans IDE."

```
@Model
public class PrimeBean implements Serializable {
    ...
    @Size(min=1, max=45)
    private String name;
    ...

    public String calculate() {
        ...
    }
}
```

14.4.4 Running the compositecomponentexample Example

You can use either NetBeans IDE or Maven to build, package, deploy, and run the compositecomponentexample example.

14.4.4.1 To Build, Package, and Deploy the compositecomponentexample Example Using NetBeans IDE

1. Make sure that GlassFish Server has been started (see Section 2.2, "Starting and Stopping GlassFish Server").

2. From the **File** menu, choose **Open Project**.

3. In the Open Project dialog box, navigate to:

   tut-install/examples/web/jsf

4. Select the compositecomponentexample folder.

5. Click **Open Project**.

6. In the **Projects** tab, right-click the compositecomponentexample project and select **Build**.

   This command builds and deploys the application.

14.4.4.2 To Build, Package, and Deploy the compositecomponentexample Example Using Maven

1. Make sure that GlassFish Server has been started (see Section 2.2, "Starting and Stopping GlassFish Server").

2. In a terminal window, go to:

   tut-install/examples/web/jsf/compositecomponentexample

3. Enter the following command to build and deploy the application:

   ```
   mvn install
   ```

14.4.4.3 To Run the compositecomponentexample Example

1. In a web browser, enter the following URL:

   ```
   http://localhost:8080/compositecomponentexample
   ```

2. On the page that appears, enter a string in the **Name, word, or phrase** field, then click **Calculate**.

   The page reports the sum of the letters and whether the sum is prime. A validation error is reported if no value is entered or if the string contains more than 45 characters.

15

Creating Custom UI Components and Other Custom Objects

JavaServer Faces technology offers a basic set of standard, reusable UI components that enable quick and easy construction of user interfaces for web applications. These components mostly map one-to-one to the elements in HTML 4. But often an application requires a component that has additional functionality or requires a completely new component. JavaServer Faces technology allows extension of standard components to enhance their functionality or to create custom components. A rich ecosystem of third-party component libraries is built on this extension capability, but it is beyond the scope of this tutorial to examine them. A web search for "JSF Component Libraries" is a good starting point to learn more about this important aspect of using JavaServer Faces technology.

In addition to extending the functionality of standard components, a component writer might want to give a page author the ability to change the appearance of the component on the page or to alter listener behavior. Alternatively, the component writer might want to render a component to a different kind of client device type, such as a smartphone or a tablet instead of a desktop computer. Enabled by the flexible JavaServer Faces architecture, a component writer can separate the definition of the component behavior from its appearance by delegating the rendering of the component to a separate renderer. In this way, a component writer can define the behavior of a custom component once but create multiple renderers, each of which defines a different way to render the component to a particular kind of client device.

A `javax.faces.component.UIComponent` is a Java class that is responsible for representing a self-contained piece of the user interface during the request-processing lifecycle. It is intended to represent the meaning of the component; the visual representation of the component is the responsibility of the javax.faces.render.Renderer. There can be multiple instances of the same UIComponent class in any given JavaServer Faces view, just as there can be multiple instances of any Java class in any given Java program.

JavaServer Faces technology provides the ability to create custom components by extending the UIComponent class, the base class for all standard UI components. A custom component can be used anywhere an ordinary component can be used, such as within a composite component. A UIComponent is identified by two names: component-family specifies the general purpose of the component (input or output, for instance), and component-type indicates the specific purpose of a component, such as a text input field or a command button.

A Renderer is a helper to the UIComponent that deals with how that specific UIComponent class should appear in a specific kind of client device. Renderers are identified by two names: render-kit-id and renderer-type. A render kit is just a bucket into which a particular group of renderers is placed, and the render-kit-id identifies the group. Most JavaServer Faces component libraries provide their own render kits.

A javax.faces.view.facelets.Tag object is a helper to the UIComponent and Renderer that allows the page author to include an instance of a UIComponent in a JavaServer Faces view. A tag represents a specific combination of component-type and renderer-type.

See Section 15.1.3, "Component, Renderer, and Tag Combinations," for information on how components, renderers, and tags interact.

This chapter uses the image map component from the Duke's Bookstore case study example to explain how you can create simple custom components, custom renderers, and associated custom tags, and take care of all the other details associated with using the components and renderers in an application. See Chapter 28, "Duke's Bookstore Case Study Example," in *The Java EE 7 Tutorial, Volume 2*, for more information about this example.

The chapter also describes how to create other custom objects: custom converters, custom listeners, and custom validators. It also describes how to bind component values and instances to data objects and how to bind custom objects to managed bean properties.

The following topics are addressed here:

- Determining Whether You Need a Custom Component or Renderer
- Understanding the Image Map Example
- Steps for Creating a Custom Component
- Creating Custom Component Classes

- Delegating Rendering to a Renderer
- Implementing an Event Listener
- Handling Events for Custom Components
- Defining the Custom Component Tag in a Tag Library Descriptor
- Using a Custom Component
- Creating and Using a Custom Converter
- Creating and Using a Custom Validator
- Binding Component Values and Instances to Managed Bean Properties
- Binding Converters, Listeners, and Validators to Managed Bean Properties

15.1 Determining Whether You Need a Custom Component or Renderer

The JavaServer Faces implementation supports a very basic set of components and associated renderers. This section helps you to decide whether you can use standard components and renderers in your application or need a custom component or custom renderer.

15.1.1 When to Use a Custom Component

A component class defines the state and behavior of a UI component. This behavior includes converting the value of a component to the appropriate markup, queuing events on components, performing validation, and any other behavior related to how the component interacts with the browser and the request-processing lifecycle.

You need to create a custom component in the following situations.

- You need to add new behavior to a standard component, such as generating an additional type of event (for example, notifying another part of the page that something changed in this component as a result of user interaction).

- You need to take a different action in the request processing of the value of a component from what is available in any of the existing standard components.

- You want to take advantage of an HTML capability offered by your target browser, but none of the standard JavaServer Faces components take advantage of the capability in the way you want, if at all. The current release does not contain standard components for complex HTML components, such as frames; however, because of the extensibility of the component architecture, you can use JavaServer Faces technology to create components like these. The Duke's Bookstore case study creates custom components that correspond to the HTML map and area tags.

- You need to render to a non-HTML client that requires extra components not supported by HTML. Eventually, the standard HTML render kit will provide support for all standard HTML components. However, if you are rendering to a different client, such as a phone, you might need to create custom components to represent the controls uniquely supported by the client. For example, some component architectures for wireless clients include support for tickers and progress bars, which are not available on an HTML client. In this case, you might also need a custom renderer along with the component, or you might need only a custom renderer.

You do not need to create a custom component in the following cases.

- You need to aggregate components to create a new component that has its own unique behavior. In this situation, you can use a composite component to combine existing standard components. For more information on composite components, see Section 8.5, "Composite Components," and Chapter 14, "Composite Components: Advanced Topics and an Example."

- You simply need to manipulate data on the component or add application-specific functionality to it. In this situation, you should create a managed bean for this purpose and bind it to the standard component rather than create a custom component. See Section 12.1, "Managed Beans in JavaServer Faces Technology," for more information on managed beans.

- You need to convert a component's data to a type not supported by its renderer. See Section 11.1, "Using the Standard Converters," for more information about converting a component's data.

- You need to perform validation on the component data. Standard validators and custom validators can be added to a component by using the validator tags from the page. See Section 11.3, "Using the Standard Validators," and Section 15.11, "Creating and Using a Custom Validator," for more information about validating a component's data.

- You need to register event listeners on components. You can either register event listeners on components using the f:valueChangeListener and f:actionListener tags, or you can point at an event-processing method on a managed bean using the component's actionListener or valueChangeListener attributes. See Section 15.6, "Implementing an Event Listener," and Section 12.3, "Writing Managed Bean Methods," for more information.

15.1.2 When to Use a Custom Renderer

A renderer, which generates the markup to display a component on a web page, allows you to separate the semantics of a component from its appearance. By keeping this separation, you can support different kinds of client devices with the same kind of authoring experience. You can think of a renderer as a "client adapter." It produces output suitable for consumption and display by the client and accepts input from the client when the user interacts with that component.

If you are creating a custom component, you need to ensure, among other things, that your component class performs these operations that are central to rendering the component:

- **Decoding**: Converting the incoming request parameters to the local value of the component

- **Encoding**: Converting the current local value of the component into the corresponding markup that represents it in the response

The JavaServer Faces specification supports two programming models for handling encoding and decoding.

- **Direct implementation**: The component class itself implements the decoding and encoding.

- **Delegated implementation**: The component class delegates the implementation of encoding and decoding to a separate renderer.

By delegating the operations to the renderer, you have the option of associating your custom component with different renderers so that you can render the component on different clients. If you don't plan to render a particular component on different clients, it may be simpler to let the component class handle the rendering. However, a separate renderer enables you to preserve the separation of semantics from appearance. The Duke's Bookstore application separates the renderers from the components, although it renders only to HTML 4 web browsers.

If you aren't sure whether you will need the flexibility offered by separate renderers but you want to use the simpler direct-implementation approach, you can actually use both models. Your component class can include some default rendering code, but it can delegate rendering to a renderer if there is one.

15.1.3 Component, Renderer, and Tag Combinations

When you create a custom component, you can create a custom renderer to go with it. To associate the component with the renderer and to reference the component from the page, you will also need a custom tag.

Although you need to write the custom component and renderer, there is no need to write code for a custom tag (called a tag handler). If you specify the component and renderer combination, Facelets creates the tag handler automatically.

In rare situations, you might use a custom renderer with a standard component rather than a custom component. Or you might use a custom tag without a renderer or a component. This section gives examples of these situations and summarizes what is required for a custom component, renderer, and tag.

You would use a custom renderer without a custom component if you wanted to add some client-side validation on a standard component. You would implement the validation code with a client-side scripting language, such as JavaScript, and then render the JavaScript with the custom renderer. In this situation, you need a custom tag to go with the renderer so that its tag handler can register the renderer on the standard component.

Custom components as well as custom renderers need custom tags associated with them. However, you can have a custom tag without a custom renderer or custom component. For example, suppose that you need to create a custom validator that requires extra attributes on the validator tag. In this case, the custom tag corresponds to a custom validator and not to a custom component or custom renderer. In any case, you still need to associate the custom tag with a server-side object.

Table 15–1 summarizes what you must or can associate with a custom component, custom renderer, or custom tag.

Table 15–1 **Requirements for Custom Components, Custom Renderers, and Custom Tags**

Custom Item	Must Have	Can Have
Custom component	Custom tag	Custom renderer or standard renderer
Custom renderer	Custom tag	Custom component or standard component
Custom JavaServer Faces tag	Some server-side object, like a component, a custom renderer, or custom validator	Custom component or standard component associated with a custom renderer

15.2 Understanding the Image Map Example

Duke's Bookstore includes a custom image map component on the index.xhtml page. This image map displays a selection of six book titles. When the user clicks one of the book titles in the image map, the application goes to a page that displays the title of the selected book as well as information about a featured book. The page allows the user to add either book (or none) to the shopping cart.

15.2.1 Why Use JavaServer Faces Technology to Implement an Image Map?

JavaServer Faces technology is an ideal framework to use for implementing this kind of image map because it can perform the work that must be done on the server without requiring you to create a server-side image map.

In general, client-side image maps are preferred over server-side image maps for several reasons. One reason is that the client-side image map allows the browser to provide immediate feedback when a user positions the mouse over a hotspot. Another reason is that client-side image maps perform better because they don't require round-trips to the server. However, in some situations, your image map might need to access the server to retrieve data or to change the appearance of nonform controls, tasks that a client-side image map cannot do.

Because the image map custom component uses JavaServer Faces technology, it has the best of both styles of image maps: It can handle the parts of the application that need to be performed on the server while allowing the other parts of the application to be performed on the client side.

15.2.2 Understanding the Rendered HTML

Here is an abbreviated version of the form part of the HTML page that the application needs to render:

```
<form id="j_idt13" name="j_idt13" method="post"
    action="/dukesbookstore/index.xhtml" ...>
  ...
  <img id="j_idt13:mapImage"
      src="/dukesbookstore/javax.faces.resource/book_all.jpg?ln=images"
      alt="Choose a Book from our Catalog"
      usemap="#bookMap" />
  ...
  <map name="bookMap">
    <area alt="Duke"
    coords="67,23,212,268"
    shape="rect"
    onmouseout="document.forms[0]['j_idt13:mapImage'].src='resources/images/book_all.jpg'"
    onmouseover="document.forms[0]['j_idt13:mapImage'].src='resources/images/book_201.jpg'"
    onclick="document.forms[0]['bookMap_current'].value='Duke'; document.forms[0].submit()"
    />
    ...
    <input type="hidden" name="bookMap_current">
  </map>
```

```
    ...
</form>
```

The img tag associates an image (book_all.jpg) with the image map referenced in the usemap attribute value.

The map tag specifies the image map and contains a set of area tags.

Each area tag specifies a region of the image map. The onmouseover, onmouseout, and onclick attributes define which JavaScript code is executed when these events occur. When the user moves the mouse over a region, the onmouseover function associated with the region displays the map with that region highlighted. When the user moves the mouse out of a region, the onmouseout function redisplays the original image. If the user clicks on a region, the onclick function sets the value of the input tag to the ID of the selected area and submits the page.

The input tag represents a hidden control that stores the value of the currently selected area between client-server exchanges so that the server-side component classes can retrieve the value.

The server-side objects retrieve the value of bookMap_current and set the locale in the javax.faces.context.FacesContext instance according to the region that was selected.

15.2.3 Understanding the Facelets Page

Here is an abbreviated form of the Facelets page that the image map component uses to generate the HTML page shown in the preceding section. It uses custom bookstore:map and bookstore:area tags to represent the custom components:

```
<h:form>
    ...
        <h:graphicImage id="mapImage"
                        name="book_all.jpg"
                        library="images"
                        alt="#{bundle.ChooseBook}"
                        usemap="#bookMap" />
        <bookstore:map id="bookMap"
                        current="map1"
                        immediate="true"
                        action="bookstore">
        <f:actionListener
            type="dukesbookstore.listeners.MapBookChangeListener"/>
        <bookstore:area id="map1" value="#{Book201}"
                            onmouseover="resources/images/book_201.jpg"
                            onmouseout="resources/images/book_all.jpg"
                            targetImage="mapImage"/>
```

```
<bookstore:area id="map2" value="#{Book202}"
                onmouseover="resources/images/book_202.jpg"
                onmouseout="resources/images/book_all.jpg"
                targetImage="mapImage"/>
    . . .
</bookstore:map>
    . . .
</h:form>
```

The `alt` attribute of the `h:graphicImage` tag maps to the localized string `"Choose a Book from our Catalog"`.

The `f:actionListener` tag within the `bookstore:map` tag points to a listener class for an action event. The `processAction` method of the listener places the book ID for the selected map area into the session map. The way this event is handled is explained more in Section 15.7, "Handling Events for Custom Components."

The `action` attribute of the `bookstore:map` tag specifies a logical outcome `String`, `"bookstore"`, which by implicit navigation rules sends the application to the page `bookstore.xhtml`. For more information on navigation, see Section 16.9, "Configuring Navigation Rules."

The `immediate` attribute of the `bookstore:map` tag is set to `true`, which indicates that the default `javax.faces.event.ActionListener` implementation should execute during the Apply Request Values phase of the request-processing lifecycle, instead of waiting for the Invoke Application phase. Because the request resulting from clicking the map does not require any validation, data conversion, or server-side object updates, it makes sense to skip directly to the Invoke Application phase.

The `current` attribute of the `bookstore:map` tag is set to the default area, which is `map1` (the book *My Early Years: Growing Up on Star7*, by Duke).

Notice that the `bookstore:area` tags do not contain any of the JavaScript, coordinate, or shape data that is displayed on the HTML page. The JavaScript is generated by the `dukesbookstore.renderers.AreaRenderer` class. The `onmouseover` and `onmouseout` attribute values indicate the image to be loaded when these events occur. How the JavaScript is generated is explained more in Section 15.4.2, "Performing Encoding."

The coordinate, shape, and alternate text data are obtained through the `value` attribute, whose value refers to an attribute in application scope. The value of this attribute is a bean, which stores the `coords`, `shape`, and `alt` data. How these beans are stored in the application scope is explained more in the next section.

15.2.4 Configuring Model Data

In a JavaServer Faces application, data such as the coordinates of a hotspot of an image map is retrieved from the `value` attribute through a bean. However, the shape and coordinates of a hotspot should be defined together because the coordinates are interpreted differently depending on what shape the hotspot is. Because a component's value can be bound only to one property, the `value` attribute cannot refer to both the shape and the coordinates.

To solve this problem, the application encapsulates all of this information in a set of `ImageArea` objects. These objects are initialized into application scope by the managed bean creation facility (see Section 16.4.1, "Using the managed-bean Element"). Here is part of the managed bean declaration for the `ImageArea` bean corresponding to the South America hotspot:

```
<managed-bean eager="true">
    ...
    <managed-bean-name>Book201</managed-bean-name>
    <managed-bean-class>
        javaeetutorial.dukesbookstore.model.ImageArea
    </managed-bean-class>
    <managed-bean-scope>application</managed-bean-scope>
    <managed-property>
        ...
        <property-name>shape</property-name>
        <value>rect</value>
    </managed-property>
    <managed-property>
        ...
        <property-name>alt</property-name>
        <value>Duke</value>
    </managed-property>
    <managed-property>
        ...
        <property-name>coords</property-name>
        <value>67,23,212,268</value>
    </managed-property>
</managed-bean>
```

For more information on initializing managed beans with the managed bean creation facility, see Section 16.2, "Application Configuration Resource File."

The `value` attributes of the `bookstore:area` tags refer to the beans in the application scope, as shown in this `bookstore:area` tag from `index.xhtml`:

```
<bookstore:area id="map1" value="#{Book201}"
            onmouseover="resources/images/book_201.jpg"
```

```
onmouseout="resources/images/book_all.jpg"
targetImage="mapImage" />
```

To reference the `ImageArea` model object bean values from the component class, you implement a `getValue` method in the component class. This method calls `super.getValue`. The superclass of *tut-install*/examples/case-studies/ dukes-bookstore/src/java/dukesbookstore/components/AreaComponent.java, `UIOutput`, has a `getValue` method that does the work of finding the `ImageArea` object associated with `AreaComponent`. The `AreaRenderer` class, which needs to render the `alt`, `shape`, and `coords` values from the `ImageArea` object, calls the `getValue` method of `AreaComponent` to retrieve the `ImageArea` object.

```
ImageArea iarea = (ImageArea) area.getValue();
```

`ImageArea` is a simple bean, so you can access the shape, coordinates, and alternative text values by calling the appropriate accessor methods of `ImageArea`. Section 15.5.1, "Creating the Renderer Class," explains how to do this in the `AreaRenderer` class.

15.2.5 Summary of the Image Map Application Classes

Table 15–2 summarizes all the classes needed to implement the image map component.

Table 15–2 **Image Map Classes**

Class	Function
AreaSelectedEvent	The `javax.faces.event.ActionEvent` indicating that an `AreaComponent` from the `MapComponent` has been selected.
AreaComponent	The class that defines `AreaComponent`, which corresponds to the `bookstore:area` custom tag.
MapComponent	The class that defines `MapComponent`, which corresponds to the `bookstore:map` custom tag.
AreaRenderer	This `javax.faces.render.Renderer` performs the delegated rendering for `AreaComponent`.
ImageArea	The bean that stores the shape and coordinates of the hotspots.
MapBookChangeListener	The action listener for the `MapComponent`.

The Duke's Bookstore source directory, called *bookstore-dir*, is *tut-install*/examples/ case-studies/dukes-bookstore/src/java/dukesbookstore/. The event and listener classes are located in *bookstore-dir*/listeners/. The component classes are located in *bookstore-dir*/`components/`. The renderer classes are located in *bookstore-dir*/`renderers/`. `ImageArea` is located in *bookstore-dir*/`model/`.

15.3 Steps for Creating a Custom Component

You can apply the following steps while developing your own custom component.

1. Create a custom component class that does the following:

   a. Overrides the `getFamily` method to return the component family, which is used to look up renderers that can render the component

   b. Includes the rendering code or delegates it to a renderer (explained in Step 2)

   c. Enables component attributes to accept expressions

   d. Queues an event on the component if the component generates events

   e. Saves and restores the component state

2. Delegate rendering to a renderer if your component does not handle the rendering. To do this:

   a. Create a custom renderer class by extending `javax.faces.render.Renderer`.

   b. Register the renderer to a render kit.

3. Register the component.

4. Create an event handler if your component generates events.

5. Create a tag library descriptor (TLD) that defines the custom tag.

See Section 16.11, "Registering a Custom Component," and Section 16.10, "Registering a Custom Renderer with a Render Kit," for information on registering the custom component and the renderer. Section 15.9, "Using a Custom Component," discusses how to use the custom component in a JavaServer Faces page.

15.4 Creating Custom Component Classes

As explained in Section 15.1.1, "When to Use a Custom Component," a component class defines the state and behavior of a UI component. The state information includes the component's type, identifier, and local value. The behavior defined by the component class includes the following:

- Decoding (converting the request parameter to the component's local value)
- Encoding (converting the local value into the corresponding markup)
- Saving the state of the component
- Updating the bean value with the local value
- Processing validation on the local value
- Queueing events

The `javax.faces.component.UIComponentBase` class defines the default behavior of a component class. All the classes representing the standard components extend from `UIComponentBase`. These classes add their own behavior definitions, as your custom component class will do.

Your custom component class must either extend `UIComponentBase` directly or extend a class representing one of the standard components. These classes are located in the `javax.faces.component` package, and their names begin with `UI`.

If your custom component serves the same purpose as a standard component, you should extend that standard component rather than directly extend `UIComponentBase`. For example, suppose you want to create an editable menu component. It makes sense to have this component extend `UISelectOne` rather than `UIComponentBase` because you can reuse the behavior already defined in `UISelectOne`. The only new functionality you need to define is to make the menu editable.

Whether you decide to have your component extend `UIComponentBase` or a standard component, you might also want your component to implement one or more of these behavioral interfaces defined in the `javax.faces.component` package:

- `ActionSource`: Indicates that the component can fire a `javax.faces.event.ActionEvent`
- `ActionSource2`: Extends `ActionSource` and allows component properties referencing methods that handle action events to use method expressions as defined by the EL
- `EditableValueHolder`: Extends `ValueHolder` and specifies additional features for editable components, such as validation and emitting value-change events
- `NamingContainer`: Mandates that each component rooted at this component has a unique ID

- `StateHolder`: Denotes that a component has state that must be saved between requests

- `ValueHolder`: Indicates that the component maintains a local value as well as the option of accessing data in the model tier

If your component extends `UIComponentBase`, it automatically implements only `StateHolder`. Because all components directly or indirectly extend `UIComponentBase`, they all implement `StateHolder`. Any component that implements `StateHolder` also implements the `StateHelper` interface, which extends `StateHolder` and defines a `Map`-like contract that makes it easy for components to save and restore a partial view state.

If your component extends one of the other standard components, it might also implement other behavioral interfaces in addition to `StateHolder`. If your component extends `UICommand`, it automatically implements `ActionSource2`. If your component extends `UIOutput` or one of the component classes that extend `UIOutput`, it automatically implements `ValueHolder`. If your component extends `UIInput`, it automatically implements `EditableValueHolder` and `ValueHolder`. See the JavaServer Faces API documentation to find out what the other component classes implement.

You can also make your component explicitly implement a behavioral interface that it doesn't already by virtue of extending a particular standard component. For example, if you have a component that extends `UIInput` and you want it to fire action events, you must make it explicitly implement `ActionSource2` because a `UIInput` component doesn't automatically implement this interface.

The Duke's Bookstore image map example has two component classes: `AreaComponent` and `MapComponent`. The `MapComponent` class extends `UICommand` and therefore implements `ActionSource2`, which means it can fire action events when a user clicks on the map. The `AreaComponent` class extends the standard component `UIOutput`. The `@FacesComponent` annotation registers the components with the JavaServer Faces implementation:

```
@FacesComponent("DemoMap")
public class MapComponent extends UICommand { ... }

@FacesComponent("DemoArea")
public class AreaComponent extends UIOutput { ... }
```

The `MapComponent` class represents the component corresponding to the `bookstore:map` tag:

```
<bookstore:map id="bookMap"
               current="map1"
               immediate="true"
```

```
                  action="bookstore">
  . . .
</bookstore:map>
```

The `AreaComponent` class represents the component corresponding to the `bookstore:area` tag:

```
<bookstore:area id="map1" value="#{Book201}"
                onmouseover="resources/images/book_201.jpg"
                onmouseout="resources/images/book_all.jpg"
                targetImage="mapImage"/>
```

`MapComponent` has one or more `AreaComponent` instances as children. Its behavior consists of the following actions:

- Retrieving the value of the currently selected area

- Defining the properties corresponding to the component's values

- Generating an event when the user clicks on the image map

- Queuing the event

- Saving its state

- Rendering the HTML `map` tag and the HTML `input` tag

`MapComponent` delegates the rendering of the HTML `map` and `input` tags to the `MapRenderer` class.

`AreaComponent` is bound to a bean that stores the shape and coordinates of the region of the image map. You will see how all this data is accessed through the value expression in Section 15.5.1, "Creating the Renderer Class." The behavior of `AreaComponent` consists of the following:

- Retrieving the shape and coordinate data from the bean

- Setting the value of the hidden tag to the `id` of this component

- Rendering the `area` tag, including the JavaScript for the `onmouseover`, `onmouseout`, and `onclick` functions

Although these tasks are actually performed by `AreaRenderer`, `AreaComponent` must delegate the tasks to `AreaRenderer`. See Section 15.5, "Delegating Rendering to a Renderer," for more information.

The rest of this section describes the tasks that `MapComponent` performs as well as the encoding and decoding that it delegates to `MapRenderer`. Section 15.7, "Handling Events for Custom Components," details how `MapComponent` handles events.

15.4.1 Specifying the Component Family

If your custom component class delegates rendering, it needs to override the getFamily method of UIComponent to return the identifier of a **component family**, which is used to refer to a component or set of components that can be rendered by a renderer or set of renderers. The component family is used along with the renderer type to look up renderers that can render the component:

```
public String getFamily() {
    return ("Map");
}
```

The component family identifier, Map, must match that defined by the component-family elements included in the component and renderer configurations in the application configuration resource file. Section 16.10, "Registering a Custom Renderer with a Render Kit," explains how to define the component family in the renderer configuration. Section 16.11, "Registering a Custom Component," explains how to define the component family in the component configuration.

15.4.2 Performing Encoding

During the Render Response phase, the JavaServer Faces implementation processes the encoding methods of all components and their associated renderers in the view. The encoding methods convert the current local value of the component into the corresponding markup that represents it in the response.

The UIComponentBase class defines a set of methods for rendering markup: encodeBegin, encodeChildren, and encodeEnd. If the component has child components, you might need to use more than one of these methods to render the component; otherwise, all rendering should be done in encodeEnd. Alternatively, you can use the encodeALL method, which encompasses all the methods.

Because MapComponent is a parent component of AreaComponent, the area tags must be rendered after the beginning map tag and before the ending map tag. To accomplish this, the MapRenderer class renders the beginning map tag in encodeBegin and the rest of the map tag in encodeEnd.

The JavaServer Faces implementation automatically invokes the encodeEnd method of AreaComponent's renderer after it invokes MapRenderer's encodeBegin method and before it invokes MapRenderer's encodeEnd method. If a component needs to perform the rendering for its children, it does this in the encodeChildren method.

Here are the encodeBegin and encodeEnd methods of MapRenderer:

```
@Override
public void encodeBegin(FacesContext context, UIComponent component)
        throws IOException {
    if ((context == null)|| (component == null)) {
        throw new NullPointerException();
    }
    MapComponent map = (MapComponent) component;
    ResponseWriter writer = context.getResponseWriter();
    writer.startElement("map", map);
    writer.writeAttribute("name", map.getId(), "id");
}

@Override
public void encodeEnd(FacesContext context, UIComponent component)
        throws IOException {
    if ((context == null) || (component == null)){
        throw new NullPointerException();
    }
    MapComponent map = (MapComponent) component;
    ResponseWriter writer = context.getResponseWriter();
    writer.startElement("input", map);
    writer.writeAttribute("type", "hidden", null);
    writer.writeAttribute("name", getName(context,map), "clientId");
    writer.endElement("input");
    writer.endElement("map");
}
```

Notice that encodeBegin renders only the beginning map tag. The encodeEnd method renders the input tag and the ending map tag.

The encoding methods accept a UIComponent argument and a javax.faces.context.FacesContext argument. The FacesContext instance contains all the information associated with the current request. The UIComponent argument is the component that needs to be rendered.

The rest of the method renders the markup to the javax.faces.context.ResponseWriter instance, which writes out the markup to the current response. This basically involves passing the HTML tag names and attribute names to the ResponseWriter instance as strings, retrieving the values of the component attributes, and passing these values to the ResponseWriter instance.

The startElement method takes a String (the name of the tag) and the component to which the tag corresponds (in this case, map). (Passing this information to the ResponseWriter instance helps design-time tools know which portions of the generated markup are related to which components.)

After calling startElement, you can call writeAttribute to render the tag's attributes. The writeAttribute method takes the name of the attribute, its value, and the name of a property or attribute of the containing component corresponding to the attribute. The last parameter can be null, and it won't be rendered.

The name attribute value of the map tag is retrieved using the getId method of UIComponent, which returns the component's unique identifier. The name attribute value of the input tag is retrieved using the getName(FacesContext, UIComponent) method of MapRenderer.

If you want your component to perform its own rendering but delegate to a renderer if there is one, include the following lines in the encoding method to check whether there is a renderer associated with this component:

```
if (getRendererType() != null) {
    super.encodeEnd(context);
    return;
}
```

If there is a renderer available, this method invokes the superclass's encodeEnd method, which does the work of finding the renderer. The MapComponent class delegates all rendering to MapRenderer, so it does not need to check for available renderers.

In some custom component classes that extend standard components, you might need to implement other methods in addition to encodeEnd. For example, if you need to retrieve the component's value from the request parameters, you must also implement the decode method.

15.4.3 Performing Decoding

During the Apply Request Values phase, the JavaServer Faces implementation processes the decode methods of all components in the tree. The decode method extracts a component's local value from incoming request parameters and uses a javax.faces.convert.Converter implementation to convert the value to a type that is acceptable to the component class.

A custom component class or its renderer must implement the decode method only if it must retrieve the local value or if it needs to queue events. The component queues the event by calling queueEvent.

Here is the decode method of MapRenderer:

```
@Override
public void decode(FacesContext context, UIComponent component) {
    if ((context == null) || (component == null)) {
        throw new NullPointerException();
    }
    MapComponent map = (MapComponent) component;
    String key = getName(context, map);
    String value = (String) context.getExternalContext().
            getRequestParameterMap().get(key);
    if (value != null)
        map.setCurrent(value);
    }
}
```

The decode method first gets the name of the hidden input field by calling getName(FacesContext, UIComponent). It then uses that name as the key to the request parameter map to retrieve the current value of the input field. This value represents the currently selected area. Finally, it sets the value of the MapComponent class's current attribute to the value of the input field.

15.4.4 Enabling Component Properties to Accept Expressions

Nearly all the attributes of the standard JavaServer Faces tags can accept expressions, whether they are value expressions or method expressions. It is recommended that you also enable your component attributes to accept expressions because it gives you much more flexibility when you write Facelets pages.

To enable the attributes to accept expressions, the component class must implement getter and setter methods for the component properties. These methods can use the facilities offered by the StateHelper interface to store and retrieve not only the values for these properties but also the state of the components across multiple requests.

Because MapComponent extends UICommand, the UICommand class already does the work of getting the ValueExpression and MethodExpression instances associated with each of the attributes that it supports. Similarly, the UIOutput class that AreaComponent extends already obtains the ValueExpression instances for its supported attributes. For both components, the simple getter and setter methods store and retrieve the key values and state for the attributes, as shown in this code fragment from `AreaComponent`:

```
enum PropertyKeys {
    alt, coords, shape, targetImage;
}
public String getAlt() {
    return (String) getStateHelper().eval(PropertyKeys.alt, null);
}
public void setAlt(String alt) {
    getStateHelper().put(PropertyKeys.alt, alt);
}
...
```

However, if you have a custom component class that extends `UIComponentBase`, you will need to implement the methods that get the `ValueExpression` and `MethodExpression` instances associated with those attributes that are enabled to accept expressions. For example, you could include a method that gets the `ValueExpression` instance for the `immediate` attribute:

```
public boolean isImmediate() {
    if (this.immediateSet) {
        return (this.immediate);
    }
    ValueExpression ve = getValueExpression("immediate");
    if (ve != null) {
        Boolean value = (Boolean) ve.getValue(
            getFacesContext().getELContext());
        return (value.booleanValue());
    } else {
        return (this.immediate);
    }
}
```

The properties corresponding to the component attributes that accept method expressions must accept and return a `MethodExpression` object. For example, if `MapComponent` extended `UIComponentBase` instead of `UICommand`, it would need to provide an `action` property that returns and accepts a `MethodExpression` object:

```
public MethodExpression getAction() {
    return (this.action);
}
public void setAction(MethodExpression action) {
    this.action = action;
}
```

15.4.5 Saving and Restoring State

As described in Section 15.4.4, "Enabling Component Properties to Accept Expressions," use of the StateHelper interface facilities allows you to save the component's state at the same time you set and retrieve property values. The StateHelper implementation allows partial state saving; it saves only the changes in the state since the initial request, not the entire state, because the full state can be restored during the Restore View phase.

Component classes that implement StateHolder may prefer to implement the saveState(FacesContext) and restoreState(FacesContext, Object) methods to help the JavaServer Faces implementation save and restore the state of components across multiple requests.

To save a set of values, you can implement the saveState(FacesContext) method. This method is called during the Render Response phase, during which the state of the response is saved for processing on subsequent requests. Here is a hypothetical method from MapComponent, which has only one attribute, current:

```
@Override
public Object saveState(FacesContext context) {
    Object values[] = new Object[2];
    values[0] = super.saveState(context);
    values[1] = current;
    return (values);
}
```

This method initializes an array, which will hold the saved state. It next saves all of the state associated with the component.

A component that implements StateHolder may also provide an implementation for restoreState(FacesContext, Object), which restores the state of the component to that saved with the saveState(FacesContext) method. The restoreState(FacesContext, Object) method is called during the Restore View phase, during which the JavaServer Faces implementation checks whether there is any state that was saved during the last Render Response phase and needs to be restored in preparation for the next postback.

Here is a hypothetical restoreState(FacesContext, Object) method from MapComponent:

```
public void restoreState(FacesContext context, Object state) {
    Object values[] = (Object[]) state;
    super.restoreState(context, values[0]);
    current = (String) values[1];
}
```

This method takes a FacesContext and an Object instance, representing the array that is holding the state for the component. This method sets the component's properties to the values saved in the Object array.

Whether or not you implement these methods in your component class, you can use the javax.faces.STATE_SAVING_METHOD context parameter to specify in the deployment descriptor where you want the state to be saved: either client or server. If state is saved on the client, the state of the entire view is rendered to a hidden field on the page. By default, the state is saved on the server.

The web applications in the Duke's Forest case study save their view state on the client. (See Chapter 30, "Duke's Forest Case Study Example," in *The Java EE 7 Tutorial, Volume 2.*)

Saving state on the client uses more bandwidth as well as more client resources, whereas saving it on the server uses more server resources. You may also want to save state on the client if you expect your users to disable cookies.

15.5 Delegating Rendering to a Renderer

Both MapComponent and AreaComponent delegate all of their rendering to a separate renderer. Section 15.4.2, "Performing Encoding," explains how MapRenderer performs the encoding for MapComponent. This section explains in detail the process of delegating rendering to a renderer using AreaRenderer, which performs the rendering for AreaComponent.

To delegate rendering, you perform these tasks.

- Create the Renderer class.

- Register the renderer with a render kit by using the @FacesRenderer annotation (or by using the application configuration resource file, as explained in Section 16.10, "Registering a Custom Renderer with a Render Kit").

- Identify the renderer type in the FacesRenderer annotation.

15.5.1 Creating the Renderer Class

When delegating rendering to a renderer, you can delegate all encoding and decoding to the renderer, or you can choose to do part of it in the component class. The AreaComponent class delegates encoding to the AreaRenderer class.

The renderer class begins with a @FacesRenderer annotation:

```
@FacesRenderer(componentFamily = "Area", rendererType = "DemoArea")
public class AreaRenderer extends Renderer {
```

The @FacesRenderer annotation registers the renderer class with the JavaServer Faces implementation as a renderer class. The annotation identifies the component family as well as the renderer type.

To perform the rendering for AreaComponent, AreaRenderer must implement an encodeEnd method. The encodeEnd method of AreaRenderer retrieves the shape, coordinates, and alternative text values stored in the ImageArea bean that is bound to AreaComponent. Suppose that the area tag currently being rendered has a value attribute value of "book203". The following line from encodeEnd gets the value of the attribute "book203" from the FacesContext instance:

```
ImageArea ia = (ImageArea)area.getValue();
```

The attribute value is the ImageArea bean instance, which contains the shape, coords, and alt values associated with the book203 AreaComponent instance. Section 15.2.4, "Configuring Model Data," describes how the application stores these values.

After retrieving the ImageArea object, the method renders the values for shape, coords, and alt by simply calling the associated accessor methods and passing the returned values to the ResponseWriter instance, as shown by these lines of code, which write out the shape and coordinates:

```
writer.startElement("area", area);
writer.writeAttribute("alt", iarea.getAlt(), "alt");
writer.writeAttribute("coords", iarea.getCoords(), "coords");
writer.writeAttribute("shape", iarea.getShape(), "shape");
```

The encodeEnd method also renders the JavaScript for the onmouseout, onmouseover, and onclick attributes. The Facelets page needs to provide only the path to the images that are to be loaded during an onmouseover or onmouseout action:

```
<bookstore:area id="map3" value="#{Book203}"
                onmouseover="resources/images/book_203.jpg"
                onmouseout="resources/images/book_all.jpg"
                targetImage="mapImage"/>
```

The AreaRenderer class takes care of generating the JavaScript for these actions, as shown in the following code from encodeEnd. The JavaScript that AreaRenderer generates for the onclick action sets the value of the hidden field to the value of the current area's component ID and submits the page.

```
sb = new StringBuffer("document.forms[0]['").append(targetImageId)
        .append("'].src='");
```

```
sb.append(
        getURI(context,
                (String) area.getAttributes().get("onmouseout")));
sb.append("'");
writer.writeAttribute("onmouseout", sb.toString(), "onmouseout");
sb = new StringBuffer("document.forms[0]['").append(targetImageId)
        .append("'].src='");
sb.append(
        getURI(context,
                (String) area.getAttributes().get("onmouseover")));
sb.append("'");
writer.writeAttribute("onmouseover", sb.toString(), "onmouseover");
sb = new StringBuffer("document.forms[0]['");
sb.append(getName(context, area));
sb.append("'].value='");
sb.append(iarea.getAlt());
sb.append("'; document.forms[0].submit()");
writer.writeAttribute("onclick", sb.toString(), "value");
writer.endElement("area");
```

By submitting the page, this code causes the JavaServer Faces lifecycle to return back to the Restore View phase. This phase saves any state information, including the value of the hidden field, so that a new request component tree is constructed. This value is retrieved by the decode method of the MapComponent class. This decode method is called by the JavaServer Faces implementation during the Apply Request Values phase, which follows the Restore View phase.

In addition to the encodeEnd method, AreaRenderer contains an empty constructor. This is used to create an instance of AreaRenderer so that it can be added to the render kit.

The @FacesRenderer annotation registers the renderer class with the JavaServer Faces implementation as a renderer class. The annotation identifies the component family as well as the renderer type.

15.5.2 Identifying the Renderer Type

During the Render Response phase, the JavaServer Faces implementation calls the getRendererType method of the component's tag handler to determine which renderer to invoke, if there is one.

You identify the type associated with the renderer in the rendererType element of the @FacesRenderer annotation for AreaRenderer as well as in the renderer-type element of the tag library descriptor.

15.6 Implementing an Event Listener

The JavaServer Faces technology supports action events and value-change events for components.

Action events occur when the user activates a component that implements `javax.faces.component.ActionSource`. These events are represented by the class `javax.faces.event.ActionEvent`.

Value-change events occur when the user changes the value of a component that implements `javax.faces.component.EditableValueHolder`. These events are represented by the class `javax.faces.event.ValueChangeEvent`.

One way to handle events is to implement the appropriate listener classes. Listener classes that handle the action events in an application must implement the interface `javax.faces.event.ActionListener`. Similarly, listeners that handle the value-change events must implement the interface `javax.faces.event.ValueChangeListener`.

This section explains how to implement the two listener classes.

To handle events generated by custom components, you must implement an event listener and an event handler and manually queue the event on the component. See Section 15.7, "Handling Events for Custom Components," for more information.

> **Note:** You do not need to create an `ActionListener` implementation to handle an event that results solely in navigating to a page and does not perform any other application-specific processing. See Section 12.3.1, "Writing a Method to Handle Navigation," for information on how to manage page navigation.

15.6.1 Implementing Value-Change Listeners

A `javax.faces.event.ValueChangeListener` implementation must include a `processValueChange(ValueChangeEvent)` method. This method processes the specified value-change event and is invoked by the JavaServer Faces implementation when the value-change event occurs. The `ValueChangeEvent` instance stores the old and the new values of the component that fired the event.

In the Duke's Bookstore case study, the `NameChanged` listener implementation is registered on the `name` `UIInput` component on the `bookcashier.xhtml` page. This listener stores into session scope the name the user entered in the field corresponding to the name component.

The `bookreceipt.xhtml` subsequently retrieves the name from the session scope:

```
<h:outputFormat title="thanks"
                value="#{bundle.ThankYouParam}">
    <f:param value="#{sessionScope.name}"/>
</h:outputFormat>
```

When the `bookreceipt.xhtml` page is loaded, it displays the name inside the message:

```
"Thank you, {0}, for purchasing your books from us."
```

Here is part of the `NameChanged` listener implementation:

```
public class NameChanged extends Object implements ValueChangeListener {

    @Override
    public void processValueChange(ValueChangeEvent event)
            throws AbortProcessingException {
        if (null != event.getNewValue()) {
            FacesContext.getCurrentInstance().getExternalContext()
                    .getSessionMap().put("name", event.getNewValue());
        }
    }
}
```

When the user enters the name in the field, a value-change event is generated, and the `processValueChange(ValueChangeEvent)` method of the `NameChanged` listener implementation is invoked. This method first gets the ID of the component that fired the event from the `ValueChangeEvent` object, and it puts the value, along with an attribute name, into the session map of the `FacesContext` instance.

Section 11.2.1, "Registering a Value-Change Listener on a Component," explains how to register this listener onto a component.

15.6.2 Implementing Action Listeners

A `javax.faces.event.ActionListener` implementation must include a `processAction(ActionEvent)` method. The `processAction(ActionEvent)` method processes the specified action event. The JavaServer Faces implementation invokes the `processAction(ActionEvent)` method when the `ActionEvent` occurs.

The Duke's Bookstore case study uses two `ActionListener` implementations, `LinkBookChangeListener` and `MapBookChangeListener`. See Section 15.7,

"Handling Events for Custom Components," for details on MapBookChangeListener.

Section 11.2.2, "Registering an Action Listener on a Component," explains how to register this listener onto a component.

15.7 Handling Events for Custom Components

As explained in Section 15.6, "Implementing an Event Listener," events are automatically queued on standard components that fire events. A custom component, on the other hand, must manually queue events from its decode method if it fires events.

Section 15.4.3, "Performing Decoding," explains how to queue an event on MapComponent using its decode method. This section explains how to write the class that represents the event of clicking on the map and how to write the method that processes this event.

As explained in Section 15.2.3, "Understanding the Facelets Page," the actionListener attribute of the bookstore:map tag points to the MapBookChangeListener class. The listener class's processAction method processes the event of clicking the image map. Here is the processAction method:

```
@Override
public void processAction(ActionEvent actionEvent)
        throws AbortProcessingException {

    AreaSelectedEvent event = (AreaSelectedEvent) actionEvent;
    String current = event.getMapComponent().getCurrent();
    FacesContext context = FacesContext.getCurrentInstance();
    String bookId = books.get(current);
    context.getExternalContext().getSessionMap().put("bookId", bookId);
}
```

When the JavaServer Faces implementation calls this method, it passes in an ActionEvent object that represents the event generated by clicking on the image map. Next, it casts it to an AreaSelectedEvent object (see *tut-install*/examples/ case-studies/dukes-bookstore/src/java/dukesbookstore/listeners/ AreaSelectedEvent.java). Then this method gets the MapComponent associated with the event. Next, it gets the value of the MapComponent object's current attribute, which indicates the currently selected area. The method then uses the value of the current attribute to get the book's ID value from a HashMap object, which is constructed elsewhere in the MapBookChangeListener class. Finally, the method places the ID obtained from the `HashMap` object into the session map for the application.

In addition to the method that processes the event, you need the event class itself. This class is very simple to write; you have it extend `ActionEvent` and provide a constructor that takes the component on which the event is queued and a method that returns the component. Here is the `AreaSelectedEvent` class used with the image map:

```
public class AreaSelectedEvent extends ActionEvent {
    public AreaSelectedEvent(MapComponent map) {
        super(map);
    }
    public MapComponent getMapComponent() {
        return ((MapComponent) getComponent());
    }
}
```

As explained in Section 15.4, "Creating Custom Component Classes," in order for `MapComponent` to fire events in the first place, it must implement `ActionSource`. Because `MapComponent` extends `UICommand`, it also implements `ActionSource`.

15.8 Defining the Custom Component Tag in a Tag Library Descriptor

To use a custom tag, you declare it in a Tag Library Descriptor (TLD). The TLD file defines how the custom tag is used in a JavaServer Faces page. The web container uses the TLD to validate the tag. The set of tags that are part of the HTML render kit are defined in the HTML_BASIC TLD, available at `http://docs.oracle.com/javaee/7/javaserverfaces/2.2/renderkitdocs/`.

The TLD file name must end with `taglib.xml`. In the Duke's Bookstore case study, the custom tags `area` and `map` are defined in the file `web/WEB-INF/bookstore.taglib.xml`.

All tag definitions must be nested inside the `facelet-taglib` element in the TLD. Each tag is defined by a `tag` element. Here are the tag definitions for the `area` and `map` components:

```
<facelet-taglib xmlns="http://xmlns.jcp.org/xml/ns/javaee"
...>
    <namespace>http://dukesbookstore</namespace>
    <tag>
        <tag-name>area</tag-name>
        <component>
            <component-type>DemoArea</component-type>
```

```
            <renderer-type>DemoArea</renderer-type>
        </component>
    </tag>
    <tag>
        <tag-name>map</tag-name>
        <component>
            <component-type>DemoMap</component-type>
            <renderer-type>DemoMap</renderer-type>
        </component>
    </tag>
</facelet-taglib>
```

The `component-type` element specifies the name defined in the `@FacesComponent` annotation, and the `renderer-type` element specifies the `rendererType` defined in the `@FacesRenderer` annotation.

The `facelet-taglib` element must also include a `namespace` element, which defines the namespace to be specified in pages that use the custom component. See Section 15.9, "Using a Custom Component," for information on specifying the namespace in pages.

The TLD file is located in the `WEB-INF` directory. In addition, an entry is included in the web deployment descriptor (`web.xml`) to identify the custom tag library descriptor file, as follows:

```
<context-param>
    <param-name>javax.faces.FACELETS_LIBRARIES</param-name>
    <param-value>/WEB-INF/bookstore.taglib.xml</param-value>
</context-param>
```

15.9 Using a Custom Component

To use a custom component in a page, you add the custom tag associated with the component to the page.

As explained in Section 15.8, "Defining the Custom Component Tag in a Tag Library Descriptor," you must ensure that the TLD that defines any custom tags is packaged in the application if you intend to use the tags in your pages. TLD files are stored in the `WEB-INF/` directory or subdirectory of the WAR file or in the `META-INF/` directory or subdirectory of a tag library packaged in a JAR file.

You also need to include a namespace declaration in the page so that the page has access to the tags. The custom tags for the Duke's Bookstore case study are defined in `bookstore.taglib.xml`. The `ui:composition` tag on the `index.xhtml` page declares the namespace defined in the tag library:

```
<ui:composition xmlns="http://www.w3.org/1999/xhtml"
                xmlns:ui="http://xmlns.jcp.org/jsf/facelets"
                xmlns:h="http://xmlns.jcp.org/jsf/html"
                xmlns:f="http://xmlns.jcp.org/jsf/core"
                xmlns:bookstore="http://dukesbookstore"
                template="./bookstoreTemplate.xhtml">
```

Finally, to use a custom component in a page, you add the component's tag to the page.

The Duke's Bookstore case study includes a custom image map component on the `index.xhtml` page. This component allows you to select a book by clicking on a region of the image map:

```
...
<h:graphicImage id="mapImage"
                name="book_all.jpg"
                library="images
                alt="#{bundle.chooseLocale}"
                usemap="#bookMap" />
<bookstore:map id="bookMap"
                current="map1"
                immediate="true"
                action="bookstore">
    <f:actionListener
        type="javaeetutorial.dukesbookstore.listeners.MapBookChangeListener" />
    <bookstore:area id="map1" value="#{Book201}"
                    onmouseover="resources/images/book_201.jpg"
                    onmouseout="resources/images/book_all.jpg"
                    targetImage="mapImage" />
    ...
    <bookstore:area id="map6" value="#{Book207}"
                    onmouseover="resources/images/book_207.jpg"
                    onmouseout="resources/images//book_all.jpg"
                    targetImage="mapImage" />
</bookstore:map>
```

The standard `h:graphicImage` tag associates an image (`book_all.jpg`) with an image map that is referenced in the `usemap` attribute value.

The custom `bookstore:map` tag that represents the custom component, `MapComponent`, specifies the image map and contains a set of `bookstore:area` tags. Each custom `bookstore:area` tag represents a custom `AreaComponent` and specifies a region of the image map.

On the page, the onmouseover and onmouseout attributes specify the image that is displayed when the user performs the actions described by the attributes. The custom renderer also renders an onclick attribute.

In the rendered HTML page, the onmouseover, onmouseout, and onclick attributes define which JavaScript code is executed when these events occur. When the user moves the mouse over a region, the onmouseover function associated with the region displays the map with that region highlighted. When the user moves the mouse out of a region, the onmouseout function redisplays the original image. When the user clicks a region, the onclick function sets the value of a hidden input tag to the ID of the selected area and submits the page.

When the custom renderer renders these attributes in HTML, it also renders the JavaScript code. The custom renderer also renders the entire onclick attribute rather than letting the page author set it.

The custom renderer that renders the HTML map tag also renders a hidden input component that holds the current area. The server-side objects retrieve the value of the hidden input field and set the locale in the FacesContext instance according to which region was selected.

15.10 Creating and Using a Custom Converter

A JavaServer Faces converter class converts strings to objects and objects to strings as required. Several standard converters are provided by JavaServer Faces for this purpose. See Section 11.1, "Using the Standard Converters," for more information on these included converters.

As explained in Section 7.4.3, "Conversion Model," if the standard converters included with JavaServer Faces cannot perform the data conversion that you need, you can create a custom converter to perform this specialized conversion. This implementation, at a minimum, must define how to convert data both ways between the two views of the data described in Section 7.4.3, "Conversion Model."

All custom converters must implement the javax.faces.convert.Converter interface. This section explains how to implement this interface to perform a custom data conversion.

The Duke's Bookstore case study uses a custom Converter implementation, located in *tut-install*/examples/case-studies/dukes-bookstore/src/java/ dukesbookstore/converters/CreditCardConverter.java, to convert the data entered in the Credit Card Number field on the bookcashier.xhtml page. It strips blanks and hyphens from the text string and formats it so that a blank space separates every four characters.

Another common use case for a custom converter is in a list for a nonstandard object type. In the Duke's Tutoring case study, the `Student` and `Guardian` entities require a custom converter so that they can be converted to and from a `UISelectItems` input component. (See Chapter 29, "Duke's Tutoring Case Study Example," in *The Java EE 7 Tutorial, Volume 2*.)

15.10.1 Creating a Custom Converter

The `CreditCardConverter` custom converter class is created as follows:

```
@FacesConverter("ccno")
public class CreditCardConverter implements Converter { ... }
```

The `@FacesConverter` annotation registers the custom converter class as a converter with the name of `ccno` with the JavaServer Faces implementation. Alternatively, you can register the converter with entries in the application configuration resource file, as shown in Section 16.8, "Registering a Custom Converter."

To define how the data is converted from the presentation view to the model view, the `Converter` implementation must implement the `getAsObject(FacesContext, UIComponent, String)` method from the `Converter` interface. Here is the implementation of this method from `CreditCardConverter`:

```
@Override
public Object getAsObject(FacesContext context,
        UIComponent component, String newValue)
        throws ConverterException {

    if (newValue.isEmpty()) {
        return null;
    }
    // Since this is only a String to String conversion,
    // this conversion does not throw ConverterException.

    String convertedValue = newValue.trim();
    if ( (convertedValue.contains("-")) || (convertedValue.contains(" "))) {
        char[] input = convertedValue.toCharArray();
        StringBuilder builder = new StringBuilder(input.length);
        for (int i = 0; i < input.length; ++i) {
            if ((input[i] == '-') || (input[i] == ' ')) {
            } else {
                builder.append(input[i]);
            }
        }
        convertedValue = builder.toString();
```

```
    }
    return convertedValue;
}
```

During the Apply Request Values phase, when the components' decode methods are processed, the JavaServer Faces implementation looks up the component's local value in the request and calls the getAsObject method. When calling this method, the JavaServer Faces implementation passes in the current FacesContext instance, the component whose data needs conversion, and the local value as a String. The method then writes the local value to a character array, trims the hyphens and blanks, adds the rest of the characters to a String, and returns the String.

To define how the data is converted from the model view to the presentation view, the Converter implementation must implement the getAsString(FacesContext, UIComponent, Object) method from the Converter interface. Here is an implementation of this method:

```
@Override
public String getAsString(FacesContext context,
        UIComponent component, Object value)
        throws ConverterException {

    String inputVal = null;
    if ( value == null ) {
        return "";
    }
    // value must be of a type that can be cast to a String.
    try {
        inputVal = (String)value;
    } catch (ClassCastException ce) {
        FacesMessage errMsg = new FacesMessage(CONVERSION_ERROR_MESSAGE_ID);
        FacesContext.getCurrentInstance().addMessage(null, errMsg);
        throw new ConverterException(errMsg.getSummary());
    }
    // insert spaces after every four characters for better
    // readability if they are not already present.
    char[] input = inputVal.toCharArray();
    StringBuilder builder = new StringBuilder(input.length + 3);
    for (int i = 0; i < input.length; ++i) {
        if ((i % 4) == 0 && (i != 0)) {
            if ((input[i] != ' ') || (input[i] != '-')){
                builder.append(" ");
                // if there are any "-"'s convert them to blanks.
            } else if (input[i] == '-') {
                builder.append(" ");
```

```
            }
        }
        builder.append(input[i]);
    }
    String convertedValue = builder.toString();
    return convertedValue;
}
```

During the Render Response phase, in which the components' encode methods are called, the JavaServer Faces implementation calls the getAsString method in order to generate the appropriate output. When the JavaServer Faces implementation calls this method, it passes in the current FacesContext, the UIComponent whose value needs to be converted, and the bean value to be converted. Because this converter does a String-to-String conversion, this method can cast the bean value to a String.

If the value cannot be converted to a String, the method throws an exception, passing an error message from the resource bundle that is registered with the application. Section 16.5, "Registering Application Messages," explains how to register custom error messages with the application.

If the value can be converted to a String, the method reads the String to a character array and loops through the array, adding a space after every four characters.

You can also create a custom converter with a @FacesConverter annotation that specifies the forClass attribute, as shown in the following example from the Duke's Tutoring case study:

```
@FacesConverter(forClass=Guardian.class, value="guardian")
public class GuardianConverter extends EntityConverter
        implements Converter {
    ...
```

The forClass attribute registers the converter as the default converter for the Guardian class. Therefore, whenever that class is specified by a value attribute of an input component, the converter is invoked automatically.

A converter class can be a separate Java POJO class, as in the Duke's Bookstore case study. If it needs to access objects defined in a managed bean class, however, it can be a subclass of a JavaServer Faces managed bean, as in the address-book persistence example, in which the converters use an enterprise bean that is injected into the managed bean class.

15.10.2 Using a Custom Converter

To apply the data conversion performed by a custom converter to a particular component's value, you must do one of the following.

- Reference the converter from the component tag's `converter` attribute.

- Nest an `f:converter` tag inside the component's tag and reference the custom converter from one of the `f:converter` tag's attributes.

If you are using the component tag's `converter` attribute, this attribute must reference the `Converter` implementation's identifier or the fully-qualified class name of the converter. Section 15.10, "Creating and Using a Custom Converter," explains how to implement a custom converter.

The identifier for the credit card converter class is `ccno`, the value specified in the `@FacesConverter` annotation:

```
@FacesConverter("ccno")
public class CreditCardConverter implements Converter { ...
```

Therefore, the `CreditCardConverter` instance can be registered on the `ccno` component as shown in the following example:

```
<h:inputText id="ccno"
             size="19"
             converter="ccno"
             value="#{cashierBean.creditCardNumber}"
             required="true"
             requiredMessage="#{bundle.ReqCreditCard}">
    ...
</h:inputText>
```

By setting the `converter` attribute of a component's tag to the converter's identifier or its class name, you cause that component's local value to be automatically converted according to the rules specified in the `Converter` implementation.

Instead of referencing the converter from the component tag's `converter` attribute, you can reference the converter from an `f:converter` tag nested inside the component's tag. To reference the custom converter using the `f:converter` tag, you do one of the following.

- Set the `f:converter` tag's `converterId` attribute to the `Converter` implementation's identifier defined in the `@FacesConverter` annotation or in

the application configuration resource file. This method is shown in
bookcashier.xhtml:

```
<h:inputText id="ccno"
             size="19"
             value="#{cashierBean.creditCardNumber}"
             required="true"
             requiredMessage="#{bundle.ReqCreditCard}">
    <f:converter converterId="ccno"/>
    <f:validateRegex
        pattern="\d{16}|\d{4} \d{4} \d{4} \d{4}|\d{4}-\d{4}-\d{4}-\d{4}"/>
</h:inputText>
```

- Bind the Converter implementation to a managed bean property using the
  f:converter tag's binding attribute, as described in Section 15.13, "Binding
  Converters, Listeners, and Validators to Managed Bean Properties."

The JavaServer Faces implementation calls the converter's getAsObject method to
strip spaces and hyphens from the input value. The getAsString method is called
when the bookcashier.xhtml page is redisplayed; this happens if the user orders
more than $100 worth of books.

In the Duke's Tutoring case study, each converter is registered as the converter for
a particular class. The converter is automatically invoked whenever that class is
specified by a value attribute of an input component. In the following example,
the itemValue attribute (highlighted in **bold**) calls the converter for the Guardian
class:

```
<h:selectManyListbox id="selectGuardiansMenu"
                     title="#{bundle['action.add.guardian']}"
                     value="#{guardianManager.selectedGuardians}"
                     size="5"
                     converter="guardian">
    <f:selectItems value="#{guardianManager.allGuardians}"
                   var="selectedGuardian"
                   itemLabel="#{selectedGuardian.name}"
                   itemValue="#{selectedGuardian}" />
</h:selectManyListbox>
```

15.11 Creating and Using a Custom Validator

If the standard validators or Bean Validation don't perform the validation
checking you need, you can create a custom validator to validate user input. As

explained in Section 7.4.5, "Validation Model," there are two ways to implement validation code.

- Implement a managed bean method that performs the validation.

- Provide an implementation of the `javax.faces.validator.Validator` interface to perform the validation.

Section 12.3.3, "Writing a Method to Perform Validation," explains how to implement a managed bean method to perform validation. The rest of this section explains how to implement the `Validator` interface.

If you choose to implement the `Validator` interface and you want to allow the page author to configure the validator's attributes from the page, you also must specify a custom tag for registering the validator on a component.

If you prefer to configure the attributes in the `Validator` implementation, you can forgo specifying a custom tag and instead let the page author register the validator on a component using the `f:validator` tag, as described in Section 15.11.3, "Using a Custom Validator."

You can also create a managed bean property that accepts and returns the `Validator` implementation you create, as described in Section 12.2.3, "Writing Properties Bound to Converters, Listeners, or Validators." You can use the `f:validator` tag's binding attribute to bind the `Validator` implementation to the managed bean property.

Usually, you will want to display an error message when data fails validation. You need to store these error messages in a resource bundle.

After creating the resource bundle, you have two ways to make the messages available to the application. You can queue the error messages onto the `FacesContext` programmatically, or you can register the error messages in the application configuration resource file, as explained in Section 16.5, "Registering Application Messages."

For example, an e-commerce application might use a general-purpose custom validator called `FormatValidator.java` to validate input data against a format pattern that is specified in the custom validator tag. This validator would be used with a Credit Card Number field on a Facelets page. Here is the custom validator tag:

```
<mystore:formatValidator
    formatPatterns="9999999999999999|9999 9999 9999 9999|9999-9999-9999-9999"/>
```

According to this validator, the data entered in the field must be one of the following:

■ A 16-digit number with no spaces

■ A 16-digit number with a space between every four digits

■ A 16-digit number with hyphens between every four digits

The f:validateRegex tag makes a custom validator unnecessary in this situation. However, the rest of this section describes how this validator would be implemented and how to specify a custom tag so that the page author could register the validator on a component.

15.11.1 Implementing the Validator Interface

A Validator implementation must contain a constructor, a set of accessor methods for any attributes on the tag, and a validate method, which overrides the validate method of the Validator interface.

The hypothetical FormatValidator class also defines accessor methods for setting the formatPatterns attribute, which specifies the acceptable format patterns for input into the fields. The setter method calls the parseFormatPatterns method, which separates the components of the pattern string into a string array, formatPatternsList.

```
public String getFormatPatterns() {
    return (this.formatPatterns);
}

public void setFormatPatterns(String formatPatterns) {
    this.formatPatterns = formatPatterns;
    parseFormatPatterns();
}
```

In addition to defining accessor methods for the attributes, the class overrides the validate method of the Validator interface. This method validates the input and also accesses the custom error messages to be displayed when the String is invalid.

The validate method performs the actual validation of the data. It takes the FacesContext instance, the component whose data needs to be validated, and the value that needs to be validated. A validator can validate only data of a component that implements javax.faces.component.EditableValueHolder.

Here is an implementation of the `validate` method:

```
@FacesValidator
public class FormatValidator implements Validator, StateHolder {
    ...
    public void validate(FacesContext context, UIComponent component,
                         Object toValidate) {

        boolean valid = false;
        String value = null;
        if ((context == null) || (component == null)) {
            throw new NullPointerException();
        }
        if (!(component instanceof UIInput)) {
            return;
        }
        if ( null == formatPatternsList || null == toValidate) {
            return;
        }
        value = toValidate.toString();
        // validate the value against the list of valid patterns.
        Iterator patternIt = formatPatternsList.iterator();
        while (patternIt.hasNext()) {
            valid = isFormatValid(
                ((String)patternIt.next()), value);
            if (valid) {
                break;
            }
        }
        if ( !valid ) {
            FacesMessage errMsg =
                new FacesMessage(FORMAT_INVALID_MESSAGE_ID);
            FacesContext.getCurrentInstance().addMessage(null, errMsg);
            throw new ValidatorException(errMsg);
        }
    }
}
```

The `@FacesValidator` annotation registers the `FormatValidator` class as a validator with the JavaServer Faces implementation. The `validate` method gets the local value of the component and converts it to a `String`. It then iterates over the `formatPatternsList` list, which is the list of acceptable patterns that was parsed from the `formatPatterns` attribute of the custom validator tag.

While iterating over the list, this method checks the pattern of the component's local value against the patterns in the list. If the pattern of the local value does not match any pattern in the list, this method generates an error message. It then

creates a `javax.faces.application.FacesMessage` and queues it on the
`FacesContext` for display, using a `String` that represents the key in the
`Properties` file:

```
public static final String FORMAT_INVALID_MESSAGE_ID =
    "FormatInvalid";
}
```

Finally, the method passes the message to the constructor of
`javax.faces.validator.ValidatorException`.

When the error message is displayed, the format pattern will be substituted for
the {0} in the error message, which, in English, is as follows:

```
Input must match one of the following patterns: {0}
```

You may wish to save and restore state for your validator, although state saving is
not usually necessary. To do so, you will need to implement the `StateHolder`
interface as well as the `Validator` interface. To implement `StateHolder`, you
would need to implement its four methods: `saveState(FacesContext)`,
`restoreState(FacesContext, Object)`, `isTransient`, and
`setTransient(boolean)`. See Section 15.4.5, "Saving and Restoring State," for
more information.

15.11.2 Specifying a Custom Tag

If you implemented a `Validator` interface rather than implementing a managed
bean method that performs the validation, you need to do one of the following.

- Allow the page author to specify the `Validator` implementation to use with
  the `f:validator` tag. In this case, the `Validator` implementation must define
  its own properties. Section 15.11.3, "Using a Custom Validator," explains how
  to use the `f:validator` tag.

- Specify a custom tag that provides attributes for configuring the properties of
  the validator from the page.

To create a custom tag, you need to add the tag to the tag library descriptor for the
application, `bookstore.taglib.xml`:

```
<tag>
    <tag-name>validator</tag-name>
    <validator>
        <validator-id>formatValidator</validator-id>
        <validator-class>
            dukesbookstore.validators.FormatValidator
        </validator-class>
```

```
      </validator>
  </tag>
```

The `tag-name` element defines the name of the tag as it must be used in a Facelets page. The `validator-id` element identifies the custom validator. The `validator-class` element wires the custom tag to its implementation class.

Section 15.11.3, "Using a Custom Validator," explains how to use the custom validator tag on the page.

15.11.3 Using a Custom Validator

To register a custom validator on a component, you must do one of the following.

- Nest the validator's custom tag inside the tag of the component whose value you want to be validated.

- Nest the standard `f:validator` tag within the tag of the component and reference the custom `Validator` implementation from the `f:validator` tag.

Here is a hypothetical custom `formatValidator` tag for the Credit Card Number field, nested within the `h:inputText` tag:

```
<h:inputText id="ccno" size="19"
  ...
  required="true">
  <mystore:formatValidator
   formatPatterns="9999999999999999|9999 9999 9999 9999|9999-9999-9999-9999"/>
</h:inputText>
<h:message styleClass="validationMessage" for="ccno"/>
```

This tag validates the input of the `ccno` field against the patterns defined by the page author in the `formatPatterns` attribute.

You can use the same custom validator for any similar component by simply nesting the custom validator tag within the component tag.

If the application developer who created the custom validator prefers to configure the attributes in the `Validator` implementation rather than allow the page author to configure the attributes from the page, the developer will not create a custom tag for use with the validator.

In this case, the page author must nest the `f:validator` tag inside the tag of the component whose data needs to be validated. Then the page author needs to do one of the following.

- Set the `f:validator` tag's `validatorId` attribute to the ID of the validator that is defined in the application configuration resource file.

- Bind the custom `Validator` implementation to a managed bean property using the `f:validator` tag's `binding` attribute, as described in Section 15.13, "Binding Converters, Listeners, and Validators to Managed Bean Properties."

The following tag registers a hypothetical validator on a component using an `f:validator` tag and references the ID of the validator:

```
<h:inputText id="name" value="#{CustomerBean.name}"
        size="10" ...>
    <f:validator validatorId="customValidator" />
    ...
</h:inputText>
```

15.12 Binding Component Values and Instances to Managed Bean Properties

A component tag can wire its data to a managed bean by one of the following methods:

- Binding its component's value to a bean property

- Binding its component's instance to a bean property

To bind a component's value to a managed bean property, a component tag's `value` attribute uses an EL value expression. To bind a component instance to a bean property, a component tag's `binding` attribute uses a value expression.

When a component instance is bound to a managed bean property, the property holds the component's local value. Conversely, when a component's value is bound to a managed bean property, the property holds the value stored in the managed bean. This value is updated with the local value during the Update Model Values phase of the lifecycle. There are advantages to both of these methods.

Binding a component instance to a bean property has the following advantages.

- The managed bean can programmatically modify component attributes.

- The managed bean can instantiate components rather than let the page author do so.

Binding a component's value to a bean property has the following advantages.

- The page author has more control over the component attributes.

- The managed bean has no dependencies on the JavaServer Faces API (such as the component classes), allowing for greater separation of the presentation layer from the model layer.

- The JavaServer Faces implementation can perform conversions on the data based on the type of the bean property without the developer needing to apply a converter.

In most situations, you will bind a component's value rather than its instance to a bean property. You'll need to use a component binding only when you need to change one of the component's attributes dynamically. For example, if an application renders a component only under certain conditions, it can set the component's `rendered` property accordingly by accessing the property to which the component is bound.

When referencing the property using the component tag's `value` attribute, you need to use the proper syntax. For example, suppose a managed bean called `MyBean` has this `int` property:

```
protected int currentOption = null;
public int getCurrentOption(){ ... }
public void setCurrentOption(int option){ ... }
```

The `value` attribute that references this property must have this value-binding expression:

```
#{myBean.currentOption}
```

In addition to binding a component's value to a bean property, the `value` attribute can specify a literal value or can map the component's data to any primitive (such as `int`), structure (such as an array), or collection (such as a list), independent of a JavaBeans component. Table 15–3 lists some example value-binding expressions that you can use with the `value` attribute.

Table 15–3 ***Examples of Value-Binding Expressions***

Value	Expression
A Boolean	`cart.numberOfItems > 0`
A property initialized from a context initialization parameter	`initParam.quantity`
A bean property	`cashierBean.name`
A value in an array	`books[3]`
A value in a collection	`books["fiction"]`
A property of an object in an array of objects	`books[3].price`

The next two sections explain how to use the `value` attribute to bind a component's value to a bean property or other data objects and how to use the `binding` attribute to bind a component instance to a bean property.

15.12.1 Binding a Component Value to a Property

To bind a component's value to a managed bean property, you specify the name of the bean and the property using the `value` attribute.

This means that the first part of the EL value expression must match the name of the managed bean up to the first period (`.`) and the part of the value expression after the period must match the property of the managed bean.

For example, in the Duke's Bookstore case study, the `h:dataTable` tag in `bookcatalog.xhtml` sets the value of the component to the value of the `books` property of the `BookstoreBean` backing bean, whose name is `store`:

```
<h:dataTable id="books"
             value="#{store.books}"
             var="book"
             headerClass="list-header"
             styleClass="list-background"
             rowClasses="list-row-even, list-row-odd"
             border="1"
             summary="#{bundle.BookCatalog}">
```

The value is obtained by calling the backing bean's `getBooks` method, which in turn calls the `BookRequestBean` session bean's `getBooks` method.

If you use the application configuration resource file to configure managed beans instead of defining them in managed bean classes, the name of the bean in the `value` expression must match the `managed-bean-name` element of the managed bean declaration up to the first period (`.`) in the expression. Similarly, the part of the value expression after the period must match the name specified in the corresponding `property-name` element in the application configuration resource file.

For example, consider this managed bean configuration, which configures the `ImageArea` bean corresponding to the top-left book in the image map on the `index.html` page of the Duke's Bookstore case study:

```
<managed-bean eager="true">
    ...
    <managed-bean-name>Book201</managed-bean-name>
    <managed-bean-class>dukesbookstore.model.ImageArea</managed-bean-class>
    <managed-bean-scope>application</managed-bean-scope>
    <managed-property>
```

```
      . . .
      <property-name>shape</property-name>
      <value>rect</value>
  </managed-property>
  <managed-property>
      . . .
      <property-name>alt</property-name>
      <value>Duke</value>
  </managed-property>
  . . .
```

This example configures a bean called `Book201`, which has several properties, one of which is called `shape`.

Although the `bookstore:area` tags on the `index.xhtml` page do not bind to an `ImageArea` property (they bind to the bean itself), you could refer to the property using a value expression from the `value` attribute of the component's tag:

```
<h:outputText value="#{Book201.shape}" />
```

See Section 16.4, "Configuring Managed Beans," for information on how to configure beans in the application configuration resource file.

15.12.2 Binding a Component Value to an Implicit Object

One external data source that a `value` attribute can refer to is an implicit object.

The `bookreceipt.xhtml` page of the Duke's Bookstore case study has a reference to an implicit object:

```
<h:outputFormat title="thanks"
                value="#{bundle.ThankYouParam}">
    <f:param value="#{sessionScope.name}"/>
</h:outputFormat>
```

This tag gets the name of the customer from the session scope and inserts it into the parameterized message at the key `ThankYouParam` from the resource bundle. For example, if the name of the customer is Gwen Canigetit, this tag will render:

```
Thank you, Gwen Canigetit, for purchasing your books from us.
```

Retrieving values from other implicit objects is done in a similar way to the example shown in this section. Table 15–4 lists the implicit objects to which a value attribute can refer. All of the implicit objects, except for the scope objects, are read-only and therefore should not be used as values for a `UIInput` component.

Table 15–4   Implicit Objects

Implicit Object	What It Is
applicationScope	A Map of the application scope attribute values, keyed by attribute name
cookie	A Map of the cookie values for the current request, keyed by cookie name
facesContext	The FacesContext instance for the current request
header	A Map of HTTP header values for the current request, keyed by header name
headerValues	A Map of String arrays containing all the header values for HTTP headers in the current request, keyed by header name
initParam	A Map of the context initialization parameters for this web application
param	A Map of the request parameters for this request, keyed by parameter name
paramValues	A Map of String arrays containing all the parameter values for request parameters in the current request, keyed by parameter name
requestScope	A Map of the request attributes for this request, keyed by attribute name
sessionScope	A Map of the session attributes for this request, keyed by attribute name
view	The root UIComponent in the current component tree stored in the FacesRequest for this request

15.12.3 Binding a Component Instance to a Bean Property

A component instance can be bound to a bean property using a value expression with the binding attribute of the component's tag. You usually bind a component instance rather than its value to a bean property if the bean must dynamically change the component's attributes.

Here are two tags from the bookcashier.xhtml page that bind components to bean properties:

```
<h:selectBooleanCheckbox id="fanClub"
                         rendered="false"
                         binding="#{cashierBean.specialOffer}" />
<h:outputLabel for="fanClub"
               rendered="false"
               binding="#{cashierBean.specialOfferText}"
```

```
                 value="#{bundle.DukeFanClub}"/>
</h:outputLabel>
```

The `h:selectBooleanCheckbox` tag renders a check box and binds the `fanClub` `UISelectBoolean` component to the `specialOffer` property of the `cashier` bean. The `h:outputLabel` tag binds the component representing the check box's label to the `specialOfferText` property of the `cashier` bean. If the application's locale is English, the `h:outputLabel` tag renders

```
I'd like to join the Duke Fan Club, free with my purchase of over $100
```

The `rendered` attributes of both tags are set to `false` to prevent the check box and its label from being rendered. If the customer makes a large order and clicks the **Submit** button, the `submit` method of `CashierBean` sets both components' `rendered` properties to `true`, causing the check box and its label to be rendered.

These tags use component bindings rather than value bindings because the managed bean must dynamically set the values of the components' `rendered` properties.

If the tags were to use value bindings instead of component bindings, the managed bean would not have direct access to the components and would therefore require additional code to access the components from the `FacesContext` instance to change the components' `rendered` properties.

Section 12.2.2, "Writing Properties Bound to Component Instances," explains how to write the bean properties bound to the example components.

15.13 Binding Converters, Listeners, and Validators to Managed Bean Properties

As described in Section 10.2, "Adding Components to a Page Using HTML Tag Library Tags," a page author can bind converter, listener, and validator implementations to managed bean properties using the `binding` attributes of the tags that are used to register the implementations on components.

This technique has similar advantages to binding component instances to managed bean properties, as described in Section 15.12, "Binding Component Values and Instances to Managed Bean Properties." In particular, binding a converter, listener, or validator implementation to a managed bean property yields the following benefits.

- The managed bean can instantiate the implementation instead of allowing the page author to do so.

- The managed bean can programmatically modify the attributes of the implementation. In the case of a custom implementation, the only other way to modify the attributes outside of the implementation class would be to create a custom tag for it and require the page author to set the attribute values from the page.

Whether you are binding a converter, listener, or validator to a managed bean property, the process is the same for any of the implementations.

- Nest the converter, listener, or validator tag within an appropriate component tag.

- Make sure that the managed bean has a property that accepts and returns the converter, listener, or validator implementation class that you want to bind to the property.

- Reference the managed bean property using a value expression from the binding attribute of the converter, listener, or validator tag.

For example, say that you want to bind the standard DateTime converter to a managed bean property because you want to set the formatting pattern of the user's input in the managed bean rather than on the Facelets page. First, the page registers the converter onto the component by nesting the f:convertDateTime tag within the component tag. Then, the page references the property with the binding attribute of the f:convertDateTime tag:

```
<h:inputText value="#{loginBean.birthDate}">
    <f:convertDateTime binding="#{loginBean.convertDate}" />
</h:inputText>
```

The convertDate property would look something like this:

```
private DateTimeConverter convertDate;
public DateTimeConverter getConvertDate() {
    ...
    return convertDate;
}
public void setConvertDate(DateTimeConverter convertDate) {
    convertDate.setPattern("EEEEEEE, MMM dd, yyyy");
    this.convertDate = convertDate;
}
```

See Section 12.2.3, "Writing Properties Bound to Converters, Listeners, or Validators," for more information on writing managed bean properties for converter, listener, and validator implementations.

16

Configuring JavaServer Faces Applications

The process of building and deploying simple JavaServer Faces applications is described in earlier chapters of this tutorial, including Chapter 6, "Getting Started with Web Applications," Chapter 8, "Introduction to Facelets," Chapter 13, "Using Ajax with JavaServer Faces Technology," and Chapter 14, "Composite Components: Advanced Topics and an Example." When you create large and complex applications, however, various additional configuration tasks are required. These tasks include the following:

- Registering managed beans with the application so that all parts of the application have access to them

- Configuring managed beans and model beans so that they are instantiated with the proper values when a page makes reference to them

- Defining navigation rules for each of the pages in the application so that the application has a smooth page flow, if nondefault navigation is needed

- Packaging the application to include all the pages, resources, and other files so that the application can be deployed on any compliant container

The following topics are addressed here:

- Using Annotations to Configure Managed Beans

- Application Configuration Resource File

- Using Faces Flows

- Configuring Managed Beans

- Registering Application Messages

- Using Default Validators

- Registering a Custom Validator

- Registering a Custom Converter

- Configuring Navigation Rules

- Registering a Custom Renderer with a Render Kit

- Registering a Custom Component

- Basic Requirements of a JavaServer Faces Application

16.1 Using Annotations to Configure Managed Beans

JavaServer Faces support for bean annotations is introduced in Chapter 7, "JavaServer Faces Technology." Bean annotations can be used for configuring JavaServer Faces applications.

The @Named (`javax.inject.Named`) annotation in a class, along with a scope annotation, automatically registers that class as a resource with the JavaServer Faces implementation. A bean that uses these annotations is a CDI managed bean.

The following shows the use of the @Named and @SessionScoped annotations in a class:

```
@Named("cart")
@SessionScoped
public class ShoppingCart ... { ... }
```

The above code snippet shows a bean that is managed by the JavaServer Faces implementation and is available for the length of the session.

You can annotate beans with any of the scopes listed in Section 16.1.1, "Using Managed Bean Scopes."

All classes will be scanned for annotations at startup unless the faces-config element in the faces-config.xml file has the metadata-complete attribute set to true.

Annotations are also available for other artifacts, such as components, converters, validators, and renderers, to be used in place of application configuration resource file entries. These are discussed, along with registration of custom listeners, custom validators, and custom converters, in Chapter 15, "Creating Custom UI Components and Other Custom Objects."

16.1.1 Using Managed Bean Scopes

You can use annotations to define the scope in which the bean will be stored. You can specify one of the following scopes for a bean class.

- **Application** (`javax.enterprise.context.ApplicationScoped`): Application scope persists across all users' interactions with a web application.

- **Session** (`javax.enterprise.context.SessionScoped`): Session scope persists across multiple HTTP requests in a web application.

- **Flow** (`javax.faces.flows.FlowScoped`): Flow scope persists during a user's interaction with a specific flow of a web application. See Section 16.3, "Using Faces Flows," for more information.

- **Request** (`javax.enterprise.context.RequestScoped`): Request scope persists during a single HTTP request in a web application.

- **Dependent** (`javax.enterprise.context.Dependent`): Indicates that the bean depends on some other bean.

You may want to use `@Dependent` when a managed bean references another managed bean. The second bean should not be in a scope (`@Dependent`) if it is supposed to be created only when it is referenced. If you define a bean as `@Dependent`, the bean is instantiated anew each time it is referenced, so it does not get saved in any scope.

If your managed bean is referenced by the `binding` attribute of a component tag, you should define the bean with a request scope. If you placed the bean in session or application scope instead, the bean would need to take precautions to ensure thread safety, because `javax.faces.component.UIComponent` instances each depend on running inside of a single thread.

If you are configuring a bean that allows attributes to be associated with the view, you can use the view scope. The attributes persist until the user has navigated to the next view.

16.2 Application Configuration Resource File

JavaServer Faces technology provides a portable configuration format (as an XML document) for configuring application resources. One or more XML documents, called *application configuration resource files*, may use this format to register and configure objects and resources and to define navigation rules for applications. An application configuration resource file is usually named `faces-config.xml`.

You need an application configuration resource file in the following cases:

- To specify configuration elements for your application that are not available through managed bean annotations, such as localized messages and navigation rules

- To override managed bean annotations when the application is deployed

The application configuration resource file must be valid against the XML schema located at `http://xmlns.jcp.org/xml/ns/javaee/web-facesconfig_2_2.xsd`.

In addition, each file must include the following information, in the following order:

- The XML version number, usually with an `encoding` attribute:

```
<?xml version="1.0" encoding='UTF-8'?>
```

- A `faces-config` tag enclosing all the other declarations:

```
<faces-config version="2.2" xmlns="http://xmlns.jcp.org/xml/ns/javaee"
              xmlns:xsi="http://www.w3.org/2001/XMLSchema-instance"
              xsi:schemaLocation="http://xmlns.jcp.org/xml/ns/javaee
              http://xmlns.jcp.org/xml/ns/javaee/web-facesconfig_2_2.xsd">
    ...
</faces-config>
```

You can have more than one application configuration resource file for an application. The JavaServer Faces implementation finds the configuration file or files by looking for the following.

- A resource named `/META-INF/faces-config.xml` in any of the JAR files in the web application's `/WEB-INF/lib/` directory and in parent class loaders. If a resource with this name exists, it is loaded as a configuration resource. This method is practical for a packaged library containing some components and renderers. In addition, any file with a name that ends in `faces-config.xml` is also considered a configuration resource and is loaded as such.

- A context initialization parameter, `javax.faces.application.CONFIG_FILES`, in your web deployment descriptor file that specifies one or more (comma-delimited) paths to multiple configuration files for your web application. This method is most often used for enterprise-scale applications that delegate to separate groups the responsibility for maintaining the file for each portion of a big application.

- A resource named `faces-config.xml` in the `/WEB-INF/` directory of your application. Simple web applications make their configuration files available in this way.

To access the resources registered with the application, an application developer can use an instance of the `javax.faces.application.Application` class, which is automatically created for each application. The `Application` instance acts as a centralized factory for resources that are defined in the XML file.

When an application starts up, the JavaServer Faces implementation creates a single instance of the `Application` class and configures it with the information you provided in the application configuration resource file.

16.2.1 Configuring Eager Application-Scoped Managed Beans

JavaServer Faces managed beans (either specified in the `faces-config.xml` file or annotated with `javax.faces.bean.ManagedBean`) are lazily instantiated. That is, that they are instantiated when a request is made from the application.

To force an application-scoped bean to be instantiated and placed in the application scope as soon as the application is started and before any request is made, the `eager` attribute of the managed bean should be set to `true`, as shown in the following examples.

The `faces-config.xml` file declaration is as follows:

```
<managed-bean eager="true">
```

The annotation is as follows:

```
@ManagedBean(eager=true)
@ApplicationScoped
```

16.2.2 Ordering of Application Configuration Resource Files

Because JavaServer Faces technology allows the use of multiple application configuration resource files stored in different locations, the order in which they are loaded by the implementation becomes important in certain situations (for example, when using application-level objects). This order can be defined through an `ordering` element and its subelements in the application configuration resource file itself. The ordering of application configuration resource files can be absolute or relative.

Absolute ordering is defined by an `absolute-ordering` element in the file. With absolute ordering, the user specifies the order in which application configuration resource files will be loaded. The following example shows an entry for absolute ordering.

File `my-faces-config.xml` contains the following elements:

```
<faces-config>
    <name>myJSF</name>
    <absolute-ordering>
        <name>A</name>
        <name>B</name>
        <name>C</name>
    </absolute-ordering>
</faces-config>
```

In this example, A, B, and C are different application configuration resource files and are to be loaded in the listed order.

If there is an `absolute-ordering` element in the file, only the files listed by the subelement `name` are processed. To process any other application configuration resource files, an `others` subelement is required. In the absence of the `others` subelement, all other unlisted files will be ignored at load time.

Relative ordering is defined by an `ordering` element and its subelements `before` and `after`. With relative ordering, the order in which application configuration resource files will be loaded is calculated by considering ordering entries from the different files. The following example shows some of these considerations. In the following example, `config-A`, `config-B`, and `config-C` are different application configuration resource files.

File `config-A` contains the following elements:

```
<faces-config>
    <name>config-A</name>
    <ordering>
        <before>
            <name>config-B</name>
        </before>
    </ordering>
</faces-config>
```

File `config-B` (not shown here) does not contain any `ordering` elements.

File `config-C` contains the following elements:

```
<faces-config>
    <name>config-C</name>
    <ordering>
        <after>
            <name>config-B</name>
```

```
        </after>
      </ordering>
    </faces-config>
```

Based on the before subelement entry, file config-A will be loaded before the config-B file. Based on the after subelement entry, file config-C will be loaded after the config-B file.

In addition, a subelement others can also be nested within the before and after subelements. If the others element is present, the specified file may receive highest or lowest preference among both listed and unlisted configuration files.

If an ordering element is not present in an application configuration file, then that file will be loaded after all the files that contain ordering elements.

16.3 Using Faces Flows

The Faces Flows feature of JavaServer Faces technology allows you to create a set of pages with a scope, FlowScoped, that is greater than request scope but less than session scope. For example, you might want to create a series of pages for the checkout process in an online store. You could create a set of self-contained pages that could be transferred from one store to another as needed.

Faces Flows are somewhat analogous to subroutines in procedural programming, in the following ways.

- Like a subroutine, a flow has a well defined entry point, list of parameters, and return value. However, unlike a subroutine, a flow can return multiple values.

- Like a subroutine, a flow has a scope, allowing information to be available only during the invocation of the flow. Such information is not available outside the scope of the flow and does not consume any resources once the flow returns.

- Like a subroutine, a flow may call other flows before returning. The invocation of flows is maintained in a call stack: a new flow causes a push onto the stack, and a return causes a pop.

An application can have any number of flows. Each flow includes a set of pages and, usually, one or more managed beans scoped to that flow. Each flow has a starting point, called a start node, and an exit point, called a return node.

The data in a flow is scoped to that flow alone, but you can pass data from one flow to another by specifying parameters and calling the other flow.

Flows can be nested, so that if you call one flow from another and then exit the second flow, you return to the calling flow rather than to the second flow's return node.

You can configure a flow programmatically, by creating a class annotated @FlowDefinition, or you can configure a flow by using a configuration file. The configuration file can be limited to one flow, or you can use the faces-config.xml file to put all the flows in one place, if you have many flows in an application. The programmatic configuration places the code closer to the rest of the flow code and enables you to modularize the flows.

Figure 16–1 shows two flows and illustrates how they interact.

Figure 16–1   Two Faces Flows and Their Interactions

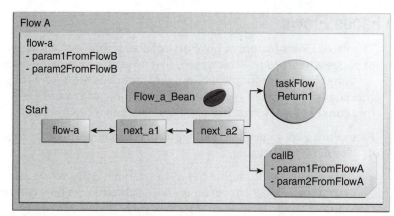

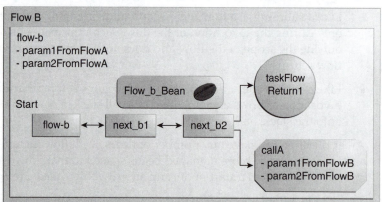

In this figure, Flow A has a start node named flow-a and two additional pages, next_a1 and next_a2. From next_a2, a user can either exit the flow using the defined return node, `taskFlowReturn1`, or call Flow B, passing two parameters. Flow A also defines two inbound parameters that it can accept from Flow B. Flow B is identical to Flow A except for the names of the flow and files. Each flow also has an associated managed bean; the beans are `Flow_a_Bean` and `Flow_b_Bean`.

16.3.1 Packaging Flows in an Application

Typically, you package flows in a web application using a directory structure that modularizes the flows. In the `src/main/webapp` directory of a Maven project, for example, you would place the Facelets files that are outside the flow at the top level as usual. Then the `webapp` files for each flow would be in a separate directory, and the Java files would be under `src/main/java`. For example, the files for the application shown in Figure 16–1 might look like this:

```
src/main/webapp/
    index.xhtml
    return.xhtml
    WEB_INF/
        beans.xml
        web.xml
    flow-a/
        flow-a.xhtml
        next_a1.xhtml
        next_a2.xhtml
    flow-b/
        flow-b-flow.xml
        next_b1.xhtml
        next_b2.xhtml
src/main/java/javaeetutorial/flowexample
            FlowA.java
            Flow_a_Bean.java
            Flow_b_Bean.java
```

In this example, `flow-a` is defined programmatically in `FlowA.java`, while `flow-b` is defined by the configuration file `flow-b-flow.xml`.

16.3.2 The Simplest Possible Flow: The simple-flow Example Application

The `simple-flow` example application demonstrates the most basic building blocks of a Faces Flows application and illustrates some of the conventions that make it easy to get started with iterative development using flows. You may want to start with a simple example like this one and build upon it.

This example provides an **implicit flow definition** by including an empty configuration file. A configuration file that has content, or a class annotated @FlowDefinition, provides an **explicit flow definition**.

The source code for this application is in the *tut-install*/examples/web/jsf/ simple-flow/ directory.

The file layout of the simple-flow example looks like this:

```
src/main/webapp
    index.xhtml
    simple-flow-return.xhtml
    WEB_INF/
        web.xml
    simple-flow
        simple-flow-flow.xml
        simple-flow.xhtml
        simple-flow-page2.xhtml
```

The simple-flow example has an empty configuration file, which is by convention named *flow-name*-flow.xml. The flow does not require any configuration for the following reasons.

- The flow does not call another flow, nor does it pass parameters to another flow.

- The flow uses default names for the first page of the flow, *flow-name*.xhtml, and the return page, *flow-name*-return.xhtml.

This example has only four Facelets pages.

- index.xhtml, the start page, which contains almost nothing but a button that navigates to the first page of the flow:

  ```
  <p><h:commandButton value="Enter Flow" action="simple-flow"/></p>
  ```

- simple-flow.xhtml and simple-flow-page2.xhtml, the two pages of the flow itself. In the absence of an explicit flow definition, the page whose name is the same as the name of the flow is assumed to be the start node of the flow. In this case, the flow is named simple-flow, so the page named simple-flow.xhtml is assumed to be the start node of the flow. The start node is the node navigated to upon entry into the flow. It can be thought of as the home page of the flow.

The `simple-flow.xhtml` page asks you to enter a flow-scoped value and provides a button that navigates to the next page of the flow:

```
<p>Value: <h:inputText id="input" value="#{flowScope.value}" /></p>

<p><h:commandButton value="Next" action="simple-flow-page2" /></p>
```

The second page, which can have any name, displays the flow-scoped value and provides a button that navigates to the return page:

```
<p>Value: #{flowScope.value}</p>

<p><h:commandButton value="Return" action="simple-flow-return" /></p>
```

- `simple-flow-return.xhtml`, the return page. The return page, which by convention is named *flow-name*`-return.xhtml`, must be located outside of the flow. This page displays the flow-scoped value, to show that it has no value outside of the flow, and provides a link that navigates to the `index.xhtml` page:

```
<p>Value (should be empty):
    "<h:outputText id="output" value="#{flowScope.value}" />"</p>

<p><h:link outcome="index" value="Back to Start" /></p>
```

The Facelets pages use only flow-scoped data, so the example does not need a managed bean.

16.3.2.1 To Build, Package, and Deploy the simple-flow Example Using NetBeans IDE

1. Make sure that GlassFish Server has been started (see Section 2.2, "Starting and Stopping GlassFish Server").

2. From the **File** menu, choose **Open Project**.

3. In the Open Project dialog box, navigate to:

   tut-install/examples/web/jsf

4. Select the `simple-flow` folder.

5. Click **Open Project**.

6. In the **Projects** tab, right-click the `simple-flow` project and select **Build**.

   This command builds and packages the application into a WAR file, `simple-flow.war`, that is located in the `target` directory. It then deploys the application to the server.

16.3.2.2 To Build, Package, and Deploy the simple-flow Example Using Maven

1. Make sure that GlassFish Server has been started (see Section 2.2, "Starting and Stopping GlassFish Server").

2. In a terminal window, go to:

   `tut-install/examples/web/jsf/simple-flow/`

3. Enter the following command:

   ```
   mvn install
   ```

   This command builds and packages the application into a WAR file, `simple-flow.war`, that is located in the `target` directory. It then deploys the application to the server.

16.3.2.3 To Run the simple-flow Example

1. Enter the following URL in your web browser:

   `http://localhost:8080/simple-flow`

2. On the `index.xhtml` page, click **Enter Flow**.

3. On the first page of the flow, enter any string in the **Value** field, then click **Next**.

4. On the second page of the flow, you can see the value you entered. Click **Return**.

5. On the return page, an empty pair of quotation marks encloses the inaccessible value. Click **Back to Start** to return to the `index.xhtml` page.

16.3.3 The checkout-module Example Application

The `checkout-module` example application is considerably more complex than `simple-flow`. It shows how you might use the Faces Flows feature to implement a checkout module for an online store.

Like the hypothetical example in Figure 16–1 on page 312, the example application contains two flows, each of which can call the other. Both flows have explicit flow definitions. One flow, `checkoutFlow`, is specified programmatically. The other flow, `joinFlow`, is specified in a configuration file.

The source code for this application is in the *tut-install*/examples/web/jsf/checkout-module/ directory.

For the `checkout-module` application, the directory structure is as follows (there is also a `src/main/webapp/resources` directory with a stylesheet and an image):

```
src/main/webapp/
    index.xhtml
    exithome.xhtml
    WEB_INF/
        beans.xml
        web.xml
    checkoutFlow/
        checkoutFlow.xhtml
        checkoutFlow2.xhtml
        checkoutFlow3.xhtml
        checkoutFlow4.xhtml
    joinFlow/
        joinFlow-flow.xml
        joinFlow.xhtml
        joinFlow2.xhtml
src/main/java/javaeetutorial/checkoutmodule
            CheckoutBean.java
            CheckoutFlow.java
            CheckoutFlowBean.java
            JoinFlowBean.java
```

For the example, `index.xhtml` is the beginning page for the application as well as the return node for the checkout flow. The `exithome.xhtml` page is the return node for the join flow.

The configuration file `joinFlow-flow.xml` defines the join flow, and the source file `CheckoutFlow.java` defines the checkout flow.

The checkout flow contains four Facelets pages, whereas the join flow contains two.

The managed beans scoped to each flow are `CheckoutFlowBean.java` and `JoinFlowBean.java`, whereas `CheckoutBean.java` is the backing bean for the `index.html` page.

16.3.3.1 The Facelets Pages for the checkout-module Example

The starting page for the example, `index.xhtml`, summarizes the contents of a hypothetical shopping cart. It allows the user to click either of two buttons to enter one of the two flows:

```
<p><h:commandButton value="Check Out" action="checkoutFlow"/></p>
...
<p><h:commandButton value="Join" action="joinFlow"/></p>
```

This page is also the return node for the checkout flow.

The Facelets page `exithome.xhtml` is the return node for the join flow. This page has a button that allows you to return to the `index.xhtml` page.

The four Facelets pages within the checkout flow, starting with `checkoutFlow.xhtml` and ending with `checkoutFlow4.xhtml`, allow you to proceed to the next page or, in some cases, to return from the flow. The `checkoutFlow.xhtml` page allows you to access parameters passed from the join flow through the flow scope. These appear as empty quotation marks if you have not called the checkout flow from the join flow.

```
<p>If you called this flow from the Join flow, you can see these parameters:
    "<h:outputText value="#{flowScope.param1Value}"/>" and
    "<h:outputText value="#{flowScope.param2Value}"/>"
</p>
```

Only `checkoutFlow2.xhtml` has a button to return to the previous page, but moving between pages is generally permitted within flows. Here are the buttons for `checkoutFlow2.xhtml`:

```
<p><h:commandButton value="Continue" action="checkoutFlow3"/></p>
<p><h:commandButton value="Go Back" action="checkoutFlow"/></p>
<p><h:commandButton value="Exit Flow" action="returnFromCheckoutFlow"/></p>
```

The action `returnFromCheckoutFlow` is defined in the configuration source code file, `CheckoutFlow.java`.

The final page of the checkout flow, `checkoutFlow4.xhtml`, contains a button that calls the join flow:

```
<p><h:commandButton value="Join" action="calljoin"/></p>
<p><h:commandButton value="Exit Flow" action="returnFromCheckoutFlow"/></p>
```

The `calljoin` action is also defined in the configuration source code file, `CheckoutFlow.java`. This action enters the join flow, passing two parameters from the checkout flow.

The two pages in the join flow, `joinFlow.xhtml` and `joinFlow2.xhtml`, are similar to those in the checkout flow. The second page has a button to call the checkout flow as well as one to return from the join flow:

```
<p><h:commandButton value="Check Out" action="callcheckoutFlow"/></p>
<p><h:commandButton value="Exit Flow" action="returnFromJoinFlow"/></p>
```

For this flow, the actions `callcheckoutFlow` and `returnFromJoinFlow` are defined in the configuration file `joinFlow-flow.xml`.

16.3.3.2 Using a Configuration File to Configure a Flow

If you use an application configuration resource file to configure a flow, it must be named *flowName*-flow.xml. In this example, the join flow uses a configuration file named joinFlow-flow.xml. The file is a faces-config file that specifies a flow-definition element. This element must define the flow name using the id attribute. Under the flow-definition element, there must be a flow-return element that specifies the return point for the flow. Any inbound parameters are specified with inbound-parameter elements. If the flow calls another flow, the call-flow element must use the flow-reference element to name the called flow and may use the outbound-parameter element to specify any outbound parameters.

The configuration file for the join flow looks like this:

```
<faces-config version="2.2" xmlns="http://xmlns.jcp.org/xml/ns/javaee"
            xmlns:xsi="http://www.w3.org/2001/XMLSchema-instance"
            xsi:schemaLocation="http://xmlns.jcp.org/xml/ns/javaee \
            http://xmlns.jcp.org/xml/ns/javaee/web-facesconfig_2_2.xsd">


    <flow-definition id="joinFlow">
        <flow-return id="returnFromJoinFlow">
            <from-outcome>#{joinFlowBean.returnValue}</from-outcome>
        </flow-return>

        <inbound-parameter>
            <name>param1FromCheckoutFlow</name>
            <value>#{flowScope.param1Value}</value>
        </inbound-parameter>
        <inbound-parameter>
            <name>param2FromCheckoutFlow</name>
            <value>#{flowScope.param2Value}</value>
        </inbound-parameter>

        <flow-call id="callcheckoutFlow">
            <flow-reference>
                <flow-id>checkoutFlow</flow-id>
            </flow-reference>
            <outbound-parameter>
                <name>param1FromJoinFlow</name>
                <value>param1 joinFlow value</value>
            </outbound-parameter>
            <outbound-parameter>
                <name>param2FromJoinFlow</name>
                <value>param2 joinFlow value</value>
            </outbound-parameter>
        </flow-call>
```

```
        </flow-definition>
    </faces-config>
```

The id attribute of the flow-definition element defines the name of the flow as joinFlow. The value of the id attribute of the flow-return element identifies the name of the return node, and its value is defined in the from-outcome element as the returnValue property of the flow-scoped managed bean for the join flow, JoinFlowBean.

The names and values of the inbound parameters are retrieved from the flow scope in order (flowScope.param1Value, flowScope.param2Value), based on the way they were defined in the checkout flow configuration.

The flow-call element defines how the join flow calls the checkout flow. The id attribute of the element, callcheckoutFlow, defines the action of calling the flow. Within the flow-call element, the flow-reference element defines the actual name of the flow to call, checkoutFlow. The outbound-parameter elements define the parameters to be passed when checkoutFlow is called. Here they are just arbitrary strings.

16.3.3.3 Using a Java Class to Configure a Flow

If you use a Java class to configure a flow, it must have the name of the flow. The class for the checkout flow is called CheckoutFlow.java.

```java
import java.io.Serializable;
import javax.enterprise.inject.Produces;
import javax.faces.flow.Flow;
import javax.faces.flow.builder.FlowBuilder;
import javax.faces.flow.builder.FlowBuilderParameter;
import javax.faces.flow.builder.FlowDefinition;

class CheckoutFlow implements Serializable {

    private static final long serialVersionUID = 1L;

    @Produces
    @FlowDefinition
    public Flow defineFlow(@FlowBuilderParameter FlowBuilder flowBuilder) {

        String flowId = "checkoutFlow";
        flowBuilder.id("", flowId);
        flowBuilder.viewNode(flowId,
                "/" + flowId + "/" + flowId + ".xhtml").
                markAsStartNode();
```

```
flowBuilder.returnNode("returnFromCheckoutFlow").
        fromOutcome("#{checkoutFlowBean.returnValue}");

flowBuilder.inboundParameter("param1FromJoinFlow",
        "#{flowScope.param1Value}");
flowBuilder.inboundParameter("param2FromJoinFlow",
        "#{flowScope.param2Value}");

flowBuilder.flowCallNode("calljoin").flowReference("", "joinFlow").
        outboundParameter("param1FromCheckoutFlow",
            "#{checkoutFlowBean.name}").
        outboundParameter("param2FromCheckoutFlow",
            "#{checkoutFlowBean.city}");
    return flowBuilder.getFlow();
    }
}
```

The class performs actions that are almost identical to those performed by the configuration file `joinFlow-flow.xml`. It contains a single method, `defineFlow`, as a producer method with the `@FlowDefinition` qualifier that returns a `javax.faces.flow.Flow` class. The `defineFlow` method takes one parameter, a `FlowBuilder` with the qualifier `@FlowBuilderParameter`, which is passed in from the JavaServer Faces implementation. The method then calls methods from the `javax.faces.flow.Builder.FlowBuilder` class to configure the flow.

First, the method defines the flow id as `checkoutFlow`. Then, it explicitly defines the start node for the flow. By default, this is the name of the flow with a `.xhtml` suffix.

The method then defines the return node similarly to the way the configuration file does. The `returnNode` method sets the name of the return node as `returnFromCheckoutFlow`, and the chained `fromOutcome` method specifies its value as the `returnValue` property of the flow-scoped managed bean for the checkout flow, `CheckoutFlowBean`.

The `inboundParameter` method sets the names and values of the inbound parameters from the join flow, which are retrieved from the flow scope in order (`flowScope.param1Value`, `flowScope.param2Value`), based on the way they were defined in the join flow configuration.

The `flowCallNode` method defines how the checkout flow calls the join flow. The argument, `calljoin`, specifies the action of calling the flow. The chained `flowReference` method defines the actual name of the flow to call, `joinFlow`, then calls `outboundParameter` methods to define the parameters to be passed when `joinFlow` is called. Here they are values from the `CheckoutFlowBean` managed bean.

Finally, the `defineFlow` method calls the `getFlow` method and returns the result.

16.3.3.4 The Flow-Scoped Managed Beans

Each of the two flows has a managed bean that defines properties for the pages within the flow. For example, the `CheckoutFlowBean` defines properties whose values are entered by the user on both the `checkoutFlow.xhtml` page and the `checkoutFlow3.xhtml` page.

Each managed bean has a `getReturnValue` method that sets the value of the return node. For the `CheckoutFlowBean`, the return node is the `index.xhtml` page, specified using implicit navigation:

```
public String getReturnValue() {
    return "index";
}
```

For the `JoinFlowBean`, the return node is the `exithome.xhtml` page.

16.3.3.5 To Build, Package, and Deploy the checkout-module Example Using NetBeans IDE

1. Make sure that GlassFish Server has been started (see Section 2.2, "Starting and Stopping GlassFish Server").

2. From the **File** menu, choose **Open Project**.

3. In the Open Project dialog box, navigate to:

   tut-install/examples/web/jsf

4. Select the `checkout-module` folder.

5. Click **Open Project**.

6. In the **Projects** tab, right-click the `checkout-module` project and select **Build**.

   This command builds and packages the application into a WAR file, `checkout-module.war`, that is located in the `target` directory. It then deploys the application to the server.

16.3.3.6 To Build, Package, and Deploy the checkout-module Example Using Maven

1. Make sure that GlassFish Server has been started (see Section 2.2, "Starting and Stopping GlassFish Server").

2. In a terminal window, go to:

   `tut-install/examples/web/jsf/checkout-module/`

3. Enter the following command:

   `mvn install`

   This command builds and packages the application into a WAR file, `checkout-module.war`, that is located in the `target` directory. It then deploys the application to the server.

16.3.3.7 To Run the checkout-module Example

1. Enter the following URL in your web browser:

   `http://localhost:8080/checkout-module`

2. The `index.xhtml` page presents hypothetical results of the shopping expedition. Click either **Check Out** or **Join** to enter one of the two flows.

3. Follow the flow, providing input as needed and choosing whether to continue, go back, or exit the flow.

   In the checkout flow, only one of the input fields is validated (the credit card field expects 16 digits), so you can enter any values you like. The join flow does not require you to check any boxes in its checkbox menus.

4. On the last page of a flow, select the option to enter the other flow. This allows you to view the inbound parameters from the previous flow.

5. Because flows are nested, if you click **Exit Flow** from a called flow, you will return to the first page of the calling flow. (You may see a warning, which you can ignore.) Click **Exit Flow** on that page to go to the specified return node.

16.4 Configuring Managed Beans

When a page references a managed bean for the first time, the JavaServer Faces implementation initializes it either based on a @Named annotation and scope annotation in the bean class or according to its configuration in the application configuration resource file. For information on using annotations to initialize beans, see Section 16.1, "Using Annotations to Configure Managed Beans."

You can use either annotations or the application configuration resource file to instantiate managed beans that are used in a JavaServer Faces application and to store them in scope. The managed bean creation facility is configured in the application configuration resource file using `managed-bean` XML elements to define each bean. This file is processed at application startup time. For information on using this facility, see Section 16.4.1, "Using the managed-bean Element."

Managed beans created in the application configuration resource file are JavaServer Faces managed beans, not CDI managed beans.

With the managed bean creation facility, you can

- Create beans in one centralized file that is available to the entire application, rather than conditionally instantiate beans throughout the application

- Customize a bean's properties without any additional code

- Customize a bean's property values directly from within the configuration file so that it is initialized with these values when it is created

- Using `value` elements, set a property of one managed bean to be the result of evaluating another value expression

This section shows you how to initialize beans using the managed bean creation facility. See Section 12.2, "Writing Bean Properties," and Section 12.3, "Writing Managed Bean Methods," for information on programming managed beans.

16.4.1 Using the managed-bean Element

A managed bean is initiated in the application configuration resource file using a `managed-bean` element, which represents an instance of a bean class that must exist in the application. At runtime, the JavaServer Faces implementation processes the `managed-bean` element. If a page references the bean and no bean instance exists, the JavaServer Faces implementation instantiates the bean as specified by the element configuration.

Here is a managed bean configuration from the Duke's Bookstore case study (see Chapter 28, "Duke's Bookstore Case Study Example," in *The Java EE 7 Tutorial, Volume 2*):

```
<managed-bean eager="true">
    <managed-bean-name>Book201</managed-bean-name>
    <managed-bean-class>dukesbookstore.model.ImageArea</managed-bean-class>
    <managed-bean-scope>application</managed-bean-scope>
    <managed-property>
        <property-name>shape</property-name>
        <value>rect</value>
    </managed-property>
    <managed-property>
        <property-name>alt</property-name>
        <value>Duke</value>
```

```
        </managed-property>
        <managed-property>
            <property-name>coords</property-name>
            <value>67,23,212,268</value>
        </managed-property>
</managed-bean>
```

The `managed-bean-name` element defines the key under which the bean will be stored in a scope. For a component's value to map to this bean, the component tag's `value` attribute must match the `managed-bean-name` up to the first period.

The `managed-bean-class` element defines the fully qualified name of the JavaBeans component class used to instantiate the bean.

The `managed-bean` element can contain zero or more `managed-property` elements, each corresponding to a property defined in the bean class. These elements are used to initialize the values of the bean properties. If you don't want a particular property initialized with a value when the bean is instantiated, do not include a `managed-property` definition for it in your application configuration resource file.

If a `managed-bean` element does not contain other `managed-bean` elements, it can contain one `map-entries` element or `list-entries` element. The `map-entries` element configures a set of beans that are instances of `Map`. The `list-entries` element configures a set of beans that are instances of `List`.

In the following example, the `newsletters` managed bean, representing a `UISelectItems` component, is configured as an `ArrayList` that represents a set of `SelectItem` objects. Each `SelectItem` object is in turn configured as a managed bean with properties:

```
<managed-bean>
    <managed-bean-name>newsletters</managed-bean-name>
    <managed-bean-class>java.util.ArrayList</managed-bean-class>
    <managed-bean-scope>application</managed-bean-scope>
    <list-entries>
        <value-class>javax.faces.model.SelectItem</value-class>
        <value>#{newsletter0}</value>
        <value>#{newsletter1}</value>
        <value>#{newsletter2}</value>
        <value>#{newsletter3}</value>
    </list-entries>
</managed-bean>
<managed-bean>
    <managed-bean-name>newsletter0</managed-bean-name>
    <managed-bean-class>javax.faces.model.SelectItem</managed-bean-class>
    <managed-bean-scope>none</managed-bean-scope>
    <managed-property>
```

```
                <property-name>label</property-name>
                <value>Duke's Quarterly</value>
        </managed-property>
        <managed-property>
                <property-name>value</property-name>
                <value>200</value>
        </managed-property>
</managed-bean>
...
```

This approach may be useful for quick-and-dirty creation of selection item lists before a development team has had time to create such lists from the database. Note that each of the individual newsletter beans has a `managed-bean-scope` setting of `none` so that they will not themselves be placed into any scope.

See Section 16.4.2.4, "Initializing Array and List Properties," for more information on configuring collections as beans.

To map to a property defined by a `managed-property` element, you must ensure that the part of a component tag's `value` expression after the period matches the `managed-property` element's `property-name` element. Section 16.4.2, "Initializing Properties Using the managed-property Element," explains in more detail how to use the `managed-property` element. See Section 16.4.2.5, "Initializing Managed Bean Properties," for an example of initializing a managed bean property.

16.4.2 Initializing Properties Using the managed-property Element

A `managed-property` element must contain a `property-name` element, which must match the name of the corresponding property in the bean. A `managed-property` element must also contain one of a set of elements that defines the value of the property. This value must be of the same type as that defined for the property in the corresponding bean. Which element you use to define the value depends on the type of the property defined in the bean. Table 16–1 lists all the elements that are used to initialize a value.

Table 16–1 **Subelements of managed-property Elements That Define Property Values**

Element	Value It Defines
list-entries	Defines the values in a list
map-entries	Defines the values of a map
null-value	Explicitly sets the property to null
value	Defines a single value, such as a String, int, or JavaServer Faces EL expression

Section 16.4.1, "Using the managed-bean Element," includes an example of initializing an int property (a primitive type) using the value subelement. You also use the value subelement to initialize String and other reference types. The rest of this section describes how to use the value subelement and other subelements to initialize properties of Java Enum types, Map, array, and Collection, as well as initialization parameters.

16.4.2.1 Referencing a Java Enum Type

A managed bean property can also be a Java Enum type (see http://docs.oracle.com/javase/7/docs/api/java/lang/Enum.html). In this case, the value element of the managed-property element must be a String that matches one of the String constants of the Enum. In other words, the String must be one of the valid values that can be returned if you were to call valueOf(Class, String) on enum, where Class is the Enum class and String is the contents of the value subelement. For example, suppose the managed bean property is the following:

```
public enum Suit { Hearts, Spades, Diamonds, Clubs }
...
public Suit getSuit() { ... return Suit.Hearts; }
```

Assuming you want to configure this property in the application configuration resource file, the corresponding managed-property element looks like this:

```
<managed-property>
    <property-name>Suit</property-name>
    <value>Hearts</value>
</managed-property>
```

When the system encounters this property, it iterates over each of the members of the enum and calls toString() on each member until it finds one that is exactly equal to the value from the value element.

16.4.2.2 Referencing a Context Initialization Parameter

Another powerful feature of the managed bean creation facility is the ability to reference implicit objects from a managed bean property.

Suppose you have a page that accepts data from a customer, including the customer's address. Suppose also that most of your customers live in a particular area code. You can make the area code component render this area code by saving it in an implicit object and referencing it when the page is rendered.

You can save the area code as an initial default value in the context initParam implicit object by adding a context parameter to your web application and setting its value in the deployment descriptor. For example, to set a context parameter called `defaultAreaCode` to 650, add a `context-param` element to the deployment descriptor and give the parameter the name `defaultAreaCode` and the value 650.

Next, write a `managed-bean` declaration that configures a property that references the parameter:

```
<managed-bean>
    <managed-bean-name>customer</managed-bean-name>
        <managed-bean-class>CustomerBean</managed-bean-class>
        <managed-bean-scope>request</managed-bean-scope>
        <managed-property>
            <property-name>areaCode</property-name>
                <value>#{initParam.defaultAreaCode}</value>
            </managed-property>
            ...
</managed-bean>
```

To access the area code at the time the page is rendered, refer to the property from the `area` component tag's `value` attribute:

```
<h:inputText id=area value="#{customer.areaCode}"
```

Values are retrieved from other implicit objects in a similar way.

16.4.2.3 Initializing Map Properties

The `map-entries` element is used to initialize the values of a bean property with a type of `Map` if the `map-entries` element is used within a `managed-property` element. A `map-entries` element contains an optional `key-class` element, an optional `value-class` element, and zero or more `map-entry` elements.

Each of the `map-entry` elements must contain a `key` element and either a `null-value` or `value` element. Here is an example that uses the `map-entries` element:

```
<managed-bean>
    ...
    <managed-property>
        <property-name>prices</property-name>
        <map-entries>
            <map-entry>
                <key>My Early Years: Growing Up on *7</key>
                <value>30.75</value>
            </map-entry>
            <map-entry>
                <key>Web Servers for Fun and Profit</key>
                <value>40.75</value>
```

```
            </map-entry>
        </map-entries>
    </managed-property>
</managed-bean>
```

The map created from this `map-entries` tag contains two entries. By default, all the keys and values are converted to `String`. If you want to specify a different type for the keys in the map, embed the `key-class` element just inside the `map-entries` element:

```
<map-entries>
    <key-class>java.math.BigDecimal</key-class>
    ...
</map-entries>
```

This declaration will convert all the keys into `java.math.BigDecimal`. Of course, you must make sure that the keys can be converted to the type you specify. The key from the example in this section cannot be converted to a `BigDecimal`, because it is a `String`.

If you want to specify a different type for all the values in the map, include the `value-class` element after the `key-class` element:

```
<map-entries>
    <key-class>int</key-class>
    <value-class>java.math.BigDecimal</value-class>
    ...
</map-entries>
```

Note that this tag sets only the type of all the `value` subelements.

Each `map-entry` in the preceding example includes a `value` subelement. The `value` subelement defines a single value, which will be converted to the type specified in the bean.

Instead of using a `map-entries` element, it is also possible to assign the entire map using a `value` element that specifies a map-typed expression.

16.4.2.4 Initializing Array and List Properties

The `list-entries` element is used to initialize the values of an array or `List` property. Each individual value of the array or `List` is initialized using a `value` or `null-value` element. Here is an example:

```
<managed-bean>
    ...
    <managed-property>
        <property-name>books</property-name>
```

```
        <list-entries>
            <value-class>java.lang.String</value-class>
            <value>Web Servers for Fun and Profit</value>
            <value>#{myBooks.bookId[3]}</value>
            <null-value/>
        </list-entries>
    </managed-property>
</managed-bean>
```

This example initializes an array or a List. The type of the corresponding property in the bean determines which data structure is created. The list-entries element defines the list of values in the array or List. The value element specifies a single value in the array or List and can reference a property in another bean. The null-value element will cause the setBooks method to be called with an argument of null. A null property cannot be specified for a property whose data type is a Java primitive, such as int or boolean.

16.4.2.5 Initializing Managed Bean Properties

Sometimes you might want to create a bean that also references other managed beans so that you can construct a graph or a tree of beans. For example, suppose you want to create a bean representing a customer's information, including the mailing address and street address, each of which is also a bean. The following managed-bean declarations create a CustomerBean instance that has two AddressBean properties: one representing the mailing address and the other representing the street address. This declaration results in a tree of beans with CustomerBean as its root and the two AddressBean objects as children.

```
<managed-bean>
    <managed-bean-name>customer</managed-bean-name>
    <managed-bean-class>
        com.example.mybeans.CustomerBean
    </managed-bean-class>
    <managed-bean-scope> request </managed-bean-scope>
    <managed-property>
        <property-name>mailingAddress</property-name>
        <value>#{addressBean}</value>
    </managed-property>
    <managed-property>
        <property-name>streetAddress</property-name>
        <value>#{addressBean}</value>
    </managed-property>
    <managed-property>
        <property-name>customerType</property-name>
        <value>New</value>
    </managed-property>
```

```
</managed-bean>
<managed-bean>
    <managed-bean-name>addressBean</managed-bean-name>
    <managed-bean-class>
        com.example.mybeans.AddressBean
    </managed-bean-class>
    <managed-bean-scope> none </managed-bean-scope>
    <managed-property>
        <property-name>street</property-name>
        <null-value/>
    <managed-property>
    ...
</managed-bean>
```

The first `CustomerBean` declaration (with the `managed-bean-name` of `customer`) creates a `CustomerBean` in request scope. This bean has two properties, `mailingAddress` and `streetAddress`. These properties use the `value` element to reference a bean named `addressBean`.

The second managed bean declaration defines an `AddressBean` but does not create it, because its `managed-bean-scope` element defines a scope of `none`. Recall that a scope of `none` means that the bean is created only when something else references it. Because both the `mailingAddress` and the `streetAddress` properties reference `addressBean` using the `value` element, two instances of `AddressBean` are created when `CustomerBean` is created.

When you create an object that points to other objects, do not try to point to an object with a shorter life span, because it might be impossible to recover that scope's resources when it goes away. A session-scoped object, for example, cannot point to a request-scoped object. And objects with `none` scope have no effective life span managed by the framework, so they can point only to other `none`-scoped objects. Table 16–2 outlines all of the allowed connections.

Table 16–2   Allowable Connections between Scoped Objects

An Object of This Scope	May Point to an Object of This Scope
none	none
application	none, application
session	none, application, session
request	none, application, session, request, view
view	none, application, session, view

Be sure not to allow cyclical references between objects. For example, neither of the AddressBean objects in the preceding example should point back to the CustomerBean object, because CustomerBean already points to the AddressBean objects.

16.4.3 Initializing Maps and Lists

In addition to configuring Map and List properties, you can also configure a Map and a List directly so that you can reference them from a tag rather than referencing a property that wraps a Map or a List.

16.5 Registering Application Messages

Application messages can include any strings displayed to the user as well as custom error messages (which are displayed by the message and messages tags) for your custom converters or validators. To make messages available at application startup time, do one of the following:

- Queue an individual message onto the javax.faces.context.FacesContext instance programmatically, as described in Section 16.5.1, "Using FacesMessage to Create a Message"

- Register all the messages with your application using the application configuration resource file

Here is the section of the faces-config.xml file that registers the messages for the Duke's Bookstore case study application:

```
<application>
    <resource-bundle>
        <base-name>
            javaeetutorial.dukesbookstore.web.messages.Messages
        </base-name>
        <var>bundle</var>
    </resource-bundle>
    <locale-config>
        <default-locale>en</default-locale>
        <supported-locale>es</supported-locale>
        <supported-locale>de</supported-locale>
        <supported-locale>fr</supported-locale>
    </locale-config>
</application>
```

This set of elements causes the application to be populated with the messages that are contained in the specified resource bundle.

The `resource-bundle` element represents a set of localized messages. It must contain the fully qualified path to the resource bundle containing the localized messages (in this case, `dukesbookstore.web.messages.Messages`). The `var` element defines the EL name by which page authors refer to the resource bundle.

The `locale-config` element lists the default locale and the other supported locales. The `locale-config` element enables the system to find the correct locale based on the browser's language settings.

The `supported-locale` and `default-locale` tags accept the lowercase, two-character codes defined by ISO 639-1 (see `http://www.loc.gov/standards/iso639-2/php/English_list.php`). Make sure that your resource bundle actually contains the messages for the locales you specify with these tags.

To access the localized message, the application developer merely references the key of the message from the resource bundle.

You can pull localized text into an `alt` tag for a graphic image, as in the following example:

```
<h:graphicImage id="mapImage"
                name="book_all.jpg"
                library="images"
                alt="#{bundle.ChooseBook}"
                usemap="#bookMap" />
```

The `alt` attribute can accept value expressions. In this case, the `alt` attribute refers to localized text that will be included in the alternative text of the image rendered by this tag.

16.5.1 Using FacesMessage to Create a Message

Instead of registering messages in the application configuration resource file, you can access the `java.util.ResourceBundle` directly from managed bean code. The code snippet below locates an email error message:

```
String message = "";
...
message = ExampleBean.loadErrorMessage(context,
    ExampleBean.EX_RESOURCE_BUNDLE_NAME,
        "EMailError");
context.addMessage(toValidate.getClientId(context),
    new FacesMessage(message));
```

These lines call the bean's `loadErrorMessage` method to get the message from the ResourceBundle. Here is the `loadErrorMessage` method:

```
public static String loadErrorMessage(FacesContext context,
    String basename, String key) {
  if ( bundle == null ) {
      try {
         bundle = ResourceBundle.getBundle(basename,
               context.getViewRoot().getLocale());
      } catch (Exception e) {
         return null;
      }
  }
  return bundle.getString(key);
}
```

16.5.2 Referencing Error Messages

A JavaServer Faces page uses the `message` or `messages` tags to access error messages, as explained in Section 10.2.13, "Displaying Error Messages with the h:message and h:messages Tags."

The error messages these tags access include

- The standard error messages that accompany the standard converters and validators that ship with the API (see Section 2.5.2.4 of the JavaServer Faces specification for a complete list of standard error messages)

- Custom error messages contained in resource bundles registered with the application by the application architect using the `resource-bundle` element in the configuration file

When a converter or validator is registered on an input component, the appropriate error message is automatically queued on the component.

A page author can override the error messages queued on a component by using the following attributes of the component's tag:

- `converterMessage`: References the error message to display when the data on the enclosing component cannot be converted by the converter registered on this component

- `requiredMessage`: References the error message to display when no value has been entered into the enclosing component

- `validatorMessage`: References the error message to display when the data on the enclosing component cannot be validated by the validator registered on this component

All three attributes are enabled to take literal values and value expressions. If an attribute uses a value expression, this expression references the error message in a resource bundle. This resource bundle must be made available to the application in one of the following ways:

- By the application architect using the `resource-bundle` element in the configuration file

- By the page author using the `f:loadBundle` tag

Conversely, the `resource-bundle` element must be used to make available to the application those resource bundles containing custom error messages that are queued on the component as a result of a custom converter or validator being registered on the component.

The following tags show how to specify the `requiredMessage` attribute using a value expression to reference an error message:

```
<h:inputText id="ccno" size="19"
    required="true"
    requiredMessage="#{customMessages.ReqMessage}">
    ...
</h:inputText>
<h:message styleClass="error-message" for="ccno"/>
```

The value expression used by `requiredMessage` in this example references the error message with the `ReqMessage` key in the resource bundle `customMessages`.

This message replaces the corresponding message queued on the component and will display wherever the `message` or `messages` tag is placed on the page.

16.6 Using Default Validators

In addition to the validators you declare on the components, you can also specify zero or more default validators in the application configuration resource file. The default validator applies to all `javax.faces.component.UIInput` instances in a view or component tree and is appended after the local defined validators. Here is an example of a default validator registered in the application configuration resource file:

```
<faces-config>
    <application>
        <default-validators>
            <validator-id>javax.faces.Bean</validator-id>
        </default-validators>
    <application/>
</faces-config>
```

16.7 Registering a Custom Validator

If the application developer provides an implementation of the
javax.faces.validator.Validator interface to perform validation, you must
register this custom validator either by using the @FacesValidator annotation, as
described in Section 15.11.1, "Implementing the Validator Interface," or by using
the validator XML element in the application configuration resource file:

```
<validator>
    ...
    <validator-id>FormatValidator</validator-id>
    <validator-class>
        myapplication.validators.FormatValidator
    </validator-class>
    <attribute>
        ...
        <attribute-name>formatPatterns</attribute-name>
        <attribute-class>java.lang.String</attribute-class>
    </attribute>
</validator>
```

Attributes specified in a validator tag override any settings in the
@FacesValidator annotation.

The validator-id and validator-class elements are required subelements. The
validator-id element represents the identifier under which the Validator class
should be registered. This ID is used by the tag class corresponding to the custom
validator tag.

The validator-class element represents the fully qualified class name of the
Validator class.

The attribute element identifies an attribute associated with the Validator
implementation. It has required attribute-name and attribute-class
subelements. The attribute-name element refers to the name of the attribute as it
appears in the validator tag. The attribute-class element identifies the Java
type of the value associated with the attribute.

Section 15.11, "Creating and Using a Custom Validator," explains how to
implement the Validator interface.

Section 15.11.3, "Using a Custom Validator," explains how to reference the
validator from the page.

16.8 Registering a Custom Converter

As is the case with a custom validator, if the application developer creates a custom converter, you must register it with the application either by using the @FacesConverter annotation, as described in Section 15.10.1, "Creating a Custom Converter," or by using the converter XML element in the application configuration resource file. Here is a hypothetical converter configuration for CreditCardConverter from the Duke's Bookstore case study:

```
<converter>
    <description>
        Converter for credit card numbers that normalizes
        the input to a standard format
    </description>
    <converter-id>CreditCardConverter</converter-id>
    <converter-class>
        dukesbookstore.converters.CreditCardConverter
    </converter-class>
</converter>
```

Attributes specified in a converter tag override any settings in the @FacesConverter annotation.

The converter element represents a javax.faces.convert.Converter implementation and contains required converter-id and converter-class elements.

The converter-id element identifies an ID that is used by the converter attribute of a UI component tag to apply the converter to the component's data. Section 15.10.2, "Using a Custom Converter," includes an example of referencing the custom converter from a component tag.

The converter-class element identifies the Converter implementation.

Section 15.10, "Creating and Using a Custom Converter," explains how to create a custom converter.

16.9 Configuring Navigation Rules

Navigation between different pages of a JavaServer Faces application, such as choosing the next page to be displayed after a button or link component is clicked, is defined by a set of rules. Navigation rules can be implicit, or they can be explicitly defined in the application configuration resource file. For more information on implicit navigation rules, see Section 7.5, "Navigation Model."

Each navigation rule specifies how to navigate from one page to another page or set of pages. The JavaServer Faces implementation chooses the proper navigation rule according to which page is currently displayed.

After the proper navigation rule is selected, the choice of which page to access next from the current page depends on two factors:

- The action method invoked when the component was clicked
- The logical outcome referenced by the component's tag or returned from the action method

The outcome can be anything the developer chooses, but Table 16–3 lists some outcomes commonly used in web applications.

Table 16–3 **Common Outcome Strings**

Outcome	What It Means
success	Everything worked. Go on to the next page.
failure	Something is wrong. Go on to an error page.
login	The user needs to log in first. Go on to the login page.
no results	The search did not find anything. Go to the search page again.

Usually, the action method performs some processing on the form data of the current page. For example, the method might check whether the user name and password entered in the form match the user name and password on file. If they match, the method returns the outcome success. Otherwise, it returns the outcome failure. As this example demonstrates, both the method used to process the action and the outcome returned are necessary to determine the correct page to access.

Here is a navigation rule that could be used with the example just described:

```
<navigation-rule>
    <from-view-id>/login.xhtml</from-view-id>
    <navigation-case>
        <from-action>#{LoginForm.login}</from-action>
        <from-outcome>success</from-outcome>
        <to-view-id>/storefront.xhtml</to-view-id>
    </navigation-case>
    <navigation-case>
        <from-action>#{LoginForm.logon}</from-action>
        <from-outcome>failure</from-outcome>
        <to-view-id>/logon.xhtml</to-view-id>
```

```
    </navigation-case>
</navigation-rule>
```

This navigation rule defines the possible ways to navigate from `login.xhtml`. Each `navigation-case` element defines one possible navigation path from `login.xhtml`. The first `navigation-case` says that if `LoginForm.login` returns an outcome of `success`, then `storefront.xhtml` will be accessed. The second `navigation-case` says that `login.xhtml` will be re-rendered if `LoginForm.login` returns `failure`.

The configuration of an application's page flow consists of a set of navigation rules. Each rule is defined by the `navigation-rule` element in the `faces-config.xml` file.

Each `navigation-rule` element corresponds to one component tree identifier defined by the optional `from-view-id` element. This means that each rule defines all the possible ways to navigate from one particular page in the application. If there is no `from-view-id` element, the navigation rules defined in the `navigation-rule` element apply to all the pages in the application. The `from-view-id` element also allows wildcard matching patterns. For example, this `from-view-id` element says that the navigation rule applies to all the pages in the `books` directory:

```
<from-view-id>/books/*</from-view-id>
```

A `navigation-rule` element can contain zero or more `navigation-case` elements. The `navigation-case` element defines a set of matching criteria. When these criteria are satisfied, the application will navigate to the page defined by the `to-view-id` element contained in the same `navigation-case` element.

The navigation criteria are defined by optional `from-outcome` and `from-action` elements. The `from-outcome` element defines a logical outcome, such as `success`. The `from-action` element uses a method expression to refer to an action method that returns a `String`, which is the logical outcome. The method performs some logic to determine the outcome and returns the outcome.

The `navigation-case` elements are checked against the outcome and the method expression in the following order.

1. Cases specifying both a `from-outcome` value and a `from-action` value. Both of these elements can be used if the action method returns different outcomes depending on the result of the processing it performs.

2. Cases specifying only a `from-outcome` value. The `from-outcome` element must match either the outcome defined by the `action` attribute of the `javax.faces.component.UICommand` component or the outcome returned by the method referred to by the `UICommand` component.

3. Cases specifying only a `from-action` value. This value must match the `action` expression specified by the component tag.

When any of these cases is matched, the component tree defined by the `to-view-id` element will be selected for rendering.

16.10 Registering a Custom Renderer with a Render Kit

When the application developer creates a custom renderer, as described in Section 15.5, "Delegating Rendering to a Renderer," you must register it using the appropriate render kit. Because the image map application implements an HTML image map, the `AreaRenderer` and `MapRenderer` classes in the Duke's Bookstore case study should be registered using the HTML render kit.

You register the renderer either by using the `@FacesRenderer` annotation, as described in Section 15.5.1, "Creating the Renderer Class," or by using the `render-kit` element of the application configuration resource file. Here is a hypothetical configuration of `AreaRenderer`:

```
<render-kit>
    <renderer>
        <component-family>Area</component-family>
        <renderer-type>DemoArea</renderer-type>
        <renderer-class>
            dukesbookstore.renderers.AreaRenderer
        </renderer-class>
        <attribute>
            <attribute-name>onmouseout</attribute-name>
            <attribute-class>java.lang.String</attribute-class>
        </attribute>
        <attribute>
            <attribute-name>onmouseover</attribute-name>
            <attribute-class>java.lang.String</attribute-class>
        </attribute>
        <attribute>
            <attribute-name>styleClass</attribute-name>
            <attribute-class>java.lang.String</attribute-class>
        </attribute>
    </renderer>
    ...
```

Attributes specified in a `renderer` tag override any settings in the `@FacesRenderer` annotation.

The `render-kit` element represents a javax.faces.render.RenderKit implementation. If no `render-kit-id` is specified, the default HTML render kit is assumed. The `renderer` element represents a `javax.faces.render.Renderer` implementation. By nesting the `renderer` element inside the `render-kit` element, you are registering the renderer with the `RenderKit` implementation associated with the `render-kit` element.

The `renderer-class` is the fully qualified class name of the `Renderer`.

The `component-family` and `renderer-type` elements are used by a component to find renderers that can render it. The `component-family` identifier must match that returned by the component class's `getFamily` method. The component family represents a component or set of components that a particular renderer can render. The `renderer-type` must match that returned by the `getRendererType` method of the tag handler class.

By using the component family and renderer type to look up renderers for components, the JavaServer Faces implementation allows a component to be rendered by multiple renderers and allows a renderer to render multiple components.

Each of the `attribute` tags specifies a render-dependent attribute and its type. The `attribute` element doesn't affect the runtime execution of your application. Rather, it provides information to tools about the attributes the `Renderer` supports.

The object responsible for rendering a component (be it the component itself or a renderer to which the component delegates the rendering) can use facets to aid in the rendering process. These facets allow the custom component developer to control some aspects of rendering the component. Consider this custom component tag example:

```
<d:dataScroller>
    <f:facet name="header">
        <h:panelGroup>
            <h:outputText value="Account Id"/>
            <h:outputText value="Customer Name"/>
            <h:outputText value="Total Sales"/>
        </h:panelGroup>
    </f:facet>
    <f:facet name="next">
        <h:panelGroup>
            <h:outputText value="Next"/>
            <h:graphicImage url="/images/arrow-right.gif" />
        </h:panelGroup>
    </f:facet>
    ...
</d:dataScroller>
```

The dataScroller component tag includes a component that will render the header and a component that will render the **Next** button. If the renderer associated with this component renders the facets, you can include the following facet elements in the renderer element:

```
<facet>
    <description>This facet renders as the header of the table. It should be
        a panelGroup with the same number of columns as the data.
    </description>
    <display-name>header</display-name>
    <facet-name>header</facet-name>
</facet>
<facet>
    <description>This facet renders as the content of the "next" button in
        the scroller. It should be a panelGroup that includes an outputText
        tag that has the text "Next" and a right arrow icon.
    </description>
    <display-name>Next</display-name>
    <facet-name>next</facet-name>
</facet>
```

If a component that supports facets provides its own rendering and you want to include facet elements in the application configuration resource file, you need to put them in the component's configuration rather than the renderer's configuration.

16.11 Registering a Custom Component

In addition to registering custom renderers (as explained in the preceding section), you also must register the custom components that are usually associated with the custom renderers. You use either a @FacesComponent annotation, as described in Section 15.4, "Creating Custom Component Classes," or the component element of the application configuration resource file.

Here is a hypothetical component element from the application configuration resource file that registers AreaComponent:

```
<component>
    <component-type>DemoArea</component-type>
    <component-class>
        dukesbookstore.components.AreaComponent
    </component-class>
    <property>
        <property-name>alt</property-name>
        <property-class>java.lang.String</property-class>
    </property>
```

```
<property>
    <property-name>coords</property-name>
    <property-class>java.lang.String</property-class>
</property>
<property>
    <property-name>shape</property-name>
    <property-class>java.lang.String</property-class>
</property>
</component>
```

Attributes specified in a `component` tag override any settings in the `@FacesComponent` annotation.

The `component-type` element indicates the name under which the component should be registered. Other objects referring to this component use this name. For example, the `component-type` element in the configuration for `AreaComponent` defines a value of `DemoArea`, which matches the value returned by the `AreaTag` class's `getComponentType` method.

The `component-class` element indicates the fully qualified class name of the component. The `property` elements specify the component properties and their types.

If the custom component can include facets, you can configure the facets in the component configuration using `facet` elements, which are allowed after the `component-class` elements. See Section 16.10, "Registering a Custom Renderer with a Render Kit," for further details on configuring facets.

16.12 Basic Requirements of a JavaServer Faces Application

In addition to configuring your application, you must satisfy other requirements of JavaServer Faces applications, including properly packaging all the necessary files and providing a deployment descriptor. This section describes how to perform these administrative tasks.

JavaServer Faces applications can be packaged in a WAR file, which must conform to specific requirements to execute across different containers. At a minimum, a WAR file for a JavaServer Faces application may contain the following:

- A web application deployment descriptor, called `web.xml`, to configure resources required by a web application (required)

- A specific set of JAR files containing essential classes (optional)

- A set of application classes, JavaServer Faces pages, and other required resources, such as image files

A WAR file may also contain:

- An application configuration resource file, which configures application resources

- A set of tag library descriptor files

For example, a Java Server Faces web application WAR file using Facelets typically has the following directory structure:

```
$PROJECT_DIR
[Web Pages]
+- /[xhtml or html documents]
+- /resources
+- /WEB-INF
   +- /web.xml
   +- /beans.xml (optional)
   +- /classes (optional)
   +- /lib (optional)
   +- /faces-config.xml (optional)
   +- /*.taglib.xml (optional)
   +- /glassfish-web.xml (optional)
```

The web.xml file (or web deployment descriptor), the set of JAR files, and the set of application files must be contained in the WEB-INF directory of the WAR file.

16.12.1 Configuring an Application with a Web Deployment Descriptor

Web applications are commonly configured using elements contained in the web application deployment descriptor, web.xml. The deployment descriptor for a JavaServer Faces application must specify certain configurations, including the following:

- The servlet used to process JavaServer Faces requests

- The servlet mapping for the processing servlet

- The path to the configuration resource file, if it exists and is not located in a default location

The deployment descriptor can also include other, optional configurations, such as those that

- Specify where component state is saved

- Encrypt state saved on the client

- Compress state saved on the client

- Restrict access to pages containing JavaServer Faces tags

- Turn on XML validation

- Specify the Project Stage

- Verify custom objects

This section gives more details on these configurations. Where appropriate, it also describes how you can make these configurations using NetBeans IDE.

16.12.1.1 Identifying the Servlet for Lifecycle Processing

A requirement of a JavaServer Faces application is that all requests to the application that reference previously saved JavaServer Faces components must go through `javax.faces.webapp.FacesServlet`. A `FacesServlet` instance manages the request-processing lifecycle for web applications and initializes the resources required by JavaServer Faces technology.

Before a JavaServer Faces application can launch its first web page, the web container must invoke the `FacesServlet` instance in order for the application lifecycle process to start. See Section 7.6, "The Lifecycle of a JavaServer Faces Application," for more information.

The following example shows the default configuration of the `FacesServlet`:

```
<servlet>
    <servlet-name>Faces Servlet</servlet-name>
    <servlet-class>javax.faces.webapp.FacesServlet</servlet-class>
</servlet>
```

You will provide a mapping configuration entry to make sure that the `FacesServlet` instance is invoked. The mapping to `FacesServlet` can be a prefix mapping, such as `/faces/*`, or an extension mapping, such as `*.xhtml`. The mapping is used to identify a page as having JavaServer Faces content. Because of this, the URL to the first page of the application must include the URL pattern mapping.

The following elements specify a prefix mapping:

```
<servlet-mapping>
    <servlet-name>Faces Servlet</servlet-name>
    <url-pattern>/faces/*</url-pattern>
</servlet-mapping>
...
<welcome-file-list>
    <welcome-file>faces/greeting.xhtml</welcome-file>
</welcome-file-list>
```

The following elements, used in the tutorial examples, specify an extension mapping:

```
<servlet-mapping>
    <servlet-name>Faces Servlet</servlet-name>
    <url-pattern>*.xhtml</url-pattern>
</servlet-mapping>
...
<welcome-file-list>
    <welcome-file>index.xhtml</welcome-file>
</welcome-file-list>
```

When you use this mechanism, users access the application as shown in the following example:

```
http://localhost:8080/guessNumber
```

In the case of extension mapping, if a request comes to the server for a page with an .xhtml extension, the container will send the request to the FacesServlet instance, which will expect a corresponding page of the same name containing the content to exist.

If you are using NetBeans IDE to create your application, a web deployment descriptor is automatically created for you with default configurations. If you created your application without an IDE, you can create a web deployment descriptor.

16.12.1.2 To Specify a Path to an Application Configuration Resource File

As explained in Section 16.2, "Application Configuration Resource File," an application can have multiple application configuration resource files. If these files are not located in the directories that the implementation searches by default or the files are not named faces-config.xml, you need to specify paths to these files.

To specify these paths using NetBeans IDE, do the following.

1. Expand the node of your project in the **Projects** tab.

2. Expand the **Web Pages** and **WEB-INF** nodes that are under the project node.

3. Double-click web.xml.

4. After the web.xml file appears in the editor, click **General** at the top of the editor window.

5. Expand the **Context Parameters** node.

6. Click **Add**.

7. In the Add Context Parameter dialog box:

    a. Enter `javax.faces.CONFIG_FILES` in the **Parameter Name** field.

    b. Enter the path to your configuration file in the **Parameter Value** field.

    c. Click **OK**.

8. Repeat steps 1 through 7 for each configuration file.

16.12.1.3 To Specify Where State Is Saved

For all the components in a web application, you can specify in your deployment descriptor where you want the state to be saved, on either client or server. You do this by setting a context parameter in your deployment descriptor. By default, state is saved on the server, so you need to specify this context parameter only if you want to save state on the client. See Section 15.4.5, "Saving and Restoring State," for information on the advantages and disadvantages of each location.

To specify where state is saved using NetBeans IDE, do the following.

1. Expand the node of your project in the **Projects** tab.

2. Expand the **Web Pages** and **WEB-INF** nodes under the project node.

3. Double-click `web.xml`.

4. After the `web.xml` file appears in the editor window, click **General** at the top of the editor window.

5. Expand the **Context Parameters** node.

6. Click **Add**.

7. In the Add Context Parameter dialog box:

    a. Enter `javax.faces.STATE_SAVING_METHOD` in the **Parameter Name** field.

    b. Enter `client` or `server` in the **Parameter Value** field.

    c. Click **OK**.

If state is saved on the client, the state of the entire view is rendered to a hidden field on the page. The JavaServer Faces implementation saves the state on the server by default. The Duke's Forest case study saves its state on the client. (See Chapter 30, "Duke's Forest Case Study Example," in *The Java EE 7 Tutorial, Volume 2*.)

16.12.2 Configuring Project Stage

Project Stage is a context parameter identifying the status of a JavaServer Faces application in the software lifecycle. The stage of an application can affect the behavior of the application. For example, error messages can be displayed during the Development stage but suppressed during the Production stage.

The possible Project Stage values are as follows:

- Development

- UnitTest

- SystemTest

- Production

Project Stage is configured through a context parameter in the web deployment descriptor file. Here is an example:

```
<context-param>
    <param-name>javax.faces.PROJECT_STAGE</param-name>
    <param-value>Development</param-value>
</context-param>
```

If no Project Stage is defined, the default stage is Production. You can also add custom stages according to your requirements.

16.12.3 Including the Classes, Pages, and Other Resources

When packaging web applications using the included build scripts, you'll notice that the scripts package resources in the following ways.

- All web pages are placed at the top level of the WAR file.

- The faces-config.xml file and the web.xml file are packaged in the WEB-INF directory.

- All packages are stored in the WEB-INF/classes/ directory.

- All application JAR files are packaged in the WEB-INF/lib/ directory.

- All resource files are either under the root of the web application /resources directory or in the web application's classpath, the META-INF/resources/ *resourceIdentifier* directory. For more information on resources, see Section 8.6, "Web Resources."

When packaging your own applications, you can use NetBeans IDE or you can use XML files such as those created for Maven. You can modify the XML files to fit your situation. However, you can continue to package your WAR files by using the directory structure described in this section, because this technique complies with the commonly accepted practice for packaging web applications.

17

Java Servlet Technology

Java Servlet technology provides dynamic, user-oriented content in web applications using a request-response programming model.

The following topics are addressed here:

- What Is a Servlet?
- Servlet Lifecycle
- Sharing Information
- Creating and Initializing a Servlet
- Writing Service Methods
- Filtering Requests and Responses
- Invoking Other Web Resources
- Accessing the Web Context
- Maintaining Client State
- Finalizing a Servlet
- Uploading Files with Java Servlet Technology
- Asynchronous Processing
- Nonblocking I/O
- Protocol Upgrade Processing
- The mood Example Application
- The fileupload Example Application

- The dukeetf Example Application

- Further Information about Java Servlet Technology

17.1 What Is a Servlet?

A servlet is a Java programming language class used to extend the capabilities of servers that host applications accessed by means of a request-response programming model. Although servlets can respond to any type of request, they are commonly used to extend the applications hosted by web servers. For such applications, Java Servlet technology defines HTTP-specific servlet classes.

The javax.servlet and javax.servlet.http packages provide interfaces and classes for writing servlets. All servlets must implement the Servlet interface, which defines lifecycle methods. When implementing a generic service, you can use or extend the GenericServlet class provided with the Java Servlet API. The HttpServlet class provides methods, such as doGet and doPost, for handling HTTP-specific services.

17.2 Servlet Lifecycle

The lifecycle of a servlet is controlled by the container in which the servlet has been deployed. When a request is mapped to a servlet, the container performs the following steps.

1. If an instance of the servlet does not exist, the web container:

   a. Loads the servlet class

   b. Creates an instance of the servlet class

   c. Initializes the servlet instance by calling the init method (initialization is covered in Section 17.4, "Creating and Initializing a Servlet")

2. The container invokes the service method, passing request and response objects. Service methods are discussed in Section 17.5, "Writing Service Methods."

If it needs to remove the servlet, the container finalizes the servlet by calling the servlet's destroy method. For more information, see Section 17.10, "Finalizing a Servlet."

17.2.1 Handling Servlet Lifecycle Events

You can monitor and react to events in a servlet's lifecycle by defining listener objects whose methods get invoked when lifecycle events occur. To use these listener objects, you must define and specify the listener class.

17.2.1.1 Defining the Listener Class

You define a listener class as an implementation of a listener interface. Table 17–1 lists the events that can be monitored and the corresponding interface that must be implemented. When a listener method is invoked, it is passed an event that contains information appropriate to the event. For example, the methods in the `HttpSessionListener` interface are passed an `HttpSessionEvent`, which contains an `HttpSession`.

Table 17–1   Servlet Lifecycle Events

Object	Event	Listener Interface and Event Class
Web context	Initialization and destruction	`javax.servlet.ServletContextListener` and `ServletContextEvent`
Web context	Attribute added, removed, or replaced	`javax.servlet.ServletContextAttributeListener` and `ServletContextAttributeEvent`
Session	Creation, invalidation, activation, passivation, and timeout	`javax.servlet.http.HttpSessionListener`, `javax.servlet.http.HttpSessionActivationListener`, and `HttpSessionEvent`
Session	Attribute added, removed, or replaced	`javax.servlet.http.HttpSessionAttributeListener` and `HttpSessionBindingEvent`
Request	A servlet request has started being processed by web components	`javax.servlet.ServletRequestListener` and `ServletRequestEvent`
Request	Attribute added, removed, or replaced	`javax.servlet.ServletRequestAttributeListener` and `ServletRequestAttributeEvent`

Use the `@WebListener` annotation to define a listener to get events for various operations on the particular web application context. Classes annotated with `@WebListener` must implement one of the following interfaces:

```
javax.servlet.ServletContextListener
javax.servlet.ServletContextAttributeListener
javax.servlet.ServletRequestListener
javax.servlet.ServletRequestAttributeListener
```

```
javax.servlet..http.HttpSessionListener
javax.servlet..http.HttpSessionAttributeListener
```

For example, the following code snippet defines a listener that implements two of these interfaces:

```
import javax.servlet.ServletContextAttributeListener;
import javax.servlet.ServletContextListener;
import javax.servlet.annotation.WebListener;

@WebListener()
public class SimpleServletListener implements ServletContextListener,
        ServletContextAttributeListener {
    ...
```

17.2.2 Handling Servlet Errors

Any number of exceptions can occur when a servlet executes. When an exception occurs, the web container generates a default page containing the following message:

```
A Servlet Exception Has Occurred
```

But you can also specify that the container should return a specific error page for a given exception.

17.3 Sharing Information

Web components, like most objects, usually work with other objects to accomplish their tasks. Web components can do so by doing the following.

- Using private helper objects (for example, JavaBeans components).

- Sharing objects that are attributes of a public scope.

- Using a database.

- Invoking other web resources. The Java Servlet technology mechanisms that allow a web component to invoke other web resources are described in Section 17.7, "Invoking Other Web Resources."

17.3.1 Using Scope Objects

Collaborating web components share information by means of objects that are maintained as attributes of four scope objects. You access these attributes by using the getAttribute and setAttribute methods of the class representing the scope. Table 17–2 lists the scope objects.

Table 17–2   *Scope Objects*

Scope Object	Class	Accessible From
Web context	`javax.servlet.ServletContext`	Web components within a web context. See Section 17.8, "Accessing the Web Context."
Session	`javax.servlet.http.HttpSession`	Web components handling a request that belongs to the session. See Section 17.9, "Maintaining Client State."
Request	Subtype of `javax.servlet.ServletRequest`	Web components handling the request.
Page	`javax.servlet.jsp.JspContext`	The JSP page that creates the object.

17.3.2 Controlling Concurrent Access to Shared Resources

In a multithreaded server, shared resources can be accessed concurrently. In addition to scope object attributes, shared resources include in-memory data, such as instance or class variables, and external objects, such as files, database connections, and network connections.

Concurrent access can arise in several situations.

- Multiple web components accessing objects stored in the web context.

- Multiple web components accessing objects stored in a session.

- Multiple threads within a web component accessing instance variables. A web container will typically create a thread to handle each request. To ensure that a servlet instance handles only one request at a time, a servlet can implement the SingleThreadModel interface. If a servlet implements this interface, no two threads will execute concurrently in the servlet's service method. A web container can implement this guarantee by synchronizing access to a single instance of the servlet or by maintaining a pool of web component instances and dispatching each new request to a free instance. This interface does not prevent synchronization problems that result from web components' accessing shared resources, such as static class variables or external objects.

When resources can be accessed concurrently, they can be used in an inconsistent fashion. You prevent this by controlling the access using the synchronization techniques described in the Threads lesson at `http://docs.oracle.com/javase/tutorial/essential/concurrency/`.

17.4 Creating and Initializing a Servlet

Use the `@WebServlet` annotation to define a servlet component in a web application. This annotation is specified on a class and contains metadata about the servlet being declared. The annotated servlet must specify at least one URL pattern. This is done by using the `urlPatterns` or `value` attribute on the annotation. All other attributes are optional, with default settings. Use the `value` attribute when the only attribute on the annotation is the URL pattern; otherwise, use the `urlPatterns` attribute when other attributes are also used.

Classes annotated with `@WebServlet` must extend the `javax.servlet.http.HttpServlet` class. For example, the following code snippet defines a servlet with the URL pattern `/report`:

```
import javax.servlet.annotation.WebServlet;
import javax.servlet.http.HttpServlet;

@WebServlet("/report")
public class MoodServlet extends HttpServlet {
    ...
```

The web container initializes a servlet after loading and instantiating the servlet class and before delivering requests from clients. To customize this process to allow the servlet to read persistent configuration data, initialize resources, and perform any other one-time activities, you can either override the `init` method of the `Servlet` interface or specify the `initParams` attribute of the `@WebServlet` annotation. The `initParams` attribute contains a `@WebInitParam` annotation. If it cannot complete its initialization process, a servlet throws an `UnavailableException`.

Use an initialization parameter to provide data needed by a particular servlet. By contrast, a context parameter provides data that is available to all components of a web application.

17.5 Writing Service Methods

The service provided by a servlet is implemented in the `service` method of a `GenericServlet`, in the do*Method* methods (where *Method* can take the value `Get`, `Delete`, `Options`, `Post`, `Put`, or `Trace`) of an `HttpServlet` object, or in any other protocol-specific methods defined by a class that implements the `Servlet` interface. The term **service method** is used for any method in a servlet class that provides a service to a client.

The general pattern for a service method is to extract information from the request, access external resources, and then populate the response, based on that information. For HTTP servlets, the correct procedure for populating the response is to do the following:

1. Retrieve an output stream from the response.

2. Fill in the response headers.

3. Write any body content to the output stream.

Response headers must always be set before the response has been committed. The web container will ignore any attempt to set or add headers after the response has been committed. The next two sections describe how to get information from requests and generate responses.

17.5.1 Getting Information from Requests

A request contains data passed between a client and the servlet. All requests implement the ServletRequest interface. This interface defines methods for accessing the following information:

- Parameters, which are typically used to convey information between clients and servlets

- Object-valued attributes, which are typically used to pass information between the web container and a servlet or between collaborating servlets

- Information about the protocol used to communicate the request and about the client and server involved in the request

- Information relevant to localization

You can also retrieve an input stream from the request and manually parse the data. To read character data, use the BufferedReader object returned by the request's getReader method. To read binary data, use the ServletInputStream returned by getInputStream.

HTTP servlets are passed an HTTP request object, HttpServletRequest, which contains the request URL, HTTP headers, query string, and so on. An HTTP request URL contains the following parts:

```
http://[host]:[port][request-path]?[query-string]
```

The request path is further composed of the following elements.

- **Context path**: A concatenation of a forward slash (/) with the context root of the servlet's web application.

- **Servlet path**: The path section that corresponds to the component alias that activated this request. This path starts with a forward slash (/).

- **Path info**: The part of the request path that is not part of the context path or the servlet path.

You can use the getContextPath, getServletPath, and getPathInfo methods of the HttpServletRequest interface to access this information. Except for URL encoding differences between the request URI and the path parts, the request URI is always comprised of the context path plus the servlet path plus the path info.

Query strings are composed of a set of parameters and values. Individual parameters are retrieved from a request by using the getParameter method. There are two ways to generate query strings.

- A query string can explicitly appear in a web page.
- A query string is appended to a URL when a form with a GET HTTP method is submitted.

17.5.2 Constructing Responses

A response contains data passed between a server and the client. All responses implement the ServletResponse interface. This interface defines methods that allow you to do the following.

- Retrieve an output stream to use to send data to the client. To send character data, use the PrintWriter returned by the response's getWriter method. To send binary data in a Multipurpose Internet Mail Extensions (MIME) body response, use the ServletOutputStream returned by getOutputStream. To mix binary and text data, as in a multipart response, use a ServletOutputStream and manage the character sections manually.

- Indicate the content type (for example, text/html) being returned by the response with the setContentType(String) method. This method must be called before the response is committed. A registry of content type names is kept by the Internet Assigned Numbers Authority (IANA) at http://www.iana.org/assignments/media-types/.

- Indicate whether to buffer output with the setBufferSize(int) method. By default, any content written to the output stream is immediately sent to the client. Buffering allows content to be written before anything is sent back to the client, thus providing the servlet with more time to set appropriate status codes and headers or forward to another web resource. The method must be called before any content is written or before the response is committed.

- Set localization information, such as locale and character encoding. See Chapter 20, "Internationalizing and Localizing Web Applications," for details.

HTTP response objects, `javax.servlet.http.HttpServletResponse`, have fields representing HTTP headers, such as the following.

- Status codes, which are used to indicate the reason a request is not satisfied or that a request has been redirected.

- Cookies, which are used to store application-specific information at the client. Sometimes, cookies are used to maintain an identifier for tracking a user's session (see Section 17.9.4, "Session Tracking").

17.6 Filtering Requests and Responses

A **filter** is an object that can transform the header and content (or both) of a request or response. Filters differ from web components in that filters usually do not themselves create a response. Instead, a filter provides functionality that can be "attached" to any kind of web resource. Consequently, a filter should not have any dependencies on a web resource for which it is acting as a filter; this way, it can be composed with more than one type of web resource.

The main tasks that a filter can perform are as follows.

- Query the request and act accordingly.

- Block the request-and-response pair from passing any further.

- Modify the request headers and data. You do this by providing a customized version of the request.

- Modify the response headers and data. You do this by providing a customized version of the response.

- Interact with external resources.

Applications of filters include authentication, logging, image conversion, data compression, encryption, tokenizing streams, XML transformations, and so on.

You can configure a web resource to be filtered by a chain of zero, one, or more filters in a specific order. This chain is specified when the web application containing the component is deployed and is instantiated when a web container loads the component.

17.6.1 Programming Filters

The filtering API is defined by the `Filter`, `FilterChain`, and `FilterConfig` interfaces in the `javax.servlet` package. You define a filter by implementing the `Filter` interface.

Use the @WebFilter annotation to define a filter in a web application. This annotation is specified on a class and contains metadata about the filter being declared. The annotated filter must specify at least one URL pattern. This is done by using the urlPatterns or value attribute on the annotation. All other attributes are optional, with default settings. Use the value attribute when the only attribute on the annotation is the URL pattern; use the urlPatterns attribute when other attributes are also used.

Classes annotated with the @WebFilter annotation must implement the javax.servlet.Filter interface.

To add configuration data to the filter, specify the initParams attribute of the @WebFilter annotation. The initParams attribute contains a @WebInitParam annotation. The following code snippet defines a filter, specifying an initialization parameter:

```
import javax.servlet.Filter;
import javax.servlet.annotation.WebFilter;
import javax.servlet.annotation.WebInitParam;

@WebFilter(filterName = "TimeOfDayFilter",
urlPatterns = {"/*"},
initParams = {
    @WebInitParam(name = "mood", value = "awake")})
public class TimeOfDayFilter implements Filter {
    ...
```

The most important method in the Filter interface is doFilter, which is passed request, response, and filter chain objects. This method can perform the following actions.

■   Examine the request headers.

■   Customize the request object if the filter wishes to modify request headers or data.

■   Customize the response object if the filter wishes to modify response headers or data.

■   Invoke the next entity in the filter chain. If the current filter is the last filter in the chain that ends with the target web component or static resource, the next entity is the resource at the end of the chain; otherwise, it is the next filter that was configured in the WAR. The filter invokes the next entity by calling the doFilter method on the chain object, passing in the request and response it was called with or the wrapped versions it may have created. Alternatively, the filter can choose to block the request by not making the call to invoke the next entity. In the latter case, the filter is responsible for filling out the response.

- Examine response headers after invoking the next filter in the chain.

- Throw an exception to indicate an error in processing.

In addition to doFilter, you must implement the init and destroy methods. The init method is called by the container when the filter is instantiated. If you wish to pass initialization parameters to the filter, you retrieve them from the FilterConfig object passed to init.

17.6.2 Programming Customized Requests and Responses

There are many ways for a filter to modify a request or a response. For example, a filter can add an attribute to the request or can insert data in the response.

A filter that modifies a response must usually capture the response before it is returned to the client. To do this, you pass a stand-in stream to the servlet that generates the response. The stand-in stream prevents the servlet from closing the original response stream when it completes and allows the filter to modify the servlet's response.

To pass this stand-in stream to the servlet, the filter creates a response wrapper that overrides the getWriter or getOutputStream method to return this stand-in stream. The wrapper is passed to the doFilter method of the filter chain. Wrapper methods default to calling through to the wrapped request or response object.

To override request methods, you wrap the request in an object that extends either ServletRequestWrapper or HttpServletRequestWrapper. To override response methods, you wrap the response in an object that extends either ServletResponseWrapper or HttpServletResponseWrapper.

17.6.3 Specifying Filter Mappings

A web container uses filter mappings to decide how to apply filters to web resources. A filter mapping matches a filter to a web component by name or to web resources by URL pattern. The filters are invoked in the order in which filter mappings appear in the filter mapping list of a WAR. You specify a filter mapping list for a WAR in its deployment descriptor by either using NetBeans IDE or coding the list by hand with XML.

If you want to log every request to a web application, you map the hit counter filter to the URL pattern /*.

You can map a filter to one or more web resources, and you can map more than one filter to a web resource. This is illustrated in Figure 17–1, in which filter F1 is mapped to servlets S1, S2, and S3; filter F2 is mapped to servlet S2; and filter F3 is mapped to servlets S1 and S2.

Figure 17–1   Filter-to-Servlet Mapping

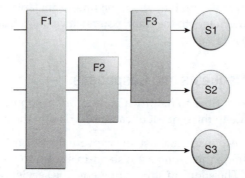

Recall that a filter chain is one of the objects passed to the doFilter method of a filter. This chain is formed indirectly by means of filter mappings. The order of the filters in the chain is the same as the order in which filter mappings appear in the web application deployment descriptor.

When a filter is mapped to servlet S1, the web container invokes the doFilter method of F1. The doFilter method of each filter in S1's filter chain is invoked by the preceding filter in the chain by means of the chain.doFilter method. Because S1's filter chain contains filters F1 and F3, F1's call to chain.doFilter invokes the doFilter method of filter F3. When F3's doFilter method completes, control returns to F1's doFilter method.

17.6.3.1 To Specify Filter Mappings Using NetBeans IDE

1. Expand the application's project node in the **Project** tab.

2. Expand the **Web Pages** and **WEB-INF** nodes under the project node.

3. Double-click web.xml.

4. Click **Filters** at the top of the editor window.

5. Expand the **Servlet Filters** node in the editor window.

6. Click **Add Filter Element** to map the filter to a web resource by name or by URL pattern.

7. In the Add Servlet Filter dialog box, enter the name of the filter in the **Filter Name** field.

8. Click **Browse** to locate the servlet class to which the filter applies.

   You can include wildcard characters so that you can apply the filter to more than one servlet.

9. Click **OK**.

10. To constrain how the filter is applied to requests, follow these steps.

    a. Expand the **Filter Mappings** node.

    b. Select the filter from the list of filters.

    c. Click **Add**.

    d. In the Add Filter Mapping dialog box, select one of the following dispatcher types:

       – **REQUEST**: Only when the request comes directly from the client

       – **ASYNC**: Only when the asynchronous request comes from the client

       – **FORWARD**: Only when the request has been forwarded to a component (see Section 17.7.2, "Transferring Control to Another Web Component")

       – **INCLUDE**: Only when the request is being processed by a component that has been included (see Section 17.7.1, "Including Other Resources in the Response")

       – **ERROR**: Only when the request is being processed with the error page mechanism (see Section 17.2.2, "Handling Servlet Errors")

    You can direct the filter to be applied to any combination of the preceding situations by selecting multiple dispatcher types. If no types are specified, the default option is **REQUEST**.

17.7 Invoking Other Web Resources

Web components can invoke other web resources both indirectly and directly. A web component indirectly invokes another web resource by embedding a URL that points to another web component in content returned to a client. While it is executing, a web component directly invokes another resource by either including the content of another resource or forwarding a request to another resource.

To invoke a resource available on the server that is running a web component, you must first obtain a RequestDispatcher object by using the getRequestDispatcher("URL") method. You can get a RequestDispatcher object from either a request or the web context; however, the two methods have slightly different behavior. The method takes the path to the requested resource as an argument. A request can take a relative path (that is, one that does not begin with a /), but the web context requires an absolute path. If the resource is not available or if the server has not implemented a RequestDispatcher object for that type of resource, getRequestDispatcher will return null. Your servlet should be prepared to deal with this condition.

17.7.1 Including Other Resources in the Response

It is often useful to include another web resource, such as banner content or copyright information, in the response returned from a web component. To include another resource, invoke the include method of a RequestDispatcher object:

```
include(request, response);
```

If the resource is static, the include method enables programmatic server-side includes. If the resource is a web component, the effect of the method is to send the request to the included web component, execute the web component, and then include the result of the execution in the response from the containing servlet. An included web component has access to the request object but is limited in what it can do with the response object.

- It can write to the body of the response and commit a response.

- It cannot set headers or call any method, such as setCookie, that affects the headers of the response.

17.7.2 Transferring Control to Another Web Component

In some applications, you might want to have one web component do preliminary processing of a request and have another component generate the response. For example, you might want to partially process a request and then transfer to another component, depending on the nature of the request.

To transfer control to another web component, you invoke the forward method of a RequestDispatcher. When a request is forwarded, the request URL is set to the path of the forwarded page. The original URI and its constituent parts are saved as the following request attributes:

- javax.servlet.forward.request_uri

- javax.servlet.forward.context_path

- `javax.servlet.forward.servlet_path`
- `javax.servlet.forward.path_info`
- `javax.servlet.forward.query_string`

The `forward` method should be used to give another resource responsibility for replying to the user. If you have already accessed a `ServletOutputStream` or `PrintWriter` object within the servlet, you cannot use this method; doing so throws an `IllegalStateException`.

17.8 Accessing the Web Context

The context in which web components execute is an object that implements the `ServletContext` interface. You retrieve the web context by using the `getServletContext` method. The web context provides methods for accessing

- Initialization parameters
- Resources associated with the web context
- Object-valued attributes
- Logging capabilities

The counter's access methods are synchronized to prevent incompatible operations by servlets that are running concurrently. A filter retrieves the counter object by using the context's `getAttribute` method. The incremented value of the counter is recorded in the log.

17.9 Maintaining Client State

Many applications require that a series of requests from a client be associated with one another. For example, a web application can save the state of a user's shopping cart across requests. Web-based applications are responsible for maintaining such state, called a **session**, because HTTP is stateless. To support applications that need to maintain state, Java Servlet technology provides an API for managing sessions and allows several mechanisms for implementing sessions.

17.9.1 Accessing a Session

Sessions are represented by an `HttpSession` object. You access a session by calling the `getSession` method of a request object. This method returns the current session associated with this request; or, if the request does not have a session, this method creates one.

17.9.2 Associating Objects with a Session

You can associate object-valued attributes with a session by name. Such attributes are accessible by any web component that belongs to the same web context *and* is handling a request that is part of the same session.

Recall that your application can notify web context and session listener objects of servlet lifecycle events (Section 17.2.1, "Handling Servlet Lifecycle Events"). You can also notify objects of certain events related to their association with a session, such as the following.

- When the object is added to or removed from a session. To receive this notification, your object must implement the `javax.servlet.http.HttpSessionBindingListener` interface.

- When the session to which the object is attached will be passivated or activated. A session will be passivated or activated when it is moved between virtual machines or saved to and restored from persistent storage. To receive this notification, your object must implement the `javax.servlet.http.HttpSessionActivationListener` interface.

17.9.3 Session Management

Because an HTTP client has no way to signal that it no longer needs a session, each session has an associated timeout so that its resources can be reclaimed. The timeout period can be accessed by using a session's `getMaxInactiveInterval` and `setMaxInactiveInterval` methods.

- To ensure that an active session is not timed out, you should periodically access the session by using service methods because this resets the session's time-to-live counter.

- When a particular client interaction is finished, you use the session's `invalidate` method to invalidate a session on the server side and remove any session data.

17.9.3.1 To Set the Timeout Period Using NetBeans IDE

To set the timeout period in the deployment descriptor using NetBeans IDE, follow these steps.

1. Open the project if you haven't already.

2. Expand the node of your project in the **Projects** tab.

3. Expand the **Web Pages** and **WEB-INF** nodes that are under the project node.

4. Double-click `web.xml`.

5. Click **General** at the top of the editor.

6. In the **Session Timeout** field, enter an integer value.

   The integer value represents the number of minutes of inactivity that must pass before the session times out.

17.9.4 Session Tracking

To associate a session with a user, a web container can use several methods, all of which involve passing an identifier between the client and the server. The identifier can be maintained on the client as a cookie, or the web component can include the identifier in every URL that is returned to the client.

If your application uses session objects, you must ensure that session tracking is enabled by having the application rewrite URLs whenever the client turns off cookies. You do this by calling the response's encodeURL(URL) method on all URLs returned by a servlet. This method includes the session ID in the URL only if cookies are disabled; otherwise, the method returns the URL unchanged.

17.10 Finalizing a Servlet

The web container may determine that a servlet should be removed from service (for example, when a container wants to reclaim memory resources or when it is being shut down). In such a case, the container calls the destroy method of the Servlet interface. In this method, you release any resources the servlet is using and save any persistent state. The destroy method releases the database object created in the init method.

A servlet's service methods should all be complete when a servlet is removed. The server tries to ensure this by calling the destroy method only after all service requests have returned or after a server-specific grace period, whichever comes first. If your servlet has operations that may run longer than the server's grace period, the operations could still be running when destroy is called. You must make sure that any threads still handling client requests complete.

The remainder of this section explains how to do the following.

- Keep track of how many threads are currently running the service method.

- Provide a clean shutdown by having the destroy method notify long-running threads of the shutdown and wait for them to complete.

- Have the long-running methods poll periodically to check for shutdown and, if necessary, stop working, clean up, and return.

17.10.1 Tracking Service Requests

To track service requests, include in your servlet class a field that counts the number of service methods that are running. The field should have synchronized access methods to increment, decrement, and return its value:

```
public class ShutdownExample extends HttpServlet {
    private int serviceCounter = 0;
    ...
    // Access methods for serviceCounter
    protected synchronized void enteringServiceMethod() {
        serviceCounter++;
    }
    protected synchronized void leavingServiceMethod() {
        serviceCounter--;
    }
    protected synchronized int numServices() {
        return serviceCounter;
    }
}
```

The service method should increment the service counter each time the method is entered and should decrement the counter each time the method returns. This is one of the few times that your HttpServlet subclass should override the service method. The new method should call super.service to preserve the functionality of the original service method:

```
protected void service(HttpServletRequest req,
                        HttpServletResponse resp)
                        throws ServletException,IOException {
    enteringServiceMethod();
    try {
        super.service(req, resp);
    } finally {
        leavingServiceMethod();
    }
}
```

17.10.2 Notifying Methods to Shut Down

To ensure a clean shutdown, your destroy method should not release any shared resources until all the service requests have completed. One part of doing this is to check the service counter. Another part is to notify long-running methods that it is time to shut down. For this notification, another field is required. The field should have the usual access methods:

```
public class ShutdownExample extends HttpServlet {
    private boolean shuttingDown;
    ...
    //Access methods for shuttingDown
    protected synchronized void setShuttingDown(boolean flag) {
        shuttingDown = flag;
    }
    protected synchronized boolean isShuttingDown() {
        return shuttingDown;
    }
}
```

Here is an example of the destroy method using these fields to provide a clean shutdown:

```
public void destroy() {
    /* Check to see whether there are still service methods /*
    /* running, and if there are, tell them to stop. */
    if (numServices()> 0) {
        setShuttingDown(true);
    }

    /* Wait for the service methods to stop. */
    while (numServices()> 0) {
        try {
            Thread.sleep(interval);
        } catch (InterruptedException e) {
        }
    }
}
```

17.10.3 Creating Polite Long-Running Methods

The final step in providing a clean shutdown is to make any long-running methods behave politely. Methods that might run for a long time should check the value of the field that notifies them of shutdowns and should interrupt their work, if necessary:

```
public void doPost(...) {
    ...
    for(i = 0; ((i < lotsOfStuffToDo) &&
        !isShuttingDown()); i++) {
        try {
            partOfLongRunningOperation(i);
```

```
                    } catch (InterruptedException e) {
                        ...
                    }
                }
            }
```

17.11 Uploading Files with Java Servlet Technology

Supporting file uploads is a very basic and common requirement for many web applications. In prior versions of the Servlet specification, implementing file upload required the use of external libraries or complex input processing. The Java Servlet specification now helps to provide a viable solution to the problem in a generic and portable way. Java Servlet technology now supports file upload out of the box, so any web container that implements the specification can parse multipart requests and make mime attachments available through the HttpServletRequest object.

A new annotation, javax.servlet.annotation.MultipartConfig, is used to indicate that the servlet on which it is declared expects requests to be made using the multipart/form-data MIME type. Servlets that are annotated with @MultipartConfig can retrieve the Part components of a given multipart/form-data request by calling the request.getPart(String name) or request.getParts() method.

17.11.1 The @MultipartConfig Annotation

The @MultipartConfig annotation supports the following optional attributes.

- location: An absolute path to a directory on the file system. The location attribute does not support a path relative to the application context. This location is used to store files temporarily while the parts are processed or when the size of the file exceeds the specified fileSizeThreshold setting. The default location is "".

- fileSizeThreshold: The file size in bytes after which the file will be temporarily stored on disk. The default size is 0 bytes.

- MaxFileSize: The maximum size allowed for uploaded files, in bytes. If the size of any uploaded file is greater than this size, the web container will throw an exception (IllegalStateException). The default size is unlimited.

- maxRequestSize: The maximum size allowed for a multipart/form-data request, in bytes. The web container will throw an exception if the overall size of all uploaded files exceeds this threshold. The default size is unlimited.

For, example, the @MultipartConfig annotation could be constructed as follows:

```
@MultipartConfig(location="/tmp", fileSizeThreshold=1024*1024,
    maxFileSize=1024*1024*5, maxRequestSize=1024*1024*5*5)
```

Instead of using the @MultipartConfig annotation to hard-code these attributes in your file upload servlet, you could add the following as a child element of the servlet configuration element in the web.xml file:

```
<multipart-config>
    <location>/tmp</location>
    <max-file-size>20848820</max-file-size>
    <max-request-size>418018841</max-request-size>
    <file-size-threshold>1048576</file-size-threshold>
</multipart-config>
```

17.11.2 The getParts and getPart Methods

The Servlet specification supports two additional HttpServletRequest methods:

- Collection<Part> getParts()

- Part getPart(String name)

The request.getParts() method returns collections of all Part objects. If you have more than one input of type file, multiple Part objects are returned. Because Part objects are named, the getPart(String name) method can be used to access a particular Part. Alternatively, the getParts() method, which returns an Iterable<Part>, can be used to get an Iterator over all the Part objects.

The javax.servlet.http.Part interface is a simple one, providing methods that allow introspection of each Part. The methods do the following:

- Retrieve the name, size, and content-type of the Part

- Query the headers submitted with a Part

- Delete a Part

- Write a Part out to disk

For example, the Part interface provides the write(String filename) method to write the file with the specified name. The file can then be saved in the directory that is specified with the location attribute of the @MultipartConfig annotation or, in the case of the fileupload example, in the location specified by the Destination field in the form.

17.12 Asynchronous Processing

Web containers in application servers normally use a server thread per client request. Under heavy load conditions, containers need a large amount of threads to serve all the client requests. Scalability limitations include running out of memory or exhausting the pool of container threads. To create scalable web applications, you must ensure that no threads associated with a request are sitting idle, so the container can use them to process new requests.

There are two common scenarios in which a thread associated with a request can be sitting idle.

- The thread needs to wait for a resource to become available or process data before building the response. For example, an application may need to query a database or access data from a remote web service before generating the response.

- The thread needs to wait for an event before generating the response. For example, an application may have to wait for a JMS message, new information from another client, or new data available in a queue before generating the response.

These scenarios represent blocking operations that limit the scalability of web applications. Asynchronous processing refers to assigning these blocking operations to a new thread and retuning the thread associated with the request immediately to the container.

17.12.1 Asynchronous Processing in Servlets

Java EE provides asynchronous processing support for servlets and filters. If a servlet or a filter reaches a potentially blocking operation when processing a request, it can assign the operation to an asynchronous execution context and return the thread associated with the request immediately to the container without generating a response. The blocking operation completes in the asynchronous execution context in a different thread, which can generate a response or dispatch the request to another servlet.

To enable asynchronous processing on a servlet, set the parameter asyncSupported to true on the @WebServlet annotation as follows:

```
@WebServlet(urlPatterns={"/asyncservlet"}, asyncSupported=true)
public class AsyncServlet extends HttpServlet { ... }
```

The javax.servlet.AsyncContext class provides the functionality that you need to perform asynchronous processing inside service methods. To obtain an instance of `AsyncContext`, call the `startAsync()` method on the request object of your service method; for example:

```
public void doGet(HttpServletRequest req, HttpServletResponse resp) {
    ...
    AsyncContext acontext = req.startAsync();
    ...
}
```

This call puts the request into asynchronous mode and ensures that the response is not committed after exiting the service method. You have to generate the response in the asynchronous context after the blocking operation completes or dispatch the request to another servlet.

Table 17–3 describes the basic functionality provided by the `AsyncContext` class.

Table 17–3   Functionality Provided by the AsyncContext Class

Method Signature	Description
`void start(Runnable run)`	The container provides a different thread in which the blocking operation can be processed.
	You provide code for the blocking operation as a class that implements the `Runnable` interface. You can provide this class as an inner class when calling the `start` method or use another mechanism to pass the `AsyncContext` instance to your class.
`ServletRequest getRequest()`	Returns the request used to initialize this asynchronous context. In the example above, the request is the same as in the service method.
	You can use this method inside the asynchronous context to obtain parameters from the request.
`ServletResponse getResponse()`	Returns the response used to initialize this asynchronous context. In the example above, the response is the same as in the service method.
	You can use this method inside the asynchronous context to write to the response with the results of the blocking operation.

Table 17–3   (Cont.) Functionality Provided by the AsyncContext Class

Method Signature	Description
`void complete()`	Completes the asynchronous operation and closes the response associated with this asynchronous context.
	You call this method after writing to the response object inside the asynchronous context.
`void dispatch(String path)`	Dispatches the request and response objects to the given path.
	You use this method to have another servlet write to the response after the blocking operation completes.

17.12.2 Waiting for a Resource

This section demonstrates how to use the functionality provided by the AsyncContext class for the following use case:

1. A servlet receives a parameter from a GET request.

2. The servlet uses a resource, such as a database or a web service, to retrieve information based on the value of the parameter. The resource can be slow at times, so this may be a blocking operation.

3. The servlet generates a response using the result from the resource.

The following code shows a basic servlet that does not use asynchronous processing:

```
@WebServlet(urlPatterns={"/syncservlet"})
public class SyncServlet extends HttpServlet {
    private MyRemoteResource resource;
    @Override
    public void init(ServletConfig config) {
        resource = MyRemoteResource.create("config1=x,config2=y");
    }

    @Override
    public void doGet(HttpServletRequest request,
                      HttpServletResponse response) {
        response.setContentType("text/html;charset=UTF-8");
        String param = request.getParameter("param");
        String result = resource.process(param);
        /* ... print to the response ... */
    }
}
```

The following code shows the same servlet using asynchronous processing:

```
@WebServlet(urlPatterns={"/asyncservlet"}, asyncSupported=true)
public class AsyncServlet extends HttpServlet {
    /* ... Same variables and init method as in SyncServlet ... */

    @Override
    public void doGet(HttpServletRequest request,
                      HttpServletResponse response) {
        response.setContentType("text/html;charset=UTF-8");
        final AsyncContext acontext = request.startAsync();
        acontext.start(new Runnable() {
            public void run() {
                String param = acontext.getRequest().getParameter("param");
                String result = resource.process(param);
                HttpServletResponse response = acontext.getResponse();
                /* ... print to the response ... */
                acontext.complete();
            }
        }
    }
}
```

`AsyncServlet` adds `asyncSupported=true` to the `@WebServlet` annotation. The rest of the differences are inside the service method.

- `request.startAsync()` causes the request to be processed asynchronously; the response is not sent to the client at the end of the service method.

- `acontext.start(new Runnable() {...})` gets a new thread from the container.

- The code inside the `run()` method of the inner class executes in the new thread. The inner class has access to the asynchronous context to read parameters from the request and write to the response. Calling the `complete()` method of the asynchronous context commits the response and sends it to the client.

The service method of `AsyncServlet` returns immediately, and the request is processed in the asynchronous context.

17.13 Nonblocking I/O

Web containers in application servers normally use a server thread per client request. To develop scalable web applications, you must ensure that threads associated with client requests are never sitting idle waiting for a blocking operation to complete. Asynchronous processing (see Section 17.12, "Asynchronous Processing") provides a mechanism to execute application-specific blocking operations in a new thread, returning the thread associated with the request immediately to the container. Even if you use asynchronous processing for all the application-specific blocking operations inside your service methods, threads associated with client requests can be momentarily sitting idle because of input/output considerations.

For example, if a client is submitting a large HTTP POST request over a slow network connection, the server can read the request faster than the client can provide it. Using traditional I/O, the container thread associated with this request would be sometimes sitting idle waiting for the rest of the request.

Java EE provides nonblocking I/O support for servlets and filters when processing requests in asynchronous mode. The following steps summarize how to use nonblocking I/O to process requests and write responses inside service methods.

1. Put the request in asynchronous mode as described in Section 17.12, "Asynchronous Processing."

2. Obtain an input stream and/or an output stream from the request and response objects in the service method.

3. Assign a read listener to the input stream and/or a write listener to the output stream.

4. Process the request and the response inside the listener's callback methods.

Table 17–4 and Table 17–5 describe the methods available in the servlet input and output streams for nonblocking I/O support. Table 17–6 describes the interfaces for read listeners and write listeners.

Table 17–4   Nonblocking I/O Support in javax.servlet.ServletInputStream

Method	Description
void setReadListener(ReadListener rl)	Associates this input stream with a listener object that contains callback methods to read data asynchronously. You provide the listener object as an anonymous class or use another mechanism to pass the input stream to the read listener object.
boolean isReady()	Returns true if data can be read without blocking.
boolean isFinished()	Returns true when all the data has been read.

Table 17–5   Nonblocking I/O Support in javax.servlet.ServletOutputStream

Method	Description
void setWriteListener(WriteListener wl)	Associates this output stream with a listener object that contains callback methods to write data asynchronously. You provide the write listener object as an anonymous class or use another mechanism to pass the output stream to the write listener object.
boolean isReady()	Returns true if data can be written without blocking.

Table 17–6   Listener Interfaces for Nonblocking I/O Support

Interface	Methods	Description
ReadListener	void onDataAvailable() void onAllDataRead() void onError(Throwable t)	A ServletInputStream instance calls these methods on its listener when there is data available to read, when all the data has been read, or when there is an error.
WriteListener	void onWritePossible() void onError(Throwable t)	A ServletOutputStream instance calls these methods on its listener when it is possible to write data without blocking or when there is an error.

17.13.1 Reading a Large HTTP POST Request Using Nonblocking I/O

The code in this section shows how to read a large HTTP POST request inside a servlet by putting the request in asynchronous mode (as described in Section 17.12, "Asynchronous Processing") and using the nonblocking I/O functionality from Table 17–4 and Table 17–6.

```
@WebServlet(urlPatterns={"/asyncioservlet"}, asyncSupported=true)
public class AsyncIOServlet extends HttpServlet {
    @Override
    public void doPost(HttpServletRequest request,
                       HttpServletResponse response)
                       throws IOException {
        final AsyncContext acontext = request.startAsync();
        final ServletInputStream input = request.getInputStream();

        input.setReadListener(new ReadListener() {
            byte buffer[] = new byte[4*1024];
            StringBuilder sbuilder = new StringBuilder();
```

```
    @Override
    public void onDataAvailable() {
        try {
            do {
                int length = input.read(buffer);
                sbuilder.append(new String(buffer, 0, length));
            } while(input.isReady());
        } catch (IOException ex) { ... }
    }
    @Override
    public void onAllDataRead() {
        try {
            acontext.getResponse().getWriter()
                                   .write("...the response...");
        } catch (IOException ex) { ... }
        acontext.complete();
    }
    @Override
    public void onError(Throwable t) { ... }
    });
    }
}
```

This example declares the web servlet with asynchronous support using the
@WebServlet annotation parameter asyncSupported=true. The service method
first puts the request in asynchronous mode by calling the startAsync() method
of the request object, which is required in order to use nonblocking I/O. Then, the
service method obtains an input stream associated with the request and assigns a
read listener defined as an inner class. The listener reads parts of the request as
they become available and then writes some response to the client when it
finishes reading the request.

17.14 Protocol Upgrade Processing

In HTTP/1.1, clients can request to switch to a different protocol on the current
connection by using the Upgrade header field. If the server accepts the request to
switch to the protocol indicated by the client, it generates an HTTP response with
status 101 (switching protocols). After this exchange, the client and the server
communicate using the new protocol.

For example, a client can make an HTTP request to switch to the XYZP protocol as follows:

```
GET /xyzpresource HTTP/1.1
Host: localhost:8080
Accept: text/html
Upgrade: XYZP
Connection: Upgrade
OtherHeaderA: Value
```

The client can specify parameters for the new protocol using HTTP headers. The server can accept the request and generate a response as follows:

```
HTTP/1.1 101 Switching Protocols
Upgrade: XYZP
Connection: Upgrade
OtherHeaderB: Value

(XYZP data)
```

Java EE supports the HTTP protocol upgrade functionality in servlets, as described in Table 17–7.

Table 17–7   Protocol Upgrade Support

Class or Interface	Method
HttpServletRequest	HttpUpgradeHandler upgrade(Class handler)
	The upgrade method starts the protocol upgrade processing. This method instantiates a class that implements the HttpUpgradeHandler interface and delegates the connection to it.
	You call the upgrade method inside a service method when accepting a request from a client to switch protocols.
HttpUpgradeHandler	void init(WebConnection wc)
	The init method is called when the servlet accepts the request to switch protocols. You implement this method and obtain input and output streams from the WebConnection object to implement the new protocol.
HttpUpgradeHandler	void destroy()
	The destroy method is called when the client disconnects. You implement this method and free any resources associated with processing the new protocol.

Table 17–7   (Cont.) Protocol Upgrade Support

Class or Interface	Method
WebConnection	ServletInputStream getInputStream()
	The getInputStream method provides access to the input stream of the connection. You can use nonblocking I/O (see Section 17.13, "Nonblocking I/O") with the returned stream to implement the new protocol.
WebConnection	ServletOutputStream getOutputStream()
	The getOutputStream method provides access to the output stream of the connection. You can use nonblocking I/O (see Section 17.13, "Nonblocking I/O") with the returned stream to implement the new protocol.

The following code demonstrates how to accept an HTTP protocol upgrade request from a client:

```
@WebServlet(urlPatterns={"/xyzpresource"})
public class XYZPUpgradeServlet extends HttpServlet {
   @Override
   public void doGet(HttpServletRequest request,
                     HttpServletResponse response) {
      if ("XYZP".equals(request.getHeader("Upgrade"))) {
         /* Accept upgrade request */
         response.setStatus(101);
         response.setHeader("Upgrade", "XYZP");
         response.setHeader("Connection", "Upgrade");
         response.setHeader("OtherHeaderB", "Value");
         /* Delegate the connection to the upgrade handler */
         XYZPUpgradeHandler = request.upgrade(XYZPUpgradeHandler.class);
         /* (the service method returns immediately) */
      } else {
         /* ... write error response ... */
      }
   }
}
```

The XYZPUpgradeHandler class handles the connection:

```
public class XYZPUpgradeHandler implements HttpUpgradeHandler {
   @Override
   public void init(WebConnection wc) {
      ServletInputStream input = wc.getInputStream();
      ServletOutputStream output = wc.getOutputStream();
      /* ... implement XYZP using these streams (protocol-specific) ... */
   }
```

```
@Override
public void destroy() { ... }
}
```

The class that implements `HttpUpgradeHandler` uses the streams from the current connection to communicate with the client using the new protocol. See the Servlet 3.1 specification at `http://jcp.org/en/jsr/detail?id=340` for details on HTTP protocol upgrade support.

17.15 The mood Example Application

The mood example application, located in the *tut-install*/examples/web/servlet/ mood/ directory, is a simple example that displays Duke's moods at different times during the day. The example shows how to develop a simple application by using the @WebServlet, @WebFilter, and @WebListener annotations to create a servlet, a listener, and a filter.

17.15.1 Components of the mood Example Application

The mood example application is comprised of three components: mood.web.MoodServlet, mood.web.TimeOfDayFilter, and mood.web.SimpleServletListener.

MoodServlet, the presentation layer of the application, displays Duke's mood in a graphic, based on the time of day. The @WebServlet annotation specifies the URL pattern:

```
@WebServlet("/report")
public class MoodServlet extends HttpServlet {
    ...
```

TimeOfDayFilter sets an initialization parameter indicating that Duke is awake:

```
@WebFilter(filterName = "TimeOfDayFilter",
urlPatterns = {"/*"},
initParams = {
    @WebInitParam(name = "mood", value = "awake")})
public class TimeOfDayFilter implements Filter {
    ...
```

The filter calls the doFilter method, which contains a switch statement that sets Duke's mood based on the current time.

SimpleServletListener logs changes in the servlet's lifecycle. The log entries appear in the server log.

17.15.2 Running the mood Example

You can use either NetBeans IDE or Maven to build, package, deploy, and run the mood example.

17.15.2.1 To Run the mood Example Using NetBeans IDE

1. Make sure that GlassFish Server has been started (see Section 2.2, "Starting and Stopping GlassFish Server").

2. From the **File** menu, choose **Open Project**.

3. In the Open Project dialog box, navigate to:

   `tut-install/examples/web/servlet`

4. Select the mood folder.

5. Click **Open Project**.

6. In the **Projects** tab, right-click the mood project and select **Build**.

7. In a web browser, enter the following URL:

   `http://localhost:8080/mood/report`

   The URL specifies the context root, followed by the URL pattern.

   A web page appears with the title "Servlet MoodServlet at /mood", a text string describing Duke's mood, and an illustrative graphic.

17.15.2.2 To Run the mood Example Using Maven

1. Make sure that GlassFish Server has been started (see Section 2.2, "Starting and Stopping GlassFish Server").

2. In a terminal window, go to:

   `tut-install/examples/web/servlet/mood/`

3. Enter the following command to deploy the application:

   `mvn install`

4. In a web browser, enter the following URL:

   `http://localhost:8080/mood/report`

   The URL specifies the context root, followed by the URL pattern.

A web page appears with the title "Servlet MoodServlet at /mood", a text string describing Duke's mood, and an illustrative graphic.

17.16 The fileupload Example Application

The fileupload example, located in the *tut-install*/examples/web/servlet/fileupload/ directory, illustrates how to implement and use the file upload feature.

The Duke's Forest case study provides a more complex example that uploads an image file and stores its content in a database. (See Chapter 30, "Duke's Forest Case Study Example," in *The Java EE 7 Tutorial, Volume 2*.)

17.16.1 Architecture of the fileupload Example Application

The fileupload example application consists of a single servlet and an HTML form that makes a file upload request to the servlet.

This example includes a very simple HTML form with two fields, File and Destination. The input type, file, enables a user to browse the local file system to select the file. When the file is selected, it is sent to the server as a part of a POST request. During this process, two mandatory restrictions are applied to the form with input type file.

- The enctype attribute must be set to a value of multipart/form-data.

- Its method must be POST.

When the form is specified in this manner, the entire request is sent to the server in encoded form. The servlet then uses its own means to handle the request to process the incoming file data and extract a file from the stream. The destination is the path to the location where the file will be saved on your computer. Pressing the **Upload** button at the bottom of the form posts the data to the servlet, which saves the file in the specified destination.

The HTML form in index.html is as follows:

```
<!DOCTYPE html>
<html lang="en">
    <head>
        <title>File Upload</title>
        <meta http-equiv="Content-Type" content="text/html; charset=UTF-8">
    </head>
    <body>
        <form method="POST" action="upload" enctype="multipart/form-data" >
            File:
            <input type="file" name="file" id="file" /> <br/>
```

```
            Destination:
            <input type="text" value="/tmp" name="destination"/>
            </br>
            <input type="submit" value="Upload" name="upload" id="upload" />
        </form>
    </body>
</html>
```

A POST request method is used when the client needs to send data to the server as part of the request, such as when uploading a file or submitting a completed form. In contrast, a GET request method sends a URL and headers only to the server, whereas POST requests also include a message body. This allows arbitrary length data of any type to be sent to the server. A header field in the POST request usually indicates the message body's Internet media type.

When submitting a form, the browser streams the content in, combining all parts, with each part representing a field of a form. Parts are named after the input elements and are separated from each other with string delimiters named boundary.

This is what submitted data from the fileupload form looks like, after selecting sample.txt as the file that will be uploaded to the tmp directory on the local file system:

```
POST /fileupload/upload HTTP/1.1
Host: localhost:8080
Content-Type: multipart/form-data;
boundary=-------------------------263081694432439
Content-Length: 441
-------------------------263081694432439
Content-Disposition: form-data; name="file"; filename="sample.txt"
Content-Type: text/plain

Data from sample file
-------------------------263081694432439
Content-Disposition: form-data; name="destination"

/tmp
-------------------------263081694432439
Content-Disposition: form-data; name="upload"

Upload
-------------------------263081694432439--
```

The servlet `FileUploadServlet.java` begins as follows:

```
@WebServlet(name = "FileUploadServlet", urlPatterns = {"/upload"})
@MultipartConfig
public class FileUploadServlet extends HttpServlet {
    private final static Logger LOGGER =
            Logger.getLogger(FileUploadServlet.class.getCanonicalName());
```

The `@WebServlet` annotation uses the `urlPatterns` property to define servlet mappings.

The `@MultipartConfig` annotation indicates that the servlet expects requests to be made using the multipart/form-data MIME type.

The `processRequest` method retrieves the destination and file part from the request, then calls the `getFileName` method to retrieve the file name from the file part. The method then creates a `FileOutputStream` and copies the file to the specified destination. The error-handling section of the method catches and handles some of the most common reasons why a file would not be found. The `processRequest` and `getFileName` methods look like this:

```
protected void processRequest(HttpServletRequest request,
        HttpServletResponse response)
        throws ServletException, IOException {
    response.setContentType("text/html;charset=UTF-8");

    // Create path components to save the file
    final String path = request.getParameter("destination");
    final Part filePart = request.getPart("file");
    final String fileName = getFileName(filePart);

    OutputStream out = null;
    InputStream filecontent = null;
    final PrintWriter writer = response.getWriter();

    try {
        out = new FileOutputStream(new File(path + File.separator
                + fileName));
        filecontent = filePart.getInputStream();

        int read = 0;
        final byte[] bytes = new byte[1024];

        while ((read = filecontent.read(bytes)) != -1) {
            out.write(bytes, 0, read);
        }
        writer.println("New file " + fileName + " created at " + path);
```

```
                LOGGER.log(Level.INFO, "File{0}being uploaded to {1}",
                        new Object[]{fileName, path});
        } catch (FileNotFoundException fne) {
            writer.println("You either did not specify a file to upload or are "
                    + "trying to upload a file to a protected or nonexistent "
                    + "location.");
            writer.println("<br/> ERROR: " + fne.getMessage());

            LOGGER.log(Level.SEVERE, "Problems during file upload. Error: {0}",
                    new Object[]{fne.getMessage()});
        } finally {
            if (out != null) {
                out.close();
            }
            if (filecontent != null) {
                filecontent.close();
            }
            if (writer != null) {
                writer.close();
            }
        }
    }

    private String getFileName(final Part part) {
        final String partHeader = part.getHeader("content-disposition");
        LOGGER.log(Level.INFO, "Part Header = {0}", partHeader);
        for (String content : part.getHeader("content-disposition").split(";")){
            if (content.trim().startsWith("filename")) {
                return content.substring(
                        content.indexOf('=') + 1).trim().replace("\"", "");
            }
        }
        return null;
    }
```

17.16.2 Running the fileupload Example

You can use either NetBeans IDE or Maven to build, package, deploy, and run the fileupload example.

17.16.2.1 To Build, Package, and Deploy the fileupload Example Using NetBeans IDE

1. Make sure that GlassFish Server has been started (see Section 2.2, "Starting and Stopping GlassFish Server").

2. From the **File** menu, choose **Open Project**.

3. In the Open Project dialog box, navigate to:

    tut-install/examples/web/servlet

4. Select the fileupload folder.

5. Click **Open Project**.

6. In the **Projects** tab, right-click the fileupload project and select **Build**.

17.16.2.2 To Build, Package, and Deploy the fileupload Example Using Maven

1. Make sure that GlassFish Server has been started (see Section 2.2, "Starting and Stopping GlassFish Server").

2. In a terminal window, go to:

    tut-install/examples/web/servlet/fileupload/

3. Enter the following command to deploy the application:

    mvn install

17.16.2.3 To Run the fileupload Example

1. In a web browser, enter the following URL:

    http://localhost:8080/fileupload/

2. On the File Upload page, click **Choose File** to display a file browser window.

3. Select a file to upload and click **Open**.

    The name of the file you selected is displayed in the **File** field. If you do not select a file, an exception will be thrown.

4. In the **Destination** field, type a directory name.

    The directory must have already been created and must also be writable. If you do not enter a directory name or if you enter the name of a nonexistent or protected directory, an exception will be thrown.

5. Click **Upload** to upload the file that you selected to the directory that you specified in the **Destination** field.

    A message reports that the file was created in the directory that you specified.

6. Go to the directory that you specified in the **Destination** field and verify that the uploaded file is present.

17.17 The dukeetf Example Application

The `dukeetf` example application, located in the *tut-install*/examples/web/dukeetf/ directory, demonstrates how to use asynchronous processing in a servlet to provide data updates to web clients. The example resembles a service that provides periodic updates on the price and trading volume of an electronically traded fund (ETF).

17.17.1 Architecture of the dukeetf Example Application

The `dukeetf` example application consists of a servlet, an enterprise bean, and an HTML page.

- The servlet puts requests in asynchronous mode, stores them in a queue, and writes the responses when new data for price and trading volume becomes available.

- The enterprise bean updates the price and volume information once every second.

- The HTML page uses JavaScript code to make requests to the servlet for new data, parse the response from the servlet, and update the price and volume information without reloading the page.

The `dukeetf` example application uses a programming model known as **long polling**. In the traditional HTTP request and response model, the user must make an explicit request (such as clicking a link or submitting a form) to get any new information from the server, and the page has to be reloaded. Long polling provides a mechanism for web applications to push updates to clients using HTTP without the user making an explicit request. The server handles connections asynchronously, and the client uses JavaScript to make new connections. In this model, clients make a new request immediately after receiving new data, and the server keeps the connection open until new data becomes available.

17.17.1.1 The Servlet

The `DukeETFServlet` class uses asynchronous processing:

```
@WebServlet(urlPatterns={"/dukeetf"}, asyncSupported=true)
public class DukeETFServlet extends HttpServlet {
    ...
}
```

In the following code example, the `init` method initializes a queue to hold client requests and starts a new thread. The thread updates the price and trading volume information every second with random increments and sends the new values as plain text to all connected clients:

```java
@Override
public void init(ServletConfig config) {
    /* Queue for requests */
    requestQueue = new ConcurrentLinkedQueue<AsyncContext>();
    /* Set the price and volume periodically,
       Send the information to all connected clients. */
    Executors.newSingleThreadExecutor().execute(new Runnable() {
        public void run() {
            Random random = new Random();
            while (true) {
                /* Set price and volume */
                price += 1.0*(random.nextInt(100)-50)/100.0;
                volume += random.nextInt(5000) - 2500;
                /* Send information to all clients */
                for (AsyncContext acontext : requestQueue) {
                    try {
                        PrintWriter writer = acontext.getResponse()
                                                     .getWriter();
                        writer.printf("%.2f, %d", price, volume);
                        acontext.complete();
                    } catch (IOException ex) {}
                }
                /* Wait */
                try { Thread.sleep(DELAY_MS); } catch (Exception e) {}
            }
        }
    });
}
```

The preceding code does not require an enterprise bean for this example, but it contains several bad practices.

- The servlet contains business logic (updating the price and volume information). You should normally use enterprise beans to implement business logic.

- The servlet creates a new thread. You should use threads provided by the container whenever possible instead of manually creating new threads.

- The servlet calls `Thread.sleep` inside a `while` loop to simulate periodic events. You should use the timer service from the enterprise Java beans (EJB) container to schedule periodic notifications.

The following code replaces the previous `init` method and adds the `send` method:

```java
@Override
public void init(ServletConfig config) {
    /* Queue for requests */
    requestQueue = new ConcurrentLinkedQueue<>();
    /* Register with the enterprise bean that provides
     * price/volume updates */
    pvbean.registerServlet(this);
}

/* PriceVolumeBean calls this method every second to send updates */
public void send(double price, int volume) {
    /* Send update to all connected clients */
    for (AsyncContext acontext : requestQueue) {
        try {
            String msg = String.format("%.2f, %d", price, volume);
            PrintWriter writer = acontext.getResponse().getWriter();
            writer.write(msg);
            logger.log(Level.INFO, "Sent: {0}", msg);
            /* Close the connection
             * The client (JavaScript) makes a new one instantly */
            acontext.complete();
        } catch (IOException ex) {
            logger.log(Level.INFO, ex.toString());
        }
    }
}
```

The service method puts client requests in asynchronous mode and adds a listener to each request. The listener is implemented as an anonymous class that removes the request from the queue when the servlet finishes writing a response or when there is an error. Finally, the service method adds the request to the request queue created in the `init` method. The service method is as follows:

```java
@Override
public void doGet(HttpServletRequest request,
                  HttpServletResponse response) {
    response.setContentType("text/html");
    /* Put request in async mode */
    final AsyncContext acontext = request.startAsync();
    /* Remove from the queue when done */
    acontext.addListener(new AsyncListener() {
        public void onComplete(AsyncEvent ae) throws IOException {
            requestQueue.remove(acontext);
        }
```

```
        public void onTimeout(AsyncEvent ae) throws IOException {
            requestQueue.remove(acontext);
        }
        public void onError(AsyncEvent ae) throws IOException {
            requestQueue.remove(acontext);
        }
        public void onStartAsync(AsyncEvent ae) throws IOException {}
    });
    /* Add to the queue */
    requestQueue.add(acontext);
}
```

17.17.1.2 The Enterprise Bean

The PriceVolumeBean class is an enterprise bean that uses the timer service from the container to update the price and volume information and call the servlet's send method once every second:

```
@Startup
@Singleton
public class PriceVolumeBean {
    /* Use the container's timer service */
    @Resource TimerService tservice;
    private DukeETFServlet servlet;
    ...
    @PostConstruct
    public void init() {
        /* Initialize the EJB and create a timer */
        random = new Random();
        servlet = null;
        tservice.createIntervalTimer(1000, 1000, new TimerConfig());
    }

    public void registerServlet(DukeETFServlet servlet) {
        /* Associate a servlet to send updates to */
        this.servlet = servlet;
    }

    @Timeout
    public void timeout() {
        /* Adjust price and volume and send updates */
        price += 1.0*(random.nextInt(100)-50)/100.0;
        volume += random.nextInt(5000) - 2500;
        if (servlet != null)
            servlet.send(price, volume);
    }
}
```

See Section 5.4, "Using the Timer Service," in *The Java EE 7 Tutorial, Volume 2*, for more information on the timer service.

17.17.1.3 The HTML Page

The HTML page consists of a table and some JavaScript code. The table contains two fields referenced from JavaScript code:

```
<html xmlns="http://www.w3.org/1999/xhtml">
<head>...</head>
<body onload="makeAjaxRequest();">
  ...
  <table>
    ...
    <tr>
    ...
      <td id="price">--.--</td>
    </tr>
    <tr>
    ...
      <td id="volume">--</td>
    </tr>
  </table>
</body>
</html>
```

The JavaScript code uses the XMLHttpRequest API, which provides functionality for transferring data between a client and a server. The script makes an asynchronous request to the servlet and designates a callback method. When the server provides a response, the callback method updates the fields in the table and makes a new request. The JavaScript code is as follows:

```
var ajaxRequest;
function updatePage() {
    if (ajaxRequest.readyState === 4) {
        var arraypv = ajaxRequest.responseText.split(",");
        document.getElementById("price").innerHTML = arraypv[0];
        document.getElementById("volume").innerHTML = arraypv[1];
        makeAjaxRequest();
    }
}
function makeAjaxRequest() {
    ajaxRequest = new XMLHttpRequest();
    ajaxRequest.onreadystatechange = updatePage;
    ajaxRequest.open("GET", "http://localhost:8080/dukeetf/dukeetf",
                    true);
```

```
        ajaxRequest.send(null);
}
```

The XMLHttpRequest API is supported by most modern browsers, and it is widely used in Ajax web client development (Asynchronous JavaScript and XML).

See Section 18.11, "The dukeetf2 Example Application," for an equivalent version of this example implemented using a WebSocket endpoint.

17.17.2 Running the dukeetf Example Application

This section describes how to run the dukeetf example application using NetBeans IDE and from the command line.

17.17.2.1 To Run the dukeetf Example Application Using NetBeans IDE

1. Make sure that GlassFish Server has been started (see Section 2.2, "Starting and Stopping GlassFish Server").

2. From the **File** menu, choose **Open Project**.

3. In the Open Project dialog box, navigate to:

    tut-install/examples/web/servlet

4. Select the dukeetf folder.

5. Click **Open Project**.

6. In the **Projects** tab, right-click the dukeetf project and select **Run**.

    This command builds and packages the application into a WAR file (dukeetf.war) located in the target directory, deploys it to the server, and launches a web browser window with the following URL:

    http://localhost:8080/dukeetf/

    Open the same URL in a different web browser to see how both pages get price and volume updates simultaneously.

17.17.2.2 To Run the dukeetf Example Application Using Maven

1. Make sure that GlassFish Server has been started (see Section 2.2, "Starting and Stopping GlassFish Server").

2. In a terminal window, go to:

    tut-install/examples/web/servlet/dukeetf/

3. Enter the following command to deploy the application:

```
mvn install
```

4. Open a web browser window to the following URL:

```
http://localhost:8080/dukeetf/
```

Open the same URL in a different web browser to see how both pages get price and volume updates simultaneously.

17.18 Further Information about Java Servlet Technology

For more information on Java Servlet technology, see the Java Servlet 3.1 specification at `http://jcp.org/en/jsr/detail?id=340`.

18

Java API for WebSocket

This chapter describes the Java API for WebSocket (JSR 356), which provides support for creating WebSocket applications. WebSocket is an application protocol that provides full-duplex communications between two peers over the TCP protocol.

In the traditional request-response model used in HTTP, the client requests resources, and the server provides responses. The exchange is always initiated by the client; the server cannot send any data without the client requesting it first. This model worked well for the World Wide Web when clients made occasional requests for documents that changed infrequently, but the limitations of this approach are increasingly relevant as content changes quickly and users expect a more interactive experience on the Web. The WebSocket protocol addresses these limitations by providing a full-duplex communication channel between the client and the server. Combined with other client technologies, such as JavaScript and HTML5, WebSocket enables web applications to deliver a richer user experience.

The following topics are addressed here:

- Introduction to WebSocket
- Creating WebSocket Applications in the Java EE Platform
- Programmatic Endpoints
- Annotated Endpoints
- Sending and Receiving Messages
- Maintaining Client State
- Using Encoders and Decoders
- Path Parameters

- Handling Errors

- Specifying an Endpoint Configurator Class

- The dukeetf2 Example Application

- The websocketbot Example Application

- Further Information about WebSocket

18.1 Introduction to WebSocket

In a WebSocket application, the server publishes a WebSocket **endpoint**, and the client uses the endpoint's URI to connect to the server. The WebSocket protocol is symmetrical after the connection has been established; the client and the server can send messages to each other at any time while the connection is open, and they can close the connection at any time. Clients usually connect only to one server, and servers accept connections from multiple clients.

The WebSocket protocol has two parts: handshake and data transfer. The client initiates the handshake by sending a request to a WebSocket endpoint using its URI. The handshake is compatible with existing HTTP-based infrastructure: web servers interpret it as an HTTP connection upgrade request. An example handshake from a client looks like this:

```
GET /path/to/websocket/endpoint HTTP/1.1
Host: localhost
Upgrade: websocket
Connection: Upgrade
Sec-WebSocket-Key: xqBt3ImNzJbYqRINxEFlkg==
Origin: http://localhost
Sec-WebSocket-Version: 13
```

An example handshake from the server in response to the client looks like this:

```
HTTP/1.1 101 Switching Protocols
Upgrade: websocket
Connection: Upgrade
Sec-WebSocket-Accept: K7DJLdLooIwIG/MOpvWFB3y3FE8=
```

The server applies a known operation to the value of the Sec-WebSocket-Key header to generate the value of the Sec-WebSocket-Accept header. The client applies the same operation to the value of the Sec-WebSocket-Key header, and the connection is established successfully if the result matches the value received from the server. The client and the server can send messages to each other after a successful handshake.

WebSocket supports text messages (encoded as UTF-8) and binary messages. The control frames in WebSocket are *close*, *ping*, and *pong* (a response to a *ping* frame). Ping and pong frames may also contain application data.

WebSocket endpoints are represented by URIs that have the following form:

```
ws://host:port/path?query
wss://host:port/path?query
```

The `ws` scheme represents an unencrypted WebSocket connection, and the `wss` scheme represents an encrypted connection. The `port` component is optional; the default port number is 80 for unencrypted connections and 443 for encrypted connections. The `path` component indicates the location of an endpoint within a server. The `query` component is optional.

Modern web browsers implement the WebSocket protocol and provide a JavaScript API to connect to endpoints, send messages, and assign callback methods for WebSocket events (such as opened connections, received messages, and closed connections).

18.2 Creating WebSocket Applications in the Java EE Platform

The Java EE platform includes the Java API for WebSocket (JSR 356), which enables you to create, configure, and deploy WebSocket endpoints in web applications. The WebSocket client API specified in JSR 356 also enables you to access remote WebSocket endpoints from any Java application.

The Java API for WebSocket consists of the following packages.

- The `javax.websocket.server` package contains annotations, classes, and interfaces to create and configure server endpoints.

- The `javax.websocket` package contains annotations, classes, interfaces, and exceptions that are common to client and server endpoints.

WebSocket endpoints are instances of the `javax.websocket.Endpoint` class. The Java API for WebSocket enables you to create two kinds of endpoints: programmatic endpoints and annotated endpoints. To create a **programmatic endpoint**, you extend the `Endpoint` class and override its lifecycle methods. To create an **annotated endpoint**, you decorate a Java class and some of its methods with the annotations provided by the packages mentioned previously. After you have created an endpoint, you deploy it to an specific URI in the application so that remote clients can connect to it.

> **Note:** In most cases, it is easier to create and deploy an annotated endpoint than a programmatic endpoint. This chapter provides a simple example of a programmatic endpoint, but it focuses on annotated endpoints.

The process for creating and deploying a WebSocket endpoint follows.

1. Create an endpoint class.

2. Implement the lifecycle methods of the endpoint.

3. Add your business logic to the endpoint.

4. Deploy the endpoint inside a web application.

The process is slightly different for programmatic endpoints and annotated endpoints, and it is covered in detail in the following sections.

> **Note:** As opposed to servlets, WebSocket endpoints are instantiated multiple times. The container creates an instance of an endpoint per connection to its deployment URI. Each instance is associated with one and only one connection. This facilitates keeping user state for each connection and makes development easier, because there is only one thread executing the code of an endpoint instance at any given time.

18.3 Programmatic Endpoints

The following example shows how to create an endpoint by extending the `Endpoint` class:

```
public class EchoEndpoint extends Endpoint {
    @Override
    public void onOpen(final Session session, EndpointConfig config) {
        session.addMessageHandler(new MessageHandler.Whole<String>() {
            @Override
            public void onMessage(String msg) {
                try {
                    session.getBasicRemote().sendText(msg);
                } catch (IOException e) { ... }
            }
        });
    }
}
```

This endpoint echoes every message received. The Endpoint class defines three lifecycle methods: onOpen, onClose, and onError. The EchoEndpoint class implements the onOpen method, which is the only abstract method in the Endpoint class.

The Session parameter represents a conversation between this endpoint and the remote endpoint. The addMessageHandler method registers message handlers, and the getBasicRemote method returns an object that represents the remote endpoint. The Session interface is covered in detail in the rest of this chapter.

The message handler is implemented as an anonymous inner class. The onMessage method of the message handler is invoked when the endpoint receives a text message.

To deploy this programmatic endpoint, use the following code in your Java EE application:

```
ServerEndpointConfig.Builder.create(EchoEndpoint.class, "/echo").build();
```

When you deploy your application, the endpoint is available at

```
ws://host:port/application/echo
```

For example, it might be available at the following location:

```
ws://localhost:8080/echoapp/echo
```

18.4 Annotated Endpoints

The following example shows how to create the same endpoint from Section 18.3, "Programmatic Endpoints," using annotations instead:

```
@ServerEndpoint("/echo")
public class EchoEndpoint {
   @OnMessage
   public void onMessage(Session session, String msg) {
      try {
         session.getBasicRemote().sendText(msg);
      } catch (IOException e) { ... }
   }
}
```

The annotated endpoint is simpler than the equivalent programmatic endpoint, and it is deployed automatically with the application to the relative path defined in the ServerEndpoint annotation. Instead of having to create an additional class for the message handler, this example uses the OnMessage annotation to designate the method invoked to handle messages.

Table 18–1 lists the annotations available in the `javax.websocket` package to designate the methods that handle lifecycle events. The examples in the table show the most common parameters for these methods. See the API reference for details on what combinations of parameters are allowed in each case.

Table 18–1   WebSocket Endpoint Lifecycle Annotations

Annotation	Event	Example

OnOpen	Connection opened	`@OnOpen`
		`public void open(Session session,`
		`                  EndpointConfig conf) { }`

OnMessage	Message received	`@OnMessage`
		`public void message(Session session,`
		`                    String msg) { }`

OnError	Connection error	`@OnError`
		`public void error(Session session,`
		`                  Throwable error) { }`

OnClose	Connection closed	`@OnClose`
		`public void close(Session session,`
		`                  CloseReason reason) { }`

18.5 Sending and Receiving Messages

WebSocket endpoints can send and receive text and binary messages. In addition, they can also send ping frames and receive pong frames. This section describes how to use the `Session` and `RemoteEndpoint` interfaces to send messages to the connected peer and how to use the `OnMessage` annotation to receive messages from it.

18.5.1 Sending Messages

Follow these steps to send messages in an endpoint.

1. Obtain the `Session` object from the connection.

    The `Session` object is available as a parameter in the annotated lifecycle methods of the endpoint, like those in Table 18–1. When your message is a response to a message from the peer, you have the `Session` object available inside the method that received the message (the method annotated with `@OnMessage`). If you have to send messages that are not responses, store the `Session` object as an instance variable of the endpoint class in the method annotated with `@OnOpen` so that you can access it from other methods.

2. Use the `Session` object to obtain a `RemoteEndpoint` object.

The `Session.getBasicRemote` method and the `Session.getAsyncRemote` method return `RemoteEndpoint.Basic` and `RemoteEndpoint.Async` objects respectively. The `RemoteEndpoint.Basic` interface provides blocking methods to send messages; the `RemoteEndpoint.Async` interface provides nonblocking methods.

3. Use the `RemoteEndpoint` object to send messages to the peer.

The following list shows some of the methods you can use to send messages to the peer.

- `void RemoteEndpoint.Basic.sendText(String text)`

  Send a text message to the peer. This method blocks until the whole message has been transmitted.

- `void RemoteEndpoint.Basic.sendBinary(ByteBuffer data)`

  Send a binary message to the peer. This method blocks until the whole message has been transmitted.

- `void RemoteEndpoint.sendPing(ByteBuffer appData)`

  Send a ping frame to the peer.

- `void RemoteEndpoint.sendPong(ByteBuffer appData)`

  Send a pong frame to the peer.

The example in Section 18.4, "Annotated Endpoints," demonstrates how to use this procedure to reply to every incoming text message.

18.5.1.1 Sending Messages to All Peers Connected to an Endpoint

Each instance of an endpoint class is associated with one and only one connection and peer; however, there are cases in which an endpoint instance needs to send messages to all connected peers. Examples include chat applications and online auctions. The `Session` interface provides the `getOpenSessions` method for this purpose. The following example demonstrates how to use this method to forward incoming text messages to all connected peers:

```
@ServerEndpoint("/echoall")
public class EchoAllEndpoint {
  @OnMessage
  public void onMessage(Session session, String msg) {
    try {
      for (Session sess : session.getOpenSessions()) {
        if (sess.isOpen())
          sess.getBasicRemote().sendText(msg);
      }
```

```
        } catch (IOException e) { ... }
    }
}
```

18.5.2 Receiving Messages

The OnMessage annotation designates methods that handle incoming messages.
You can have at most three methods annotated with @OnMessage in an endpoint,
one for each message type: text, binary, and pong. The following example
demonstrates how to designate methods to receive all three types of messages:

```
@ServerEndpoint("/receive")
public class ReceiveEndpoint {
    @OnMessage
    public void textMessage(Session session, String msg) {
        System.out.println("Text message: " + msg);
    }
    @OnMessage
    public void binaryMessage(Session session, ByteBuffer msg) {
        System.out.println("Binary message: " + msg.toString());
    }
    @OnMessage
    public void pongMessage(Session session, PongMessage msg) {
        System.out.println("Pong message: " +
                            msg.getApplicationData().toString());
    }
}
```

18.6 Maintaining Client State

Because the container creates an instance of the endpoint class for every
connection, you can define and use instance variables to store client state
information. In addition, the Session.getUserProperties method provides a
modifiable map to store user properties. For example, the following endpoint
replies to incoming text messages with the contents of the previous message from
each client:

```
@ServerEndpoint("/delayedecho")
public class DelayedEchoEndpoint {
    @OnOpen
    public void open(Session session) {
        session.getUserProperties().put("previousMsg", " ");
    }
    @OnMessage
    public void message(Session session, String msg) {
```

```
        String prev = (String) session.getUserProperties()
                                 .get("previousMsg");
        session.getUserProperties().put("previousMsg", msg);
        try {
           session.getBasicRemote().sendText(prev);
        } catch (IOException e) { ... }
    }
}
```

To store information common to all connected clients, you can use class (static) variables; however, you are responsible for ensuring thread-safe access to them.

18.7 Using Encoders and Decoders

The Java API for WebSocket provides support for converting between WebSocket messages and custom Java types using encoders and decoders. An encoder takes a Java object and produces a representation that can be transmitted as a WebSocket message; for example, encoders typically produce JSON, XML, or binary representations. A decoder performs the reverse function; it reads a WebSocket message and creates a Java object.

This mechanism simplifies WebSocket applications, because it decouples the business logic from the serialization and deserialization of objects.

18.7.1 Implementing Encoders to Convert Java Objects into WebSocket Messages

The procedure to implement and use encoders in endpoints follows.

1. Implement one of the following interfaces:

    - Encoder.Text<T> for text messages

    - Encoder.Binary<T> for binary messages

    These interfaces specify the encode method. Implement an encoder class for each custom Java type that you want to send as a WebSocket message.

2. Add the names of your encoder implementations to the encoders optional parameter of the ServerEndpoint annotation.

3. Use the sendObject(Object data) method of the RemoteEndpoint.Basic or RemoteEndpoint.Async interfaces to send your objects as messages. The container looks for an encoder that matches your type and uses it to convert the object to a WebSocket message.

For example, if you have two Java types (MessageA and MessageB) that you want to send as text messages, implement the Encoder.Text<MessageA> and Encoder.Text<MessageB> interfaces as follows:

```
public class MessageATextEncoder implements Encoder.Text<MessageA> {
    @Override
    public void init(EndpointConfig ec) { }
    @Override
    public void destroy() { }
    @Override
    public String encode(MessageA msgA) throws EncodeException {
        // Access msgA's properties and convert to JSON text...
        return msgAJsonString;
    }
}
```

Implement Encoder.Text<MessageB> similarly. Then, add the encoders parameter to the ServerEndpoint annotation as follows:

```
@ServerEndpoint(
    value = "/myendpoint",
    encoders = { MessageATextEncoder.class, MessageBTextEncoder.class }
)
public class EncEndpoint { ... }
```

Now, you can send MessageA and MessageB objects as WebSocket messages using the sendObject method as follows:

```
MessageA msgA = new MessageA(...);
MessageB msgB = new MessageB(...);
session.getBasicRemote.sendObject(msgA);
session.getBasicRemote.sendObject(msgB);
```

As in this example, you can have more than one encoder for text messages and more than one encoder for binary messages. Like endpoints, encoder instances are associated with one and only one WebSocket connection and peer, so there is only one thread executing the code of an encoder instance at any given time.

18.7.2 Implementing Decoders to Convert WebSocket Messages into Java Objects

The procedure to implement and use decoders in endpoints follows.

1. Implement one of the following interfaces:

   - Decoder.Text<T> for text messages

   - Decoder.Binary<T> for binary messages

These interfaces specify the `willDecode` and `decode` methods.

Note: Unlike with encoders, you can specify at most *one* decoder for binary messages and *one* decoder for text messages.

---

2. Add the names of your decoder implementations to the `decoders` optional parameter of the `ServerEndpoint` annotation.

3. Use the `OnMessage` annotation in the endpoint to designate a method that takes your custom Java type as a parameter. When the endpoint receives a message that can be decoded by one of the decoders you specified, the container calls the method annotated with `@OnMessage` that takes your custom Java type as a parameter if this method exists.

For example, if you have two Java types (`MessageA` and `MessageB`) that you want to send and receive as text messages, define them so that they extend a common class (`Message`). Because you can only define one decoder for text messages, implement a decoder for the `Message` class as follows:

```
public class MessageTextDecoder implements Decoder.Text<Message> {
    @Override
    public void init(EndpointConfig ec) { }
    @Override
    public void destroy() { }
    @Override
    public Message decode(String string) throws DecodeException {
        // Read message...
        if ( /* message is an A message */ )
            return new MessageA(...);
        else if ( /* message is a B message */ )
            return new MessageB(...);
    }
    @Override
    public boolean willDecode(String string) {
        // Determine if the message can be converted into either a
        // MessageA object or a MessageB object...
        return canDecode;
    }
}
```

Then, add the `decoder` parameter to the `ServerEndpoint` annotation as follows:

```
@ServerEndpoint(
    value = "/myendpoint",
    encoders = { MessageATextEncoder.class, MessageBTextEncoder.class },
    decoders = { MessageTextDecoder.class }
```

```
)
public class EncDecEndpoint { ... }
```

Now, define a method in the endpoint class that receives `MessageA` and `MessageB` objects as follows:

```
@OnMessage
public void message(Session session, Message msg) {
    if (msg instanceof MessageA) {
        // We received a MessageA object...
    } else if (msg instanceof MessageB) {
        // We received a MessageB object...
    }
}
```

Like endpoints, decoder instances are associated with one and only one WebSocket connection and peer, so there is only one thread executing the code of a decoder instance at any given time.

18.8 Path Parameters

The `ServerEndpoint` annotation enables you to use URI templates to specify parts of an endpoint deployment URI as application parameters. For example, consider this endpoint:

```
@ServerEndpoint("/chatrooms/{room-name}")
public class ChatEndpoint {
    ...
}
```

If the endpoint is deployed inside a web application called `chatapp` at a local Java EE server in port 8080, clients can connect to the endpoint using any of the following URIs:

```
http://localhost:8080/chatapp/chatrooms/currentnews
http://localhost:8080/chatapp/chatrooms/music
http://localhost:8080/chatapp/chatrooms/cars
http://localhost:8080/chatapp/chatrooms/technology
```

Annotated endpoints can receive path parameters as arguments in methods annotated with `@OnOpen`, `@OnMessage`, and `@OnClose`. In this example, the endpoint uses the parameter in the `@OnOpen` method to determine which chat room the client wants to join:

```
@ServerEndpoint("/chatrooms/{room-name}")
public class ChatEndpoint {
```

```
@OnOpen
public void open(Session session,
                 EndpointConfig c,
                 @PathParam("room-name") String roomName) {
    // Add the client to the chat room of their choice ...
    }
}
```

The path parameters used as arguments in these methods can be strings, primitive types, or the corresponding wrapper types.

18.9 Handling Errors

To designate a method that handles errors in an annotated WebSocket endpoint, decorate it with @OnError:

```
@ServerEndpoint("/testendpoint")
public class TestEndpoint {
    ...
    @OnError
    public void error(Session session, Throwable t) {
        t.printStackTrace();
        ...
    }
}
```

This method is invoked when there are connection problems, runtime errors from message handlers, or conversion errors when decoding messages.

18.10 Specifying an Endpoint Configurator Class

The Java API for WebSocket enables you to configure how the container creates server endpoint instances. You can provide custom endpoint configuration logic to

- Access the details of the initial HTTP request for a WebSocket connection

- Perform custom checks on the Origin HTTP header

- Modify the WebSocket handshake response

- Choose a WebSocket subprotocol from those requested by the client

- Control the instantiation and initialization of endpoint instances

To provide custom endpoint configuration logic, you extend the ServerEndpointConfig.Configurator class and override some of its methods. In the endpoint class, you specify the configurator class using the `configurator` parameter of the `ServerEndpoint` annotation.

For example, the following configurator class makes the handshake request object available to endpoint instances:

```
public class CustomConfigurator extends ServerEndpointConfig.Configurator {

    @Override
    public void modifyHandshake(ServerEndpointConfig conf,
                                HandshakeRequest req,
                                HandshakeResponse resp) {

        conf.getUserProperties().put("handshakereq", req);
    }
}
```

The following endpoint class configures endpoint instances with the custom configurator, which enables them to access the handshake request object:

```
@ServerEndpoint(
    value = "/myendpoint",
    configurator = CustomConfigurator.class
)
public class MyEndpoint {

    @OnOpen
    public void open(Session s, EndpointConfig conf) {
        HandshakeRequest req = (HandshakeRequest) conf.getUserProperties()
                                                      .get("handshakereq");
        Map<String,List<String>> headers = req.getHeaders();
        ...
    }
}
```

The endpoint class can use the handshake request object to access the details of the initial HTTP request, such as its headers or the `HttpSession` object.

For more information on endpoint configuration, see the API reference for the `ServerEndpointConfig.Configurator` class.

18.11 The dukeetf2 Example Application

The `dukeetf2` example application, located in the *tut-install*/examples/web/websocket/dukeetf2/ directory, demonstrates how to use a WebSocket endpoint to provide data updates to web clients. The example resembles a service that provides periodic updates on the price and trading volume of an electronically traded fund (ETF).

18.11.1 Architecture of the dukeetf2 Sample Application

The dukeetf2 example application consists of a WebSocket endpoint, an enterprise bean, and an HTML page.

- The endpoint accepts connections from clients and sends them updates when new data for price and trading volume becomes available.

- The enterprise bean updates the price and volume information once every second.

- The HTML page uses JavaScript code to connect to the WebSocket endpoint, parse incoming messages, and update the price and volume information without reloading the page.

18.11.1.1 The Endpoint

The WebSocket endpoint is implemented in the ETFEndpoint class, which stores all connected sessions in a queue and provides a method that the enterprise bean calls when there is new information available to send:

```
@ServerEndpoint("/dukeetf")
public class ETFEndpoint {
    private static final Logger logger = Logger.getLogger("ETFEndpoint");
    /* Queue for all open WebSocket sessions */
    static Queue<Session> queue = new ConcurrentLinkedQueue<>();

    /* PriceVolumeBean calls this method to send updates */
    public static void send(double price, int volume) {
        String msg = String.format("%.2f, %d", price, volume);
        try {
            /* Send updates to all open WebSocket sessions */
            for (Session session : queue) {
                session.getBasicRemote().sendText(msg);
                logger.log(Level.INFO, "Sent: {0}", msg);
            }
        } catch (IOException e) {
            logger.log(Level.INFO, e.toString());
        }
    }
    ...
}
```

The lifecycle methods of the endpoint add and remove sessions to and from the queue:

```
@ServerEndpoint("/dukeetf")
public class ETFEndpoint {
    ...
    @OnOpen
    public void openConnection(Session session) {
        /* Register this connection in the queue */
        queue.add(session);
        logger.log(Level.INFO, "Connection opened.");
    }

    @OnClose
    public void closedConnection(Session session) {
        /* Remove this connection from the queue */
        queue.remove(session);
        logger.log(Level.INFO, "Connection closed.");
    }

    @OnError
    public void error(Session session, Throwable t) {
        /* Remove this connection from the queue */
        queue.remove(session);
        logger.log(Level.INFO, t.toString());
        logger.log(Level.INFO, "Connection error.");
    }
}
```

18.11.1.2 The Enterprise Bean

The enterprise bean uses the timer service to generate new price and volume information every second:

```
@Startup
@Singleton
public class PriceVolumeBean {
    /* Use the container's timer service */
    @Resource TimerService tservice;
    private Random random;
    private volatile double price = 100.0;
    private volatile int volume = 300000;
    private static final Logger logger = Logger.getLogger("PriceVolumeBean");

    @PostConstruct
    public void init() {
        /* Initialize the EJB and create a timer */
```

```
        logger.log(Level.INFO, "Initializing EJB.");
        random = new Random();
        tservice.createIntervalTimer(1000, 1000, new TimerConfig());
    }

    @Timeout
    public void timeout() {
        /* Adjust price and volume and send updates */
        price += 1.0*(random.nextInt(100)-50)/100.0;
        volume += random.nextInt(5000) - 2500;
        ETFEndpoint.send(price, volume);
    }
}
```

The enterprise bean calls the send method of the ETFEndpoint class in the timeout method. See Section 5.4, "Using the Timer Service," in *The Java EE 7 Tutorial, Volume 2*, for more information on the timer service.

18.11.1.3 The HTML Page

The HTML page consists of a table and some JavaScript code. The table contains two fields referenced from JavaScript code:

```
<!DOCTYPE html>
<html>
<head>...</head>
<body>
  ...
  <table>
    ...
    <td id="price">--.--</td>
    ...
    <td id="volume">--</td>
    ...
  </table>
</body>
</html>
```

The JavaScript code uses the WebSocket API to connect to the server endpoint and to designate a callback method for incoming messages. The callback method updates the page with the new information:

```
var wsocket;
function connect() {
    wsocket = new WebSocket("ws://localhost:8080/dukeetf2/dukeetf");
    wsocket.onmessage = onMessage;
}
```

```
function onMessage(evt) {
    var arraypv = evt.data.split(",");
    document.getElementById("price").innerHTML = arraypv[0];
    document.getElementById("volume").innerHTML = arraypv[1];
}
window.addEventListener("load", connect, false);
```

The WebSocket API is supported by most modern browsers, and it is widely used in HTML5 web client development.

18.11.2 Running the dukeetf2 Example Application

This section describes how to run the dukeetf2 example application using NetBeans IDE and from the command line.

18.11.2.1 To Run the dukeetf2 Example Application Using NetBeans IDE

1. Make sure that GlassFish Server has been started (see Section 2.2, "Starting and Stopping GlassFish Server").

2. From the **File** menu, choose **Open Project**.

3. In the Open Project dialog box, navigate to:

   tut-install/examples/web/websocket

4. Select the dukeetf2 folder.

5. Click **Open Project**.

6. In the **Projects** tab, right-click the dukeetf2 project and select **Run**.

   This command builds and packages the application into a WAR file (dukeetf2.war) located in the target/ directory, deploys it to the server, and launches a web browser window with the following URL:

   http://localhost:8080/dukeetf2/

   Open the same URL on a different web browser tab or window to see how both pages get price and volume updates simultaneously.

18.11.2.2 To Run the dukeetf2 Example Application Using Maven

1. Make sure that GlassFish Server has been started (see Section 2.2, "Starting and Stopping GlassFish Server").

2. In a terminal window, go to:

   tut-install/examples/web/websocket/dukeetf2/

3. Enter the following command to deploy the application:

   ```
   mvn install
   ```

4. Open a web browser window and type the following address:

   ```
   http://localhost:8080/dukeetf2/
   ```

   Open the same URL on a different web browser tab or window to see how both pages get price and volume updates simultaneously.

18.12 The websocketbot Example Application

The websocketbot example application, located in the *tut-install*/examples/web/ websocket/websocketbot/ directory, demonstrates how to use a WebSocket endpoint to implement a chat. The example resembles a chat room in which many users can join and have a conversation. Users can ask simple questions to a bot agent that is always available in the chat room.

18.12.1 Architecture of the websocketbot Example Application

The websocketbot example application consists of the following elements:

- A CDI bean (BotBean) that contains the logic for the bot agent to reply to messages

- A WebSocket endpoint (BotEndpoint) that implements the chat room

- A set of classes (Message, ChatMessage, InfoMessage, JoinMessage, and UsersMessage) that represent application messages

- A set of classes (ChatMessageEncoder, InfoMessageEncoder, JoinMessageEncoder, and UsersMessageEncoder) that encode application messages into WebSocket text messages as JSON data

- A class (MessageDecoder) the parses WebSocket text messages as JSON data and decodes them into JoinMessage or ChatMessage objects

- An HTML page (index.html) that uses JavaScript code to implement the client for the chat room

18.12.1.1 The CDI Bean

The CDI bean (BotBean) is a Java class that contains the respond method. This method compares the incoming chat message with a set of predefined questions and returns a chat response.

```
@Named
public class BotBean {
    public String respond(String msg) { ... }
}
```

18.12.1.2 The WebSocket Endpoint

The WebSocket endpoint (BotEndpoint) is an annotated endpoint that performs the following functions:

- Receives messages from clients

- Forwards messages to clients

- Maintains a list of connected clients

- Invokes the bot agent functionality

The endpoint specifies its deployment URI and the message encoders and decoders using the ServerEndpoint annotation. The endpoint obtains an instance of the BotBean class and a managed executor service resource through dependency injection:

```
@ServerEndpoint(
    value = "/websocketbot",
    decoders = { MessageDecoder.class },
    encoders = { JoinMessageEncoder.class, ChatMessageEncoder.class,
                 InfoMessageEncoder.class, UsersMessageEncoder.class }
)
/* There is a BotEndpoint instance per connection */
public class BotEndpoint {
    private static final Logger logger = Logger.getLogger("BotEndpoint");
    /* Bot functionality bean */
    @Inject private BotBean botbean;
    /* Executor service for asynchronous processing */
    @Resource(name="comp/DefaultManagedExecutorService")
    private ManagedExecutorService mes;

    @OnOpen
    public void openConnection(Session session) {
        logger.log(Level.INFO, "Connection opened.");
    } ...
}
```

The message method processes incoming messages from clients. The decoder converts incoming text messages into JoinMessage or ChatMessage objects, which inherit from the Message class. The message method receives a Message object as a parameter:

```
@OnMessage
public void message(Session session, Message msg) {
    logger.log(Level.INFO, "Received: {0}", msg.toString());

    if (msg instanceof JoinMessage) {
        /* Add the new user and notify everybody */
        JoinMessage jmsg = (JoinMessage) msg;
        session.getUserProperties().put("name", jmsg.getName());
        session.getUserProperties().put("active", true);
        logger.log(Level.INFO, "Received: {0}", jmsg.toString());
        sendAll(session, new InfoMessage(jmsg.getName() +
                " has joined the chat"));
        sendAll(session, new ChatMessage("Duke", jmsg.getName(),
                "Hi there!!"));
        sendAll(session, new UsersMessage(this.getUserList(session)));

    } else if (msg instanceof ChatMessage) {
        /* Forward the message to everybody */
        ChatMessage cmsg = (ChatMessage) msg;
        logger.log(Level.INFO, "Received: {0}", cmsg.toString());
        sendAll(session, cmsg);
        if (cmsg.getTarget().compareTo("Duke") == 0) {
            /* The bot replies to the message */
            mes.submit(new Runnable() {
                @Override
                public void run() {
                    String resp = botbean.respond(cmsg.getMessage());
                    sendAll(session, new ChatMessage("Duke",
                            cmsg.getName(), resp));
                }
            });
        }
    }
}
```

If the message is a join message, the endpoint adds the new user to the list and notifies all connected clients. If the message is a chat message, the endpoint forwards it to all connected clients.

If a chat message is for the bot agent, the endpoint obtains a response using the BotBean instance and sends it to all connected clients. The sendAll method is similar to the example in Section 18.5.1.1, "Sending Messages to All Peers Connected to an Endpoint."

Asynchronous Processing and Concurrency Considerations

The WebSocket endpoint calls the `BotBean.respond` method to obtain a response from the bot. In this example, this is a blocking operation; the user that sent the associated message would not be able to send or receive other chat messages until the operation completes. To avoid this problem, the endpoint obtains an executor service from the container and executes the blocking operation in a different thread using the `ManagedExecutorService.submit` method from Concurrency Utilities for Java EE.

The Java API for WebSocket specification requires that Java EE implementations instantiate endpoint classes once per connection. This facilitates the development of WebSocket endpoints, because you are guaranteed that only one thread is executing the code in a WebSocket endpoint class at any given time. When you introduce a new thread in an endpoint, as in this example, you must ensure that variables and methods accessed by more than one thread are thread safe. In this example, the code in `BotBean` is thread safe, and the `BotEndpoint.sendAll` method has been declared `synchronized`.

See Chapter 27, "Concurrency Utilities for Java EE," in *The Java EE 7 Tutorial, Volume 2*, for more information on the managed executor service and Concurrency Utilities for Java EE.

18.12.1.3 The Application Messages

The classes that represent application messages (`Message`, `ChatMessage`, `InfoMessage`, `JoinMessage`, and `UsersMessage`) contain only properties and getter and setter methods. For example, the `ChatMessage` class looks like this:

```
public class ChatMessage extends Message {
    private String name;
    private String target;
    private String message;
    /* ... Constructor, getters, and setters ... */
}
```

18.12.1.4 The Encoder Classes

The encoder classes convert application message objects into JSON text using the Java API for JSON Processing. For example, the `ChatMessageEncoder` class is implemented as follows:

```
/* Encode a ChatMessage as JSON.
 * For example, (new ChatMessage("Peter","Duke","How are you?"))
 * is encoded as follows:
 * {"type":"chat","target":"Duke","message":"How are you?"}
 */
```

```java
public class ChatMessageEncoder implements Encoder.Text<ChatMessage> {
    @Override
    public void init(EndpointConfig ec) { }
    @Override
    public void destroy() { }
    @Override
    public String encode(ChatMessage chatMessage) throws EncodeException {
        // Access properties in chatMessage and write JSON text...
    }
}
```

See Chapter 19, "JSON Processing," for more information on the Java API for
JSON Processing.

18.12.1.5 The Message Decoder

The message decoder (MessageDecoder) class converts WebSocket text messages
into application messages by parsing JSON text. It is implemented as follows:

```java
/* Decode a JSON message into a JoinMessage or a ChatMessage.
 * For example, the incoming message
 * {"type":"chat","name":"Peter","target":"Duke","message":"How are you?"}
 * is decoded as (new ChatMessage("Peter", "Duke", "How are you?"))
 */
public class MessageDecoder implements Decoder.Text<Message> {
    /* Stores the name-value pairs from a JSON message as a Map */
    private Map<String,String> messageMap;

    @Override
    public void init(EndpointConfig ec) { }
    @Override
    public void destroy() { }

    /* Create a new Message object if the message can be decoded */
    @Override
    public Message decode(String string) throws DecodeException {
        Message msg = null;
        if (willDecode(string)) {
            switch (messageMap.get("type")) {
                case "join":
                    msg = new JoinMessage(messageMap.get("name"));
                    break;
                case "chat":
                    msg = new ChatMessage(messageMap.get("name"),
                                          messageMap.get("target"),
                                          messageMap.get("message"));
        }
```

```
        } else {
            throw new DecodeException(string, "[Message] Can't decode.");
        }
        return msg;
    }

    /* Decode a JSON message into a Map and check if it contains
     * all the required fields according to its type. */
    @Override
    public boolean willDecode(String string) {
        // Convert JSON data from the message into a name-value map...
        // Check if the message has all the fields for its message type...
    }
}
```

18.12.1.6 The HTML Page

The HTML page (index.html) contains a field for the user name. After the user types a name and clicks **Join**, three text areas are available: one to type and send messages, one for the chat room, and one with the list of users. The page also contains a WebSocket console that shows the messages sent and received as JSON text.

The JavaScript code on the page uses the WebSocket API to connect to the endpoint, send messages, and designate callback methods. The WebSocket API is supported by most modern browsers and is widely used for web client development with HTML5.

18.12.2 Running the websocketbot Example Application

This section describes how to run the websocketbot example application using NetBeans IDE and from the command line.

18.12.2.1 To Run the websocketbot Example Application Using NetBeans IDE

1. Make sure that GlassFish Server has been started (see Section 2.2, "Starting and Stopping GlassFish Server").

2. From the **File** menu, choose **Open Project**.

3. In the Open Project dialog box, navigate to:

    tut-install/examples/web/websocket

4. Select the websocketbot folder.

5. Click **Open Project**.

6. In the **Projects** tab, right-click the `websocketbot` project and select **Run**.

   This command builds and packages the application into a WAR file, `websocketbot.war`, located in the `target/` directory; deploys it to the server; and launches a web browser window with the following URL:

   ```
   http://localhost:8080/websocketbot/
   ```

   See Section 18.12.2.3, "To Test the websocketbot Example Application," for more information.

18.12.2.2 To Run the websocketbot Example Application Using Maven

1. Make sure that GlassFish Server has been started (see Section 2.2, "Starting and Stopping GlassFish Server").

2. In a terminal window, go to:

   ```
   tut-install/examples/web/websocket/websocketbot/
   ```

3. Enter the following command to deploy the application:

   ```
   mvn install
   ```

4. Open a web browser window and type the following address:

   ```
   http://localhost:8080/websocketbot/
   ```

   See Section 18.12.2.3, "To Test the websocketbot Example Application," for more information.

18.12.2.3 To Test the websocketbot Example Application

1. On the main page, type your name on the first text field and press the Enter key.

   The list of connected users appears on the text area on the right. The text area on the left is the chat room.

2. Type a message on the text area below the login button. For example, type the messages in bold and press enter to obtain responses similar to the following:

   ```
   [--Peter has joined the chat--]
   Duke: @Peter Hi there!!
   Peter: @Duke how are you?
   Duke: @Peter I'm doing great, thank you!
   Peter: @Duke when is your birthday?
   Duke: @Peter My birthday is on May 23rd. Thanks for asking!
   ```

3. Join the chat from another browser window by copying and pasting the URI on the address bar and joining with a different name.

    The new user name appears in the list of users in both browser windows. You can send messages from either window and see how they appear in the other.

4. Click **Show WebSocket Console**.

    The console shows the messages sent and received as JSON text.

18.13 Further Information about WebSocket

For more information on WebSocket in Java EE, see the Java API for WebSocket specification:

```
http://www.jcp.org/en/jsr/detail?id=356
```

19

JSON Processing

This chapter describes the Java API for JSON Processing (JSR 353). JSON is a data exchange format widely used in web services and other connected applications. JSR 353 provides an API to parse, transform, and query JSON data using the object model or the streaming model.

The following topics are addressed here:

- Introduction to JSON
- JSON Processing in the Java EE Platform
- Using the Object Model API
- Using the Streaming API
- JSON in Java EE RESTful Web Services
- The jsonpmodel Example Application
- The jsonpstreaming Example Application
- Further Information about the Java API for JSON Processing

19.1 Introduction to JSON

JSON is a text-based data exchange format derived from JavaScript that is used in web services and other connected applications. The following sections provide an introduction to JSON syntax, an overview of JSON uses, and a description of the most common approaches to generate and parse JSON.

19.1.1 JSON Syntax

JSON defines only two data structures: objects and arrays. An object is a set of name-value pairs, and an array is a list of values. JSON defines seven value types: *string, number, object, array, true, false,* and *null.*

The following example shows JSON data for a sample object that contains name-value pairs. The value for the name "phoneNumbers" is an array whose elements are two objects:

```
{
    "firstName": "Duke",
    "lastName": "Java",
    "age": 18,
    "streetAddress": "100 Internet Dr",
    "city": "JavaTown",
    "state": "JA",
    "postalCode": "12345",
    "phoneNumbers": [
        { "Mobile": "111-111-1111" },
        { "Home": "222-222-2222" }
    ]
}
```

JSON has the following syntax.

- Objects are enclosed in braces ({}), their name-value pairs are separated by a comma (,), and the name and value in a pair are separated by a colon (:). Names in an object are strings, whereas values may be of any of the seven value types, including another object or an array.

- Arrays are enclosed in brackets ([]), and their values are separated by a comma (,). Each value in an array may be of a different type, including another array or an object.

- When objects and arrays contain other objects or arrays, the data has a tree-like structure.

19.1.2 Uses of JSON

JSON is often used as a common format to serialize and deserialize data in applications that communicate with each other over the Internet. These applications are created using different programming languages and run in very different environments. JSON is suited to this scenario because it is an open standard, it is easy to read and write, and it is more compact than other representations.

RESTful web services use JSON extensively as the format for the data inside requests and responses. The HTTP header used to indicate that the content of a request or a response is JSON data is

```
Content-Type: application/json
```

JSON representations are usually more compact than XML representations because JSON does not have closing tags. Unlike XML, JSON does not have a widely accepted schema for defining and validating the structure of JSON data.

19.1.3 Generating and Parsing JSON Data

For generating and parsing JSON data, there are two programming models, which are similar to those used for XML documents.

- The object model creates a tree that represents the JSON data in memory. The tree can then be navigated, analyzed, or modified. This approach is the most flexible and allows for processing that requires access to the complete contents of the tree. However, it is often slower than the streaming model and requires more memory. The object model generates JSON output by navigating the entire tree at once.

- The streaming model uses an event-based parser that reads JSON data one element at a time. The parser generates events and stops for processing when an object or an array begins or ends, when it finds a key, or when it finds a value. Each element can be processed or discarded by the application code, and then the parser proceeds to the next event. This approach is adequate for local processing, in which the processing of an element does not require information from the rest of the data. The streaming model generates JSON output to a given stream by making a function call with one element at a time.

There are many JSON generators and parsers available for different programming languages and environments. Section 19.2, "JSON Processing in the Java EE Platform," describes the functionality provided by the Java API for JSON Processing (JSR 353).

19.2 JSON Processing in the Java EE Platform

Java EE includes support for JSR 353, which provides an API to parse, transform, and query JSON data using the object model or the streaming model described in Section 19.1.3, "Generating and Parsing JSON Data." The Java API for JSON Processing contains the following packages.

- The javax.json package contains a reader interface, a writer interface, and a model builder interface for the object model. This package also contains other utility classes and Java types for JSON elements. Table 19–1 lists the main classes and interfaces in this package.

- The `javax.json.stream` package contains a parser interface and a generator interface for the streaming model. Table 19–2 lists the main classes and interfaces in this package.

Table 19–1   Main Classes and Interfaces in javax.json

Class or Interface	Description
Json	Contains static methods to create instances of JSON parsers, builders, and generators. This class also contains methods to create parser, builder, and generator factory objects.
JsonReader	Reads JSON data from a stream and creates an object model in memory.
JsonObjectBuilder JsonArrayBuilder	Create an object model or an array model in memory by adding elements from application code.
JsonWriter	Writes an object model from memory to a stream.
JsonValue	Represents an element (such as an object, an array, or a value) in JSON data.
JsonStructure	Represents an object or an array in JSON data. This interface is a subtype of JsonValue.
JsonObject JsonArray	Represent an object or an array in JSON data. These two interfaces are subtypes of JsonStructure.
JsonString JsonNumber	Represent data types for elements in JSON data. These two interfaces are subtypes of JsonValue.
JsonException	Indicates that a problem occurred during JSON processing.

Table 19–2   Main Classes and Interfaces in javax.json.stream

Class or Interface	Description
JsonParser	Represents an event-based parser that can read JSON data from a stream or from an object model.
JsonGenerator	Writes JSON data to a stream one element at a time.

19.3 Using the Object Model API

This section describes four use cases of the object model API: creating an object model from JSON data, creating an object model from application code, navigating an object model, and writing an object model to a stream.

19.3.1 Creating an Object Model from JSON Data

The following code demonstrates how to create an object model from JSON data in a text file:

```
import java.io.FileReader;
import javax.json.Json;
import javax.json.JsonReader;
import javax.json.JsonStructure;
...
JsonReader reader = Json.createReader(new FileReader("jsondata.txt"));
JsonStructure jsonst = reader.read();
```

The object reference jsonst can be either of type JsonObject or of type JsonArray, depending on the contents of the file. JsonObject and JsonArray are subtypes of JsonStructure. This reference represents the top of the tree and can be used to navigate the tree or to write it to a stream as JSON data.

19.3.2 Creating an Object Model from Application Code

The following code demonstrates how to create an object model from application code:

```
import javax.json.Json;
import javax.json.JsonObject;
...
JsonObject model = Json.createObjectBuilder()
    .add("firstName", "Duke")
    .add("lastName", "Java")
    .add("age", 18)
    .add("streetAddress", "100 Internet Dr")
    .add("city", "JavaTown")
    .add("state", "JA")
    .add("postalCode", "12345")
    .add("phoneNumbers", Json.createArrayBuilder()
      .add(Json.createObjectBuilder()
        .add("type", "mobile")
        .add("number", "111-111-1111"))
      .add(Json.createObjectBuilder()
        .add("type", "home")
```

```
          .add("number", "222-222-2222")))
   .build();
```

The object reference `model` represents the top of the tree, which is created by nesting calls to the `add` methods and built by calling the `build` method. The `JsonObjectBuilder` class contains the following `add` methods:

```
JsonObjectBuilder add(String name, BigDecimal value)
JsonObjectBuilder add(String name, BigInteger value)
JsonObjectBuilder add(String name, boolean value)
JsonObjectBuilder add(String name, double value)
JsonObjectBuilder add(String name, int value)
JsonObjectBuilder add(String name, JsonArrayBuilder builder)
JsonObjectBuilder add(String name, JsonObjectBuilder builder)
JsonObjectBuilder add(String name, JsonValue value)
JsonObjectBuilder add(String name, long value)
JsonObjectBuilder add(String name, String value)
JsonObjectBuilder addNull(String name)
```

The `JsonArrayBuilder` class contains similar `add` methods that do not have a name (key) parameter. You can nest arrays and objects by passing a new `JsonArrayBuilder` object or a new `JsonObjectBuilder` object to the corresponding `add` method, as shown in this example.

The resulting tree represents the JSON data from Section 19.1.1, "JSON Syntax."

19.3.3 Navigating an Object Model

The following code demonstrates a simple approach to navigating an object model:

```
import javax.json.JsonValue;
import javax.json.JsonObject;
import javax.json.JsonArray;
import javax.json.JsonNumber;
import javax.json.JsonString;
...
public static void navigateTree(JsonValue tree, String key) {
   if (key != null)
      System.out.print("Key " + key + ": ");
   switch(tree.getValueType()) {
      case OBJECT:
         System.out.println("OBJECT");
         JsonObject object = (JsonObject) tree;
         for (String name : object.keySet())
            navigateTree(object.get(name), name);
         break;
```

```
            case ARRAY:
                System.out.println("ARRAY");
                JsonArray array = (JsonArray) tree;
                for (JsonValue val : array)
                    navigateTree(val, null);
                break;
            case STRING:
                JsonString st = (JsonString) tree;
                System.out.println("STRING " + st.getString());
                break;
            case NUMBER:
                JsonNumber num = (JsonNumber) tree;
                System.out.println("NUMBER " + num.toString());
                break;
            case TRUE:
            case FALSE:
            case NULL:
                System.out.println(tree.getValueType().toString());
                break;
        }
}
```

The method `navigateTree` can be used with the models built in Section 19.3.1, "Creating an Object Model from JSON Data," and Section 19.3.2, "Creating an Object Model from Application Code," as follows:

```
navigateTree(model, null);
```

The `navigateTree` method takes two arguments: a JSON element and a key. The key is used only to help print the key-value pairs inside objects. Elements in a tree are represented by the `JsonValue` type. If the element is an object or an array, a new call to this method is made for every element contained in the object or array. If the element is a value, it is printed to the standard output.

The `JsonValue.getValueType` method identifies the element as an object, an array, or a value. For objects, the `JsonObject.keySet` method returns a set of strings that contains the keys in the object, and the `JsonObject.get(String name)` method returns the value of the element whose key is name. For arrays, `JsonArray` implements the `List<JsonValue>` interface. You can use enhanced `for` loops with the `Set<String>` instance returned by `JsonObject.keySet` and with instances of `JsonArray`, as shown in this example.

The `navigateTree` method for the model built in Section 19.3.2, "Creating an Object Model from Application Code," produces the following output:

```
OBJECT
Key firstName: STRING Duke
Key lastName: STRING Java
Key age: NUMBER 18
Key streetAddress: STRING 100 Internet Dr
Key city: STRING JavaTown
Key state: STRING JA
Key postalCode: STRING 12345
Key phoneNumbers: ARRAY
OBJECT
Key type: STRING mobile
Key number: STRING 111-111-1111
OBJECT
Key type: STRING home
Key number: STRING 222-222-2222
```

19.3.4 Writing an Object Model to a Stream

The object models created in Section 19.3.1, "Creating an Object Model from JSON Data," and Section 19.3.2, "Creating an Object Model from Application Code," can be written to a stream using the `JsonWriter` class as follows:

```
import java.io.StringWriter;
import javax.json.JsonWriter;
...
StringWriter stWriter = new StringWriter();
JsonWriter jsonWriter = Json.createWriter(stWriter);
jsonWriter.writeObject(model);
jsonWriter.close();

String jsonData = stWriter.toString();
System.out.println(jsonData);
```

The `Json.createWriter` method takes an output stream as a parameter. The `JsonWriter.writeObject` method writes the object to the stream. The `JsonWriter.close` method closes the underlying output stream.

The following example uses `try-with-resources` to close the JSON writer automatically:

```
StringWriter stWriter = new StringWriter();
try (JsonWriter jsonWriter = Json.createWriter(stWriter)) {
   jsonWriter.writeObject(model);
}
```

```
String jsonData = stWriter.toString();
System.out.println(jsonData);
```

19.4 Using the Streaming API

This section describes two use cases of the streaming API:

- Reading JSON data using a parser
- Writing JSON data using a generator

19.4.1 Reading JSON Data Using a Parser

The streaming API is the most efficient approach for parsing JSON text. The following code demonstrates how to create a `JsonParser` object and how to parse JSON data using events:

```
import javax.json.Json;
import javax.json.stream.JsonParser;
...
JsonParser parser = Json.createParser(new StringReader(jsonData));
while (parser.hasNext()) {
   JsonParser.Event event = parser.next();
   switch(event) {
      case START_ARRAY:
      case END_ARRAY:
      case START_OBJECT:
      case END_OBJECT:
      case VALUE_FALSE:
      case VALUE_NULL:
      case VALUE_TRUE:
         System.out.println(event.toString());
         break;
      case KEY_NAME:
         System.out.print(event.toString() + " " +
                          parser.getString() + " - ");
         break;
      case VALUE_STRING:
      case VALUE_NUMBER:
         System.out.println(event.toString() + " " +
                            parser.getString());
         break;
   }
}
```

This example consists of three steps.

1. Obtain a parser instance by calling the `Json.createParser` static method.

2. Iterate over the parser events with the `JsonParser.hasNext` and the `JsonParser.next` methods.

3. Perform local processing for each element.

The example shows the ten possible event types from the parser. The parser's next method advances it to the next event. For the event types KEY_NAME, VALUE_STRING, and VALUE_NUMBER, you can obtain the content of the element by calling the method `JsonParser.getString`. For VALUE_NUMBER events, you can also use the following methods:

- `JsonParser.isIntegralNumber`

- `JsonParser.getInt`

- `JsonParser.getLong`

- `JsonParser.getBigDecimal`

See the Java EE 7 API reference for the `javax.json.stream.JsonParser` interface for more information.

The output of this example is the following:

```
START_OBJECT
KEY_NAME firstName - VALUE_STRING Duke
KEY_NAME lastName - VALUE_STRING Java
KEY_NAME age - VALUE_NUMBER 18
KEY_NAME streetAddress - VALUE_STRING 100 Internet Dr
KEY_NAME city - VALUE_STRING JavaTown
KEY_NAME state - VALUE_STRING JA
KEY_NAME postalCode - VALUE_STRING 12345
KEY_NAME phoneNumbers - START_ARRAY
START_OBJECT
KEY_NAME type - VALUE_STRING mobile
KEY_NAME number - VALUE_STRING 111-111-1111
END_OBJECT
START_OBJECT
KEY_NAME type - VALUE_STRING home
KEY_NAME number - VALUE_STRING 222-222-2222
END_OBJECT
END_ARRAY
END_OBJECT
```

19.4.2 Writing JSON Data Using a Generator

The following code demonstrates how to write JSON data to a file using the streaming API:

```
FileWriter writer = new FileWriter("test.txt");
JsonGenerator gen = Json.createGenerator(writer);
gen.writeStartObject()
    .write("firstName", "Duke")
    .write("lastName", "Java")
    .write("age", 18)
    .write("streetAddress", "100 Internet Dr")
    .write("city", "JavaTown")
    .write("state", "JA")
    .write("postalCode", "12345")
    .writeStartArray("phoneNumbers")
      .writeStartObject()
        .write("type", "mobile")
        .write("number", "111-111-1111")
      .writeEnd()
      .writeStartObject()
        .write("type", "home")
        .write("number", "222-222-2222")
      .writeEnd()
    .writeEnd()
.writeEnd();
gen.close();
```

This example obtains a JSON generator by calling the `Json.createGenerator` static method, which takes a writer or an output stream as a parameter. The example writes JSON data to the `test.txt` file by nesting calls to the `write`, `writeStartArray`, `writeStartObject`, and `writeEnd` methods. The `JsonGenerator.close` method closes the underlying writer or output stream.

19.5 JSON in Java EE RESTful Web Services

This section explains how the Java API for JSON Processing is related to other Java EE packages that provide JSON support for RESTful web services. See Chapter 29, "Building RESTful Web Services with JAX-RS," for more information on RESTful web services.

Jersey, the reference implementation for JAX-RS (JSR 311) included in GlassFish Server, provides support for binding JSON data from RESTful resource methods to Java objects using JAXB, as described in Section 31.7, "Using JAX-RS with JAXB." However, JSON support is not part of JAX-RS (JSR 311) or JAXB (JSR 222), so that procedure may not work for Java EE implementations other than GlassFish Server.

The Java API for JSON Processing (JSR 353) does not explicitly support JSON binding in Java. A future JSR (JSON Binding) that is similar to JAXB for XML is under consideration for a future release of Java EE.

You can still use the Java API for JSON Processing with JAX-RS resource methods. For more information, see the sample code for JSON Processing included with the Java EE 7 SDK.

19.6 The jsonpmodel Example Application

This section describes how to build and run the jsonpmodel example application. This example is a web application that demonstrates how to create an object model from form data, how to parse JSON data, and how write JSON data using the object model API.

The jsonpmodel example application is in the *tut-install*/examples/web/jsonp/ jsonpmodel directory.

19.6.1 Components of the jsonpmodel Example Application

The jsonpmodel example application contains the following files.

- Three JavaServer Faces pages.

    - The index.xhtml page contains a form to collect information.

    - The modelcreated.xhtml page contains a text area that displays JSON data.

    - The parsejson.xhtml page contains a table that shows the elements of the object model.

- The ObjectModelBean.java managed bean, which is a session-scoped managed bean that stores the data from the form and directs the navigation between the Facelets pages. This file also contains code that uses the JSON object model API.

The code used in ObjectModelBean.java to create an object model from the data in the form is similar to the example in Section 19.3.2, "Creating an Object Model from Application Code." The code to write JSON output from the model is similar to the example in Section 19.3.4, "Writing an Object Model to a Stream." The code to navigate the object model tree is similar to the example in Section 19.3.3, "Navigating an Object Model."

19.6.2 Running the jsonpmodel Example Application

This section describes how to run the jsonpmodel example application using NetBeans IDE and from the command line.

19.6.2.1 To Run the jsonpmodel Example Application Using NetBeans IDE

1. Make sure that GlassFish Server has been started (see Section 2.2, "Starting and Stopping GlassFish Server").

2. From the **File** menu, choose **Open Project**.

3. In the Open Project dialog box, navigate to:

   tut-install/examples/web/jsonp

4. Select the jsonpmodel folder.

5. Click **Open Project**.

6. In the **Projects** tab, right-click the jsonpmodel project and select **Run**.

   This command builds and packages the application into a WAR file (jsonpmodel.war) located in the target/ directory, deploys it to the server, and opens a web browser window with the following URL:

   http://localhost:8080/jsonpmodel/

7. Edit the data on the page and click **Create a JSON Object** to submit the form. The following page shows a JSON object that contains the data from the form.

8. Click **Parse JSON**. The following page contains a table that lists the nodes of the object model tree.

19.6.2.2 To Run the jsonpmodel Example Application Using Maven

1. Make sure that GlassFish Server has been started (see Section 2.2, "Starting and Stopping GlassFish Server").

2. In a terminal window, go to:

   tut-install/examples/web/jsonp/jsonpmodel/

3. Enter the following command to deploy the application:

   mvn install

4. Open a web browser window at the following URL:

   http://localhost:8080/jsonpmodel/

5. Edit the data on the page and click **Create a JSON Object** to submit the form. The following page shows a JSON object that contains the data from the form.

6. Click **Parse JSON**. The following page contains a table that lists the nodes of the object model tree.

19.7 The jsonpstreaming Example Application

This section describes how to build and run the `jsonpstreaming` example application. This example is a web application that demonstrates how to create JSON data from form data, how to parse JSON data, and how to write JSON output using the streaming API.

The `jsonpstreaming` example application is in the *tut-install*/examples/web/jsonp/jsonpstreaming directory.

19.7.1 Components of the jsonpstreaming Example Application

The `jsonpstreaming` example application contains the following files.

- Three JavaServer Faces pages.

    - The `index.xhtml` page contains a form to collect information.

    - The `filewritten.xhtml` page contains a text area that displays JSON data.

    - The `parsed.xhtml` page contains a table that lists the events from the parser.

- The `StreamingBean.java` managed bean, a session-scoped managed bean that stores the data from the form and directs the navigation between the Facelets pages. This file also contains code that uses the JSON streaming API.

The code used in `StreamingBean.java` to write JSON data to a file is similar to the example in Section 19.4.2, "Writing JSON Data Using a Generator." The code to parse JSON data from a file is similar to the example in Section 19.4.1, "Reading JSON Data Using a Parser."

19.7.2 Running the jsonpstreaming Example Application

This section describes how to run the `jsonpstreaming` example application using NetBeans IDE and from the command line.

19.7.2.1 To Run the jsonpstreaming Example Application Using NetBeans IDE

1. Make sure that GlassFish Server has been started (see Section 2.2, "Starting and Stopping GlassFish Server").

2. From the **File** menu, choose **Open Project**.

3. In the Open Project dialog box, navigate to:

   tut-install/examples/web/jsonp

4. Select the jsonpstreaming folder.

5. Click **Open Project**.

6. In the **Projects** tab, right-click the jsonpstreaming project and select **Run**.

   This command builds and packages the application into a WAR file (jsonpstreaming.war) located in the target directory, deploys it to the server, and opens a web browser window with the following URL:

   http://localhost:8080/jsonpstreaming/

7. Edit the data on the page and click **Write a JSON Object to a File** to submit the form and write a JSON object to a text file. The following page shows the contents of the text file.

8. Click **Parse JSON from File**. The following page contains a table that lists the parser events for the JSON data in the text file.

19.7.2.2 To Run the jsonpstreaming Example Application Using Maven

1. Make sure that GlassFish Server has been started (see Section 2.2, "Starting and Stopping GlassFish Server").

2. In a terminal window, go to:

   tut-install/examples/web/jsonp/jsonpstreaming/

3. Enter the following command to deploy the application:

   mvn install

4. Open a web browser window at the following URL:

   http://localhost:8080/jsonpstreaming/

5. Edit the data on the page and click **Write a JSON Object to a File** to submit the form and write a JSON object to a text file. The following page shows the contents of the text file.

6. Click **Parse JSON from File**. The following page contains a table that lists the parser events for the JSON data in the text file.

19.8 Further Information about the Java API for JSON Processing

For more information on JSON processing in Java EE, see the Java API for JSON Processing specification:

```
http://www.jcp.org/en/jsr/detail?id=353
```

20

Internationalizing and Localizing Web Applications

The process of preparing an application to support more than one language and data format is called **internationalization**. **Localization** is the process of adapting an internationalized application to support a specific region or locale. Examples of locale-dependent information include messages and user interface labels, character sets and encoding, and date and currency formats. Although all client user interfaces should be internationalized and localized, it is particularly important for web applications because of the global nature of the web.

The following topics are addressed here:

- Java Platform Localization Classes

- Providing Localized Messages and Labels

- Date and Number Formatting

- Character Sets and Encodings

20.1 Java Platform Localization Classes

In the Java platform, `java.util.Locale` (`http://docs.oracle.com/javase/7/docs/api/java/util/Locale.html`) represents a specific geographical, political, or cultural region. The string representation of a locale consists of the international standard two-character abbreviation for language and country and an optional variant, all separated by underscore (_) characters. Examples of locale strings include `fr` (French), `de_CH` (Swiss German), and `en_US_POSIX` (English on a POSIX-compliant platform).

Locale-sensitive data is stored in a `java.util.ResourceBundle` (`http://docs.oracle.com/javase/7/docs/api/java/util/ResourceBundle.html`). A resource bundle contains key-value pairs, where the keys uniquely identify a locale-specific object in the bundle. A resource bundle can be backed by a text file (properties resource bundle) or a class (list resource bundle) containing the pairs. You construct a resource bundle instance by appending a locale string representation to a base name.

The Duke's Bookstore application (see Chapter 28, "Duke's Bookstore Case Study Example," in *The Java EE 7 Tutorial, Volume 2*) contains resource bundles with the base name `messages.properties` for the locales `de` (German), `es` (Spanish), and `fr` (French). The default locale, `en` (English), which is specified in the `faces-config.xml` file, uses the resource bundle with the base name, `messages.properties`.

For more details on internationalization and localization in the Java platform, see `http://docs.oracle.com/javase/tutorial/i18n/`.

20.2 Providing Localized Messages and Labels

Messages and labels should be tailored according to the conventions of a user's language and region. There are two approaches to providing localized messages and labels in a web application.

- Provide a version of the web page in each of the target locales and have a controller servlet dispatch the request to the appropriate page depending on the requested locale. This approach is useful if large amounts of data on a page or an entire web application need to be internationalized.

- Isolate any locale-sensitive data on a page into resource bundles, and access the data so that the corresponding translated message is fetched automatically and inserted into the page. Thus, instead of creating strings directly in your code, you create a resource bundle that contains translations and read the translations from that bundle using the corresponding key.

The Duke's Bookstore application follows the second approach. Here are a few lines from the default resource bundle `messages.properties`:

```
TitleShoppingCart=Shopping Cart
TitleReceipt=Receipt
TitleBookCatalog=Book Catalog
TitleCashier=Cashier
TitleBookDescription=Book Description
Visitor=You are visitor number
What=What We\'re Reading
```

20.2.1 Establishing the Locale

To get the correct strings for a given user, a web application either retrieves the locale (set by a browser language preference) from the request using the getLocale method, or allows the user to explicitly select the locale.

A component can explicitly set the locale by using the fmt:setLocale tag.

The locale-config element in the configuration file registers the default locale and also registers other supported locales. This element in Duke's Bookstore registers English as the default locale and indicates that German, French, and Spanish are supported locales.

```
<locale-config>
    <default-locale>en</default-locale>
    <supported-locale>es</supported-locale>
    <supported-locale>de</supported-locale>
    <supported-locale>fr</supported-locale>
</locale-config>
```

The LocaleBean in the Duke's Bookstore application uses the getLocale method to retrieve the locale.

```
public class LocaleBean {

    ...
    private FacesContext ctx = FacesContext.getCurrentInstance();
    private Locale locale = ctx.getViewRoot().getLocale();;

    ...
}
```

20.2.2 Setting the Resource Bundle

The resource bundle is set with the resource-bundle element in the configuration file. The setting for Duke's Bookstore looks like this:

```
<resource-bundle>
    <base-name>
        javaeetutorial.dukesbookstore.web.messages.Messages
    </base-name>
    <var>bundle</var>
</resource-bundle>
```

After the locale is set, the controller of a web application could retrieve the resource bundle for that locale and save it as a session attribute (see Section 17.9.2,

"Associating Objects with a Session") for use by other components or simply be used to return a text string appropriate for the selected locale:

```
public String toString(Locale locale) {
    ResourceBundle res =
        ResourceBundle.getBundle(
            "javaeetutorial.dukesbookstore.web.messages.Messages", locale);
    return res.getString(name() + ".string");
}
```

Alternatively, an application could use the f:loadBundle tag to set the resource bundle. This tag loads the correct resource bundle according to the locale stored in FacesContext:

```
<f:loadBundle basename="javaeetutorial.dukesbookstore.web.messages.Messages"
    var="bundle"/>
```

Resource bundles containing messages that are explicitly referenced from a JavaServer Faces tag attribute using a value expression must be registered using the resource-bundle element of the configuration file.

For more information on using this element, see Section 16.5, "Registering Application Messages."

20.2.3 Retrieving Localized Messages

A web component written in the Java programming language retrieves the resource bundle from the session:

```
ResourceBundle messages = (ResourceBundle)session.getAttribute("messages");
```

Then it looks up the string associated with the key person.lastName as follows:

```
messages.getString("person.lastName");
```

You can only use a message or messages tag to display messages that are queued onto a component as a result of a converter or validator being registered on the component. The following example shows a message tag that displays the error message queued on the userNo input component if the validator registered on the component fails to validate the value the user enters into the component:

```
<h:inputText id="userNo" value="#{UserNumberBean.userNumber}">
    <f:validateLongRange minimum="0" maximum="10" />
</h:inputText>
...
<h:message style="color: red; text-decoration: overline"
        id="errors1" for="userNo"/>
```

For more information on using the message or messages tags, see Section 10.2.13, "Displaying Error Messages with the h:message and h:messages Tags."

Messages that are not queued on a component and are therefore not loaded automatically are referenced using a value expression. You can reference a localized message from almost any JavaServer Faces tag attribute.

The value expression that references a message has the same notation whether you loaded the resource bundle with the loadBundle tag or registered it with the resource-bundle element in the configuration file.

The value expression notation is var.message, in which var matches the var attribute of the loadBundle tag or the var element defined in the resource-bundle element of the configuration file, and message matches the key of the message contained in the resource bundle, referred to by the var attribute.

Here is an example from bookcashier.xhtml in Duke's Bookstore:

```
<h:outputLabel for="name" value="#{bundle.Name}" />
```

Notice that bundle matches the var element from the configuration file and that Name matches the key in the resource bundle.

20.3 Date and Number Formatting

Java programs use the DateFormat.getDateInstance(int, locale) method to parse and format dates in a locale-sensitive manner. Java programs use the NumberFormat.get*XXX*Instance(locale) method, where *XXX* can be Currency, Number, or Percent, to parse and format numerical values in a locale-sensitive manner.

An application can use date/time and number converters to format dates and numbers in a locale-sensitive manner. For example, a shipping date could be converted as follows:

```
<h:outputText value="#{cashier.shipDate}">
    <f:convertDateTime dateStyle="full"/>
</h:outputText>
```

For information on JavaServer Faces converters, see Section 11.1, "Using the Standard Converters."

20.4 Character Sets and Encodings

The following sections describe character sets and character encodings.

20.4.1 Character Sets

A **character set** is a set of textual and graphic symbols, each of which is mapped to a set of nonnegative integers.

The first character set used in computing was US-ASCII. It is limited in that it can represent only American English. US-ASCII contains uppercase and lowercase Latin alphabets, numerals, punctuation, a set of control codes, and a few miscellaneous symbols.

Unicode defines a standardized, universal character set that can be extended to accommodate additions. When the Java program source file encoding doesn't support Unicode, you can represent Unicode characters as escape sequences by using the notation \u*XXXX*, where *XXXX* is the character's 16-bit representation in hexadecimal. For example, the Spanish version of a message file could use Unicode for non-ASCII characters, as follows:

```
admin.nav.main=P\u00e1gina principal de administraci\u00f3n
```

20.4.2 Character Encoding

A **character encoding** maps a character set to units of a specific width and defines byte serialization and ordering rules. Many character sets have more than one encoding. For example, Java programs can represent Japanese character sets using the EUC-JP or Shift-JIS encodings, among others. Each encoding has rules for representing and serializing a character set.

The ISO 8859 series defines 13 character encodings that can represent texts in dozens of languages. Each ISO 8859 character encoding can have up to 256 characters. ISO-8859-1 (Latin-1) comprises the ASCII character set, characters with diacritics (accents, diaereses, cedillas, circumflexes, and so on), and additional symbols.

UTF-8 (Unicode Transformation Format, 8-bit form) is a variable-width character encoding that encodes 16-bit Unicode characters as one to four bytes. A byte in UTF-8 is equivalent to 7-bit ASCII if its high-order bit is zero; otherwise, the character comprises a variable number of bytes.

UTF-8 is compatible with the majority of existing web content and provides access to the Unicode character set. Current versions of browsers and email clients support UTF-8. In addition, many web standards specify UTF-8 as their character encoding. For example, UTF-8 is one of the two required encodings for XML documents (the other is UTF-16).

Web components usually use `PrintWriter` to produce responses; `PrintWriter` automatically encodes using ISO-8859-1. Servlets can also output binary data using `OutputStream` classes, which perform no encoding. An application that uses a character set that cannot use the default encoding must explicitly set a different encoding.

Part IV

Bean Validation

Part IV explores Java API for JavaBean Validation ("Bean Validation"). This part contains the following chapters:

- Chapter 21, "Introduction to Bean Validation"
- Chapter 22, "Bean Validation: Advanced Topics"

21

Introduction to Bean Validation

Validating input received from the user to maintain data integrity is an important part of application logic. Validation of data can take place at different layers in even the simplest of applications, as shown in Section 8.3, "Developing a Simple Facelets Application: The guessnumber-jsf Example Application." The guessnumber-jsf example application validates the user input (in the h:inputText tag) for numerical data at the presentation layer and for a valid range of numbers at the business layer.

The Java API for JavaBean Validation ("Bean Validation") provides a facility for validating objects, object members, methods, and constructors. In Java EE environments, Bean Validation integrates with Java EE containers and services to allow developers to easily define and enforce validation constraints. Bean Validation is available as part of the Java EE 7 platform.

The following topics are addressed here:

- Using Bean Validation Constraints
- Validating Null and Empty Strings
- Validating Constructors and Methods
- Further Information about Bean Validation

21.1 Using Bean Validation Constraints

The Bean Validation model is supported by constraints in the form of annotations placed on a field, method, or class of a JavaBeans component, such as a managed bean.

Constraints can be built in or user defined. User-defined constraints are called custom constraints. Several built-in constraints are available in the `javax.validation.constraints` package. Table 21–1 lists all the built-in constraints. See Section 22.1, "Creating Custom Constraints," for information on creating custom constraints.

Table 21–1 *Built-In Bean Validation Constraints*

Constraint	Description	Example
@AssertFalse	The value of the field or property must be `false`.	`@AssertFalse` `boolean isUnsupported;`
@AssertTrue	The value of the field or property must be `true`.	`@AssertTrue` `boolean isActive;`
@DecimalMax	The value of the field or property must be a decimal value lower than or equal to the number in the value element.	`@DecimalMax("30.00")` `BigDecimal discount;`
@DecimalMin	The value of the field or property must be a decimal value greater than or equal to the number in the value element.	`@DecimalMin("5.00")` `BigDecimal discount;`
@Digits	The value of the field or property must be a number within a specified range. The `integer` element specifies the maximum integral digits for the number, and the `fraction` element specifies the maximum fractional digits for the number.	`@Digits(integer=6, fraction=2)` `BigDecimal price;`
@Future	The value of the field or property must be a date in the future.	`@Future` `Date eventDate;`
@Max	The value of the field or property must be an integer value lower than or equal to the number in the value element.	`@Max(10)` `int quantity;`
@Min	The value of the field or property must be an integer value greater than or equal to the number in the value element.	`@Min(5)` `int quantity;`
@NotNull	The value of the field or property must not be null.	`@NotNull` `String username;`
@Null	The value of the field or property must be null.	`@Null` `String unusedString;`

Table 21–1   (Cont.) Built-In Bean Validation Constraints

Constraint	Description	Example
@Past	The value of the field or property must be a date in the past.	```@Past``` ```Date birthday;```
@Pattern	The value of the field or property must match the regular expression defined in the regexp element.	```@Pattern(regexp="\\(\\d{3}\\)\\d{3}-\\d{4}")``` ```String phoneNumber;```
@Size	The size of the field or property is evaluated and must match the specified boundaries. If the field or property is a String, the size of the string is evaluated. If the field or property is a Collection, the size of the Collection is evaluated. If the field or property is a Map, the size of the Map is evaluated. If the field or property is an array, the size of the array is evaluated. Use one of the optional max or min elements to specify the boundaries.	```@Size(min=2, max=240)``` ```String briefMessage;```

In the following example, a constraint is placed on a field using the built-in @NotNull constraint:

```
public class Name {
    @NotNull
    private String firstname;

    @NotNull
    private String lastname;
    ...
}
```

You can also place more than one constraint on a single JavaBeans component object. For example, you can place an additional constraint for size of field on the firstname and the lastname fields:

```
public class Name {
    @NotNull
    @Size(min=1, max=16)
    private String firstname;

    @NotNull
    @Size(min=1, max=16)
    private String lastname;
```

```
    . . .
}
```

The following example shows a method with a user-defined constraint that checks for a predefined email address pattern, such as a corporate email account:

```
@ValidEmail
public String getEmailAddress() {
    return emailAddress;
}
```

For a built-in constraint, a default implementation is available. A user-defined or custom constraint needs a validation implementation. In the preceding example, the @ValidEmail custom constraint needs an implementation class.

Any validation failures are gracefully handled and can be displayed by the h:messages tag.

Any managed bean that contains Bean Validation annotations automatically gets validation constraints placed on the fields on a JavaServer Faces application's web pages.

For more information on using validation constraints, see the following:

- Chapter 22, "Bean Validation: Advanced Topics"
- Section 31.2, "Validating Resource Data with Bean Validation"
- Section 8.1.2.4, "Validating Persistent Fields and Properties," in *The Java EE 7 Tutorial, Volume 2*

21.2 Validating Null and Empty Strings

The Java programming language distinguishes between null and empty strings. An empty string is a string instance of zero length, whereas a null string has no value at all.

An empty string is represented as " ". It is a character sequence of zero characters. A null string is represented by null. It can be described as the absence of a string instance.

Managed bean elements represented as a JavaServer Faces text component such as inputText are initialized with the value of the empty string by the JavaServer Faces implementation. Validating these strings can be an issue when user input for such fields is not required. Consider the following example, in which the string `testString` is a bean variable that will be set using input entered by the user. In this case, the user input for the field is not required:

```
if (testString==null) {
    doSomething();
} else {
    doAnotherThing();
}
```

By default, the `doAnotherThing` method is called even when the user enters no data, because the `testString` element has been initialized with the value of an empty string.

In order for the Bean Validation model to work as intended, you must set the context parameter `javax.faces.INTERPRET_EMPTY_STRING_SUBMITTED_VALUES_AS_NULL` to `true` in the web deployment descriptor file, `web.xml`:

```
<context-param>
    <param-name>
        javax.faces.INTERPRET_EMPTY_STRING_SUBMITTED_VALUES_AS_NULL
    </param-name>
    <param-value>true</param-value>
</context-param>
```

This parameter enables the JavaServer Faces implementation to treat empty strings as null.

Suppose, on the other hand, that you have a `@NotNull` constraint on an element, meaning that input is required. In this case, an empty string will pass this validation constraint. However, if you set the context parameter `javax.faces.INTERPRET_EMPTY_STRING_SUBMITTED_VALUES_AS_NULL` to `true`, the value of the managed bean attribute is passed to the Bean Validation runtime as a null value, causing the `@NotNull` constraint to fail.

21.3 Validating Constructors and Methods

Bean Validation constraints may be placed on the parameters of nonstatic methods and constructors and on the return values of nonstatic methods. Static methods and constructors will not be validated:

```
public class Employee {
...
  public Employee (@NotNull String name) { ... }

  public void setSalary(
      @NotNull
      @Digits(integer=6, fraction=2) BigDecimal salary,
```

```
            @NotNull
            @ValidCurrency
            String currencyType) {
        ...
    }
    ...
}
```

In this example, the `Employee` class has a constructor constraint requiring a name and has two sets of method parameter constraints. The amount of the salary for the employee must not be null, cannot be greater than six digits to the left of the decimal point, and cannot have more than two digits to the right of the decimal place. The currency type must not be null and is validated using a custom constraint.

If you add method constraints to classes in an object hierarchy, special care must be taken to avoid unintended behavior by subtypes. See Section 22.4, "Using Method Constraints in Type Hierarchies," for more information.

21.3.1 Cross-Parameter Constraints

Constraints that apply to multiple parameters are called **cross-parameter constraints**, and may be applied at the method or constructor level:

```
@ConsistentPhoneParameters
@NotNull
public Employee (String name, String officePhone, String mobilePhone) {
    ...
}
```

In this example, a custom cross-parameter constraint, `@ConsistentPhoneParameters`, validates that the format of the phone numbers passed into the constructor match. The `@NotNull` constraint applies to all the parameters in the constructor.

Tip: Cross-parameter constraint annotations are applied directly to the method or constructor. Return value constraints are also applied directly to the method or constructor. To avoid confusion as to where the constraint applies, parameter or return value, choose a name for any custom constraints that identifies where the constraint applies.

For instance, the preceding example applies a custom constraint, `@ConsistentPhoneParameters`, that indicates that it applies to the parameters of the method or constructor.

When you create a custom constraint that applies to both method parameters and return values, the `validationAppliesTo` element of the constraint annotation may be set to `ConstraintTarget.RETURN_VALUE` or `ConstraintTarget.PARAMETERS` to explicitly set the target of the validation constraint.

21.3.2 Identifying Parameter Constraint Violations

If a `ConstraintViolationException` occurs during a method call, the Bean Validation runtime returns a parameter index to identify which parameter caused the constraint violation. The parameter index is in the form arg*PARAMETER_INDEX*, where *PARAMETER_INDEX* is an integer that starts at 0 for the first parameter of the method or constructor.

21.3.3 Adding Constraints to Method Return Values

To validate the return value for a method, you can apply constraints directly to the method or constructor declaration:

```
@NotNull
public Employee getEmployee() { ... }
```

Cross-parameter constraints are also applied at the method level. Custom constraints that could be applied to both the return value and the method parameters have an ambiguous constraint target. To avoid this ambiguity, add a validationAppliesTo element to the constraint annotation definition with the default set to either `ConstraintTarget.RETURN_VALUE` or `ConstraintTarget.PARAMETERS` to explicitly set the target of the validation constraint:

```
@Manager(validationAppliesTo=ConstraintTarget.RETURN_VALUE)
public Employee getManager(Employee employee) { ... }
```

See Section 22.1.2, "Removing Ambiguity in Constraint Targets," for more information.

21.4 Further Information about Bean Validation

For more information on Bean Validation, see

- Bean Validation 1.1 Specification:

    `http://www.jcp.org/en/jsr/detail?id=349`

- Bean Validation Specification website:

    `http://beanvalidation.org/`

22

Bean Validation: Advanced Topics

This chapter describes how to create custom constraints, custom validator messages, and constraint groups using the Java API for JavaBeans Validation (Bean Validation).

The following topics are addressed here:

- Creating Custom Constraints
- Customizing Validator Messages
- Grouping Constraints
- Using Method Constraints in Type Hierarchies

22.1 Creating Custom Constraints

Bean Validation defines annotations, interfaces, and classes to allow developers to create custom constraints.

22.1.1 Using the Built-In Constraints to Make a New Constraint

Bean Validation includes several built-in constraints that can be combined to create new, reusable constraints. This can simplify constraint definition by allowing developers to define a custom constraint made up of several built-in constraints that may then be applied to component attributes with a single annotation:

```
@Pattern.List({
  @Pattern(regexp = "[a-z0-9!#$%&'*+/=?^_`{|}~-]+(?:\\."
  +"[a-z0-9!#$%&'*+/=?^_`{|}~-]+)*"
  +"@(?:[a-z0-9](?:[a-z0-9-]*[a-z0-9])?\\.)+[a-z0-9](?:[a-z0-9-]*[a-z0-9])?")
```

```
    })
    @Constraint(validatedBy = {})
    @Documented
    @Target({ElementType.METHOD,
        ElementType.FIELD,
        ElementType.ANNOTATION_TYPE,
        ElementType.CONSTRUCTOR,
        ElementType.PARAMETER})
    @Retention(RetentionPolicy.RUNTIME)
    public @interface Email {

        String message() default "{invalid.email}";
        Class<?>[] groups() default {};
        Class<? extends Payload>[] payload() default {};

        @Target({ElementType.METHOD,
            ElementType.FIELD,
            ElementType.ANNOTATION_TYPE,
            ElementType.CONSTRUCTOR,
            ElementType.PARAMETER})
        @Retention(RetentionPolicy.RUNTIME)
        @Documented
        @interface List {
            Email[] value();
        }
    }
```

This custom constraint can then be applied to an attribute:

```
...
@Email
protected String email;
...
```

22.1.2 Removing Ambiguity in Constraint Targets

Custom constraints that can be applied to both return values and method
parameters require a validationAppliesTo element to identify the target of the
constraint:

```
@Constraint(validatedBy=MyConstraintValidator.class)
@Target({ METHOD, FIELD, TYPE, ANNOTATION_TYPE, CONSTRUCTOR, PARAMETER })
@Retention(RUNTIME)
public @interface MyConstraint {
    String message() default "{com.example.constraint.MyConstraint.message}";
    Class<?>[] groups() default {};
    ConstraintTarget validationAppliesTo() default ConstraintTarget.PARAMETERS;
```

```
    . . .
}
```

This constraint sets the `validationAppliesTo` target by default to the method parameters:

```
@MyConstraint(validationAppliesTo=ConstraintTarget.RETURN_TYPE)
public String doSomething(String param1, String param2) { ... }
```

In the preceding example, the target is set to the return value of the method.

22.2 Customizing Validator Messages

Bean Validation includes a resource bundle of default messages for the built-in constraints. These messages can be customized and can be localized for non-English-speaking locales.

22.2.1 The ValidationMessages Resource Bundle

The `ValidationMessages` resource bundle and the locale variants of this resource bundle contain strings that override the default validation messages. The `ValidationMessages` resource bundle is typically a properties file, `ValidationMessages.properties`, in the default package of an application.

22.2.1.1 Localizing Validation Messages

Locale variants of `ValidationMessages.properties` are added by appending an underscore and the locale prefix to the base name of the file. For example, the Spanish locale variant resource bundle would be `ValidationMessages_es.properties`.

22.3 Grouping Constraints

Constraints may be added to one or more groups. Constraint groups are used to create subsets of constraints so that only certain constraints will be validated for a particular object. By default, all constraints are included in the `Default` constraint group.

Constraint groups are represented by interfaces:

```
public interface Employee {}

public interface Contractor {}
```

Constraint groups can inherit from other groups:

```
public interface Manager extends Employee {}
```

When a constraint is added to an element, the constraint declares the groups to which that constraint belongs by specifying the class name of the group interface name in the groups element of the constraint:

```
@NotNull(groups=Employee.class)
Phone workPhone;
```

Multiple groups can be declared by surrounding the groups with braces ({ and }) and separating the groups' class names with commas:

```
@NotNull(groups={ Employee.class, Contractor.class })
Phone workPhone;
```

If a group inherits from another group, validating that group results in validating all constraints declared as part of the supergroup. For example, validating the Manager group results in the workPhone field being validated, because Employee is a superinterface of Manager.

22.3.1 Customizing Group Validation Order

By default, constraint groups are validated in no particular order. There are cases in which some groups should be validated before others. For example, in a particular class, basic data should be validated before more advanced data.

To set the validation order for a group, add a javax.validation.GroupSequence annotation to the interface definition, listing the order in which the validation should occur:

```
@GroupSequence({Default.class, ExpensiveValidationGroup.class})
public interface FullValidationGroup {}
```

When validating FullValidationGroup, first the Default group is validated. If all the data passes validation, then the ExpensiveValidationGroup group is validated. If a constraint is part of both the Default and the ExpensiveValidationGroup groups, the constraint is validated as part of the Default group and will not be validated on the subsequent ExpensiveValidationGroup pass.

22.4 Using Method Constraints in Type Hierarchies

If you add validation constraints to objects in an inheritance hierarchy, take special care to avoid unintended errors when using subtypes.

For a given type, subtypes should be able to be substituted without encountering errors. For example, if you have a `Person` class and an `Employee` subclass that extends `Person`, you should be able to use `Employee` instances wherever you might use `Person` instances. If `Employee` overrides a method in `Person` by adding method parameter constraints, code that works correctly with `Person` objects may throw validation exceptions with `Employee` objects.

The following code shows an *incorrect* use of method parameter constraints within a class hierarchy:

```
public class Person {
  ...
  public void setEmail(String email) { ... }
}

public class Employee extends Person {
  ...
  @Override
  public void setEmail(@Verified String email) { ... }
}
```

Adding the `@Verified` constraint to `Employee.setEmail` means that parameters that were valid with `Person.setEmail` are not valid with `Employee.setEmail`. This is called **strengthening the preconditions** (that is, the method parameters) of a subtype's method. You may not strengthen the preconditions of subtype method calls.

Similarly, the return values from method calls should not be weakened in subtypes. The following code shows an *incorrect* use of constraints on method return values in a class hierarchy:

```
public class Person {
  ...
  @Verified
  public Email getEmail() { ... }
}

public class Employee extends Person {
  ...
  @Override
  public Email getEmail() { ... }
}
```

In this example, the `Employee.getEmail` method removes the `@Verified` constraint on the return value. Return values that would not pass validation in calls to `Person.getEmail` are allowed in calls to `Employee.getEmail`. This is called

weakening the postconditions (that is, return values) of a subtype. You may not weaken the postconditions of a subtype method call.

If your type hierarchy strengthens the preconditions or weakens the postconditions of subtype method calls, the Bean Validation runtime will throw a `javax.validation.ConstraintDeclarationException`.

Classes that implement several interfaces that each have the same method signature, known as parallel types, must be aware of the constraints applied to the interfaces that they implement to avoid strengthening the preconditions:

```
public interface PaymentService {
  void processOrder(Order order, double amount);
  ...
}

public interface CreditCardPaymentService {
  void processOrder(@NotNull Order order, @NotNull double amount);
  ...
}

public class MyPaymentService implements PaymentService,
        CreditCardPaymentService {
  @Override
  public void processOrder(Order order, double amount) { ... }
  ...
}
```

In this case, `MyPaymentService` has the constraints from the `processOrder` method in `CreditCardPaymentService`, but client code that calls `PaymentService.processOrder` doesn't expect these constraints. This is another example of strengthening the preconditions of a subtype and will result in a `ConstraintDeclarationException`.

22.4.1 Rules for Using Method Constraints in Type Hierarchies

The following rules define how method validation constraints should be used in type hierarchies.

- Do not add method parameter constraints to overridden or implemented methods in a subtype.

- Do not add method parameter constraints to overridden or implemented methods in a subtype that was originally declared in several parallel types.

- You may add return value constraints to an overridden or implemented method in a subtype.

Part V

Contexts and Dependency Injection for Java EE

Part V explores Contexts and Dependency Injection for Java EE (CDI). This part contains the following chapters:

- Chapter 23, "Introduction to Contexts and Dependency Injection for Java EE"

- Chapter 24, "Running the Basic Contexts and Dependency Injection Examples"

- Chapter 25, "Contexts and Dependency Injection for Java EE: Advanced Topics"

- Chapter 26, "Running the Advanced Contexts and Dependency Injection Examples"

23

Introduction to Contexts and Dependency Injection for Java EE

Contexts and Dependency Injection for Java EE (CDI) is one of several Java EE features that help to knit together the web tier and the transactional tier of the Java EE platform. CDI is a set of services that, used together, make it easy for developers to use enterprise beans along with JavaServer Faces technology in web applications. Designed for use with stateful objects, CDI also has many broader uses, allowing developers a great deal of flexibility to integrate various kinds of components in a loosely coupled but typesafe way.

CDI 1.1 is specified by JSR 346. Related specifications that CDI uses include the following:

- JSR 330, Dependency Injection for Java
- The Managed Beans specification, an offshoot of the Java EE 7 platform specification (JSR 342)

The following topics are addressed here:

- Getting Started
- Overview of CDI
- About Beans
- About CDI Managed Beans
- Beans as Injectable Objects
- Using Qualifiers
- Injecting Beans

- Using Scopes

- Giving Beans EL Names

- Adding Setter and Getter Methods

- Using a Managed Bean in a Facelets Page

- Injecting Objects by Using Producer Methods

- Configuring a CDI Application

- Using the @PostConstruct and @PreDestroy Annotations with CDI Managed Bean Classes

- Further Information about CDI

23.1 Getting Started

Contexts and Dependency Injection (CDI) enables your objects to have their dependencies provided to them automatically, instead of creating them or receiving them as parameters. CDI also manages the lifecycle of those dependencies for you.

For example, consider the following servlet:

```
@WebServlet("/cdiservlet")
public class NewServlet extends HttpServlet {
    private Message message;

    @Override
    public void init() {
        message = new MessageB();
    }

    @Override
    public void doGet(HttpServletRequest request,
                      HttpServletResponse response)
                throws IOException {
        response.getWriter().write(message.get());
    }
}
```

This servlet needs an instance of an object that implements the Message interface:

```
public interface Message {
    public String get();
}
```

The servlet creates itself an instance of the following object:

```
public class MessageB implements Message {
    public MessageB() { }

    @Override
    public String get() {
        return "message B";
    }
}
```

Using CDI, this servlet can declare its dependency on a Message instance and have it injected automatically by the CDI runtime. The new servlet code is the following:

```
@WebServlet("/cdiservlet")
public class NewServlet extends HttpServlet {
    @Inject private Message message;

    @Override
    public void doGet(HttpServletRequest request,
                      HttpServletResponse response)
                throws IOException {
        response.getWriter().write(message.get());
    }
}
```

The CDI runtime looks for classes that implement the Message interface, finds the MessageB class, creates a new instance of it, and injects it into the servlet at runtime. To manage the lifecycle of the new instance, the CDI runtime needs to know what the scope of the instance should be. In this example, the servlet only needs the instance to process an HTTP request; the instance can then be garbage collected. This is specified using the javax.enterprise.context.RequestScoped annotation:

```
@RequestScoped
public class MessageB implements Message { ... }
```

For more information on scopes, see Section 23.8, "Using Scopes."

The MessageB class is a **CDI bean**. CDI beans are classes that CDI can instantiate, manage, and inject automatically to satisfy the dependencies of other objects. Almost any Java class can be managed and injected by CDI. For more information on beans, see Section 23.3, "About Beans." A JAR or WAR file that contains a CDI bean is a **bean archive**. For more information on packaging bean archives, see Section 23.13, "Configuring a CDI Application," and Section 25.1, "Packaging CDI Applications."

In this example, `MessageB` is the only class that implements the `Message` interface. If an application has more than one implementation of an interface, CDI provides mechanisms that you can use to select which implementation to inject. For more information, see Section 23.6, "Using Qualifiers," and Section 25.2, "Using Alternatives in CDI Applications."

23.2 Overview of CDI

The most fundamental services provided by CDI are as follows.

- **Contexts**: This service enables you to bind the lifecycle and interactions of stateful components to well-defined but extensible lifecycle contexts.

- **Dependency injection**: This service enables you to inject components into an application in a typesafe way and to choose at deployment time which implementation of a particular interface to inject.

In addition, CDI provides the following services:

- Integration with the Expression Language (EL), which allows any component to be used directly within a JavaServer Faces page or a JavaServer Pages page

- The ability to decorate injected components

- The ability to associate interceptors with components using typesafe interceptor bindings

- An event-notification model

- A web conversation scope in addition to the three standard scopes (request, session, and application) defined by the Java Servlet specification

- A complete Service Provider Interface (SPI) that allows third-party frameworks to integrate cleanly in the Java EE 7 environment

A major theme of CDI is loose coupling. CDI does the following:

- Decouples the server and the client by means of well-defined types and qualifiers, so that the server implementation may vary

- Decouples the lifecycles of collaborating components by

  - Making components contextual, with automatic lifecycle management

  - Allowing stateful components to interact like services, purely by message passing

- Completely decouples message producers from consumers, by means of events

- Decouples orthogonal concerns by means of Java EE interceptors

Along with loose coupling, CDI provides strong typing by

- Eliminating lookup using string-based names for wiring and correlations so that the compiler will detect typing errors

- Allowing the use of declarative Java annotations to specify everything, largely eliminating the need for XML deployment descriptors, and making it easy to provide tools that introspect the code and understand the dependency structure at development time

23.3 About Beans

CDI redefines the concept of a **bean** beyond its use in other Java technologies, such as the JavaBeans and Enterprise JavaBeans (EJB) technologies. In CDI, a bean is a source of contextual objects that define application state and/or logic. A Java EE component is a bean if the lifecycle of its instances may be managed by the container according to the lifecycle context model defined in the CDI specification.

More specifically, a bean has the following attributes:

- A (nonempty) set of bean types

- A (nonempty) set of qualifiers (see Section 23.6, "Using Qualifiers")

- A scope (see Section 23.8, "Using Scopes")

- Optionally, a bean EL name (see Section 23.9, "Giving Beans EL Names")

- A set of interceptor bindings

- A bean implementation

A bean type defines a client-visible type of the bean. Almost any Java type may be a bean type of a bean.

- A bean type may be an interface, a concrete class, or an abstract class and may be declared final or have final methods.

- A bean type may be a parameterized type with type parameters and type variables.

- A bean type may be an array type. Two array types are considered identical only if the element type is identical.

- A bean type may be a primitive type. Primitive types are considered to be identical to their corresponding wrapper types in `java.lang`.

- A bean type may be a raw type.

23.4 About CDI Managed Beans

A managed bean is implemented by a Java class, which is called its bean class. A top-level Java class is a managed bean if it is defined to be a managed bean by any other Java EE technology specification, such as the JavaServer Faces technology specification, or if it meets all the following conditions.

- It is not a nonstatic inner class.

- It is a concrete class or is annotated `@Decorator`.

- It is not annotated with an EJB component-defining annotation or declared as an EJB bean class in `ejb-jar.xml`.

- It has an appropriate constructor. That is, one of the following is the case.

  - The class has a constructor with no parameters.

  - The class declares a constructor annotated `@Inject`.

No special declaration, such as an annotation, is required to define a managed bean.

23.5 Beans as Injectable Objects

The concept of injection has been part of Java technology for some time. Since the Java EE 5 platform was introduced, annotations have made it possible to inject resources and some other kinds of objects into container-managed objects. CDI makes it possible to inject more kinds of objects and to inject them into objects that are not container-managed.

The following kinds of objects can be injected:

- (Almost) any Java class

- Session beans

- Java EE resources: data sources, Java Message Service topics, queues, connection factories, and the like

- Persistence contexts (Java Persistence API `EntityManager` objects)

- Producer fields

- Objects returned by producer methods

- Web service references

- Remote enterprise bean references

For example, suppose that you create a simple Java class with a method that returns a string:

```
package greetings;

public class Greeting {
    public String greet(String name) {
        return "Hello, " + name + ".";
    }
}
```

This class becomes a bean that you can then inject into another class. This bean is not exposed to the EL in this form. Section 23.9, "Giving Beans EL Names," explains how you can make a bean accessible to the EL.

23.6 Using Qualifiers

You can use qualifiers to provide various implementations of a particular bean type. A qualifier is an annotation that you apply to a bean. A qualifier type is a Java annotation defined as `@Target({METHOD, FIELD, PARAMETER, TYPE})` and `@Retention(RUNTIME)`.

For example, you could declare an `@Informal` qualifier type and apply it to another class that extends the `Greeting` class. To declare this qualifier type, you would use the following code:

```
package greetings;

import static java.lang.annotation.ElementType.FIELD;
import static java.lang.annotation.ElementType.METHOD;
import static java.lang.annotation.ElementType.PARAMETER;
import static java.lang.annotation.ElementType.TYPE;
import static java.lang.annotation.RetentionPolicy.RUNTIME;
import java.lang.annotation.Retention;
import static java.lang.annotation.RetentionPolicy.RUNTIME;
import java.lang.annotation.Target;
import javax.inject.Qualifier;

@Qualifier
@Retention(RUNTIME)
@Target({TYPE, METHOD, FIELD, PARAMETER})
public @interface Informal {}
```

You can then define a bean class that extends the `Greeting` class and uses this qualifier:

```
package greetings;

@Informal
public class InformalGreeting extends Greeting {
    public String greet(String name) {
        return "Hi, " + name + "!";
    }
}
```

Both implementations of the bean can now be used in the application.

If you define a bean with no qualifier, the bean automatically has the qualifier `@Default`. The unannotated `Greeting` class could be declared as follows:

```
package greetings;

import javax.enterprise.inject.Default;

@Default
public class Greeting {
    public String greet(String name) {
        return "Hello, " + name + ".";
    }
}
```

23.7 Injecting Beans

In order to use the beans you create, you inject them into yet another bean that can then be used by an application, such as a JavaServer Faces application. For example, you might create a bean called `Printer` into which you would inject one of the `Greeting` beans:

```
import javax.inject.Inject;

public class Printer {

    @Inject Greeting greeting;
    ...
}
```

This code injects the @Default Greeting implementation into the bean. The following code injects the @Informal implementation:

```
import javax.inject.Inject;

public class Printer {

    @Inject @Informal Greeting greeting;
    ...
}
```

More is needed for the complete picture of this bean. Its use of scope needs to be understood. In addition, for a JavaServer Faces application, the bean needs to be accessible through the EL.

23.8 Using Scopes

For a web application to use a bean that injects another bean class, the bean needs to be able to hold state over the duration of the user's interaction with the application. The way to define this state is to give the bean a scope. You can give an object any of the scopes described in Table 23–1, depending on how you are using it.

Table 23–1   CDI Scopes

Scope	Annotation	Duration
Request	@RequestScoped	A user's interaction with a web application in a single HTTP request.
Session	@SessionScoped	A user's interaction with a web application across multiple HTTP requests.
Application	@ApplicationScoped	Shared state across all users' interactions with a web application.
Dependent	@Dependent	The default scope if none is specified; it means that an object exists to serve exactly one client (bean) and has the same lifecycle as that client (bean).
Conversation	@ConversationScoped	A user's interaction with a servlet, including JavaServer Faces applications. The conversation scope exists within developer-controlled boundaries that extend it across multiple requests for long-running conversations. All long-running conversations are scoped to a particular HTTP servlet session and may not cross session boundaries.

The first three scopes are defined by both JSR 346 and the JavaServer Faces specification. The last two are defined by JSR 346.

All predefined scopes except @Dependent are contextual scopes. CDI places beans of contextual scope in the context whose lifecycle is defined by the Java EE specifications. For example, a session context and its beans exist during the lifetime of an HTTP session. Injected references to the beans are contextually aware. The references always apply to the bean that is associated with the context for the thread that is making the reference. The CDI container ensures that the objects are created and injected at the correct time as determined by the scope that is specified for these objects.

You can also define and implement custom scopes, but that is an advanced topic. Custom scopes are likely to be used by those who implement and extend the CDI specification.

A scope gives an object a well-defined lifecycle context. A scoped object can be automatically created when it is needed and automatically destroyed when the context in which it was created ends. Moreover, its state is automatically shared by any clients that execute in the same context.

Java EE components, such as servlets and enterprise beans, and JavaBeans components do not by definition have a well-defined scope. These components are one of the following:

- Singletons, such as Enterprise JavaBeans singleton beans, whose state is shared among all clients

- Stateless objects, such as servlets and stateless session beans, which do not contain client-visible state

- Objects that must be explicitly created and destroyed by their client, such as JavaBeans components and stateful session beans, whose state is shared by explicit reference passing between clients

If, however, you create a Java EE component that is a managed bean, it becomes a scoped object, which exists in a well-defined lifecycle context.

The web application for the Printer bean will use a simple request and response mechanism, so the managed bean can be annotated as follows:

```
import javax.enterprise.context.RequestScoped;
import javax.inject.Inject;

@RequestScoped
public class Printer {

    @Inject @Informal Greeting greeting;
```

```
    . . .
}
```

Beans that use session, application, or conversation scope must be serializable, but beans that use request scope do not have to be serializable.

23.9 Giving Beans EL Names

To make a bean accessible through the EL, use the `@Named` built-in qualifier:

```
import javax.enterprise.context.RequestScoped;
import javax.inject.Inject;
import javax.inject.Named;

@Named
@RequestScoped
public class Printer {

    @Inject @Informal Greeting greeting;
    . . .
}
```

The `@Named` qualifier allows you to access the bean by using the bean name, with the first letter in lowercase. For example, a Facelets page would refer to the bean as `printer`.

You can specify an argument to the `@Named` qualifier to use a nondefault name:

```
@Named("MyPrinter")
```

With this annotation, the Facelets page would refer to the bean as `MyPrinter`.

23.10 Adding Setter and Getter Methods

To make the state of the managed bean accessible, you need to add setter and getter methods for that state. The `createSalutation` method calls the bean's `greet` method, and the `getSalutation` method retrieves the result.

Once the setter and getter methods have been added, the bean is complete. The final code looks like this:

```
package greetings;

import javax.enterprise.context.RequestScoped;
import javax.inject.Inject;
import javax.inject.Named;
```

```
@Named
@RequestScoped
public class Printer {

    @Inject @Informal Greeting greeting;

    private String name;
    private String salutation;

    public void createSalutation() {
        this.salutation = greeting.greet(name);
    }

    public String getSalutation() {
        return salutation;
    }

    public void setName(String name) {
        this.name = name;
    }

    public String getName() {
        return name;
    }
}
```

23.11 Using a Managed Bean in a Facelets Page

To use the managed bean in a Facelets page, you typically create a form that uses user interface elements to call its methods and display their results. This example provides a button that asks the user to type a name, retrieves the salutation, and then displays the text in a paragraph below the button:

```
<h:form id="greetme">
   <p><h:outputLabel value="Enter your name: " for="name"/>
      <h:inputText id="name" value="#{printer.name}"/></p>
   <p><h:commandButton value="Say Hello"
                       action="#{printer.createSalutation}"/></p>
   <p><h:outputText value="#{printer.salutation}"/></p>
</h:form>
```

23.12 Injecting Objects by Using Producer Methods

Producer methods provide a way to inject objects that are not beans, objects whose values may vary at runtime, and objects that require custom initialization.

For example, if you want to initialize a numeric value defined by a qualifier named @MaxNumber, you can define the value in a managed bean and then define a producer method, getMaxNumber, for it:

```
private int maxNumber = 100;
...
@Produces @MaxNumber int getMaxNumber() {
    return maxNumber;
}
```

When you inject the object in another managed bean, the container automatically invokes the producer method, initializing the value to 100:

```
@Inject @MaxNumber private int maxNumber;
```

If the value can vary at runtime, the process is slightly different. For example, the following code defines a producer method that generates a random number defined by a qualifier called @Random:

```
private java.util.Random random =
    new java.util.Random( System.currentTimeMillis() );

java.util.Random getRandom() {
        return random;
}

@Produces @Random int next() {
    return getRandom().nextInt(maxNumber);
}
```

When you inject this object in another managed bean, you declare a contextual instance of the object:

```
@Inject @Random Instance<Integer> randomInt;
```

You then call the get method of the Instance:

```
this.number = randomInt.get();
```

23.13 Configuring a CDI Application

When your beans are annotated with a scope type, the server recognizes the application as a bean archive and no additional configuration is required. The possible scope types for CDI beans are listed in Section 23.8, "Using Scopes."

CDI uses an optional deployment descriptor named beans.xml. Like other Java EE deployment descriptors, the configuration settings in beans.xml are used in addition to annotation settings in CDI classes. The settings in beans.xml override the annotation settings if there is a conflict. An archive must contain the beans.xml deployment descriptor only in certain limited situations, described in Chapter 25, "Contexts and Dependency Injection for Java EE: Advanced Topics."

For a web application, the beans.xml deployment descriptor, if present, must be in the WEB-INF directory. For EJB modules or JAR files, the beans.xml deployment descriptor, if present, must be in the META-INF directory.

23.14 Using the @PostConstruct and @PreDestroy Annotations with CDI Managed Bean Classes

CDI managed bean classes and their superclasses support the annotations for initializing and for preparing for the destruction of a bean. These annotations are defined in JSR 250: Common Annotations for the Java platform (http://jcp.org/en/jsr/detail?id=250).

23.14.1 To Initialize a Managed Bean Using the @PostConstruct Annotation

Initializing a managed bean specifies the lifecycle callback method that the CDI framework should call after dependency injection but before the class is put into service.

1. In the managed bean class or any of its superclasses, define a method that performs the initialization that you require.

2. Annotate the declaration of the method with the javax.annotation.PostConstruct annotation.

When the managed bean is injected into a component, CDI calls the method after all injection has occurred and after all initializers have been called.

> **Note:** As mandated in JSR 250, if the annotated method is declared in a superclass, the method is called unless a subclass of the declaring class overrides the method.

The UserNumberBean managed bean in Section 24.2, "The guessnumber-cdi CDI Example," uses @PostConstruct to annotate a method that resets all bean fields:

```
@PostConstruct
public void reset () {
    this.minimum = 0;
    this.userNumber = 0;
    this.remainingGuesses = 0;
```

```
        this.maximum = maxNumber;
        this.number = randomInt.get();
    }
```

23.14.2 To Prepare for the Destruction of a Managed Bean Using the @PreDestroy Annotation

Preparing for the destruction of a managed bean specifies the lifecycle call back method that signals that an application component is about to be destroyed by the container.

1. In the managed bean class or any of its superclasses, prepare for the destruction of the managed bean.

   In this method, perform any cleanup that is required before the bean is destroyed, such as releasing a resource that the bean has been holding.

2. Annotate the declaration of the method with the `javax.annotation.PreDestroy` annotation.

CDI calls this method before starting to destroy the bean.

23.15 Further Information about CDI

For more information about CDI, see

- Contexts and Dependency Injection for Java EE specification:

  `http://jcp.org/en/jsr/detail?id=346`

- An introduction to Contexts and Dependency Injection for Java EE:

  `http://docs.jboss.org/weld/reference/latest/en-US/html/`

- Dependency Injection for Java specification:

  `http://jcp.org/en/jsr/detail?id=330`

- Managed Beans specification, which is part of the Java Platform, Enterprise Edition 7 (Java EE 7) Specification:

  `http://jcp.org/en/jsr/detail?id=342`

24

Running the Basic Contexts and Dependency Injection Examples

This chapter describes in detail how to build and run simple examples that use CDI. The examples are in the *tut-install*/examples/cdi/ directory.

To build and run the examples, you will do the following.

1. Use NetBeans IDE or the Maven tool to compile and package the example.

2. Use NetBeans IDE or the Maven tool to deploy the example.

3. Run the example in a web browser.

See Chapter 2, "Using the Tutorial Examples," for basic information on installing, building, and running the examples.

The following topics are addressed here:

- The simplegreeting CDI Example
- The guessnumber-cdi CDI Example

24.1 The simplegreeting CDI Example

The simplegreeting example illustrates some of the most basic features of CDI: scopes, qualifiers, bean injection, and accessing a managed bean in a JavaServer Faces application. When you run the example, you click a button that presents either a formal or an informal greeting, depending on how you edited one of the classes. The example includes four source files, a Facelets page and template, and configuration files.

24.1.1 The simplegreeting Source Files

The four source files for the simplegreeting example are

- The default Greeting class, shown in Section 23.5, "Beans as Injectable Objects"

- The @Informal qualifier interface definition and the InformalGreeting class that implements the interface, both shown in Section 23.6, "Using Qualifiers"

- The Printer managed bean class, which injects one of the two interfaces, shown in full in Section 23.10, "Adding Setter and Getter Methods"

The source files are located in the *tut-install*/examples/cdi/simplegreeting/src/main/java/javaeetutorial/simplegreeting directory.

24.1.2 The Facelets Template and Page

To use the managed bean in a simple Facelets application, you can use a very simple template file and index.xhtml page. The template page, template.xhtml, looks like this:

```
<?xml version='1.0' encoding='UTF-8' ?>
<!DOCTYPE html PUBLIC "-//W3C//DTD XHTML 1.0 Transitional//EN"
        "http://www.w3.org/TR/xhtml1/DTD/xhtml1-transitional.dtd">
<html lang="en"
      xmlns="http://www.w3.org/1999/xhtml"
      xmlns:h="http://xmlns.jcp.org/jsf/html"
      xmlns:ui="http://xmlns.jcp.org/jsf/facelets">
    <h:head>
        <meta http-equiv="Content-Type" content="text/html; charset=UTF-8"/>
        <h:outputStylesheet library="css" name="default.css"/>
        <title><ui:insert name="title">Default Title</ui:insert></title>
    </h:head>

    <body>
        <div id="container">
            <div id="header">
                <h2><ui:insert name="head">Head</ui:insert></h2>
            </div>

            <div id="space">
                <p></p>
            </div>

            <div id="content">
                <ui:insert name="content"/>
            </div>
```

```
            </div>
        </body>
</html>
```

To create the Facelets page, you can redefine the title and head, then add a small form to the content:

```
<!DOCTYPE html PUBLIC "-//W3C//DTD XHTML 1.0 Transitional//EN"
          "http://www.w3.org/TR/xhtml1/DTD/xhtml1-transitional.dtd">
<html lang="en"
      xmlns="http://www.w3.org/1999/xhtml"
      xmlns:ui="http://xmlns.jcp.org/jsf/facelets"
      xmlns:h="http://xmlns.jcp.org/jsf/html">
    <ui:composition template="/template.xhtml">

        <ui:define name="title">Simple Greeting</ui:define>
        <ui:define name="head">Simple Greeting</ui:define>
        <ui:define name="content">
            <h:form id="greetme">
                <p><h:outputLabel value="Enter your name: " for="name"/>
                    <h:inputText id="name" value="#{printer.name}"/></p>
                <p><h:commandButton value="Say Hello"
                                    action="#{printer.createSalutation}"/></p>
                <p><h:outputText value="#{printer.salutation}"/> </p>
            </h:form>
        </ui:define>

    </ui:composition>
</html>
```

The form asks the user to enter a name. The button is labeled **Say Hello**, and the action defined for it is to call the `createSalutation` method of the `Printer` managed bean. This method in turn calls the `greet` method of the defined `Greeting` class.

The output text for the form is the value of the greeting returned by the setter method. Depending on whether the default or the `@Informal` version of the greeting is injected, this is one of the following, where *name* is the name entered by the user:

```
Hello, name.
```

```
Hi, name!
```

The Facelets page and template are located in the *tut-install*/examples/cdi/ simplegreeting/src/main/webapp/ directory.

The simple CSS file that is used by the Facelets page is located under this directory, in the following location:

```
resources/css/default.css
```

24.1.3 Running the simplegreeting Example

You can use either NetBeans IDE or Maven to build, package, deploy, and run the `simplegreeting` application.

24.1.3.1 To Build, Package, and Deploy the simplegreeting Example Using NetBeans IDE

1. Make sure that GlassFish Server has been started (see Section 2.2, "Starting and Stopping GlassFish Server").

2. From the **File** menu, choose **Open Project**.

3. In the Open Project dialog box, navigate to:

    tut-install/examples/cdi

4. Select the `simplegreeting` folder.

5. Click **Open Project**.

6. To modify the `Printer.java` file, perform these steps:

    a. Expand the **Source Packages** node.

    b. Expand the `greetings` node.

    c. Double-click the `Printer.java` file.

    d. In the editor, comment out the `@Informal` annotation:

    ```
    @Inject
    //@Informal
    Greeting greeting;
    ```

    e. Save the file.

7. In the **Projects** tab, right-click the `simplegreeting` project and select **Build**.

    This command builds and packages the application into a WAR file, `simplegreeting.war`, located in the `target` directory, and then deploys it to GlassFish Server.

24.1.3.2 To Build, Package, and Deploy the simplegreeting Example Using Maven

1. Make sure that GlassFish Server has been started (see Section 2.2, "Starting and Stopping GlassFish Server").

2. In a terminal window, go to:

    tut-install/examples/cdi/simplegreeting/

3. Enter the following command to deploy the application:

    `mvn install`

    This command builds and packages the application into a WAR file, `simplegreeting.war`, located in the `target` directory, and then deploys it to GlassFish Server.

24.1.3.3 To Run the simplegreeting Example

1. In a web browser, enter the following URL:

    `http://localhost:8080/simplegreeting`

    The Simple Greeting page opens.

2. Enter a name in the field.

    For example, suppose that you enter `Duke`.

3. Click **Say Hello**.

    If you did not modify the `Printer.java` file, the following text string appears below the button:

    `Hi, Duke!`

    If you commented out the `@Informal` annotation in the `Printer.java` file, the following text string appears below the button:

    `Hello, Duke.`

24.2 The guessnumber-cdi CDI Example

The `guessnumber-cdi` example, somewhat more complex than the `simplegreeting` example, illustrates the use of producer methods and of session and application scope. The example is a game in which you try to guess a number in fewer than ten attempts. It is similar to the `guessnumber-jsf` example described in Chapter 8, "Introduction to Facelets," except that you can keep guessing until you get the right answer or until you use up your ten attempts.

The example includes four source files, a Facelets page and template, and configuration files. The configuration files and the template are the same as those used for the simplegreeting example.

24.2.1 The guessnumber-cdi Source Files

The four source files for the guessnumber-cdi example are

- The @MaxNumber qualifier interface
- The @Random qualifier interface
- The Generator managed bean, which defines producer methods
- The UserNumberBean managed bean

The source files are located in the *tut-install*/examples/cdi/guessnumber-cdi/ src/main/java/javaeetutorial/guessnumber directory.

24.2.1.1 The @MaxNumber and @Random Qualifier Interfaces

The @MaxNumber qualifier interface is defined as follows:

```
package guessnumber;

import java.lang.annotation.Documented;
import static java.lang.annotation.ElementType.FIELD;
import static java.lang.annotation.ElementType.METHOD;
import static java.lang.annotation.ElementType.PARAMETER;
import static java.lang.annotation.ElementType.TYPE;
import java.lang.annotation.Retention;
import static java.lang.annotation.RetentionPolicy.RUNTIME;
import java.lang.annotation.Target;
import javax.inject.Qualifier;

@Target({TYPE, METHOD, PARAMETER, FIELD})
@Retention(RUNTIME)
@Documented
@Qualifier
public @interface MaxNumber {
}
```

The @Random qualifier interface is defined as follows:

```
package guessnumber;

import java.lang.annotation.Documented;
import static java.lang.annotation.ElementType.FIELD;
import static java.lang.annotation.ElementType.METHOD;
import static java.lang.annotation.ElementType.PARAMETER;
import static java.lang.annotation.ElementType.TYPE;
import java.lang.annotation.Retention;
import static java.lang.annotation.RetentionPolicy.RUNTIME;
import java.lang.annotation.Target;
import javax.inject.Qualifier;

@Target({TYPE, METHOD, PARAMETER, FIELD})
@Retention(RUNTIME)
@Documented
@Qualifier
public @interface Random {
}
```

24.2.1.2 The Generator Managed Bean

The Generator managed bean contains the two producer methods for the application. The bean has the @ApplicationScoped annotation to specify that its context extends for the duration of the user's interaction with the application:

```
package guessnumber;

import java.io.Serializable;
import javax.enterprise.context.ApplicationScoped;
import javax.enterprise.inject.Produces;

@ApplicationScoped
public class Generator implements Serializable {

    private static final long serialVersionUID = -7213673465118041882L;

    private final java.util.Random random =
        new java.util.Random( System.currentTimeMillis() );

    private final int maxNumber = 100;

    java.util.Random getRandom() {
        return random;
    }
```

```
@Produces @Random int next() {
    return getRandom().nextInt(maxNumber + 1);
}

@Produces @MaxNumber int getMaxNumber() {
    return maxNumber;
}

}
```

24.2.1.3 The UserNumberBean Managed Bean

The UserNumberBean managed bean, the managed bean for the JavaServer Faces application, provides the basic logic for the game. This bean does the following:

- Implements setter and getter methods for the bean fields

- Injects the two qualifier objects

- Provides a reset method that allows you to begin a new game after you complete one

- Provides a check method that determines whether the user has guessed the number

- Provides a validateNumberRange method that determines whether the user's input is correct

The bean is defined as follows:

```
package guessnumber;

import java.io.Serializable;
import javax.annotation.PostConstruct;
import javax.enterprise.context.SessionScoped;
import javax.enterprise.inject.Instance;
import javax.faces.application.FacesMessage;
import javax.faces.component.UIComponent;
import javax.faces.component.UIInput;
import javax.faces.context.FacesContext;
import javax.inject.Inject;
import javax.inject.Named;

@Named
@SessionScoped
public class UserNumberBean implements Serializable {

    private static final long serialVersionUID = -7698506329160109476L;
```

```java
private int number;
private Integer userNumber;
private int minimum;
private int remainingGuesses;
@Inject
@MaxNumber
private int maxNumber;
private int maximum;
@Random
@Inject
Instance<Integer> randomInt;

public UserNumberBean() {
}

public int getNumber() {
    return number;
}

public void setUserNumber(Integer user_number) {
    userNumber = user_number;
}

public Integer getUserNumber() {
    return userNumber;
}

public int getMaximum() {
    return (this.maximum);
}

public void setMaximum(int maximum) {
    this.maximum = maximum;
}

public int getMinimum() {
    return (this.minimum);
}

public void setMinimum(int minimum) {
    this.minimum = minimum;
}

public int getRemainingGuesses() {
    return remainingGuesses;
}
```

```java
public String check() throws InterruptedException {
    if (userNumber > number) {
        maximum = userNumber - 1;
    }
    if (userNumber < number) {
        minimum = userNumber + 1;
    }
    if (userNumber == number) {
        FacesContext.getCurrentInstance().addMessage(null,
            new FacesMessage("Correct!"));
    }
    remainingGuesses--;
    return null;
}

@PostConstruct
public void reset() {
    this.minimum = 0;
    this.userNumber = 0;
    this.remainingGuesses = 10;
    this.maximum = maxNumber;
    this.number = randomInt.get();
}

public void validateNumberRange(FacesContext context,
                                UIComponent toValidate,
                                Object value) {
    int input = (Integer) value;

    if (input < minimum || input > maximum) {
        ((UIInput) toValidate).setValid(false);

        FacesMessage message = new FacesMessage("Invalid guess");
        context.addMessage(toValidate.getClientId(context), message);
    }
}
}
```

24.2.2 The Facelets Page

This example uses the same template that the simplegreeting example uses. The index.xhtml file, however, is more complex:

```
<?xml version='1.0' encoding='UTF-8' ?>
<!DOCTYPE html PUBLIC "-//W3C//DTD XHTML 1.0 Transitional//EN"
        "http://www.w3.org/TR/xhtml1/DTD/xhtml1-transitional.dtd">
<html lang="en"
```

```
        xmlns="http://www.w3.org/1999/xhtml"
        xmlns:ui="http://xmlns.jcp.org/jsf/facelets"
        xmlns:h="http://xmlns.jcp.org/jsf/html">
    <ui:composition template="/template.xhtml">

        <ui:define name="title">Guess My Number</ui:define>
        <ui:define name="head">Guess My Number</ui:define>
        <ui:define name="content">
            <h:form id="GuessMain">
                <div style="color: black; font-size: 24px;">
                    <p>I'm thinking of a number from
                 <span style="color: blue">#{userNumberBean.minimum}</span>
                    to
                 <span style="color: blue">#{userNumberBean.maximum}</span>.
                    You have
                    <span style="color: blue">
                        #{userNumberBean.remainingGuesses}
                    </span>
                    guesses.</p>
                </div>
                <h:panelGrid border="0" columns="5" style="font-size: 18px;">
                    <h:outputLabel for="inputGuess">Number:</h:outputLabel>
                    <h:inputText id="inputGuess"
                                 value="#{userNumberBean.userNumber}"
                                 required="true" size="3"
disabled="#{userNumberBean.number eq userNumberBean.userNumber or
userNumberBean.remainingGuesses le 0}"
                                 validator="#{userNumberBean.validateNumberRange}">
                    </h:inputText>
                    <h:commandButton id="GuessButton" value="Guess"
                                     action="#{userNumberBean.check}"
disabled="#{userNumberBean.number eq userNumberBean.userNumber or
userNumberBean.remainingGuesses le 0}"/>
                    <h:commandButton id="RestartButton" value="Reset"
                                     action="#{userNumberBean.reset}"
                                     immediate="true" />
                    <h:outputText id="Higher" value="Higher!"
rendered="#{userNumberBean.number gt userNumberBean.userNumber and
userNumberBean.userNumber ne 0}"
                                     style="color: #d20005"/>
                    <h:outputText id="Lower" value="Lower!"
rendered="#{userNumberBean.number lt userNumberBean.userNumber and
userNumberBean.userNumber ne 0}"
                                     style="color: #d20005"/>
                </h:panelGrid>
                <div style="color: #d20005; font-size: 14px;">
                    <h:messages id="messages" globalOnly="false"/>
```

```
                        </div>
                    </h:form>
                </ui:define>

            </ui:composition>
        </html>
```

The Facelets page presents the user with the minimum and maximum values and the number of guesses remaining. The user's interaction with the game takes place within the panelGrid table, which contains an input field, **Guess** and **Reset** buttons, and a field that appears if the guess is higher or lower than the correct number. Every time the user clicks the **Guess** button, the userNumberBean.check method is called to reset the maximum or minimum value or, if the guess is correct, to generate a FacesMessage to that effect. The method that determines whether each guess is valid is userNumberBean.validateNumberRange.

24.2.3 Running the guessnumber-cdi Example

You can use either NetBeans IDE or Maven to build, package, deploy, and run the guessnumber-cdi application.

24.2.3.1 To Build, Package, and Deploy the guessnumber-cdi Example Using NetBeans IDE

1. Make sure that GlassFish Server has been started (see Section 2.2, "Starting and Stopping GlassFish Server").

2. From the **File** menu, choose **Open Project**.

3. In the Open Project dialog box, navigate to:

   tut-install/examples/cdi

4. Select the guessnumber-cdi folder.

5. Click **Open Project**.

6. In the **Projects** tab, right-click the guessnumber-cdi project and select **Build**.

   This command builds and packages the application into a WAR file, guessnumber-cdi.war, located in the target directory, and then deploys it to GlassFish Server.

24.2.3.2 To Build, Package, and Deploy the guessnumber-cdi Example Using Maven

1. Make sure that GlassFish Server has been started (see Section 2.2, "Starting and Stopping GlassFish Server").

2. In a terminal window, go to:

    tut-install/examples/cdi/guessnumber-cdi/

3. Enter the following command to deploy the application:

    ```
    mvn install
    ```

    This command builds and packages the application into a WAR file, guessnumber-cdi.war, located in the target directory, and then deploys it to GlassFish Server.

24.2.3.3 To Run the guessnumber Example

1. In a web browser, enter the following URL:

    ```
    http://localhost:8080/guessnumber-cdi
    ```

    The Guess My Number page opens.

2. On the Guess My Number page, enter a number in the **Number** field and click **Guess**.

    The minimum and maximum values are modified, along with the remaining number of guesses.

3. Keep guessing numbers until you get the right answer or run out of guesses.

    If you get the right answer or run out of guesses, the input field and **Guess** button are grayed out.

4. Click **Reset** to play the game again with a new random number.

25

Contexts and Dependency Injection for Java EE: Advanced Topics

This chapter describes more advanced features of Contexts and Dependency Injection for Java EE (CDI). Specifically, it covers additional features CDI provides to enable loose coupling of components with strong typing, in addition to those described in Section 23.2, "Overview of CDI."

The following topics are addressed here:

- Packaging CDI Applications

- Using Alternatives in CDI Applications

- Using Producer Methods, Producer Fields, and Disposer Methods in CDI Applications

- Using Predefined Beans in CDI Applications

- Using Events in CDI Applications

- Using Interceptors in CDI Applications

- Using Decorators in CDI Applications

- Using Stereotypes in CDI Applications

25.1 Packaging CDI Applications

When you deploy a Java EE application, CDI looks for beans inside bean archives. A **bean archive** is any module that contains beans that the CDI runtime can manage and inject. There are two kinds of bean archives: explicit bean archives and implicit bean archives.

An **explicit bean archive** is an archive that contains a `beans.xml` deployment descriptor, which can be an empty file, contain no version number, or contain the version number 1.1 with the `bean-discovery-mode` attribute set to `all`. For example:

```
<?xml version="1.0" encoding="UTF-8"?>
<beans xmlns="http://xmlns.jcp.org/xml/ns/javaee"
       xmlns:xsi="http://www.w3.org/2001/XMLSchema-instance"
       xsi:schemaLocation="http://xmlns.jcp.org/xml/ns/javaee
                           http://xmlns.jcp.org/xml/ns/javaee/beans_1_1.xsd"
       version="1.1" bean-discovery-mode="all">
   ...
</beans>
```

CDI can manage and inject any bean in an explicit archive, except those annotated with `@Vetoed`.

An **implicit bean archive** is an archive that contains some beans annotated with a scope type, contains no `beans.xml` deployment descriptor, or contains a `beans.xml` deployment descriptor with the `bean-discovery-mode` attribute set to `annotated`.

In an implicit archive, CDI can only manage and inject beans annotated with a scope type.

For a web application, the `beans.xml` deployment descriptor, if present, must be in the `WEB-INF` directory. For EJB modules or JAR files, the `beans.xml` deployment descriptor, if present, must be in the `META-INF` directory.

25.2 Using Alternatives in CDI Applications

When you have more than one version of a bean that you use for different purposes, you can choose between them during the development phase by injecting one qualifier or another, as shown in Section 24.1, "The simplegreeting CDI Example."

Instead of having to change the source code of your application, however, you can make the choice at deployment time by using **alternatives**.

Alternatives are commonly used for purposes such as the following:

- To handle client-specific business logic that is determined at runtime

- To specify beans that are valid for a particular deployment scenario (for example, when country-specific sales tax laws require country-specific sales tax business logic)

- To create dummy (mock) versions of beans to be used for testing

To make a bean available for lookup, injection, or EL resolution using this mechanism, give it a `javax.enterprise.inject.Alternative` annotation and then use the `alternatives` element to specify it in the `beans.xml` file.

For example, you might want to create a full version of a bean and also a simpler version that you use only for certain kinds of testing. The example described in Section 26.1, "The encoder Example: Using Alternatives," contains two such beans, `CoderImpl` and `TestCoderImpl`. The test bean is annotated as follows:

```
@Alternative
public class TestCoderImpl implements Coder { ... }
```

The full version is not annotated:

```
public class CoderImpl implements Coder { ... }
```

The managed bean injects an instance of the `Coder` interface:

```
@Inject
Coder coder;
```

The alternative version of the bean is used by the application only if that version is declared as follows in the `beans.xml` file:

```
<beans ...>
    <alternatives>
        <class>javaeetutorial.encoder.TestCoderImpl</class>
    </alternatives>
</beans>
```

If the `alternatives` element is commented out in the `beans.xml` file, the `CoderImpl` class is used.

You can also have several beans that implement the same interface, all annotated `@Alternative`. In this case, you must specify in the `beans.xml` file which of these alternative beans you want to use. If `CoderImpl` were also annotated `@Alternative`, one of the two beans would always have to be specified in the `beans.xml` file.

The alternatives that you specify in the `beans.xml` file apply only to classes in the same archive. Use the `@Priority` annotation to specify alternatives globally for an application that consists of multiple modules, as in the following example:

```
@Alternative
@Priority(Interceptor.Priority.APPLICATION+10)
public class TestCoderImpl implements Coder { ... }
```

The alternative with higher priority value is selected if several alternative beans that implement the same interface are annotated with `@Priority`. You do not need to specify the alternative in the `beans.xml` file when you use the `@Priority` annotation.

25.2.1 Using Specialization

Specialization has a function similar to that of alternatives in that it allows you to substitute one bean for another. However, you might want to make one bean override the other in all cases. Suppose you defined the following two beans:

```
@Default @Asynchronous
public class AsynchronousService implements Service { ... }

@Alternative
public class MockAsynchronousService extends AsynchronousService { ... }
```

If you then declared `MockAsynchronousService` as an alternative in your `beans.xml` file, the following injection point would resolve to `MockAsynchronousService`:

```
@Inject Service service;
```

The following, however, would resolve to `AsynchronousService` rather than `MockAsynchronousService`, because `MockAsynchronousService` does not have the `@Asynchronous` qualifier:

```
@Inject @Asynchronous Service service;
```

To make sure that `MockAsynchronousService` was always injected, you would have to implement all bean types and bean qualifiers of `AsynchronousService`. However, if `AsynchronousService` declared a producer method or observer method, even this cumbersome mechanism would not ensure that the other bean was never invoked. Specialization provides a simpler mechanism.

Specialization happens at development time as well as at runtime. If you declare that one bean specializes another, it extends the other bean class, and at runtime the specialized bean completely replaces the other bean. If the first bean is produced by means of a producer method, you must also override the producer method.

You specialize a bean by giving it the `javax.enterprise.inject.Specializes` annotation. For example, you might declare a bean as follows:

```
@Specializes
public class MockAsynchronousService extends AsynchronousService { ... }
```

In this case, the MockAsynchronousService class will always be invoked instead of the AsynchronousService class.

Usually, a bean marked with the @Specializes annotation is also an alternative and is declared as an alternative in the beans.xml file. Such a bean is meant to stand in as a replacement for the default implementation, and the alternative implementation automatically inherits all qualifiers of the default implementation as well as its EL name, if it has one.

25.3 Using Producer Methods, Producer Fields, and Disposer Methods in CDI Applications

A **producer method** generates an object that can then be injected. Typically, you use producer methods in the following situations:

- When you want to inject an object that is not itself a bean

- When the concrete type of the object to be injected may vary at runtime

- When the object requires some custom initialization that the bean constructor does not perform

For more information on producer methods, see Section 23.12, "Injecting Objects by Using Producer Methods."

A **producer field** is a simpler alternative to a producer method; it is a field of a bean that generates an object. It can be used instead of a simple getter method. Producer fields are particularly useful for declaring Java EE resources such as data sources, JMS resources, and web service references.

A producer method or field is annotated with the javax.enterprise.inject.Produces annotation.

25.3.1 Using Producer Methods

A producer method can allow you to select a bean implementation at runtime instead of at development time or deployment time. For example, in the example described in Section 26.2, "The producermethods Example: Using a Producer Method to Choose a Bean Implementation," the managed bean defines the following producer method:

```
@Produces
@Chosen
@RequestScoped
public Coder getCoder() {
```

```
        switch (coderType) {
            case TEST:
                return new TestCoderImpl();
            case SHIFT:
                return new CoderImpl();
            default:
                return null;
        }
    }
}
```

Here, getCoder becomes in effect a getter method, and when the coder property is injected with the same qualifier and other annotations as the method, the selected version of the interface is used:

```
@Inject
@Chosen
@RequestScoped
Coder coder;
```

Specifying the qualifier is essential: It tells CDI which Coder to inject. Without it, the CDI implementation would not be able to choose between CoderImpl, TestCoderImpl, and the one returned by getCoder and would cancel deployment, informing the user of the ambiguous dependency.

25.3.2 Using Producer Fields to Generate Resources

A common use of a producer field is to generate an object such as a JDBC DataSource or a Java Persistence API EntityManager (see Chapter 8, "Introduction to the Java Persistence API," in *The Java EE 7 Tutorial, Volume 2*, for more information). The object can then be managed by the container. For example, you could create a @UserDatabase qualifier and then declare a producer field for an entity manager as follows:

```
@Produces
@UserDatabase
@PersistenceContext
private EntityManager em;
```

The @UserDatabase qualifier can be used when you inject the object into another bean, RequestBean, elsewhere in the application:

```
@Inject
@UserDatabase
EntityManager em;
...
```

Section 26.3, "The producerfields Example: Using Producer Fields to Generate Resources," shows how to use producer fields to generate an entity manager. You can use a similar mechanism to inject @Resource, @EJB, or @WebServiceRef objects.

To minimize the reliance on resource injection, specify the producer field for the resource in one place in the application, and then inject the object wherever in the application you need it.

25.3.3 Using a Disposer Method

You can use a producer method or a producer field to generate an object that needs to be removed when its work is completed. If you do, you need a corresponding **disposer method**, annotated with a @Disposes annotation. For example, you can close the entity manager as follows:

```
public void close(@Disposes @UserDatabase EntityManager em) {
    em.close();
}
```

The disposer method is called automatically when the context ends (in this case, at the end of the conversation, because RequestBean has conversation scope), and the parameter in the close method receives the object produced by the producer field.

25.4 Using Predefined Beans in CDI Applications

Java EE provides predefined beans that implement the following interfaces.

- javax.transaction.UserTransaction: A Java Transaction API (JTA) user transaction.

- java.security.Principal: The abstract notion of a principal, which represents any entity, such as an individual, a corporation, or a login ID. Whenever the injected principal is accessed, it always represents the identity of the current caller. For example, a principal is injected into a field at initialization. Later, a method that uses the injected principal is called on the object into which the principal was injected. In this situation, the injected principal represents the identity of the current caller when the method is run.

- javax.validation.Validator: A validator for bean instances. The bean that implements this interface enables a Validator object for the default bean validation object ValidatorFactory to be injected.

- javax.validation.ValidatorFactory: A factory class for returning initialized Validator instances. The bean that implements this interface enables the default bean validation ValidatorFactory object to be injected.

- `javax.servlet.http.HttpServletRequest`: An HTTP request from a client. The bean that implements this interface enables a servlet to obtain all the details of a request.

- `javax.servlet.http.HttpSession`: An HTTP session between a client and a server. The bean that implements this interface enables a servlet to access information about a session and to bind objects to a session.

- `javax.servlet.ServletContext`: A context object that servlets can use to communicate with the servlet container.

To inject a predefined bean, create an injection point to obtain an instance of the bean by using the `javax.annotation.Resource` annotation for resources or the `javax.inject.Inject` annotation for CDI beans. For the bean type, specify the class name of the interface the bean implements.

Table 25–1   Injection of Predefined Beans

Predefined Bean	Resource or CDI Bean	Injection Example
UserTransaction	Resource	@Resource UserTransaction transaction;
Principal	Resource	@Resource Principal principal;
Validator	Resource	@Resource Validator validator;
ValidatorFactory	Resource	@Resource ValidatorFactory factory;
HttpServletRequest	CDI bean	@Inject HttpServletRequest req;
HttpSession	CDI bean	@Inject HttpSession session;
ServletContext	CDI bean	@Inject ServletContext context;

Predefined beans are injected with dependent scope and the predefined default qualifier `@Default`.

For more information about injecting resources, see Section 4.1, "Resource Injection."

The following code snippet shows how to use the `@Resource` and `@Inject` annotations to inject predefined beans. This code snippet injects a user transaction and a context object into the servlet class `TransactionServlet`. The user transaction is an instance of the predefined bean that implements the `javax.transaction.UserTransaction` interface. The context object is an instance of the predefined bean that implements the `javax.servlet.ServletContext` interface.

```
import javax.annotation.Resource;
import javax.inject.Inject;
import javax.servlet.http.HttpServlet;
import javax.transaction.UserTransaction;
...
public class TransactionServlet extends HttpServlet {
    @Resource UserTransaction transaction;
    @Inject ServletContext context;
    ...
}
```

25.5 Using Events in CDI Applications

Events allow beans to communicate without any compile-time dependency. One bean can define an event, another bean can fire the event, and yet another bean can handle the event. The beans can be in separate packages and even in separate tiers of the application.

25.5.1 Defining Events

An event consists of the following:

- The event object, a Java object

- Zero or more qualifier types, the event qualifiers

For example, in the `billpayment` example described in Section 26.4, "The billpayment Example: Using Events and Interceptors," a `PaymentEvent` bean defines an event using three properties, which have setter and getter methods:

```
public String paymentType;
public BigDecimal value;
public Date datetime;

public PaymentEvent() {
}
```

The example also defines qualifiers that distinguish between two kinds of `PaymentEvent`. Every event also has the default qualifier `@Any`.

25.5.2 Using Observer Methods to Handle Events

An event handler uses an **observer method** to consume events.

Each observer method takes as a parameter an event of a specific event type that is annotated with the `@Observes` annotation and with any qualifiers for that event type. The observer method is notified of an event if the event object matches the event type and if all the qualifiers of the event match the observer method event qualifiers.

The observer method can take other parameters in addition to the event parameter. The additional parameters are injection points and can declare qualifiers.

The event handler for the billpayment example, PaymentHandler, defines two observer methods, one for each type of PaymentEvent:

```
public void creditPayment(@Observes @Credit PaymentEvent event) {
    ...
}

public void debitPayment(@Observes @Debit PaymentEvent event) {
    ...
}
```

Observer methods can also be conditional or transactional:

- A conditional observer method is notified of an event only if an instance of the bean that defines the observer method already exists in the current context. To declare a conditional observer method, specify notifyObserver=IF_EXISTS as an argument to @Observes:

  ```
  @Observes(notifyObserver=IF_EXISTS)
  ```

  To obtain the default unconditional behavior, you can specify @Observes(notifyObserver=ALWAYS).

- A transactional observer method is notified of an event during the before-completion or after-completion phase of the transaction in which the event was fired. You can also specify that the notification is to occur only after the transaction has completed successfully or unsuccessfully. To specify a transactional observer method, use any of the following arguments to @Observes:

  ```
  @Observes(during=BEFORE_COMPLETION)

  @Observes(during=AFTER_COMPLETION)

  @Observes(during=AFTER_SUCCESS)

  @Observes(during=AFTER_FAILURE)
  ```

  To obtain the default nontransactional behavior, specify @Observes(during=IN_PROGRESS).

An observer method that is called before completion of a transaction may call the `setRollbackOnly` method on the transaction instance to force a transaction rollback.

Observer methods may throw exceptions. If a transactional observer method throws an exception, the exception is caught by the container. If the observer method is nontransactional, the exception terminates processing of the event, and no other observer methods for the event are called.

25.5.3 Firing Events

To activate an event, call the `javax.enterprise.event.Event.fire` method. This method fires an event and notifies any observer methods.

In the `billpayment` example, a managed bean called `PaymentBean` fires the appropriate event by using information it receives from the user interface. There are actually four event beans, two for the event object and two for the payload. The managed bean injects the two event beans. The pay method uses a `switch` statement to choose which event to fire, using new to create the payload:

```
@Inject
@Credit
Event<PaymentEvent> creditEvent;

@Inject
@Debit
Event<PaymentEvent> debitEvent;

private static final int DEBIT = 1;
private static final int CREDIT = 2;
private int paymentOption = DEBIT;
...

@Logged
public String pay() {
    ...
    switch (paymentOption) {
        case DEBIT:
            PaymentEvent debitPayload = new PaymentEvent();
            // populate payload ...
            debitEvent.fire(debitPayload);
            break;
        case CREDIT:
            PaymentEvent creditPayload = new PaymentEvent();
            // populate payload ...
            creditEvent.fire(creditPayload);
```

```
            break;
        default:
            logger.severe("Invalid payment option!");
    }
    ...
}
```

The argument to the `fire` method is a `PaymentEvent` that contains the payload. The fired event is then consumed by the observer methods.

25.6 Using Interceptors in CDI Applications

An **interceptor** is a class used to interpose in method invocations or lifecycle events that occur in an associated target class. The interceptor performs tasks, such as logging or auditing, that are separate from the business logic of the application and are repeated often within an application. Such tasks are often called **cross-cutting** tasks. Interceptors allow you to specify the code for these tasks in one place for easy maintenance. When interceptors were first introduced to the Java EE platform, they were specific to enterprise beans. On the Java EE 7 platform, you can use them with Java EE managed objects of all kinds, including managed beans.

For information on Java EE interceptors, see Chapter 25, "Using Java EE Interceptors," in *The Java EE 7 Tutorial, Volume 2*.

An interceptor class often contains a method annotated `@AroundInvoke`, which specifies the tasks the interceptor will perform when intercepted methods are invoked. It can also contain a method annotated `@PostConstruct`, `@PreDestroy`, `@PrePassivate`, or `@PostActivate`, to specify lifecycle callback interceptors, and a method annotated `@AroundTimeout`, to specify EJB timeout interceptors. An interceptor class can contain more than one interceptor method, but it must have no more than one method of each type.

Along with an interceptor, an application defines one or more **interceptor binding types**, which are annotations that associate an interceptor with target beans or methods. For example, the `billpayment` example contains an interceptor binding type named `@Logged` and an interceptor named `LoggedInterceptor`. The interceptor binding type declaration looks something like a qualifier declaration, but it is annotated with `javax.interceptor.InterceptorBinding`:

```
@Inherited
@InterceptorBinding
@Retention(RUNTIME)
@Target({METHOD, TYPE})
public @interface Logged {}
```

An interceptor binding also has the `java.lang.annotation.Inherited` annotation, to specify that the annotation can be inherited from superclasses. The `@Inherited` annotation also applies to custom scopes (not discussed in this tutorial) but does not apply to qualifiers.

An interceptor binding type may declare other interceptor bindings.

The interceptor class is annotated with the interceptor binding as well as with the `@Interceptor` annotation. For an example, see Section 26.4.4, "The LoggedInterceptor Interceptor Class."

Every `@AroundInvoke` method takes a `javax.interceptor.InvocationContext` argument, returns a `java.lang.Object`, and throws an `Exception`. It can call `InvocationContext` methods. The `@AroundInvoke` method must call the `proceed` method, which causes the target class method to be invoked.

Once an interceptor and binding type are defined, you can annotate beans and individual methods with the binding type to specify that the interceptor is to be invoked either on all methods of the bean or on specific methods. For example, in the `billpayment` example, the `PaymentHandler` bean is annotated `@Logged`, which means that any invocation of its business methods will cause the interceptor's `@AroundInvoke` method to be invoked:

```
@Logged
@SessionScoped
public class PaymentHandler implements Serializable { ... }
```

However, in the `PaymentBean` bean, only the `pay` and `reset` methods have the `@Logged` annotation, so the interceptor is invoked only when these methods are invoked:

```
@Logged
public String pay() { ... }

@Logged
public void reset() { ... }
```

In order for an interceptor to be invoked in a CDI application, it must, like an alternative, be specified in the `beans.xml` file. For example, the `LoggedInterceptor` class is specified as follows:

```
<interceptors>
    <class>javaeetutorial.billpayment.interceptors.LoggedInterceptor</class>
</interceptors>
```

If an application uses more than one interceptor, the interceptors are invoked in the order specified in the `beans.xml` file.

The interceptors that you specify in the beans.xml file apply only to classes in the same archive. Use the @Priority annotation to specify interceptors globally for an application that consists of multiple modules, as in the following example:

```
@Logged
@Interceptor
@Priority(Interceptor.Priority.APPLICATION)
public class LoggedInterceptor implements Serializable { ... }
```

Interceptors with lower priority values are called first. You do not need to specify the interceptor in the beans.xml file when you use the @Priority annotation.

25.7 Using Decorators in CDI Applications

A **decorator** is a Java class that is annotated javax.decorator.Decorator and that has a corresponding decorators element in the beans.xml file.

A decorator bean class must also have a delegate injection point, which is annotated javax.decorator.Delegate. This injection point can be a field, a constructor parameter, or an initializer method parameter of the decorator class.

Decorators are outwardly similar to interceptors. However, they actually perform tasks complementary to those performed by interceptors. Interceptors perform cross-cutting tasks associated with method invocation and with the lifecycles of beans, but cannot perform any business logic. Decorators, on the other hand, do perform business logic by intercepting business methods of beans. This means that instead of being reusable for different kinds of applications, as are interceptors, their logic is specific to a particular application.

For example, instead of using an alternative TestCoderImpl class for the encoder example, you could create a decorator as follows:

```
@Decorator
public abstract class CoderDecorator implements Coder {

    @Inject
    @Delegate
    @Any
    Coder coder;

    public String codeString(String s, int tval) {
        int len = s.length();

        return "\"" + s + "\" becomes " + "\"" + coder.codeString(s, tval)
                + "\", " + len + " characters in length";
    }
}
```

See Section 26.5, "The decorators Example: Decorating a Bean," for an example that uses this decorator.

This simple decorator returns more detailed output than the encoded string returned by the `CoderImpl.codeString` method. A more complex decorator could store information in a database or perform some other business logic.

A decorator can be declared as an abstract class so that it does not have to implement all the business methods of the interface.

In order for a decorator to be invoked in a CDI application, it must, like an interceptor or an alternative, be specified in the `beans.xml` file. For example, the `CoderDecorator` class is specified as follows:

```
<decorators>
    <class>javaeetutorial.decorators.CoderDecorator</class>
</decorators>
```

If an application uses more than one decorator, the decorators are invoked in the order in which they are specified in the `beans.xml` file.

If an application has both interceptors and decorators, the interceptors are invoked first. This means, in effect, that you cannot intercept a decorator.

The decorators that you specify in the `beans.xml` file apply only to classes in the same archive. Use the `@Priority` annotation to specify decorators globally for an application that consists of multiple modules, as in the following example:

```
@Decorator
@Priority(Interceptor.Priority.APPLICATION)
public abstract class CoderDecorator implements Coder { ... }
```

Decorators with lower priority values are called first. You do not need to specify the decorator in the `beans.xml` when you use the `@Priority` annotation.

25.8 Using Stereotypes in CDI Applications

A **stereotype** is a kind of annotation, applied to a bean, that incorporates other annotations. Stereotypes can be particularly useful in large applications in which you have a number of beans that perform similar functions. A stereotype is a kind of annotation that specifies the following:

- A default scope

- Zero or more interceptor bindings

- Optionally, a `@Named` annotation, guaranteeing default EL naming
- Optionally, an `@Alternative` annotation, specifying that all beans with this stereotype are alternatives

A bean annotated with a particular stereotype will always use the specified annotations, so you do not have to apply the same annotations to many beans.

For example, you might create a stereotype named `Action`, using the `javax.enterprise.inject.Stereotype` annotation:

```
@RequestScoped
@Secure
@Transactional
@Named
@Stereotype
@Target(TYPE)
@Retention(RUNTIME)
public @interface Action {}
```

All beans annotated `@Action` will have request scope, use default EL naming, and have the interceptor bindings `@Transactional` and `@Secure`.

You could also create a stereotype named `Mock`:

```
@Alternative
@Stereotype
@Target(TYPE)
@Retention(RUNTIME)
public @interface Mock {}
```

All beans with this annotation are alternatives.

It is possible to apply multiple stereotypes to the same bean, so you can annotate a bean as follows:

```
@Action
@Mock
public class MockLoginAction extends LoginAction { ... }
```

It is also possible to override the scope specified by a stereotype, simply by specifying a different scope for the bean. The following declaration gives the `MockLoginAction` bean session scope instead of request scope:

```
@SessionScoped
@Action
@Mock
public class MockLoginAction extends LoginAction { ... }
```

CDI makes available a built-in stereotype called Model, which is intended for use with beans that define the model layer of a model-view-controller application architecture. This stereotype specifies that a bean is both @Named and @RequestScoped:

```
@Named
@RequestScoped
@Stereotype
@Target({TYPE, METHOD, FIELD})
@Retention(RUNTIME)
public @interface Model {}
```

26

Running the Advanced Contexts and Dependency Injection Examples

This chapter describes in detail how to build and run several advanced examples that use CDI. The examples are in the *tut-install*/examples/cdi/ directory.

To build and run the examples, you will do the following.

1. Use NetBeans IDE or the Maven tool to compile, package, and deploy the example.

2. Run the example in a web browser.

See Chapter 2, "Using the Tutorial Examples," for basic information on installing, building, and running the examples.

The following topics are addressed here:

- The encoder Example: Using Alternatives

- The producermethods Example: Using a Producer Method to Choose a Bean Implementation

- The producerfields Example: Using Producer Fields to Generate Resources

- The billpayment Example: Using Events and Interceptors

- The decorators Example: Decorating a Bean

26.1 The encoder Example: Using Alternatives

The encoder example shows how to use alternatives to choose between two beans at deployment time, as described in Section 25.2, "Using Alternatives in

CDI Applications." The example includes an interface and two implementations of it, a managed bean, a Facelets page, and configuration files.

The source files are located in the *tut-install*/examples/cdi/encoder/src/main/java/javaeetutorial/encoder/ directory.

26.1.1 The Coder Interface and Implementations

The Coder interface contains just one method, codeString, that takes two arguments: a string, and an integer value that specifies how the letters in the string should be transposed:

```
public interface Coder {

    public String codeString(String s, int tval);
}
```

The interface has two implementation classes, CoderImpl and TestCoderImpl. The implementation of codeString in CoderImpl shifts the string argument forward in the alphabet by the number of letters specified in the second argument; any characters that are not letters are left unchanged. (This simple shift code is known as a Caesar cipher because Julius Caesar reportedly used it to communicate with his generals.) The implementation in TestCoderImpl merely displays the values of the arguments. The TestCoderImpl implementation is annotated @Alternative:

```
import javax.enterprise.inject.Alternative;

@Alternative
public class TestCoderImpl implements Coder {

    @Override
    public String codeString(String s, int tval) {
        return ("input string is " + s + ", shift value is " + tval);
    }
}
```

The beans.xml file for the encoder example contains an alternatives element for the TestCoderImpl class, but by default the element is commented out:

```
<beans ...>
    <!--<alternatives>
        <class>javaeetutorial.encoder.TestCoderImpl</class>
    </alternatives>-->
</beans>
```

This means that by default, the TestCoderImpl class, annotated @Alternative, will not be used. Instead, the CoderImpl class will be used.

26.1.2 The encoder Facelets Page and Managed Bean

The simple Facelets page for the encoder example, index.xhtml, asks the user to enter the string and integer values and passes them to the managed bean, CoderBean, as coderBean.inputString and coderBean.transVal:

```
<html lang="en"
     xmlns="http://www.w3.org/1999/xhtml"
     xmlns:h="http://java.sun.com/jsf/html">
  <h:head>
     <h:outputStylesheet library="css" name="default.css"/>
     <title>String Encoder</title>
  </h:head>
  <h:body>
     <h2>String Encoder</h2>
     <p>Type a string and an integer, then click Encode.</p>
     <p>Depending on which alternative is enabled, the coder bean
        will either display the argument values or return a string that
        shifts the letters in the original string by the value you
        specify. The value must be between 0 and 26.</p>
     <h:form id="encodeit">
       <p><h:outputLabel value="Enter a string: " for="inputString"/>
          <h:inputText id="inputString"
                          value="#{coderBean.inputString}"/>
          <h:outputLabel
                       value="Enter the number of letters to shift by: "
                       for="transVal"/>
          <h:inputText id="transVal" value="#{coderBean.transVal}"/></p>
       <p><h:commandButton value="Encode"
                          action="#{coderBean.encodeString()}"/></p>
       <p><h:outputLabel value="Result: " for="outputString"/>
          <h:outputText id="outputString"
                          value="#{coderBean.codedString}"
                          style="color:blue"/></p>
       <p><h:commandButton value="Reset"
                          action="#{coderBean.reset}"/></p>
     </h:form>
     ...
  </h:body>
</html>
```

When the user clicks the **Encode** button, the page invokes the managed bean's encodeString method and displays the result, coderBean.codedString, in blue. The page also has a **Reset** button that clears the fields.

The managed bean, CoderBean, is a @RequestScoped bean that declares its input and output properties. The transVal property has three Bean Validation constraints that enforce limits on the integer value, so that if the user enters an invalid value, a default error message appears on the Facelets page. The bean also injects an instance of the `Coder` interface:

```
@Named
@RequestScoped
public class CoderBean {

    private String inputString;
    private String codedString;
    @Max(26)
    @Min(0)
    @NotNull
    private int transVal;

    @Inject
    Coder coder;
    ...
```

In addition to simple getter and setter methods for the three properties, the bean defines the `encodeString` action method called by the Facelets page. This method sets the `codedString` property to the value returned by a call to the `codeString` method of the `Coder` implementation:

```
public void encodeString() {
    setCodedString(coder.codeString(inputString, transVal));
}
```

Finally, the bean defines the `reset` method to empty the fields of the Facelets page:

```
public void reset() {
    setInputString("");
    setTransVal(0);
}
```

26.1.3 Running the encoder Example

You can use either NetBeans IDE or Maven to build, package, deploy, and run the encoder application.

26.1.3.1 To Build, Package, and Deploy the encoder Example Using NetBeans IDE

1. Make sure that GlassFish Server has been started (see Section 2.2, "Starting and Stopping GlassFish Server").

2. From the **File** menu, choose **Open Project**.

3. In the Open Project dialog box, navigate to:

   tut-install/examples/cdi

4. Select the encoder folder.

5. Click **Open Project**.

6. In the **Projects** tab, right-click the encoder project and select **Build**.

   This command builds and packages the application into a WAR file, encoder.war, located in the target directory, and then deploys it to GlassFish Server.

26.1.3.2 To Run the encoder Example Using NetBeans IDE

1. In a web browser, enter the following URL:

   http://localhost:8080/encoder

2. On the String Encoder page, enter a string and the number of letters to shift by, and then click **Encode**.

   The encoded string appears in blue on the **Result** line. For example, if you enter Java and 4, the result is Neze.

3. Now, edit the beans.xml file to enable the alternative implementation of Coder.

   a. In the **Projects** tab, under the encoder project, expand the **Web Pages** node, then expand the **WEB-INF** node.

   b. Double-click the beans.xml file to open it.

   c. Remove the comment characters that surround the alternatives element, so that it looks like this:

   ```
   <alternatives>
       <class>javaeetutorial.encoder.TestCoderImpl</class>
   </alternatives>
   ```

   d. Save the file.

4. Right-click the encoder project and select **Clean and Build**.

5. In the web browser, reenter the URL to show the String Encoder page for the redeployed project:

   http://localhost:8080/encoder/

6. Enter a string and the number of letters to shift by, and then click **Encode**.

   This time, the **Result** line displays your arguments. For example, if you enter Java and 4, the result is

   ```
   Result: input string is Java, shift value is 4
   ```

26.1.3.3 To Build, Package, and Deploy the encoder Example Using Maven

1. Make sure that GlassFish Server has been started (see Section 2.2, "Starting and Stopping GlassFish Server").

2. In a terminal window, go to:

   tut-install/examples/cdi/encoder/

3. Enter the following command to deploy the application:

   ```
   mvn install
   ```

   This command builds and packages the application into a WAR file, encoder.war, located in the target directory, and then deploys it to GlassFish Server.

26.1.3.4 To Run the encoder Example Using Maven

1. In a web browser, enter the following URL:

   ```
   http://localhost:8080/encoder/
   ```

   The String Encoder page opens.

2. Enter a string and the number of letters to shift by, and then click **Encode**.

   The encoded string appears in blue on the **Result** line. For example, if you enter Java and 4, the result is Neze.

3. Now, edit the beans.xml file to enable the alternative implementation of Coder.

   a. In a text editor, open the following file:

      tut-install/examples/cdi/encoder/src/main/webapp/WEB-INF/beans.xml

   b. Remove the comment characters that surround the alternatives element, so that it looks like this:

      ```
      <alternatives>
          <class>javaeetutorial.encoder.TestCoderImpl</class>
      </alternatives>
      ```

c. Save and close the file.

4. Enter the following command:

```
mvn clean install
```

5. In the web browser, reenter the URL to show the String Encoder page for the redeployed project:

```
http://localhost:8080/encoder
```

6. Enter a string and the number of letters to shift by, and then click **Encode**.

This time, the **Result** line displays your arguments. For example, if you enter Java and 4, the result is:

```
Result: input string is Java, shift value is 4
```

26.2 The producermethods Example: Using a Producer Method to Choose a Bean Implementation

The producermethods example shows how to use a producer method to choose between two beans at runtime, as described in Section 25.3, "Using Producer Methods, Producer Fields, and Disposer Methods in CDI Applications." It is very similar to the encoder example described in Section 26.1, "The encoder Example: Using Alternatives." The example includes the same interface and two implementations of it, a managed bean, a Facelets page, and configuration files. It also contains a qualifier type. When you run it, you do not need to edit the beans.xml file and redeploy the application to change its behavior.

The source files are located in the *tut-install*/examples/cdi/producermethods/ src/main/java/javaeetutorial/producermethods/ directory.

26.2.1 Components of the producermethods Example

The components of producermethods are very much like those for encoder, with some significant differences.

Neither implementation of the Coder bean is annotated @Alternative, and there is no beans.xml file, because it is not needed.

The Facelets page and the managed bean, CoderBean, have an additional property, coderType, that allows the user to specify at runtime which implementation to use. In addition, the managed bean has a producer method that selects the implementation using a qualifier type, @Chosen.

The bean declares two constants that specify whether the coder type is the test implementation or the implementation that actually shifts letters:

```
private final static int TEST = 1;
private final static int SHIFT = 2;
private int coderType = SHIFT; // default value
```

The producer method, annotated with @Produces and @Chosen as well as @RequestScoped (so that it lasts only for the duration of a single request and response), returns one of the two implementations based on the coderType supplied by the user:

```
@Produces
@Chosen
@RequestScoped
public Coder getCoder() {

    switch (coderType) {
        case TEST:
            return new TestCoderImpl();
        case SHIFT:
            return new CoderImpl();
        default:
            return null;
    }
}
```

Finally, the managed bean injects the chosen implementation, specifying the same qualifier as that returned by the producer method to resolve ambiguities:

```
@Inject
@Chosen
@RequestScoped
Coder coder;
```

The Facelets page contains modified instructions and a pair of options whose selected value is assigned to the property coderBean.coderType:

```
<h2>String Encoder</h2>
    <p>Select Test or Shift, enter a string and an integer, then click
        Encode.</p>
    <p>If you select Test, the TestCoderImpl bean will display the
        argument values.</p>
    <p>If you select Shift, the CoderImpl bean will return a string that
        shifts the letters in the original string by the value you specify.
        The value must be between 0 and 26.</p>
    <h:form id="encodeit">
```

```
<h:selectOneRadio id="coderType"
                  required="true"
                  value="#{coderBean.coderType}">
    <f:selectItem
        itemValue="1"
        itemLabel="Test"/>
    <f:selectItem
        itemValue="2"
        itemLabel="Shift Letters"/>
</h:selectOneRadio>
...
```

26.2.2 Running the producermethods Example

You can use either NetBeans IDE or Maven to build, package, deploy, and run the producermethods application.

26.2.2.1 To Build, Package, and Deploy the producermethods Example Using NetBeans IDE

1. Make sure that GlassFish Server has been started (see Section 2.2, "Starting and Stopping GlassFish Server").

2. From the **File** menu, choose **Open Project**.

3. In the Open Project dialog box, navigate to:

   tut-install/examples/cdi

4. Select the producermethods folder.

5. Click **Open Project**.

6. In the **Projects** tab, right-click the producermethods project and select **Build**.

   This command builds and packages the application into a WAR file, producermethods.war, located in the target directory, and then deploys it to GlassFish Server.

26.2.2.2 To Build, Package, and Deploy the producermethods Example Using Maven

1. Make sure that GlassFish Server has been started (see Section 2.2, "Starting and Stopping GlassFish Server").

2. In a terminal window, go to:

   tut-install/examples/cdi/producermethods/

3. Enter the following command to deploy the application:

```
mvn install
```

This command builds and packages the application into a WAR file, `producermethods.war`, located in the `target` directory, and then deploys it to GlassFish Server.

26.2.2.3 To Run the producermethods Example

1. In a web browser, enter the following URL:

```
http://localhost:8080/producermethods
```

2. On the String Encoder page, select either the **Test** or **Shift Letters** option, enter a string and the number of letters to shift by, and then click **Encode**.

Depending on your selection, the **Result** line displays either the encoded string or the input values you specified.

26.3 The producerfields Example: Using Producer Fields to Generate Resources

The `producerfields` example, which allows you to create a to-do list, shows how to use a producer field to generate objects that can then be managed by the container. This example generates an `EntityManager` object, but resources such as JDBC connections and datasources can also be generated this way.

The `producerfields` example is the simplest possible entity example. It also contains a qualifier and a class that generates the entity manager. It also contains a single entity, a stateful session bean, a Facelets page, and a managed bean.

The source files are located in the *tut-install*/examples/cdi/producerfields/src/main/java/javaeetutorial/producerfields/ directory.

26.3.1 The Producer Field for the producerfields Example

The most important component of the `producerfields` example is the smallest, the `db.UserDatabaseEntityManager` class, which isolates the generation of the `EntityManager` object so it can easily be used by other components in the application. The class uses a producer field to inject an `EntityManager` annotated with the `@UserDatabase` qualifier, also defined in the `db` package:

```
@Singleton
public class UserDatabaseEntityManager {
```

```
@Produces
@PersistenceContext
@UserDatabase
private EntityManager em;
...
}
```

The class does not explicitly produce a persistence unit field, but the application has a `persistence.xml` file that specifies a persistence unit. The class is annotated `javax.inject.Singleton` to specify that the injector should instantiate it only once.

The `db.UserDatabaseEntityManager` class also contains commented-out code that uses `create` and `close` methods to generate and remove the producer field:

```
/* @PersistenceContext
   private EntityManager em;

   @Produces
   @UserDatabase
   public EntityManager create() {
       return em;
   } */

   public void close(@Disposes @UserDatabase EntityManager em) {
       em.close();
   }
```

You can remove the comment indicators from this code and place them around the field declaration to test how the methods work. The behavior of the application is the same with either mechanism.

The advantage of producing the `EntityManager` in a separate class rather than simply injecting it into an enterprise bean is that the object can easily be reused in a typesafe way. Also, a more complex application can create multiple entity managers using multiple persistence units, and this mechanism isolates this code for easy maintenance, as in the following example:

```
@Singleton
public class JPAResourceProducer {
    @Produces
    @PersistenceUnit(unitName="pu3")
    @TestDatabase
    EntityManagerFactory customerDatabasePersistenceUnit;

    @Produces
    @PersistenceContext(unitName="pu3")
```

```
        @TestDatabase
        EntityManager customerDatabasePersistenceContext;

        @Produces
        @PersistenceUnit(unitName="pu4")
        @Documents
        EntityManagerFactory customerDatabasePersistenceUnit;

        @Produces
        @PersistenceContext(unitName="pu4")
        @Documents
        EntityManager docDatabaseEntityManager;"
}
```

The EntityManagerFactory declarations also allow applications to use an application-managed entity manager.

26.3.2 The producerfields Entity and Session Bean

The producerfields example contains a simple entity class, entity.ToDo, and a stateful session bean, ejb.RequestBean, that uses it.

The entity class contains three fields: an autogenerated id field, a string specifying the task, and a timestamp. The timestamp field, timeCreated, is annotated with @Temporal, which is required for persistent Date fields:

```
@Entity
public class ToDo implements Serializable {

    ...
    @Id
    @GeneratedValue(strategy = GenerationType.AUTO)
    private Long id;
    protected String taskText;
    @Temporal(TIMESTAMP)
    protected Date timeCreated;

    public ToDo() {
    }

    public ToDo(Long id, String taskText, Date timeCreated) {
        this.id = id;
        this.taskText = taskText;
        this.timeCreated = timeCreated;
    }
    ...
```

The remainder of the ToDo class contains the usual getters, setters, and other entity methods.

The RequestBean class injects the EntityManager generated by the producer method, annotated with the @UserDatabase qualifier:

```
@ConversationScoped
@Stateful
public class RequestBean {

    @Inject
    @UserDatabase
    EntityManager em;
```

It then defines two methods, one that creates and persists a single ToDo list item, and another that retrieves all the ToDo items created so far by creating a query:

```
public ToDo createToDo(String inputString) {
    ToDo toDo = null;
    Date currentTime = Calendar.getInstance().getTime();

    try {
        toDo = new ToDo();
        toDo.setTaskText(inputString);
        toDo.setTimeCreated(currentTime);
        em.persist(toDo);
        return toDo;
    } catch (Exception e) {
        throw new EJBException(e.getMessage());
    }
}


public List<ToDo> getToDos() {
    try {
        List<ToDo> toDos =
                (List<ToDo>) em.createQuery(
                "SELECT t FROM ToDo t ORDER BY t.timeCreated")
                .getResultList();
        return toDos;
    } catch (Exception e) {
        throw new EJBException(e.getMessage());
    }
}
}
```

26.3.3 The producerfields Facelets Pages and Managed Bean

The producerfields example has two Facelets pages, index.xhtml and todolist.xhtml. The simple form on the index.xhtml page asks the user only for the task. When the user clicks the **Submit** button, the listBean.createTask method is called. When the user clicks the **Show Items** button, the action specifies that the todolist.xhtml file should be displayed:

```
<h:body>
    <h2>To Do List</h2>
    <p>Enter a task to be completed.</p>
    <h:form id="todolist">
        <p><h:outputLabel value="Enter a string: " for="inputString"/>
            <h:inputText id="inputString"
                            value="#{listBean.inputString}"/></p>
        <p><h:commandButton value="Submit"
                            action="#{listBean.createTask()}"/></p>
        <p><h:commandButton value="Show Items"
                            action="todolist"/></p>
    </h:form>
    ...
</h:body>
```

The managed bean, web.ListBean, injects the ejb.RequestBean session bean. It declares the entity.ToDo entity and a list of the entity along with the input string that it passes to the session bean. The inputString is annotated with the @NotNull Bean Validation constraint, so an attempt to submit an empty string results in an error:

```
@Named
@ConversationScoped
public class ListBean implements Serializable {

    ...
    @EJB
    private RequestBean request;
    @NotNull
    private String inputString;
    private ToDo toDo;
    private List<ToDo> toDos;
```

The createTask method called by the **Submit** button calls the createToDo method of RequestBean:

```
public void createTask() {
    this.toDo = request.createToDo(inputString);
}
```

The getToDos method, which is called by the todolist.xhtml page, calls the getToDos method of RequestBean:

```
public List<ToDo> getToDos() {
    return request.getToDos();
}
```

To force the Facelets page to recognize an empty string as a null value and return an error, the web.xml file sets the context parameter javax.faces.INTERPRET_EMPTY_STRING_SUBMITTED_VALUES_AS_NULL to true:

```
<context-param>
  <param-name>
    javax.faces.INTERPRET_EMPTY_STRING_SUBMITTED_VALUES_AS_NULL
  </param-name>
  <param-value>true</param-value>
</context-param>
```

The todolist.xhtml page is a little more complicated than the index.html page. It contains a dataTable element that displays the contents of the ToDo list. The body of the page looks like this:

```
<body>
    <h2>To Do List</h2>
    <h:form id="showlist">
        <h:dataTable var="toDo"
                    value="#{listBean.toDos}"
                    rules="all"
                    border="1"
                    cellpadding="5">
            <h:column>
                <f:facet name="header">
                    <h:outputText value="Time Stamp" />
                </f:facet>
                <h:outputText value="#{toDo.timeCreated}" />
            </h:column>
            <h:column>
                <f:facet name="header">
                    <h:outputText value="Task" />
                </f:facet>
                <h:outputText value="#{toDo.taskText}" />
            </h:column>
        </h:dataTable>
        <p><h:commandButton id="back" value="Back" action="index" /></p>
    </h:form>
</body>
```

The value of the `dataTable` is `listBean.toDos`, the list returned by the managed bean's `getToDos` method, which in turn calls the session bean's `getToDos` method. Each row of the table displays the `timeCreated` and `taskText` fields of the individual task. Finally, a **Back** button returns the user to the `index.xhtml` page.

26.3.4 Running the producerfields Example

You can use either NetBeans IDE or Maven to build, package, deploy, and run the `producerfields` application.

26.3.4.1 To Build, Package, and Deploy the producerfields Example Using NetBeans IDE

1. If the database server is not already running, start it by following the instructions in Section 2.4, "Starting and Stopping the Java DB Server."

2. Make sure that GlassFish Server has been started (see Section 2.2, "Starting and Stopping GlassFish Server").

3. From the **File** menu, choose **Open Project**.

4. In the Open Project dialog box, navigate to:

    tut-install/examples/cdi

5. Select the `producerfields` folder.

6. Click **Open Project**.

7. In the **Projects** tab, right-click the `producerfields` project and select **Build**.

    This command builds and packages the application into a WAR file, `producerfields.war`, located in the `target` directory, and then deploys it to GlassFish Server.

26.3.4.2 To Build, Package, and Deploy the producerfields Example Using Maven

1. If the database server is not already running, start it by following the instructions in Section 2.4, "Starting and Stopping the Java DB Server."

2. Make sure that GlassFish Server has been started (see Section 2.2, "Starting and Stopping GlassFish Server").

3. In a terminal window, go to:

    tut-install/examples/cdi/producerfields/

4. Enter the following command to deploy the application:

```
mvn install
```

This command builds and packages the application into a WAR file, `producerfields.war`, located in the `target` directory, and then deploys it to GlassFish Server.

26.3.4.3 To Run the producerfields Example

1. In a web browser, enter the following URL:

```
http://localhost:8080/producerfields
```

2. On the Create To Do List page, enter a string in the field and click **Submit**.

You can enter additional strings and click **Submit** to create a task list with multiple items.

3. Click **Show Items**.

The To Do List page opens, showing the timestamp and text for each item you created.

4. Click **Back** to return to the Create To Do List page.

On this page, you can enter more items in the list.

26.4 The billpayment Example: Using Events and Interceptors

The `billpayment` example shows how to use both events and interceptors.

The example simulates paying an amount using a debit card or credit card. When the user chooses a payment method, the managed bean creates an appropriate event, supplies its payload, and fires it. A simple event listener handles the event using observer methods.

The example also defines an interceptor that is set on a class and on two methods of another class.

The source files are located in the *tut-install*/examples/cdi/billpayment/src/main/java/javaeetutorial/billpayment/ directory.

26.4.1 The PaymentEvent Event Class

The event class, `event.PaymentEvent`, is a simple bean class that contains a no-argument constructor. It also has a `toString` method and getter and setter methods for the payload components: a `String` for the payment type, a `BigDecimal` for the payment amount, and a `Date` for the timestamp:

```
public class PaymentEvent implements Serializable {

    ...
    public String paymentType;
    public BigDecimal value;
    public Date datetime;

    public PaymentEvent() {
    }
    @Override
    public String toString() {
        return this.paymentType
                + " = $" + this.value.toString()
                + " at " + this.datetime.toString();
    }
    ...
```

The event class is a simple bean that is instantiated by the managed bean using `new` and then populated. For this reason, the CDI container cannot intercept the creation of the bean, and hence it cannot allow interception of its getter and setter methods.

26.4.2 The PaymentHandler Event Listener

The event listener, `listener.PaymentHandler`, contains two observer methods, one for each of the two event types:

```
@Logged
@SessionScoped
public class PaymentHandler implements Serializable {

    ...
    public void creditPayment(@Observes @Credit PaymentEvent event) {
        logger.log(Level.INFO, "PaymentHandler - Credit Handler: {0}",
                event.toString());

        // call a specific Credit handler class...
    }

    public void debitPayment(@Observes @Debit PaymentEvent event) {
        logger.log(Level.INFO, "PaymentHandler - Debit Handler: {0}",
                event.toString());

        // call a specific Debit handler class...
```

```
        }
    }
```

Each observer method takes as an argument the event, annotated with @Observes and with the qualifier for the type of payment. In a real application, the observer methods would pass the event information on to another component that would perform business logic on the payment.

The qualifiers are defined in the payment package, described in Section 26.4.3, "The billpayment Facelets Pages and Managed Bean."

The PaymentHandler bean is annotated @Logged so that all its methods can be intercepted.

26.4.3 The billpayment Facelets Pages and Managed Bean

The billpayment example contains two Facelets pages, index.xhtml and the very simple response.xhtml. The body of index.xhtml looks like this:

```
<h:body>
    <h3>Bill Payment Options</h3>
    <p>Enter an amount, select Debit Card or Credit Card,
       then click Pay.</p>
    <h:form>
        <p>
        <h:outputLabel value="Amount: $" for="amt"/>
        <h:inputText id="amt" value="#{paymentBean.value}"
                     required="true"
                     requiredMessage="An amount is required."
                     maxlength="15" />
        </p>
        <h:outputLabel value="Options:" for="opt"/>
        <h:selectOneRadio id="opt" value="#{paymentBean.paymentOption}">
            <f:selectItem id="debit" itemLabel="Debit Card"
                        itemValue="1"/>
            <f:selectItem id="credit" itemLabel="Credit Card"
                        itemValue="2" />
        </h:selectOneRadio>
        <p><h:commandButton id="submit" value="Pay"
                            action="#{paymentBean.pay}" /></p>
        <p><h:commandButton value="Reset"
                            action="#{paymentBean.reset}" /></p>
    </h:form>
    ...
</h:body>
```

The input field takes a payment amount, passed to paymentBean.value. Two options ask the user to select a Debit Card or Credit Card payment, passing the integer value to paymentBean.paymentOption. Finally, the **Pay** command button's action is set to the method paymentBean.pay, and the **Reset** button's action is set to the paymentBean.reset method.

The payment.PaymentBean managed bean uses qualifiers to differentiate between the two kinds of payment event:

```
@Named
@SessionScoped
public class PaymentBean implements Serializable {

    ...
    @Inject
    @Credit
    Event<PaymentEvent> creditEvent;

    @Inject
    @Debit
    Event<PaymentEvent> debitEvent;
```

The qualifiers, @Credit and @Debit, are defined in the payment package along with PaymentBean.

Next, the PaymentBean defines the properties it obtains from the Facelets page and will pass on to the event:

```
    public static final int DEBIT = 1;
    public static final int CREDIT = 2;
    private int paymentOption = DEBIT;

    @Digits(integer = 10, fraction = 2, message = "Invalid value")
    private BigDecimal value;

    private Date datetime;
```

The paymentOption value is an integer passed in from the option component; the default value is DEBIT. The value is a BigDecimal with a Bean Validation constraint that enforces a currency value with a maximum number of digits. The timestamp for the event, datetime, is a Date object initialized when the pay method is called.

The pay method of the bean first sets the timestamp for this payment event. It then creates and populates the event payload, using the constructor for the PaymentEvent and calling the event's setter methods, using the bean properties as arguments. It then fires the event.

```
@Logged
public String pay() {
    this.setDatetime(Calendar.getInstance().getTime());
    switch (paymentOption) {
        case DEBIT:
            PaymentEvent debitPayload = new PaymentEvent();
            debitPayload.setPaymentType("Debit");
            debitPayload.setValue(value);
            debitPayload.setDatetime(datetime);
            debitEvent.fire(debitPayload);
            break;
        case CREDIT:
            PaymentEvent creditPayload = new PaymentEvent();
            creditPayload.setPaymentType("Credit");
            creditPayload.setValue(value);
            creditPayload.setDatetime(datetime);
            creditEvent.fire(creditPayload);
            break;
        default:
            logger.severe("Invalid payment option!");
    }
    return "/response.xhtml";
}
```

The pay method returns the page to which the action is redirected,
response.xhtml.

The PaymentBean class also contains a reset method that empties the value field
on the index.xhtml page and sets the payment option to the default:

```
@Logged
public void reset() {
    setPaymentOption(DEBIT);
    setValue(BigDecimal.ZERO);
}
```

In this bean, only the pay and reset methods are intercepted.

The response.xhtml page displays the amount paid. It uses a rendered
expression to display the payment method:

```
<h:body>
    <h:form>
        <h2>Bill Payment: Result</h2>
        <h3>Amount Paid with
            <h:outputText id="debit" value="Debit Card: "
                          rendered="#{paymentBean.paymentOption eq 1}" />
```

```
                    <h:outputText id="credit" value="Credit Card: "
                              rendered="#{paymentBean.paymentOption eq 2}" />
                    <h:outputText id="result" value="#{paymentBean.value}">
                        <f:convertNumber type="currency"/>
                    </h:outputText>
                </h3>
                <p><h:commandButton id="back" value="Back" action="index" /></p>
            </h:form>
        </h:body>
```

26.4.4 The LoggedInterceptor Interceptor Class

The interceptor class, LoggedInterceptor, and its interceptor binding, Logged, are both defined in the interceptor package. The Logged interceptor binding is defined as follows:

```
@Inherited
@InterceptorBinding
@Retention(RUNTIME)
@Target({METHOD, TYPE})
public @interface Logged {
}
```

The LoggedInterceptor class looks like this:

```
@Logged
@Interceptor
public class LoggedInterceptor implements Serializable {

    ...

    public LoggedInterceptor() {
    }

    @AroundInvoke
    public Object logMethodEntry(InvocationContext invocationContext)
            throws Exception {
        System.out.println("Entering method: "
                + invocationContext.getMethod().getName() + " in class "
                + invocationContext.getMethod().getDeclaringClass().getName());

        return invocationContext.proceed();
    }
}
```

The class is annotated with both the @Logged and the @Interceptor annotations. The @AroundInvoke method, logMethodEntry, takes the required

InvocationContext argument and calls the required proceed method. When a method is intercepted, logMethodEntry displays the name of the method being invoked as well as its class.

To enable the interceptor, the beans.xml file defines it as follows:

```
<interceptors>
    <class>javaeetutorial.billpayment.interceptor.LoggedInterceptor</class>
</interceptors>
```

In this application, the PaymentEvent and PaymentHandler classes are annotated @Logged, so all their methods are intercepted. In PaymentBean, only the pay and reset methods are annotated @Logged, so only those methods are intercepted.

26.4.5 Running the billpayment Example

You can use either NetBeans IDE or Maven to build, package, deploy, and run the billpayment application.

26.4.5.1 To Build, Package, and Deploy the billpayment Example Using NetBeans IDE

1. Make sure that GlassFish Server has been started (see Section 2.2, "Starting and Stopping GlassFish Server").

2. From the **File** menu, choose **Open Project**.

3. In the Open Project dialog box, navigate to:

   tut-install/examples/cdi

4. Select the billpayment folder.

5. Click **Open Project**.

6. In the **Projects** tab, right-click the billpayment project and select **Build**.

   This command builds and packages the application into a WAR file, billpayment.war, located in the target directory, and then deploys it to GlassFish Server.

26.4.5.2 To Build, Package, and Deploy the billpayment Example Using Maven

1. Make sure that GlassFish Server has been started (see Section 2.2, "Starting and Stopping GlassFish Server").

2. In a terminal window, go to:

   tut-install/examples/cdi/billpayment/

3. Enter the following command to deploy the application:

```
mvn install
```

This command builds and packages the application into a WAR file, `billpayment.war`, located in the `target` directory, and then deploys it to GlassFish Server.

26.4.5.3 To Run the billpayment Example

1. In a web browser, enter the following URL:

```
http://localhost:8080/billpayment
```

2. On the Bill Payment Options page, enter a value in the **Amount** field.

   The amount can contain up to 10 digits and include up to two decimal places. For example:

```
9876.54
```

3. Select **Debit Card** or **Credit Card** and click **Pay**.

   The Bill Payment: Result page opens, displaying the amount paid and the method of payment:

```
Amount Paid with Credit Card: $9,876.34
```

4. Click **Back** to return to the Bill Payment Options page.

   You can also click **Reset** to return to the initial page values.

5. Examine the server log output.

   In NetBeans IDE, the output is visible in the GlassFish Server **Output** tab. Otherwise, view *domain-dir*/logs/server.log.

   The output from each interceptor appears in the log, followed by the additional logger output defined by the constructor and methods:

```
INFO: Entering method: pay in class billpayment.payment.PaymentBean
INFO: PaymentHandler created.
INFO: Entering method: debitPayment in class
billpayment.listener.PaymentHandler
INFO: PaymentHandler - Debit Handler: Debit = $1234.56 at Tue Dec 14
14:50:28 EST 2010
```

26.5 The decorators Example: Decorating a Bean

The `decorators` example, which is yet another variation on the `encoder` example, shows how to use a decorator to implement additional business logic for a bean. Instead of having the user choose between two alternative implementations of an interface at deployment time or runtime, a decorator adds some additional logic to a single implementation of the interface.

The example includes an interface, an implementation of it, a decorator, an interceptor, a managed bean, a Facelets page, and configuration files.

The source files are located in the *tut-install*/examples/cdi/decorators/src/main/java/javaeetutorial/decorators/ directory.

26.5.1 Components of the decorators Example

The `decorators` example is very similar to the `encoder` example described in Section 26.1, "The encoder Example: Using Alternatives." Instead of providing two implementations of the `Coder` interface, however, this example provides only the `CoderImpl` class. The decorator class, `CoderDecorator`, rather than simply return the coded string, displays the input and output strings' values and length.

The `CoderDecorator` class, like `CoderImpl`, implements the business method of the `Coder` interface, `codeString`:

```
@Decorator
public abstract class CoderDecorator implements Coder {

    @Inject
    @Delegate
    @Any
    Coder coder;

    public String codeString(String s, int tval) {
        int len = s.length();

        return "\"" + s + "\" becomes " + "\"" + coder.codeString(s, tval)
                + "\", " + len + " characters in length";
    }
}
```

The decorator's `codeString` method calls the delegate object's `codeString` method to perform the actual encoding.

The `decorators` example includes the `Logged` interceptor binding and `LoggedInterceptor` class from the `billpayment` example. For this example, the interceptor is set on the `CoderBean.encodeString` method and the

`CoderImpl.codeString` method. The interceptor code is unchanged; interceptors are usually reusable for different applications.

Except for the interceptor annotations, the `CoderBean` and `CoderImpl` classes are identical to the versions in the `encoder` example.

The `beans.xml` file specifies both the decorator and the interceptor:

```
<decorators>
    <class>javaeetutorial.decorators.CoderDecorator</class>
</decorators>
<interceptors>
    <class>javaeetutorial.decorators.LoggedInterceptor</class>
</interceptors>
```

26.5.2 Running the decorators Example

You can use either NetBeans IDE or Maven to build, package, deploy, and run the decorators application.

26.5.2.1 To Build, Package, and Deploy the decorators Example Using NetBeans IDE

1. Make sure that GlassFish Server has been started (see Section 2.2, "Starting and Stopping GlassFish Server").

2. From the **File** menu, choose **Open Project**.

3. In the Open Project dialog box, navigate to:

    tut-install/examples/cdi

4. Select the `decorators` folder.

5. Click **Open Project**.

6. In the **Projects** tab, right-click the `decorators` project and select **Build**.

    This command builds and packages the application into a WAR file, `decorators.war`, located in the `target` directory, and then deploys it to GlassFish Server.

26.5.2.2 To Build, Package, and Deploy the decorators Example Using Maven

1. Make sure that GlassFish Server has been started (see Section 2.2, "Starting and Stopping GlassFish Server").

2. In a terminal window, go to:

    tut-install/examples/cdi/decorators/

3. Enter the following command to deploy the application:

```
mvn install
```

This command builds and packages the application into a WAR file, decorators.war, located in the target directory, and then deploys it to GlassFish Server.

26.5.2.3 To Run the decorators Example

1. In a web browser, enter the following URL:

```
http://localhost:8080/decorators
```

2. On the Decorated String Encoder page, enter a string and the number of letters to shift by, and then click **Encode**.

The output from the decorator method appears in blue on the **Result** line. For example, if you entered Java and 4, you would see the following:

```
"Java" becomes "Neze", 4 characters in length
```

3. Examine the server log output.

In NetBeans IDE, the output is visible in the GlassFish Server **Output** tab. Otherwise, view *domain-dir*/logs/server.log.

The output from the interceptors appears:

```
INFO: Entering method: encodeString in class decorators.CoderBean
INFO: Entering method: codeString in class decorators.CoderImpl
```

Part VI

Web Services

Part VI explores web services. This part contains the following chapters:

- Chapter 27, "Introduction to Web Services"
- Chapter 28, "Building Web Services with JAX-WS"
- Chapter 29, "Building RESTful Web Services with JAX-RS"
- Chapter 30, "Accessing REST Resources with the JAX-RS Client API"
- Chapter 31, "JAX-RS: Advanced Topics and an Example"

27

Introduction to Web Services

This part of the tutorial discusses Java EE 7 web services technologies. These technologies include Java API for XML Web Services (JAX-WS) and Java API for RESTful Web Services (JAX-RS).

The following topics are addressed here:

- What Are Web Services?
- Types of Web Services
- Deciding Which Type of Web Service to Use

27.1 What Are Web Services?

Web services are client and server applications that communicate over the World Wide Web's (WWW) HyperText Transfer Protocol (HTTP). As described by the World Wide Web Consortium (W3C), web services provide a standard means of interoperating between software applications running on a variety of platforms and frameworks. Web services are characterized by their great interoperability and extensibility as well as their machine-processable descriptions, thanks to the use of XML. Web services can be combined in a loosely coupled way to achieve complex operations. Programs providing simple services can interact with each other to deliver sophisticated added-value services.

27.2 Types of Web Services

On the conceptual level, a service is a software component provided through a network-accessible endpoint. The service consumer and provider use messages to exchange invocation request and response information in the form of self-containing documents that make very few assumptions about the technological capabilities of the receiver.

On a technical level, web services can be implemented in various ways. The two types of web services discussed in this section can be distinguished as "big" web services and "RESTful" web services.

27.2.1 "Big" Web Services

In the Java EE 7 platform, JAX-WS provides the functionality for "big" web services, which are described in Chapter 28, "Building Web Services with JAX-WS." Big web services use XML messages that follow the Simple Object Access Protocol (SOAP) standard, an XML language defining a message architecture and message formats. Such systems often contain a machine-readable description of the operations offered by the service, written in the Web Services Description Language (WSDL), an XML language for defining interfaces syntactically.

The SOAP message format and the WSDL interface definition language have gained widespread adoption. Many development tools, such as NetBeans IDE, can reduce the complexity of developing web service applications.

A SOAP-based design must include the following elements.

- A formal contract must be established to describe the interface that the web service offers. WSDL can be used to describe the details of the contract, which may include messages, operations, bindings, and the location of the web service. You may also process SOAP messages in a JAX-WS service without publishing a WSDL.

- The architecture must address complex nonfunctional requirements. Many web service specifications address such requirements and establish a common vocabulary for them. Examples include transactions, security, addressing, trust, coordination, and so on.

- The architecture needs to handle asynchronous processing and invocation. In such cases, the infrastructure provided by standards, such as Web Services Reliable Messaging (WSRM), and APIs, such as JAX-WS, with their client-side asynchronous invocation support, can be leveraged out of the box.

27.2.2 RESTful Web Services

In Java EE 7, JAX-RS provides the functionality for Representational State Transfer (RESTful) web services. REST is well suited for basic, ad hoc integration scenarios. RESTful web services, often better integrated with HTTP than SOAP-based services are, do not require XML messages or WSDL service-API definitions.

Project Jersey is the production-ready reference implementation for the JAX-RS specification. Jersey implements support for the annotations defined in the JAX-RS specification, making it easy for developers to build RESTful web services with Java and the Java Virtual Machine (JVM).

Because RESTful web services use existing well-known W3C and Internet Engineering Task Force (IETF) standards (HTTP, XML, URI, MIME) and have a lightweight infrastructure that allows services to be built with minimal tooling, developing RESTful web services is inexpensive and thus has a very low barrier for adoption. You can use a development tool such as NetBeans IDE to further reduce the complexity of developing RESTful web services.

A RESTful design may be appropriate when the following conditions are met.

- The web services are completely stateless. A good test is to consider whether the interaction can survive a restart of the server.

- A caching infrastructure can be leveraged for performance. If the data that the web service returns is not dynamically generated and can be cached, the caching infrastructure that web servers and other intermediaries inherently provide can be leveraged to improve performance. However, the developer must take care because such caches are limited to the HTTP GET method for most servers.

- The service producer and service consumer have a mutual understanding of the context and content being passed along. Because there is no formal way to describe the web services interface, both parties must agree out of band on the schemas that describe the data being exchanged and on ways to process it meaningfully. In the real world, most commercial applications that expose services as RESTful implementations also distribute so-called value-added toolkits that describe the interfaces to developers in popular programming languages.

- Bandwidth is particularly important and needs to be limited. REST is particularly useful for limited-profile devices, such as PDAs and mobile phones, for which the overhead of headers and additional layers of SOAP elements on the XML payload must be restricted.

- Web service delivery or aggregation into existing websites can be enabled easily with a RESTful style. Developers can use such technologies as JAX-RS and Asynchronous JavaScript with XML (Ajax) and such toolkits as Direct Web Remoting (DWR) to consume the services in their web applications. Rather than starting from scratch, services can be exposed with XML and consumed by HTML pages without significantly refactoring the existing website architecture. Existing developers will be more productive because they are adding to something they are already familiar with rather than having to start from scratch with new technology.

RESTful web services are discussed in Chapter 29, "Building RESTful Web Services with JAX-RS." This chapter contains information about generating the skeleton of a RESTful web service using both NetBeans IDE and the Maven project-management tool.

27.3 Deciding Which Type of Web Service to Use

Basically, you want to use RESTful web services for integration over the web and big web services in enterprise application–integration scenarios that have advanced quality-of-service (QoS) requirements.

- **JAX-WS**: Addresses advanced QoS requirements that commonly occur in enterprise computing. When compared to JAX-RS, JAX-WS makes it easier to support the WS-* set of protocols, which provide standards for security and reliability, among other things, and interoperate with other WS-* conforming clients and servers.

- **JAX-RS**: Makes it easier to write web applications that apply some or all of the constraints of the REST style to induce desirable properties in the application, such as loose coupling (evolving the server is easier without breaking existing clients), scalability (start small and grow), and architectural simplicity (use off-the-shelf components, such as proxies or HTTP routers). You would choose to use JAX-RS for your web application because it is easier for many types of clients to consume RESTful web services while enabling the server side to evolve and scale. Clients can choose to consume some or all aspects of the service and mash it up with other web-based services.

28

Building Web Services with JAX-WS

Java API for XML Web Services (JAX-WS) is a technology for building web services and clients that communicate using XML. JAX-WS allows developers to write message-oriented as well as Remote Procedure Call–oriented (RPC-oriented) web services.

In JAX-WS, a web service operation invocation is represented by an XML-based protocol, such as SOAP. The SOAP specification defines the envelope structure, encoding rules, and conventions for representing web service invocations and responses. These calls and responses are transmitted as SOAP messages (XML files) over HTTP.

Although SOAP messages are complex, the JAX-WS API hides this complexity from the application developer. On the server side, the developer specifies the web service operations by defining methods in an interface written in the Java programming language. The developer also codes one or more classes that implement those methods. Client programs are also easy to code. A client creates a proxy (a local object representing the service) and then simply invokes methods on the proxy. With JAX-WS, the developer does not generate or parse SOAP messages. It is the JAX-WS runtime system that converts the API calls and responses to and from SOAP messages.

With JAX-WS, clients and web services have a big advantage: the platform independence of the Java programming language. In addition, JAX-WS is not restrictive: A JAX-WS client can access a web service that is not running on the Java platform and vice versa. This flexibility is possible because JAX-WS uses technologies defined by the W3C: HTTP, SOAP, and WSDL. WSDL specifies an XML format for describing a service as a set of endpoints operating on messages.

> **Note:** Several files in the JAX-WS examples depend on the port that you specified when you installed GlassFish Server. These tutorial examples assume that the server runs on the default port, 8080. They do not run with a nondefault port setting.

The following topics are addressed here:

- Creating a Simple Web Service and Clients with JAX-WS
- Types Supported by JAX-WS
- Web Services Interoperability and JAX-WS
- Further Information about JAX-WS

28.1 Creating a Simple Web Service and Clients with JAX-WS

This section shows how to build and deploy a simple web service and two clients: an application client and a web client. The source code for the service is in the *tut-install*/examples/jaxws/helloservice-war/ directory, and the clients are in the *tut-install*/examples/jaxws/hello-appclient/ and *tut-install*/examples/jaxws/hello-webclient/ directories.

Figure 28–1 illustrates how JAX-WS technology manages communication between a web service and a client.

Figure 28–1   Communication between a JAX-WS Web Service and a Client

The starting point for developing a JAX-WS web service is a Java class annotated with the javax.jws.WebService annotation. The @WebService annotation defines the class as a web service endpoint.

A **service endpoint interface** or **service endpoint implementation** (SEI) is a Java interface or class, respectively, that declares the methods that a client can invoke on the service. An interface is not required when building a JAX-WS endpoint. The web service implementation class implicitly defines an SEI.

You may specify an explicit interface by adding the endpointInterface element to the @WebService annotation in the implementation class. You must then provide an interface that defines the public methods made available in the endpoint implementation class.

The basic steps for creating a web service and client are as follows.

1. Code the implementation class.

2. Compile the implementation class.

3. Package the files into a WAR file.

4. Deploy the WAR file. The web service artifacts, which are used to communicate with clients, are generated by GlassFish Server during deployment.

5. Code the client class.

6. Use the `wsimport` Maven goal to generate and compile the web service artifacts needed to connect to the service.

7. Compile the client class.

8. Run the client.

If you use NetBeans IDE to create a service and client, the IDE performs the `wsimport` task for you.

The sections that follow cover these steps in greater detail.

28.1.1 Requirements of a JAX-WS Endpoint

JAX-WS endpoints must follow these requirements.

- The implementing class must be annotated with either the `javax.jws.WebService` or the `javax.jws.WebServiceProvider` annotation.

- The implementing class may explicitly reference an SEI through the `endpointInterface` element of the `@WebService` annotation but is not required to do so. If no `endpointInterface` is specified in `@WebService`, an SEI is implicitly defined for the implementing class.

- The business methods of the implementing class must be public and must not be declared `static` or `final`.

- Business methods that are exposed to web service clients must be annotated with `javax.jws.WebMethod`.

- Business methods that are exposed to web service clients must have JAXB-compatible parameters and return types. See the list of JAXB default data type bindings in Section 28.2, "Types Supported by JAX-WS."

- The implementing class must not be declared `final` and must not be `abstract`.

- The implementing class must have a default public constructor.

- The implementing class must not define the `finalize` method.

- The implementing class may use the `javax.annotation.PostConstruct` or the `javax.annotation.PreDestroy` annotations on its methods for lifecycle event callbacks.

  The `@PostConstruct` method is called by the container before the implementing class begins responding to web service clients.

  The `@PreDestroy` method is called by the container before the endpoint is removed from operation.

28.1.2 Coding the Service Endpoint Implementation Class

In this example, the implementation class, `Hello`, is annotated as a web service endpoint using the `@WebService` annotation. `Hello` declares a single method named `sayHello`, annotated with the `@WebMethod` annotation, which exposes the annotated method to web service clients. The `sayHello` method returns a greeting to the client, using the name passed to it to compose the greeting. The implementation class also must define a default, public, no-argument constructor:

```
package javaeetutorial.helloservice;

import javax.jws.WebService;
import javax.jws.WebMethod;

@WebService
public class Hello {
    private final String message = "Hello, ";

    public void Hello() {
    }

    @WebMethod
    public String sayHello(String name) {
        return message + name + ".";
    }
}
```

28.1.3 Building, Packaging, and Deploying the Service

You can use either NetBeans IDE or Maven to build, package, and deploy the `helloservice-war` application.

28.1.3.1 To Build, Package, and Deploy the Service Using NetBeans IDE

1. Make sure that GlassFish Server has been started (see Section 2.2, "Starting and Stopping GlassFish Server").

2. From the **File** menu, choose **Open Project**.

3. In the Open Project dialog box, navigate to:

   tut-install/examples/jaxws

4. Select the `helloservice-war` folder.

5. Click **Open Project**.

6. In the **Projects** tab, right-click the `helloservice-war` project and select **Run**.

   This command builds and packages the application into a WAR file, `helloservice-war.war`, located in *tut-install*/examples/jaxws/ `helloservice-war/target/`, and deploys this WAR file to your GlassFish Server instance. It also opens the web service test interface at the URL shown in Section 28.1.4.1, "To Test the Service without a Client."

Next Steps

You can view the WSDL file of the deployed service by requesting the URL `http://localhost:8080/helloservice-war/HelloService?wsdl` in a web browser. Now you are ready to create a client that accesses this service.

28.1.3.2 To Build, Package, and Deploy the Service Using Maven

1. Make sure that GlassFish Server has been started (see Section 2.2, "Starting and Stopping GlassFish Server").

2. In a terminal window, go to:

   tut-install/examples/jaxws/helloservice-war/

3. Enter the following command:

   ```
   mvn install
   ```

   This command builds and packages the application into a WAR file, `helloservice-war.war`, located in *tut-install*/examples/jaxws/

`helloservice-war/target/`, and deploys this WAR file to your GlassFish Server instance.

Next Steps

You can view the WSDL file of the deployed service by requesting the URL `http://localhost:8080/helloservice-war/HelloService?wsdl` in a web browser. Now you are ready to create a client that accesses this service.

28.1.4 Testing the Methods of a Web Service Endpoint

GlassFish Server allows you to test the methods of a web service endpoint.

28.1.4.1 To Test the Service without a Client

To test the `sayHello` method of `HelloService`, follow these steps.

1. Open the web service test interface by entering the following URL in a web browser:

    `http://localhost:8080/helloservice-war/HelloService?Tester`

2. Under **Methods**, enter a name as the parameter to the `sayHello` method.

3. Click **sayHello**.

    This takes you to the `sayHello` Method invocation page.

    Under **Method returned**, you'll see the response from the endpoint.

28.1.5 A Simple JAX-WS Application Client

The `HelloAppClient` class is a stand-alone application client that accesses the `sayHello` method of `HelloService`. This call is made through a port, a local object that acts as a proxy for the remote service. The port is created at development time by the `wsimport` Maven goal, which generates JAX-WS portable artifacts based on a WSDL file.

28.1.5.1 Coding the Application Client

When invoking the remote methods on the port, the client performs these steps.

1. It uses the generated `helloservice.endpoint.HelloService` class, which represents the service at the URI of the deployed service's WSDL file:

    ```
    import javaeetutorial.helloservice.endpoint.HelloService;
    import javax.xml.ws.WebServiceRef;
    ```

```
public class HelloAppClient {
    @WebServiceRef(wsdlLocation =
        "http://localhost:8080/helloservice-war/HelloService?WSDL"")
    private static HelloService service;
```

2. It retrieves a proxy to the service, also known as a port, by invoking getHelloPort on the service:

```
javaeetutorial helloservice.endpoint.Hello port = service.getHelloPort();
```

The port implements the SEI defined by the service.

3. It invokes the port's sayHello method, passing a string to the service:

```
return port.sayHello(arg0);
```

Here is the full source of HelloAppClient.java, which is located in the *tut-install*/examples/jaxws/hello-appclient/src/main/java/javaeetutorial/hello/appclient/ directory:

```
package javaeetutorial.hello.appclient;

import javaeetutorial.helloservice.endpoint.HelloService;
import javax.xml.ws.WebServiceRef;

public class HelloAppClient {
    @WebServiceRef(wsdlLocation =
        "http://localhost:8080/helloservice-war/HelloService?WSDL"")
    private static HelloService service;

    /**
     * @param args the command line arguments
     */
    public static void main(String[] args) {
        System.out.println(sayHello("world"));
    }

    private static String sayHello(java.lang.String arg0) {
        javaeetutorial.helloservice.endpoint.Hello port =
                service.getHelloPort();
        return port.sayHello(arg0);
    }
}
```

28.1.5.2 Running the Application Client

You can use either NetBeans IDE or Maven to build, package, deploy, and run the hello-appclient application. To build the client, you must first have deployed `helloservice-war`, as described in Section 28.1.3, "Building, Packaging, and Deploying the Service."

To Run the Application Client Using NetBeans IDE

1. From the **File** menu, choose **Open Project**.

2. In the Open Project dialog box, navigate to:

   `tut-install/examples/jaxws`

3. Select the `hello-appclient` folder.

4. Click **Open Project**.

5. In the **Projects** tab, right-click the `hello-appclient` project and select **Build**.

   This command runs the `wsimport` goal, then builds, packages, and runs the client. You will see the output of the application client in the **hello-appclient** output tab:

   ```
   --- exec-maven-plugin:1.2.1:exec (run-appclient) @ hello-appclient ---
   Hello, world.
   ```

To Run the Application Client Using Maven

1. In a terminal window, go to:

   `tut-install/examples/jaxws/hello-appclient/`

2. Enter the following command:

   ```
   mvn install
   ```

   This command runs the `wsimport` goal, then builds, packages, and runs the client. The application client output looks like this:

   ```
   --- exec-maven-plugin:1.2.1:exec (run-appclient) @ hello-appclient ---
   Hello, world.
   ```

28.1.6 A Simple JAX-WS Web Client

`HelloServlet` is a servlet that, like the Java client, calls the `sayHello` method of the web service. Like the application client, it makes this call through a port.

28.1.6.1 Coding the Servlet

To invoke the method on the port, the client performs these steps.

1. It imports the `HelloService` endpoint and the `WebServiceRef` annotation:

   ```
   import javaeetutorial.helloservice.endpoint.HelloService;
   ...
   import javax.xml.ws.WebServiceRef;
   ```

2. It defines a reference to the web service by specifying the WSDL location:

   ```
   @WebServiceRef(wsdlLocation =
     "http://localhost:8080/helloservice-war/HelloService?WSDL")
   ```

3. It declares the web service, then defines a private method that calls the `sayHello` method on the port:

   ```
   private HelloService service;
   ...
   private String sayHello(java.lang.String arg0) {
       javaeetutorial.helloservice.endpoint.Hello port =
               service.getHelloPort();
       return port.sayHello(arg0);
   }
   ```

4. In the servlet, it calls this private method:

   ```
   out.println("<p>" + sayHello("world") + "</p>");
   ```

The significant parts of the `HelloServlet` code follow. The code is located in the *tut-install*/examples/jaxws/src/java/hello-webclient/ directory:

```
import javaeetutorial.helloservice.endpoint.HelloService;
import java.io.IOException;
import java.io.PrintWriter;
import javax.servlet.ServletException;
import javax.servlet.annotation.WebServlet;
import javax.servlet.http.HttpServlet;
import javax.servlet.http.HttpServletRequest;
import javax.servlet.http.HttpServletResponse;
import javax.xml.ws.WebServiceRef;

@WebServlet(name="HelloServlet", urlPatterns={"/HelloServlet"})
public class HelloServlet extends HttpServlet {
    @WebServiceRef(wsdlLocation =
      "http://localhost:8080/helloservice-war/HelloService?WSDL")
    private HelloService service;
```

```
/**
 * Processes requests for both HTTP <code>GET</code>
 *    and <code>POST</code> methods.
 * @param request servlet request
 * @param response servlet response
 * @throws ServletException if a servlet-specific error occurs
 * @throws IOException if an I/O error occurs
 */
protected void processRequest(HttpServletRequest request,
        HttpServletResponse response)
throws ServletException, IOException {
    response.setContentType("text/html;charset=UTF-8");
    try (PrintWriter out = response.getWriter()) {

        out.println("<html lang=\"en\">");
        out.println("<head>");
        out.println("<title>Servlet HelloServlet</title>");
        out.println("</head>");
        out.println("<body>");
        out.println("<h1>Servlet HelloServlet at " +
            request.getContextPath () + "</h1>");
        out.println("<p>" + sayHello("world") + "</p>");
        out.println("</body>");
        out.println("</html>");
    }
}

// doGet and doPost methods, which call processRequest, and
//    getServletInfo method

private String sayHello(java.lang.String arg0) {
    javaeetutorial.helloservice.endpoint.Hello port =
            service.getHelloPort();
    return port.sayHello(arg0);
}
}
```

28.1.6.2 Running the Web Client

You can use either NetBeans IDE or Maven to build, package, deploy, and run the hello-webclient application. To build the client, you must first have deployed helloservice-war, as described in Section 28.1.3, "Building, Packaging, and Deploying the Service."

To Run the Web Client Using NetBeans IDE

1. From the **File** menu, choose **Open Project**.

2. In the Open Project dialog box, navigate to:

   tut-install/examples/jaxws

3. Select the hello-webclient folder.

4. Click **Open Project**.

5. In the **Projects** tab, right-click the hello-webclient project and select **Build**.

   This task runs the wsimport goal, builds and packages the application into a WAR file, hello-webclient.war, located in the target directory, and deploys it to GlassFish Server.

6. In a web browser, enter the following URL:

   http://localhost:8080/hello-webclient/HelloServlet

   The output of the sayHello method appears in the window.

To Run the Web Client Using Maven

1. In a terminal window, go to:

   tut-install/examples/jaxws/hello-webclient/

2. Enter the following command:

   mvn install

   This command runs the wsimport goal, then build and packages the application into a WAR file, hello-webclient.war, located in the target directory. The WAR file is then deployed to GlassFish Server.

3. In a web browser, enter the following URL:

   http://localhost:8080/hello-webclient/HelloServlet

   The output of the sayHello method appears in the window.

28.2 Types Supported by JAX-WS

JAX-WS delegates the mapping of Java programming language types to and from XML definitions to JAXB. Application developers don't need to know the details of these mappings but should be aware that not every class in the Java language can be used as a method parameter or return type in JAX-WS.

The following sections explain the default schema-to-Java and Java-to-schema data type bindings.

28.2.1 Schema-to-Java Mapping

The Java language provides a richer set of data types than XML schema.
Table 28–1 lists the mapping of XML data types to Java data types in JAXB.

Table 28–1   Mapping of XML Data Types to Java Data Types in JAXB

XML Schema Type	Java Data Type
xsd:string	java.lang.String
xsd:integer	java.math.BigInteger
xsd:int	int
xsd:long	long
xsd:short	short
xsd:decimal	java.math.BigDecimal
xsd:float	float
xsd:double	double
xsd:boolean	boolean
xsd:byte	byte
xsd:QName	javax.xml.namespace.QName
xsd:dateTime	javax.xml.datatype.XMLGregorianCalendar
xsd:base64Binary	byte[]
xsd:hexBinary	byte[]
xsd:unsignedInt	long
xsd:unsignedShort	int
xsd:unsignedByte	short
xsd:time	javax.xml.datatype.XMLGregorianCalendar
xsd:date	javax.xml.datatype.XMLGregorianCalendar
xsd:g	javax.xml.datatype.XMLGregorianCalendar
xsd:anySimpleType	java.lang.Object
xsd:anySimpleType	java.lang.String
xsd:duration	javax.xml.datatype.Duration
xsd:NOTATION	javax.xml.namespace.QName

28.2.2 Java-to-Schema Mapping

Table 28–2 shows the default mapping of Java classes to XML data types.

Table 28–2   Mapping of Java Classes to XML Data Types in JAXB

Java Class	XML Data Type
java.lang.String	xs:string
java.math.BigInteger	xs:integer
java.math.BigDecimal	xs:decimal
java.util.Calendar	xs:dateTime
java.util.Date	xs:dateTime
javax.xml.namespace.QName	xs:QName
java.net.URI	xs:string
javax.xml.datatype.XMLGregorianCalendar	xs:anySimpleType
javax.xml.datatype.Duration	xs:duration
java.lang.Object	xs:anyType
java.awt.Image	xs:base64Binary
javax.activation.DataHandler	xs:base64Binary
javax.xml.transform.Source	xs:base64Binary
java.util.UUID	xs:string

28.3 Web Services Interoperability and JAX-WS

JAX-WS supports the Web Services Interoperability (WS-I) Basic Profile Version 1.1. The WS-I Basic Profile is a document that clarifies the SOAP 1.1 and WSDL 1.1 specifications to promote SOAP interoperability. For links related to WS-I, see Section 28.4, "Further Information about JAX-WS."

To support WS-I Basic Profile Version 1.1, the JAX-WS runtime supports doc/literal and rpc/literal encodings for services, static ports, dynamic proxies, and the Dynamic Invocation Interface (DII).

28.4 Further Information about JAX-WS

For more information about JAX-WS and related technologies, see

- Java API for XML Web Services 2.2 specification:

  `http://jcp.org/en/jsr/detail?id=224`

- JAX-WS home:

  `https://jax-ws.java.net/`

- Simple Object Access Protocol (SOAP) 1.2 W3C Note:

  `http://www.w3.org/TR/soap/`

- Web Services Description Language (WSDL) 1.1 W3C Note:

  `http://www.w3.org/TR/wsdl`

- WS-I Basic Profile 1.2 and 2.0:

  `http://www.ws-i.org`

29

Building RESTful Web Services with JAX-RS

This chapter describes the REST architecture, RESTful web services, and the Java API for RESTful Web Services (JAX-RS, defined in JSR 339).

JAX-RS makes it easy for developers to build RESTful web services using the Java programming language.

The following topics are addressed here:

- What Are RESTful Web Services?

- Creating a RESTful Root Resource Class

- Example Applications for JAX-RS

- Further Information about JAX-RS

29.1 What Are RESTful Web Services?

RESTful web services are loosely coupled, lightweight web services that are particularly well suited for creating APIs for clients spread out across the internet. Representational State Transfer (REST) is an architectural style of client-server application centered around the **transfer** of **representations** of **resources** through requests and responses. In the REST architectural style, data and functionality are considered resources and are accessed using **Uniform Resource Identifiers (URIs)**, typically links on the Web. The resources are represented by documents and are acted upon by using a set of simple, well-defined operations.

For example, a REST resource might be the current weather conditions for a city. The representation of that resource might be an XML document, an image file, or an HTML page. A client might retrieve a particular representation, modify the resource by updating its data, or delete the resource entirely.

The REST architectural style is designed to use a stateless communication protocol, typically HTTP. In the REST architecture style, clients and servers exchange representations of resources by using a standardized interface and protocol.

The following principles encourage RESTful applications to be simple, lightweight, and fast.

- **Resource identification through URI**: A RESTful web service exposes a set of resources that identify the targets of the interaction with its clients. Resources are identified by URIs, which provide a global addressing space for resource and service discovery. See Section 29.2.3, "The @Path Annotation and URI Path Templates," for more information.

- **Uniform interface**: Resources are manipulated using a fixed set of four create, read, update, delete operations: PUT, GET, POST, and DELETE. PUT creates a new resource, which can be then deleted by using DELETE. GET retrieves the current state of a resource in some representation. POST transfers a new state onto a resource. See Section 29.2.4, "Responding to HTTP Methods and Requests," for more information.

- **Self-descriptive messages**: Resources are decoupled from their representation so that their content can be accessed in a variety of formats, such as HTML, XML, plain text, PDF, JPEG, JSON, and other document formats. Metadata about the resource is available and used, for example, to control caching, detect transmission errors, negotiate the appropriate representation format, and perform authentication or access control. See Section 29.2.4, "Responding to HTTP Methods and Requests," and Section 29.2.4.2, "Using Entity Providers to Map HTTP Response and Request Entity Bodies," for more information.

- **Stateful interactions through links**: Every interaction with a resource is stateless; that is, request messages are self-contained. Stateful interactions are based on the concept of explicit state transfer. Several techniques exist to exchange state, such as URI rewriting, cookies, and hidden form fields. State can be embedded in response messages to point to valid future states of the interaction. See Section 29.2.4.2, "Using Entity Providers to Map HTTP Response and Request Entity Bodies," for more information.

29.2 Creating a RESTful Root Resource Class

Root resource classes are "plain old Java objects" (POJOs) that are either annotated with @Path or have at least one method annotated with @Path or a **request method designator**, such as @GET, @PUT, @POST, or @DELETE. **Resource methods** are methods of a resource class annotated with a request method designator. This section explains how to use JAX-RS to annotate Java classes to create RESTful web services.

29.2.1 Developing RESTful Web Services with JAX-RS

JAX-RS is a Java programming language API designed to make it easy to develop applications that use the REST architecture.

The JAX-RS API uses Java programming language annotations to simplify the development of RESTful web services. Developers decorate Java programming language class files with JAX-RS annotations to define resources and the actions that can be performed on those resources. JAX-RS annotations are runtime annotations; therefore, runtime reflection will generate the helper classes and artifacts for the resource. A Java EE application archive containing JAX-RS resource classes will have the resources configured, the helper classes and artifacts generated, and the resource exposed to clients by deploying the archive to a Java EE server.

Table 29–1 lists some of the Java programming annotations that are defined by JAX-RS, with a brief description of how each is used. Further information on the JAX-RS APIs can be viewed at http://docs.oracle.com/javaee/7/api/.

Table 29–1   Summary of JAX-RS Annotations

Annotation	Description
@Path	The @Path annotation's value is a relative URI path indicating where the Java class will be hosted: for example, /helloworld. You can also embed variables in the URIs to make a URI path template. For example, you could ask for the name of a user and pass it to the application as a variable in the URI: /helloworld/{username}.
@GET	The @GET annotation is a request method designator and corresponds to the similarly named HTTP method. The Java method annotated with this request method designator will process HTTP GET requests. The behavior of a resource is determined by the HTTP method to which the resource is responding.

Table 29–1   *(Cont.)* **Summary of JAX-RS Annotations**

Annotation	Description
@POST	The @POST annotation is a request method designator and corresponds to the similarly named HTTP method. The Java method annotated with this request method designator will process HTTP POST requests. The behavior of a resource is determined by the HTTP method to which the resource is responding.
@PUT	The @PUT annotation is a request method designator and corresponds to the similarly named HTTP method. The Java method annotated with this request method designator will process HTTP PUT requests. The behavior of a resource is determined by the HTTP method to which the resource is responding.
@DELETE	The @DELETE annotation is a request method designator and corresponds to the similarly named HTTP method. The Java method annotated with this request method designator will process HTTP DELETE requests. The behavior of a resource is determined by the HTTP method to which the resource is responding.
@HEAD	The @HEAD annotation is a request method designator and corresponds to the similarly named HTTP method. The Java method annotated with this request method designator will process HTTP HEAD requests. The behavior of a resource is determined by the HTTP method to which the resource is responding.
@PathParam	The @PathParam annotation is a type of parameter that you can extract for use in your resource class. URI path parameters are extracted from the request URI, and the parameter names correspond to the URI path template variable names specified in the @Path class-level annotation.
@QueryParam	The @QueryParam annotation is a type of parameter that you can extract for use in your resource class. Query parameters are extracted from the request URI query parameters.
@Consumes	The @Consumes annotation is used to specify the MIME media types of representations a resource can consume that were sent by the client.
@Produces	The @Produces annotation is used to specify the MIME media types of representations a resource can produce and send back to the client: for example, "text/plain".

Table 29–1 *(Cont.)* **Summary of JAX-RS Annotations**

Annotation	Description
@Provider	The @Provider annotation is used for anything that is of interest to the JAX-RS runtime, such as MessageBodyReader and MessageBodyWriter. For HTTP requests, the MessageBodyReader is used to map an HTTP request entity body to method parameters. On the response side, a return value is mapped to an HTTP response entity body by using a MessageBodyWriter. If the application needs to supply additional metadata, such as HTTP headers or a different status code, a method can return a Response that wraps the entity and that can be built using Response.ResponseBuilder.
@ApplicationPath	The @ApplicationPath annotation is used to define the URL mapping for the application. The path specified by @ApplicationPath is the base URI for all resource URIs specified by @Path annotations in the resource class. You may only apply @ApplicationPath to a subclass of javax.ws.rs.core.Application.

29.2.2 Overview of a JAX-RS Application

The following code sample is a very simple example of a root resource class that uses JAX-RS annotations:

```
package javaeetutorial.hello;

import javax.ws.rs.Consumes;
import javax.ws.rs.GET;
import javax.ws.rs.PUT;
import javax.ws.rs.Path;
import javax.ws.rs.Produces;
import javax.ws.rs.core.Context;
import javax.ws.rs.core.UriInfo;

/**
 * Root resource (exposed at "helloworld" path)
 */
@Path("helloworld")
public class HelloWorld {
    @Context
    private UriInfo context;

    /** Creates a new instance of HelloWorld */
    public HelloWorld() {}

    /**
      * Retrieves representation of an instance of helloWorld.HelloWorld
```

```
 * @return an instance of java.lang.String
 */
@GET
@Produces("text/html")
public String getHtml() {
    return "<html lang=\"en\"><body><h1>Hello, World!!</h1></body></html>";
}
}
```

The following sections describe the annotations used in this example.

- The @Path annotation's value is a relative URI path. In the preceding example, the Java class will be hosted at the URI path /helloworld. This is an extremely simple use of the @Path annotation, with a static URI path. Variables can be embedded in the URIs. **URI path templates** are URIs with variables embedded within the URI syntax.

- The @GET annotation is a request method designator, along with @POST, @PUT, @DELETE, and @HEAD, defined by JAX-RS and corresponding to the similarly named HTTP methods. In the example, the annotated Java method will process HTTP GET requests. The behavior of a resource is determined by the HTTP method to which the resource is responding.

- The @Produces annotation is used to specify the MIME media types a resource can produce and send back to the client. In this example, the Java method will produce representations identified by the MIME media type "text/html".

- The @Consumes annotation is used to specify the MIME media types a resource can consume that were sent by the client. The example could be modified to set the message returned by the getHtml method, as shown in this code example:

```
@POST
@Consumes("text/html")
public void postHtml(String message) {
    // Store the message
}
```

29.2.3 The @Path Annotation and URI Path Templates

The @Path annotation identifies the URI path template to which the resource responds and is specified at the class or method level of a resource. The @Path annotation's value is a partial URI path template relative to the base URI of the server on which the resource is deployed, the context root of the application, and the URL pattern to which the JAX-RS runtime responds.

URI path templates are URIs with variables embedded within the URI syntax. These variables are substituted at runtime in order for a resource to respond to a request based on the substituted URI. Variables are denoted by braces ({ and }). For example, look at the following @Path annotation:

```
@Path("/users/{username}")
```

In this kind of example, a user is prompted to type his or her name, and then a JAX-RS web service configured to respond to requests to this URI path template responds. For example, if the user types the user name "Galileo," the web service responds to the following URL:

```
http://example.com/users/Galileo
```

To obtain the value of the user name, the @PathParam annotation may be used on the method parameter of a request method, as shown in the following code example:

```
@Path("/users/{username}")
public class UserResource {

    @GET
    @Produces("text/xml")
    public String getUser(@PathParam("username") String userName) { ... }
}
```

By default, the URI variable must match the regular expression "[^/]+?". This variable may be customized by specifying a different regular expression after the variable name. For example, if a user name must consist only of lowercase and uppercase alphanumeric characters, override the default regular expression in the variable definition:

```
@Path("users/{username: [a-zA-Z][a-zA-Z_0-9]*}")
```

In this example, the username variable will match only user names that begin with one uppercase or lowercase letter and zero or more alphanumeric characters and the underscore character. If a user name does not match that template, a 404 (Not Found) response will be sent to the client.

A @Path value isn't required to have leading or trailing slashes (/). The JAX-RS runtime parses URI path templates the same way, whether or not they have leading or trailing slashes.

A URI path template has one or more variables, with each variable name surrounded by braces: { to begin the variable name and } to end it. In the preceding example, username is the variable name. At runtime, a resource configured to respond to the preceding URI path template will attempt to process the URI data that corresponds to the location of {username} in the URI as the variable data for username.

For example, if you want to deploy a resource that responds to the URI path template http://example.com/myContextRoot/resources/{name1}/{name2}/, you must first deploy the application to a Java EE server that responds to requests to the http://example.com/myContextRoot URI and then decorate your resource with the following @Path annotation:

```
@Path("/{name1}/{name2}/")
public class SomeResource { ... }
```

In this example, the URL pattern for the JAX-RS helper servlet, specified in web.xml, is the default:

```
<servlet-mapping>
        <servlet-name>javax.ws.rs.core.Application</servlet-name>
        <url-pattern>/resources/*</url-pattern>
</servlet-mapping>
```

A variable name can be used more than once in the URI path template.

If a character in the value of a variable would conflict with the reserved characters of a URI, the conflicting character should be substituted with percent encoding. For example, spaces in the value of a variable should be substituted with %20.

When defining URI path templates, be careful that the resulting URI after substitution is valid.

Table 29–2 lists some examples of URI path template variables and how the URIs are resolved after substitution. The following variable names and values are used in the examples:

- name1: james

- name2: gatz

- name3:

- location: Main%20Street

- question: why

> **Note:** The value of the name3 variable is an empty string.

Table 29–2   Examples of URI Path Templates

URI Path Template	URI After Substitution
`http://example.com/{name1}/{name2}/`	`http://example.com/james/gatz/`
`http://example.com/{question}/{question}/{question}/`	`http://example.com/why/why/why/`
`http://example.com/maps/{location}`	`http://example.com/maps/Main%20Street`
`http://example.com/{name3}/home/`	`http://example.com//home/`

29.2.4 Responding to HTTP Methods and Requests

The behavior of a resource is determined by the HTTP methods (typically, GET, POST, PUT, or DELETE) to which the resource is responding.

29.2.4.1 The Request Method Designator Annotations

Request method designator annotations are runtime annotations, defined by JAX-RS, that correspond to the similarly named HTTP methods. Within a resource class file, HTTP methods are mapped to Java programming language methods by using the request method designator annotations. The behavior of a resource is determined by which HTTP method the resource is responding to. JAX-RS defines a set of request method designators for the common HTTP methods GET, POST, PUT, DELETE, and HEAD; you can also create your own custom request method designators. Creating custom request method designators is outside the scope of this document.

The following example shows the use of the PUT method to create or update a storage container:

```
@PUT
public Response putContainer() {
    System.out.println("PUT CONTAINER " + container);
    URI uri = uriInfo.getAbsolutePath();
    Container c = new Container(container, uri.toString());

    Response r;
    if (!MemoryStore.MS.hasContainer(c)) {
        r = Response.created(uri).build();
    } else {
        r = Response.noContent().build();
    }

    MemoryStore.MS.createContainer(c);
    return r;
}
```

By default, the JAX-RS runtime will automatically support the methods HEAD and OPTIONS if not explicitly implemented. For HEAD, the runtime will invoke the implemented GET method, if present, and ignore the response entity, if set. For OPTIONS, the `Allow` response header will be set to the set of HTTP methods supported by the resource. In addition, the JAX-RS runtime will return a Web Application Definition Language (WADL) document describing the resource; see `http://www.w3.org/Submission/wadl/` for more information.

Methods decorated with request method designators must return `void`, a Java programming language type, or a `javax.ws.rs.core.Response` object. Multiple parameters may be extracted from the URI by using the `@PathParam` or `@QueryParam` annotations, as described in Section 29.2.6, "Extracting Request Parameters." Conversion between Java types and an entity body is the responsibility of an entity provider, such as `MessageBodyReader` or `MessageBodyWriter`. Methods that need to provide additional metadata with a response should return an instance of the `Response` class. The `ResponseBuilder` class provides a convenient way to create a `Response` instance using a builder pattern. The HTTP PUT and POST methods expect an HTTP request body, so you should use a `MessageBodyReader` for methods that respond to PUT and POST requests.

Both `@PUT` and `@POST` can be used to create or update a resource. POST can mean anything, so when using POST, it is up to the application to define the semantics. PUT has well-defined semantics. When using PUT for creation, the client declares the URI for the newly created resource.

PUT has very clear semantics for creating and updating a resource. The representation the client sends must be the same representation that is received using a GET, given the same media type. PUT does not allow a resource to be partially updated, a common mistake when attempting to use the PUT method. A common application pattern is to use POST to create a resource and return a `201` response with a location header whose value is the URI to the newly created resource. In this pattern, the web service declares the URI for the newly created resource.

29.2.4.2 Using Entity Providers to Map HTTP Response and Request Entity Bodies

Entity providers supply mapping services between representations and their associated Java types. The two types of entity providers are `MessageBodyReader` and `MessageBodyWriter`. For HTTP requests, the `MessageBodyReader` is used to map an HTTP request entity body to method parameters. On the response side, a return value is mapped to an HTTP response entity body by using a `MessageBodyWriter`. If the application needs to supply additional metadata, such as HTTP headers or a different status code, a method can return a `Response` that wraps the entity and that can be built by using `Response.ResponseBuilder`.

Table 29–3 shows the standard types that are supported automatically for HTTP request and response entity bodies. You need to write an entity provider only if you are not choosing one of these standard types.

Table 29–3 Types Supported for HTTP Request and Response Entity Bodies

Java Type	Supported Media Types
`byte[]`	All media types (`*/*`)
`java.lang.String`	All text media types (`text/*`)
`java.io.InputStream`	All media types (`*/*`)
`java.io.Reader`	All media types (`*/*`)
`java.io.File`	All media types (`*/*`)
`javax.activation.DataSource`	All media types (`*/*`)
`javax.xml.transform.Source`	XML media types (`text/xml`, `application/xml`, and `application/*+xml`)
`javax.xml.bind.JAXBElement` and application-supplied JAXB classes	XML media types (`text/xml`, `application/xml`, and `application/*+xml`)
`MultivaluedMap<String, String>`	Form content (`application/x-www-form-urlencoded`)
`StreamingOutput`	All media types (`*/*`), `MessageBodyWriter` only

The following example shows how to use `MessageBodyReader` with the `@Consumes` and `@Provider` annotations:

```
@Consumes("application/x-www-form-urlencoded")
@Provider
public class FormReader implements MessageBodyReader<NameValuePair> { ... }
```

The following example shows how to use `MessageBodyWriter` with the `@Produces` and `@Provider` annotations:

```
@Produces("text/html")
@Provider
public class FormWriter implements
        MessageBodyWriter<Hashtable<String, String>> { ... }
```

The following example shows how to use `ResponseBuilder`:

```
@GET
public Response getItem() {
    System.out.println("GET ITEM " + container + " " + item);

    Item i = MemoryStore.MS.getItem(container, item);
    if (i == null)
        throw new NotFoundException("Item not found");
    Date lastModified = i.getLastModified().getTime();
    EntityTag et = new EntityTag(i.getDigest());
    ResponseBuilder rb = request.evaluatePreconditions(lastModified, et);
    if (rb != null)
        return rb.build();

    byte[] b = MemoryStore.MS.getItemData(container, item);
    return Response.ok(b, i.getMimeType()).
            lastModified(lastModified).tag(et).build();
}
```

29.2.5 Using @Consumes and @Produces to Customize Requests and Responses

The information sent to a resource and then passed back to the client is specified as a MIME media type in the headers of an HTTP request or response. You can specify which MIME media types of representations a resource can respond to or produce by using the following annotations:

- `javax.ws.rs.Consumes`

- `javax.ws.rs.Produces`

By default, a resource class can respond to and produce all MIME media types of representations specified in the HTTP request and response headers.

29.2.5.1 The @Produces Annotation

The `@Produces` annotation is used to specify the MIME media types or representations a resource can produce and send back to the client. If `@Produces` is applied at the class level, all the methods in a resource can produce the specified MIME types by default. If applied at the method level, the annotation overrides any `@Produces` annotations applied at the class level.

If no methods in a resource are able to produce the MIME type in a client request, the JAX-RS runtime sends back an HTTP "406 Not Acceptable" error.

The value of `@Produces` is an array of `String` of MIME types or a comma-separated list of `MediaType` constants. For example:

```
@Produces({"image/jpeg,image/png"})
```

The following example shows how to apply `@Produces` at both the class and method levels:

```
@Path("/myResource")
@Produces("text/plain")
public class SomeResource {
    @GET
    public String doGetAsPlainText() { ... }

    @GET
    @Produces("text/html")
    public String doGetAsHtml() { ... }
}
```

The `doGetAsPlainText` method defaults to the MIME media type of the `@Produces` annotation at the class level. The `doGetAsHtml` method's `@Produces` annotation overrides the class-level `@Produces` setting and specifies that the method can produce HTML rather than plain text.

`@Produces` can also use the constants defined in the `javax.ws.rs.core.MediaType` class to specify the media type. For example, specifying `MediaType.APPLICATION_XML` is equivalent to specifying `"application/xml"`:

```
@Produces(MediaType.APPLICATION_XML)
@GET
public Customer getCustomer() { ... }
```

If a resource class is capable of producing more than one MIME media type, the resource method chosen will correspond to the most acceptable media type as declared by the client. More specifically, the `Accept` header of the HTTP request declares what is most acceptable. For example, if the `Accept` header is `Accept: text/plain`, the `doGetAsPlainText` method will be invoked. Alternatively, if the `Accept` header is `Accept: text/plain;q=0.9, text/html`, which declares that the client can accept media types of `text/plain` and `text/html` but prefers the latter, the `doGetAsHtml` method will be invoked.

More than one media type may be declared in the same `@Produces` declaration. The following code example shows how this is done:

```
@Produces({"application/xml", "application/json"})
public String doGetAsXmlOrJson() { ... }
```

The `doGetAsXmlOrJson` method will get invoked if either of the media types `application/xml` or `application/json` is acceptable. If both are equally acceptable, the former will be chosen because it occurs first. The preceding examples refer explicitly to MIME media types for clarity. It is possible to refer to constant values, which may reduce typographical errors. For more information, see the API documentation for the constant field values of `javax.ws.rs.core.MediaType`.

29.2.5.2 The @Consumes Annotation

The `@Consumes` annotation is used to specify which MIME media types of representations a resource can accept, or consume, from the client. If `@Consumes` is applied at the class level, all the response methods accept the specified MIME types by default. If applied at the method level, `@Consumes` overrides any `@Consumes` annotations applied at the class level.

If a resource is unable to consume the MIME type of a client request, the JAX-RS runtime sends back an HTTP 415 ("Unsupported Media Type") error.

The value of `@Consumes` is an array of `String` of acceptable MIME types or a comma-separated list of `MediaType` constants. For example:

```
@Consumes({"text/plain,text/html"})
```

This is the equivalent of:

```
@Consumes({MediaType.TEXT_PLAIN,MediaType.TEXT_HTML})
```

The following example shows how to apply `@Consumes` at both the class and method levels:

```
@Path("/myResource")
@Consumes("multipart/related")
public class SomeResource {
    @POST
    public String doPost(MimeMultipart mimeMultipartData) { ... }

    @POST
    @Consumes("application/x-www-form-urlencoded")
    public String doPost2(FormURLEncodedProperties formData) { ... }
}
```

The `doPost` method defaults to the MIME media type of the `@Consumes` annotation at the class level. The `doPost2` method overrides the class level `@Consumes` annotation to specify that it can accept URL-encoded form data.

If no resource methods can respond to the requested MIME type, an HTTP 415 ("Unsupported Media Type") error is returned to the client.

The `HelloWorld` example discussed previously in this section can be modified to set the message by using `@Consumes`, as shown in the following code example:

```
@POST
@Consumes("text/html")
public void postHtml(String message) {
    // Store the message
}
```

In this example, the Java method will consume representations identified by the MIME media type `text/plain`. Note that the resource method returns `void`. This means that no representation is returned and that a response with a status code of HTTP 204 ("No Content") will be returned.

29.2.6 Extracting Request Parameters

Parameters of a resource method may be annotated with parameter-based annotations to extract information from a request. A previous example presented the use of the `@PathParam` parameter to extract a path parameter from the path component of the request URL that matched the path declared in `@Path`.

You can extract the following types of parameters for use in your resource class:

- Query
- URI path
- Form
- Cookie
- Header
- Matrix

Query parameters are extracted from the request URI query parameters and are specified by using the `javax.ws.rs.QueryParam` annotation in the method parameter arguments. The following example demonstrates using `@QueryParam` to extract query parameters from the `Query` component of the request URL:

```
@Path("smooth")
@GET
public Response smooth(
        @DefaultValue("2") @QueryParam("step") int step,
        @DefaultValue("true") @QueryParam("min-m") boolean hasMin,
        @DefaultValue("true") @QueryParam("max-m") boolean hasMax,
```

```
@DefaultValue("true") @QueryParam("last-m") boolean hasLast,
@DefaultValue("blue") @QueryParam("min-color") ColorParam minColor,
@DefaultValue("green") @QueryParam("max-color") ColorParam maxColor,
@DefaultValue("red") @QueryParam("last-color") ColorParam lastColor
) { ... }
```

If the query parameter step exists in the query component of the request URI, the value of step will be extracted and parsed as a 32-bit signed integer and assigned to the step method parameter. If step does not exist, a default value of 2, as declared in the @DefaultValue annotation, will be assigned to the step method parameter. If the step value cannot be parsed as a 32-bit signed integer, an HTTP 400 ("Client Error") response is returned.

User-defined Java programming language types may be used as query parameters. The following code example shows the ColorParam class used in the preceding query parameter example:

```
public class ColorParam extends Color {
    public ColorParam(String s) {
        super(getRGB(s));
    }

    private static int getRGB(String s) {
        if (s.charAt(0) == '#') {
            try {
                Color c = Color.decode("0x" + s.substring(1));
                return c.getRGB();
            } catch (NumberFormatException e) {
                throw new WebApplicationException(400);
            }
        } else {
            try {
                Field f = Color.class.getField(s);
                return ((Color)f.get(null)).getRGB();
            } catch (Exception e) {
                throw new WebApplicationException(400);
            }
        }
    }
}
```

The constructor for ColorParam takes a single String parameter.

Both @QueryParam and @PathParam can be used only on the following Java types.

- All primitive types except char.

- All wrapper classes of primitive types except Character.

- Any class with a constructor that accepts a single `String` argument.

- Any class with the static method named `valueOf(String)` that accepts a single `String` argument.

- `List<T>`, `Set<T>`, or `SortedSet<T>`, where T matches the already listed criteria. Sometimes, parameters may contain more than one value for the same name. If this is the case, these types may be used to obtain all values.

If `@DefaultValue` is not used in conjunction with `@QueryParam`, and the query parameter is not present in the request, the value will be an empty collection for `List`, `Set`, or `SortedSet`; null for other object types; and the default for primitive types.

URI path parameters are extracted from the request URI, and the parameter names correspond to the URI path template variable names specified in the `@Path` class-level annotation. URI parameters are specified using the `javax.ws.rs.PathParam` annotation in the method parameter arguments. The following example shows how to use `@Path` variables and the `@PathParam` annotation in a method:

```
@Path("/{username}")
public class MyResourceBean {
    ...
    @GET
    public String printUsername(@PathParam("username") String userId) { ... }
}
```

In the preceding snippet, the URI path template variable name `username` is specified as a parameter to the `printUsername` method. The `@PathParam` annotation is set to the variable name `username`. At runtime, before `printUsername` is called, the value of `username` is extracted from the URI and cast to a `String`. The resulting `String` is then available to the method as the `userId` variable.

If the URI path template variable cannot be cast to the specified type, the JAX-RS runtime returns an HTTP 400 ("Bad Request") error to the client. If the `@PathParam` annotation cannot be cast to the specified type, the JAX-RS runtime returns an HTTP 404 ("Not Found") error to the client.

The `@PathParam` parameter and the other parameter-based annotations (`@MatrixParam`, `@HeaderParam`, `@CookieParam`, and `@FormParam`) obey the same rules as `@QueryParam`.

Cookie parameters, indicated by decorating the parameter with `javax.ws.rs.CookieParam`, extract information from the cookies declared in cookie-related HTTP headers. **Header parameters**, indicated by decorating the parameter with `javax.ws.rs.HeaderParam`, extract information from the HTTP headers. **Matrix parameters**, indicated by decorating the parameter with `javax.ws.rs.MatrixParam`, extract information from URL path segments.

Form parameters, indicated by decorating the parameter with `javax.ws.rs.FormParam`, extract information from a request representation that is of the MIME media type `application/x-www-form-urlencoded` and conforms to the encoding specified by HTML forms, as described in `http://w3.org/TR/html401/interact/forms.html#h-17.13.4.1`. This parameter is very useful for extracting information sent by POST in HTML forms.

The following example extracts the `name` form parameter from the POST form data:

```
@POST
@Consumes("application/x-www-form-urlencoded")
public void post(@FormParam("name") String name) {
    // Store the message
}
```

To obtain a general map of parameter names and values for query and path parameters, use the following code:

```
@GET
public String get(@Context UriInfo ui) {
    MultivaluedMap<String, String> queryParams = ui.getQueryParameters();
    MultivaluedMap<String, String> pathParams = ui.getPathParameters();
}
```

The following method extracts header and cookie parameter names and values into a map:

```
@GET
public String get(@Context HttpHeaders hh) {
    MultivaluedMap<String, String> headerParams = hh.getRequestHeaders();
    Map<String, Cookie> pathParams = hh.getCookies();
}
```

In general, `@Context` can be used to obtain contextual Java types related to the request or response.

For form parameters, it is possible to do the following:

```
@POST
@Consumes("application/x-www-form-urlencoded")
public void post(MultivaluedMap<String, String> formParams) {
    // Store the message
}
```

29.2.7 Configuring JAX-RS Applications

A JAX-RS application consists of at least one resource class packaged within a WAR file. The base URI from which an application's resources respond to requests can be set one of two ways:

- Using the `@ApplicationPath` annotation in a subclass of `javax.ws.rs.core.Application` packaged within the WAR

- Using the `servlet-mapping` tag within the WAR's `web.xml` deployment descriptor

29.2.7.1 Configuring a JAX-RS Application Using a Subclass of Application

Create a subclass of `javax.ws.rs.core.Application` to manually configure the environment in which the REST resources defined in your resource classes are run, including the base URI. Add a class-level `@ApplicationPath` annotation to set the base URI:

```
@ApplicationPath("/webapi")
public class MyApplication extends Application { ... }
```

In the preceding example, the base URI is set to `/webapi`, which means that all resources defined within the application are relative to `/webapi`.

By default, all the resources in an archive will be processed for resources. Override the `getClasses` method to manually register the resource classes in the application with the JAX-RS runtime:

```
@Override
public Set<Class<?>> getClasses() {
    final Set<Class<?>> classes = new HashSet<>();
    // register root resource
    classes.add(MyResource.class);
    return classes;
}
```

29.2.7.2 Configuring the Base URI in web.xml

The base URI for a JAX-RS application can be set using a `servlet-mapping` tag in the `web.xml` deployment descriptor, using the `Application` class name as the servlet:

```
<servlet-mapping>
    <servlet-name>javax.ws.rs.core.Application</servlet-name>
    <url-pattern>/webapi/*</url-pattern>
</servlet-mapping>
```

This setting will also override the path set by `@ApplicationPath` when using an `Application` subclass:

```
<servlet-mapping>
    <servlet-name>com.example.rest.MyApplication</servlet-name>
    <url-pattern>/services/*</url-pattern>
</servlet-mapping>
```

29.3 Example Applications for JAX-RS

This section provides an introduction to creating, deploying, and running your own JAX-RS applications. This section demonstrates the steps that are needed to create, build, deploy, and test a very simple web application that uses JAX-RS annotations.

29.3.1 Creating a Simple RESTful Web Service

This section explains how to use NetBeans IDE to create a RESTful web service using a Maven archetype. The archetype generates a skeleton for the application, and you simply need to implement the appropriate method.

You can find a version of this application at *tut-install*/examples/jaxrs/hello/.

29.3.1.1 To Create a RESTful Web Service Using NetBeans IDE

1. Ensure you have installed the tutorial archetypes as described in Section 2.7.1, "Installing the Tutorial Archetypes."

2. In NetBeans IDE, create a simple web application using the `jaxrs-service-archetype` Maven archetype. This archetype creates a very simple "Hello, World" web application.

   a. From the **File** menu, choose **New Project**.

   b. From **Categories**, select **Maven**. From **Projects**, select **Project From Archetype**. Click **Next**.

   c. Under **Search** enter `jaxrs-service`, select the `jaxrs-service-archetype`, and click **Next**.

   d. Under **Project Name** enter `HelloWorldApplication`, set the **Project Location**, and set the **Package** name to `javaeetutorial.hello`, and click **Finish**.

   The project is created.

3. In `HelloWorld.java`, find the `getHtml()` method. Replace the `//TODO` comment with the following text, so that the finished product resembles the following method:

```
@GET
@Produces("text/html")
public String getHtml() {
    return "<html lang=\"en\"><body><h1>Hello, World!!</body></h1></html>";
}
```

> **Note:** Because the MIME type produced is HTML, you can use HTML tags in your return statement.

4. Make sure that GlassFish Server has been started (see Section 2.2, "Starting and Stopping GlassFish Server").

5. Right-click the `HelloWorldApplication` project in the **Projects** pane and select **Build**.

This will build and deploy the application to GlassFish Server.

6. In a browser, open the following URL:

```
http://localhost:8080/HelloWorldApplication/HelloWorldApplication
```

A browser window opens and displays the return value of `Hello, World!!`

For other sample applications that demonstrate deploying and running JAX-RS applications using NetBeans IDE, see Section 29.3.2, "The rsvp Example Application," and *Your First Cup: An Introduction to the Java EE Platform* at `http://docs.oracle.com/javaee/7/firstcup/doc/`. You may also look at the tutorials on the NetBeans IDE tutorial site, such as the one titled "Getting Started with RESTful Web Services" at `https://netbeans.org/kb/docs/websvc/rest.html`. This tutorial includes a section on creating a CRUD application from a database. Create, read, update, and delete (CRUD) are the four basic functions of persistent storage and relational databases.

29.3.2 The rsvp Example Application

The `rsvp` example application, located in the *tut-install*/`examples/jaxrs/rsvp/` directory, allows invitees to an event to indicate whether they will attend. The events, people invited to the event, and the responses to the invite are stored in a Java DB database using the Java Persistence API. The JAX-RS resources in `rsvp` are exposed in a stateless session enterprise bean.

29.3.2.1 Components of the rsvp Example Application

The three enterprise beans in the rsvp example application are
rsvp.ejb.ConfigBean, rsvp.ejb.StatusBean, and rsvp.ejb.ResponseBean.

ConfigBean is a singleton session bean that initializes the data in the database.

StatusBean exposes a JAX-RS resource for displaying the current status of all
invitees to an event. The URI path template is declared first on the class and then
on the getEvent method:

```
@Stateless
@Named
@Path("/status")
public class StatusBean {
    ...
    @GET
    @Produces({MediaType.APPLICATION_XML, MediaType.APPLICATION_JSON})
    @Path("{eventId}/")
    public Event getEvent(@PathParam("eventId") Long eventId) { ... )
```

The combination of the two @Path annotations results in the following URI path
template:

```
@Path("/status/{eventId}/")
```

The URI path variable eventId is a @PathParam variable in the getEvent method,
which responds to HTTP GET requests and has been annotated with @GET. The
eventId variable is used to look up all the current responses in the database for
that particular event.

ResponseBean exposes a JAX-RS resource for setting an invitee's response to a
particular event. The URI path template for ResponseBean is declared as follows:

```
@Path("/{eventId}/{inviteId}")
```

Two URI path variables are declared in the path template: eventId and inviteId.
As in StatusBean, eventId is the unique ID for a particular event. Each invitee to
that event has a unique ID for the invitation, and that is the inviteId. Both of
these path variables are used in two JAX-RS methods in ResponseBean:
getResponse and putResponse. The getResponse method responds to HTTP GET
requests and displays the invitee's current response and a form to change the
response.

The javaeetutorial.rsvp.rest.RsvpApplication class defines the root
application path for the resources by applying the javax.ws.rs.ApplicationPath
annotation at the class level.

```
@ApplicationPath("/webapi")
public class RsvpApplication extends Application {
}
```

An invitee who wants to change his or her response selects the new response and submits the form data, which is processed as an HTTP POST request by the putResponse method. The new response is extracted from the HTTP POST request and stored as the userResponse string. The putResponse method uses userResponse, eventId, and inviteId to update the invitee's response in the database.

The events, people, and responses in rsvp are encapsulated in Java Persistence API entities. The rsvp.entity.Event, rsvp.entity.Person, and rsvp.entity.Response entities respectively represent events, invitees, and responses to an event.

The rsvp.util.ResponseEnum class declares an enumerated type that represents all the possible response statuses an invitee may have.

The web application also includes two CDI managed beans, StatusManager and EventManager, which use the JAX-RS Client API to call the resources exposed in StatusBean and ResponseBean. For information on how the Client API is used in rsvp, see Section 30.2.1, "The Client API in the rsvp Example Application."

29.3.2.2 Running the rsvp Example Application

Both NetBeans IDE and Maven can be used to deploy and run the rsvp example application.

To Run the rsvp Example Application Using NetBeans IDE

1. If the database server is not already running, start it by following the instructions in Section 2.4, "Starting and Stopping the Java DB Server."

2. Make sure that GlassFish Server has been started (see Section 2.2, "Starting and Stopping GlassFish Server").

3. From the **File** menu, choose **Open Project**.

4. In the Open Project dialog box, navigate to:

    tut-install/examples/jaxrs

5. Select the rsvp folder.

6. Click **Open Project**.

7. Right-click the rsvp project in the **Projects** tab and select **Run**.

The project will be compiled, assembled, and deployed to GlassFish Server. A web browser window will open to the following URL:

```
http://localhost:8080/rsvp/index.xhtml
```

8. In the web browser window, click the **Event status** link for the Duke's Birthday event.

   You'll see the current invitees and their responses.

9. Click the current response of one of the invitees in the Status column of the table, select a new response, and click **Update your status**.

   The invitee's new status should now be displayed in the table of invitees and their response statuses.

To Run the rsvp Example Application Using Maven

1. If the database server is not already running, start it by following the instructions in Section 2.4, "Starting and Stopping the Java DB Server."

2. Make sure that GlassFish Server has been started (see Section 2.2, "Starting and Stopping GlassFish Server").

3. In a terminal window, go to:

   ```
   tut-install/examples/jaxrs/rsvp/
   ```

4. Enter the following command:

   ```
   mvn install
   ```

   This command builds, assembles, and deploys rsvp to GlassFish Server.

5. Open a web browser window to the following URL:

   ```
   http://localhost:8080/rsvp/
   ```

6. In the web browser window, click the **Event status** link for the Duke's Birthday event.

   You'll see the current invitees and their responses.

7. Click the current response of one of the invitees in the Status column of the table, select a new response, and click **Update your status**.

   The invitee's new status should now be displayed in the table of invitees and their response statuses.

29.3.3 Real-World Examples

Most blog sites use RESTful web services. These sites involve downloading XML files, in RSS or Atom format, that contain lists of links to other resources. Other websites and web applications that use REST-like developer interfaces to data include Twitter and Amazon S3 (Simple Storage Service). With Amazon S3, buckets and objects can be created, listed, and retrieved using either a REST-style HTTP interface or a SOAP interface. The examples that ship with Jersey include a storage service example with a RESTful interface.

29.4 Further Information about JAX-RS

For more information about RESTful web services and JAX-RS, see

- "Fielding Dissertation: Chapter 5: Representational State Transfer (REST)":

  http://www.ics.uci.edu/~fielding/pubs/dissertation/
  rest_arch_style.htm

- *RESTful Web Services*, by Leonard Richardson and Sam Ruby, available from O'Reilly Media:

  http://shop.oreilly.com/product/9780596529260.do

- JSR 339: JAX-RS 2.0: The Java API for RESTful Web Services:

  http://jcp.org/en/jsr/detail?id=339

- Jersey project:

  https://jersey.java.net/

30

Accessing REST Resources with the JAX-RS Client API

This chapter describes the JAX-RS Client API and includes examples of how to access REST resources using the Java programming language.

JAX-RS provides a client API for accessing REST resources from other Java applications.

The following topics are addressed here:

- Overview of the Client API
- Using the Client API in the JAX-RS Example Applications
- Advanced Features of the Client API

30.1 Overview of the Client API

The JAX-RS Client API provides a high-level API for accessing any REST resources, not just JAX-RS services. The Client API is defined in the `javax.ws.rs.client` package.

30.1.1 Creating a Basic Client Request Using the Client API

The following steps are needed to access a REST resource using the Client API.

1. Obtain an instance of the `javax.ws.rs.client.Client` interface.
2. Configure the `Client` instance with a target.

3. Create a request based on the target.

4. Invoke the request.

The Client API is designed to be fluent, with method invocations chained together to configure and submit a request to a REST resource in only a few lines of code:

```
Client client = ClientBuilder.newClient();
String name = client.target("http://example.com/webapi/hello")
        .request(MediaType.TEXT_PLAIN)
        .get(String.class);
```

In this example, the client instance is first created by calling the `javax.ws.rs.client.ClientBuilder.newClient` method. Then, the request is configured and invoked by chaining method calls together in one line of code. The `Client.target` method sets the target based on a URI. The `javax.ws.rs.client.WebTarget.request` method sets the media type for the returned entity. The `javax.ws.rs.client.Invocation.Builder.get` method invokes the service using an HTTP GET request, setting the type of the returned entity to `String`.

30.1.1.1 Obtaining the Client Instance

The `Client` interface defines the actions and infrastructure a REST client requires to consume a RESTful web service. Instances of `Client` are obtained by calling the `ClientBuilder.newClient` method:

```
Client client = ClientBuilder.newClient();
```

Use the `close` method to close `Client` instances after all the invocations for the target resource have been performed:

```
Client client = ClientBuilder.newClient();
...
client.close();
```

`Client` instances are heavyweight objects. For performance reasons, limit the number of `Client` instances in your application, as the initialization and destruction of these instances may be expensive in your runtime environment.

30.1.1.2 Setting the Client Target

The target of a client, the REST resource at a particular URI, is represented by an instance of the `javax.ws.rs.client.WebTarget` interface. You obtain a `WebTarget` instance by calling the `Client.target` method and passing in the URI of the target REST resource.

```
Client client = ClientBuilder.newClient();
WebTarget myResource = client.target("http://example.com/webapi");
```

For complex REST resources, it may be beneficial to create several instances of `WebTarget`. In the following example, a base target is used to construct several other targets that represent different services provided by a REST resource:

```
Client client = ClientBuilder.newClient();
WebTarget base = client.target("http://example.com/webapi");
// WebTarget at http://example.com/webapi/read
WebTarget read = base.path("read");
// WebTarget at http://example.com/webapi/write
WebTarget write = base.path("write");
```

The `WebTarget.path` method creates a new `WebTarget` instance by appending the current target URI with the path that was passed in.

30.1.1.3 Setting Path Parameters in Targets

Path parameters in client requests can be specified as URI template parameters, similar to the template parameters used when defining a resource URI in a JAX-RS service. Template parameters are specified by surrounding the template variable with braces ({}). Call the `WebTarget.queryParam` method on the target to set the parameters by passing in the template parameter name and value or values:

```
WebTarget myResource = client.target("http://example.com/webapi/read")
        .path("{userName}");
Response response = myResource.queryParam("userName", "janedoe")
        .request(...)
        .get();
```

30.1.1.4 Invoking the Request

After setting and applying any configuration options to the target, call one of the `WebTarget.request` methods to begin creating the request. This is usually accomplished by passing to `WebTarget.request` the accepted media response type for the request either as a string of the MIME type or using one of the constants in `javax.ws.rs.core.MediaType`. The `WebTarget.request` method returns an instance of `javax.ws.rs.client.Invocation.Builder`, a helper object that provides methods for preparing the client request:

```
Client client = ClientBuilder.newClient();
WebTarget myResource = client.target("http://example.com/webapi/read");
Invocation.Builder builder = myResource.request(MediaType.TEXT_PLAIN);
```

Using a MediaType constant is equivalent to using the string defining the MIME type:

```
Invocation.Builder builder = myResource.request("text/plain");
```

After setting the media type, invoke the request by calling one of the methods of the Invocation.Builder instance that corresponds to the type of HTTP request the target REST resource expects. These methods are:

- get()
- post()
- delete()
- put()
- head()
- options()

For example, if the target REST resource is for an HTTP GET request, call the Invocation.Builder.get method. The return type should correspond to the entity returned by the target REST resource:

```
Client client = ClientBuilder.newClient();
WebTarget myResource = client.target("http://example.com/webapi/read");
String response = myResource.request(MediaType.TEXT_PLAIN)
        .get(String.class);
```

If the target REST resource is expecting an HTTP POST request, call the Invocation.Builder.post method:

```
Client client = ClientBuilder.newClient();
StoreOrder order = new StoreOrder(...);
WebTarget myResource = client.target("http://example.com/webapi/write");
TrackingNumber trackingNumber = myResource.request(MediaType.APPLICATION_XML)
        .post(Entity.xml(order), TrackingNumber.class);
```

In the preceding example, the return type is a custom class and is retrieved by setting the type in the Invocation.Builder.post(Entity<?> entity, Class<T> responseType) method as a parameter.

If the return type is a collection, use javax.ws.rs.core.GenericType<T> as the response type parameter, where T is the collection type:

```
List<StoreOrder> orders = client.target("http://example.com/webapi/read")
        .path("allOrders")
        .request(MediaType.APPLICATION_XML)
        .get(new GenericType<List<StoreOrder>>() {});
```

This example shows how methods are chained together in the Client API to simplify how requests are configured and invoked.

30.2 Using the Client API in the JAX-RS Example Applications

The `rsvp` and `customer` examples use the Client API to call JAX-RS services. This section describes how each example application uses the Client API.

30.2.1 The Client API in the rsvp Example Application

The `rsvp` application allows users to respond to event invitations using JAX-RS resources, as explained in Section 29.3.2, "The rsvp Example Application." The web application uses the Client API in CDI backing beans to interact with the service resources, and the Facelets web interface displays the results.

The `StatusManager` CDI backing bean retrieves all the current events in the system. The client instance used in the backing bean is obtained in the constructor:

```
public StatusManager() {
    this.client = ClientBuilder.newClient();
}
```

The `StatusManager.getEvents` method returns a collection of all the current events in the system by calling the resource at `http://localhost:8080/rsvp/webapi/status/all`, which returns an XML document with entries for each event. The Client API automatically unmarshals the XML and creates a `List<Event>` instance:

```
public List<Event> getEvents() {
    List<Event> returnedEvents = null;
    try {
        returnedEvents = client.target(baseUri)
                .path("all")
                .request(MediaType.APPLICATION_XML)
                .get(new GenericType<List<Event>>() {
        });
        if (returnedEvents == null) {
            logger.log(Level.SEVERE, "Returned events null.");
        } else {
            logger.log(Level.INFO, "Events have been returned.");
        }
    } catch (WebApplicationException ex) {
        throw new WebApplicationException(Response.Status.NOT_FOUND);
    }
    ...
```

```
            return returnedEvents;
    }
```

The `StatusManager.changeStatus` method is used to update the attendee's response. It creates an HTTP POST request to the service with the new response. The body of the request is an XML document:

```
public String changeStatus(ResponseEnum userResponse,
            Person person, Event event) {
    String navigation;
    try {
        logger.log(Level.INFO,
                "changing status to {0} for {1} {2} for event ID {3}.",
                new Object[]{userResponse,
                    person.getFirstName(),
                    person.getLastName(),
                    event.getId().toString()});
        client.target(baseUri)
                .path(event.getId().toString())
                .path(person.getId().toString())
                .request(MediaType.APPLICATION_XML)
                .post(Entity.xml(userResponse.getLabel()));
        navigation = "changedStatus";
    } catch (ResponseProcessingException ex) {
        logger.log(Level.WARNING, "couldn''t change status for {0} {1}",
                new Object[]{person.getFirstName(),
                    person.getLastName()});
        logger.log(Level.WARNING, ex.getMessage());
        navigation = "error";
    }
    return navigation;
}
```

30.2.2 The Client API in the customer Example Application

The `customer` example application stores customer data in a database and exposes the resource as XML, as explained in Section 31.8, "The customer Example Application." The service resource exposes methods that create customers and retrieve all the customers. A Facelets web application acts as a client for the service resource, with a form for creating customers and displaying the list of customers in a table.

The `CustomerBean` stateless session bean uses the JAX-RS Client API to interface with the service resource. The `CustomerBean.createCustomer` method takes the `Customer` entity instance created by the Facelets form and makes a POST call to the service URI.

```
public String createCustomer(Customer customer) {
    if (customer == null) {
        logger.log(Level.WARNING, "customer is null.");
        return "customerError";
    }
    String navigation;
    Response response =
            client.target("http://localhost:8080/customer/webapi/Customer")
            .request(MediaType.APPLICATION_XML)
            .post(Entity.entity(customer, MediaType.APPLICATION_XML),
                    Response.class);
    if (response.getStatus() == Status.CREATED.getStatusCode()) {
        navigation = "customerCreated";
    } else {
        logger.log(Level.WARNING,
            "couldn''t create customer with id {0}. Status returned was {1}",
            new Object[]{customer.getId(), response.getStatus()});
        FacesContext context = FacesContext.getCurrentInstance();
        context.addMessage(null,
                new FacesMessage("Could not create customer."));
        navigation = "customerError";
    }
    return navigation;
}
```

The XML request entity is created by calling the `Invocation.Builder.post`
method, passing in a new `Entity` instance from the `Customer` instance, and
specifying the media type as `MediaType.APPLICATION_XML`.

The `CustomerBean.retrieveCustomer` method retrieves a `Customer` entity
instance from the service by appending the customer's ID to the service URI:

```
public String retrieveCustomer(String id) {
    String navigation;
    Customer customer =
            client.target("http://localhost:8080/customer/webapi/Customer")
            .path(id)
            .request(MediaType.APPLICATION_XML)
            .get(Customer.class);
    if (customer == null) {
        navigation = "customerError";
    } else {
        navigation = "customerRetrieved";
    }
    return navigation;
}
```

The `CustomerBean.retrieveAllCustomers` method retrieves a collection of customers as a `List<Customer>` instance. This list is then displayed as a table in the Facelets web application:

```java
public List<Customer> retrieveAllCustomers() {
    List<Customer> customers =
            client.target("http://localhost:8080/customer/webapi/Customer")
            .path("all")
            .request(MediaType.APPLICATION_XML)
            .get(new GenericType<List<Customer>>() {
            });
    return customers;
}
```

Because the response type is a collection, the `Invocation.Builder.get` method is called by passing in a new instance of `GenericType<List<Customer>>`.

30.3 Advanced Features of the Client API

This section describes some of the advanced features of the JAX-RS Client API.

30.3.1 Configuring the Client Request

Additional configuration options may be added to the client request after it is created but before it is invoked.

30.3.1.1 Setting Message Headers in the Client Request

You can set HTTP headers on the request by calling the `Invocation.Builder.header` method:

```java
Client client = ClientBuilder.newClient();
WebTarget myResource = client.target("http://example.com/webapi/read");
String response = myResource.request(MediaType.TEXT_PLAIN)
        .header("myHeader", "The header value")
        .get(String.class);
```

If you need to set multiple headers on the request, call the `Invocation.Builder.headers` method and pass in a `javax.ws.rs.core.MultivaluedMap` instance with the name-value pairs of the HTTP headers. Calling the `headers` method replaces all the existing headers with the headers supplied in the `MultivaluedMap` instance:

```java
Client client = ClientBuilder.newClient();
WebTarget myResource = client.target("http://example.com/webapi/read");
```

```
MultivaluedMap<String, Object> myHeaders =
    new MultivaluedMap<>("myHeader", "The header value");
myHeaders.add(...);
String response = myResource.request(MediaType.TEXT_PLAIN)
        .headers(myHeaders)
        .get(String.class);
```

The MultivaluedMap interface lets you specify multiple values for a given key:

```
MultivaluedMap<String, Object> myHeaders =
    new MultivaluedMap<String, Object>();
List<String> values = new ArrayList<>();
values.add(...);
myHeaders.add("myHeader", values);
```

30.3.1.2 Setting Cookies in the Client Request

You can add HTTP cookies to the request by calling the
Invocation.Builder.cookie method, which takes a name-value pair as
parameters:

```
Client client = ClientBuilder.newClient();
WebTarget myResource = client.target("http://example.com/webapi/read");
String response = myResource.request(MediaType.TEXT_PLAIN)
        .cookie("myCookie", "The cookie value")
        .get(String.class);
```

The javax.ws.rs.core.Cookie class encapsulates the attributes of an HTTP
cookie, including the name, value, path, domain, and RFC specification version of
the cookie. In the following example, the Cookie object is configured with a
name-value pair, a path, and a domain:

```
Client client = ClientBuilder.newClient();
WebTarget myResource = client.target("http://example.com/webapi/read");
Cookie myCookie = new Cookie("myCookie", "The cookie value",
    "/webapi/read", "example.com");
String response = myResource.request(MediaType.TEXT_PLAIN)
        .cookie(myCookie)
        .get(String.class);
```

30.3.1.3 Adding Filters to the Client

You can register custom filters with the client request or the response received
from the target resource. To register filter classes when the Client instance is
created, call the Client.register method:

```
Client client = ClientBuilder.newClient().register(MyLoggingFilter.class);
```

In the preceding example, all invocations that use this Client instance have the MyLoggingFilter filter registered with them.

You can also register the filter classes on the target by calling WebTarget.register:

```
Client client = ClientBuilder.newClient().register(MyLoggingFilter.class);
WebTarget target = client.target("http://example.com/webapi/secure")
        .register(MyAuthenticationFilter.class);
```

In the preceding example, both the MyLoggingFilter and MyAuthenticationFilter filters are attached to the invocation.

Request and response filter classes implement the javax.ws.rs.client.ClientRequestFilter and javax.ws.rs.client.ClientResponseFilter interfaces, respectively. Both of these interfaces define a single method, filter. All filters must be annotated with javax.ws.rs.ext.Provider.

The following class is a logging filter for both client requests and client responses:

```
@Provider
public class MyLoggingFilter implements ClientRequestFilter,
        ClientResponseFilter {
    static final Logger logger = Logger.getLogger(...);

    // implement the ClientRequestFilter.filter method
    @Override
    public void filter(ClientRequestContext requestContext)
            throws IOException {
        logger.log(...);
        ...
    }

    // implement the ClientResponseFilter.filter method
    @Override
    public void filter(ClientRequestContext requestContext,
            ClientResponseContext responseContext) throws IOException {
        logger.log(...);
        ...
    }
}
```

If the invocation must be stopped while the filter is active, call the context object's abortWith method, and pass in a javax.ws.rs.core.Response instance from within the filter.

```
@Override
public void filter(ClientRequestContext requestContext) throws IOException {
    ...
    Response response = new Response();
    response.status(500);
    requestContext.abortWith(response);
}
```

30.3.2 Asynchronous Invocations in the Client API

In networked applications, network issues can affect the perceived performance of the application, particularly in long-running or complicated network calls. Asynchronous processing helps prevent blocking and makes better use of an application's resources.

In the JAX-RS Client API, the `Invocation.Builder.async` method is used when constructing a client request to indicate that the call to the service should be performed asynchronously. An asynchronous invocation returns control to the caller immediately, with a return type of `java.util.concurrent.Future<T>` (part of the Java SE concurrency API) and with the type set to the return type of the service call. `Future<T>` objects have methods to check if the asynchronous call has been completed, to retrieve the final result, to cancel the invocation, and to check if the invocation has been cancelled.

The following example shows how to invoke an asynchronous request on a resource:

```
Client client = ClientBuilder.newClient();
WebTarget myResource = client.target("http://example.com/webapi/read");
Future<String> response = myResource.request(MediaType.TEXT_PLAIN)
        .async()
        .get(String.class);
```

30.3.2.1 Using Custom Callbacks in Asynchronous Invocations

The `InvocationCallback` interface defines two methods, `completed` and `failed`, that are called when an asynchronous invocation either completes successfully or fails, respectively. You may register an `InvocationCallback` instance on your request by creating a new instance when specifying the request method.

The following example shows how to register a callback object on an asynchronous invocation:

```
Client client = ClientBuilder.newClient();
WebTarget myResource = client.target("http://example.com/webapi/read");
```

```
Future<Customer> fCustomer = myResource.request(MediaType.TEXT_PLAIN)
    .async()
    .get(new InvocationCallback<Customer>() {
        @Override
        public void completed(Customer customer) {
        // Do something with the customer object
        }
        @Override
         public void failed(Throwable throwable) {
        // handle the error
        }
    });
```

JAX-RS: Advanced Topics and an Example

The Java API for RESTful Web Services (JAX-RS, defined in JSR 339) is designed to make it easy to develop applications that use the REST architecture. This chapter describes advanced features of JAX-RS. If you are new to JAX-RS, see Chapter 29, "Building RESTful Web Services with JAX-RS," before you proceed with this chapter.

JAX-RS is integrated with Contexts and Dependency Injection for Java EE (CDI), Enterprise JavaBeans (EJB) technology, and Java Servlet technology.

The following topics are addressed here:

- Annotations for Field and Bean Properties of Resource Classes

- Validating Resource Data with Bean Validation

- Subresources and Runtime Resource Resolution

- Integrating JAX-RS with EJB Technology and CDI

- Conditional HTTP Requests

- Runtime Content Negotiation

- Using JAX-RS with JAXB

- The customer Example Application

31.1 Annotations for Field and Bean Properties of Resource Classes

JAX-RS annotations for resource classes let you extract specific parts or values from a Uniform Resource Identifier (URI) or request header.

JAX-RS provides the annotations listed in Table 31–1.

Table 31–1   Advanced JAX-RS Annotations

Annotation	Description
@Context	Injects information into a class field, bean property, or method parameter
@CookieParam	Extracts information from cookies declared in the cookie request header
@FormParam	Extracts information from a request representation whose content type is application/x-www-form-urlencoded
@HeaderParam	Extracts the value of a header
@MatrixParam	Extracts the value of a URI matrix parameter
@PathParam	Extracts the value of a URI template parameter
@QueryParam	Extracts the value of a URI query parameter

31.1.1 Extracting Path Parameters

URI path templates are URIs with variables embedded within the URI syntax. The @PathParam annotation lets you use variable URI path fragments when you call a method.

The following code snippet shows how to extract the last name of an employee when the employee's email address is provided:

```
@Path("/employees/{firstname}.{lastname}@{domain}.com")
public class EmpResource {

  @GET
  @Produces("text/xml")
  public String getEmployeelastname(@PathParam("lastname") String lastName) {
    ...
  }
}
```

In this example, the @Path annotation defines the URI variables (or path parameters) {firstname}, {lastname}, and {domain}. The @PathParam in the method parameter of the request method extracts the last name from the email address.

If your HTTP request is `GET /employees/john.doe@example.com`, the value "doe" is injected into `{lastname}`.

You can specify several path parameters in one URI.

You can declare a regular expression with a URI variable. For example, if it is required that the last name must consist only of lowercase and uppercase characters, you can declare the following regular expression:

```
@Path("/employees/{firstname}.{lastname[a-zA-Z]*}@{domain}.com")
```

If the last name does not match the regular expression, a 404 response is returned.

31.1.2 Extracting Query Parameters

Use the `@QueryParam` annotation to extract query parameters from the query component of the request URI.

For instance, to query all employees who have joined within a specific range of years, use a method signature like the following:

```
@Path("/employees/")
@GET
public Response getEmployees(
        @DefaultValue("2003") @QueryParam("minyear") int minyear,
        @DefaultValue("2013") @QueryParam("maxyear") int maxyear) { ... }
```

This code snippet defines two query parameters, `minyear` and `maxyear`. The following HTTP request would query for all employees who have joined between 2003 and 2013:

```
GET /employees?maxyear=2013&minyear=2003
```

The `@DefaultValue` annotation defines a default value, which is to be used if no values are provided for the query parameters. By default, JAX-RS assigns a null value for `Object` values and zero for primitive data types. You can use the `@DefaultValue` annotation to eliminate null or zero values and define your own default values for a parameter.

31.1.3 Extracting Form Data

Use the `@FormParam` annotation to extract form parameters from HTML forms. For example, the following form accepts the name, address, and manager's name of an employee:

```
<FORM action="http://example.com/employees/" method="post">
  <p>
```

```
      <fieldset>
        Employee name: <INPUT type="text" name="empname" tabindex="1">
        Employee address: <INPUT type="text" name="empaddress" tabindex="2">
        Manager name: <INPUT type="text" name="managername" tabindex="3">
      </fieldset>
    </p>
</FORM>
```

Use the following code snippet to extract the manager name from this HTML form:

```
@POST
@Consumes("application/x-www-form-urlencoded")
public void post(@FormParam("managername") String managername) {
    // Store the value
    ...
}
```

To obtain a map of form parameter names to values, use a code snippet like the following:

```
@POST
@Consumes("application/x-www-form-urlencoded")
public void post(MultivaluedMap<String, String> formParams) {
    // Store the message
}
```

31.1.4 Extracting the Java Type of a Request or Response

The javax.ws.rs.core.Context annotation retrieves the Java types related to a request or response.

The javax.ws.rs.core.UriInfo interface provides information about the components of a request URI. The following code snippet shows how to obtain a map of query and path parameter names to values:

```
@GET
public String getParams(@Context UriInfo ui) {
    MultivaluedMap<String, String> queryParams = ui.getQueryParameters();
    MultivaluedMap<String, String> pathParams = ui.getPathParameters();
}
```

The javax.ws.rs.core.HttpHeaders interface provides information about request headers and cookies. The following code snippet shows how to obtain a map of header and cookie parameter names to values:

```
@GET
public String getHeaders(@Context HttpHeaders hh) {
```

```
MultivaluedMap<String, String> headerParams = hh.getRequestHeaders();
MultivaluedMap<String, Cookie> pathParams = hh.getCookies();
}
```

31.2 Validating Resource Data with Bean Validation

JAX-RS supports the Bean Validation to verify JAX-RS resource classes. This support consists of:

- Adding constraint annotations to resource method parameters
- Ensuring entity data is valid when the entity is passed in as a parameter

31.2.1 Using Constraint Annotations on Resource Methods

Bean Validation constraint annotations may be applied to parameters for a resource. The server will validate the parameters and either pass or throw a `javax.validation.ValidationException`:

```
@POST
@Path("/createUser")
@Consumes(MediaType.APPLICATION_FORM_URLENCODED)
public void createUser(@NotNull @FormParam("username") String username,
                       @NotNull @FormParam("firstName") String firstName,
                       @NotNull @FormParam("lastName") String lastName,
                       @Email @FormParam("email") String email) { ... }
```

In the preceding example, the built-in constraint `@NotNull` is applied to the username, firstName, and lastName form fields. The user-defined `@Email` constraint validates that the email address supplied by the email form field is correctly formatted.

The constraints may also be applied to fields within a resource class:

```
@Path("/createUser")
public class CreateUserResource {
  @NotNull
  @FormParam("username")
  private String username;

  @NotNull
  @FormParam("firstName")
  private String firstName;

  @NotNull
  @FormParam("lastName")
  private String lastName;
```

```
@Email
@FormParam("email")
private String email;
...
}
```

In the preceding example, the same constraints that were applied to the method parameters in the previous example are applied to the class fields. The behavior is the same in both examples.

Constraints may also be applied to a resource class's JavaBeans properties by adding the constraint annotations to the getter method:

```
@Path("/createuser")
public class CreateUserResource {
  private String username;

  @FormParam("username")
  public void setUsername(String username) {
    this.username = username;
  }

  @NotNull
  public String getUsername() {
    return username;
  }
  ...
}
```

Constraints may also be applied at the resource class level. In the following example, @PhoneRequired is a user-defined constraint that ensures that a user enters at least one phone number. That is, either homePhone or mobilePhone can be null, but not both:

```
@Path("/createUser")
@PhoneRequired
public class CreateUserResource {
  @FormParam("homePhone")
  private Phone homePhone;

  @FormParam("mobilePhone")
  private Phone mobilePhone;
  ...
}
```

31.2.2 Validating Entity Data

Classes that contain validation constraint annotations may be used in method parameters in a resource class. To validate these entity classes, use the `@Valid` annotation on the method parameter. For example, the following class is a user-defined class containing both standard and user-defined validation constraints:

```
@PhoneRequired
public class User {
  @NotNull
  private String username;

  private Phone homePhone;

  private Phone mobilePhone;
  ...
}
```

This entity class is used as a parameter to a resource method:

```
@Path("/createUser")
public class CreateUserResource {
  ...
  @POST
  @Consumers(MediaType.APPLICATION_XML)
  public void createUser(@Valid User user) { ... }
  ...
}
```

The `@Valid` annotation ensures that the entity class is validated at runtime. Additional user-defined constraints can also trigger validation of an entity:

```
@Path("/createUser")
public class CreateUserResource {
  ...
  @POST
  @Consumers(MediaType.APPLICATION_XML)
  public void createUser(@ActiveUser User user) { ... }
  ...
}
```

In the preceding example, the user-defined `@ActiveUser` constraint is applied to the `User` class in addition to the `@PhoneRequired` and `@NotNull` constraints defined within the entity class.

If a resource method returns an entity class, validation may be triggered by applying the @Valid or any other user-defined constraint annotation to the resource method:

```
@Path("/getUser")
public class GetUserResource {
  ...
  @GET
  @Path("{username}")
  @Produces(MediaType.APPLICATION_XML)
  @ActiveUser
  @Valid
  public User getUser(@PathParam("username") String username) {
    // find the User
    return user;
  }
  ...
}
```

As in the previous example, the @ActiveUser constraint is applied to the returned entity class as well as the @PhoneRequired and @NotNull constraints defined within the entity class.

31.2.3 Validation Exception Handling and Response Codes

If a javax.validation.ValidationException or any subclass of ValidationException except ConstraintValidationException is thrown, the JAX-RS runtime will respond to the client request with a 500 (Internal Server Error) HTTP status code.

If a ConstraintValidationException is thrown, the JAX-RS runtime will respond to the client with one of the following HTTP status codes:

- 500 (Internal Server Error) if the exception was thrown while validating a method return type
- 400 (Bad Request) in all other cases

31.3 Subresources and Runtime Resource Resolution

You can use a resource class to process only a part of the URI request. A root resource can then implement subresources that can process the remainder of the URI path.

A resource class method that is annotated with @Path is either a subresource method or a subresource locator.

- A subresource method is used to handle requests on a subresource of the corresponding resource.

- A subresource locator is used to locate subresources of the corresponding resource.

31.3.1 Subresource Methods

A **subresource method** handles an HTTP request directly. The method must be annotated with a request method designator, such as @GET or @POST, in addition to @Path. The method is invoked for request URIs that match a URI template created by concatenating the URI template of the resource class with the URI template of the method.

The following code snippet shows how a subresource method can be used to extract the last name of an employee when the employee's email address is provided:

```
@Path("/employeeinfo")
public class EmployeeInfo {

    public employeeinfo() {}

    @GET
    @Path("/employees/{firstname}.{lastname}@{domain}.com")
    @Produces("text/xml")
    public String getEmployeeLastName(
            @PathParam("lastname") String lastName) { ... }
}
```

The getEmployeeLastName method returns doe for the following GET request:

```
GET /employeeinfo/employees/john.doe@example.com
```

31.3.2 Subresource Locators

A **subresource locator** returns an object that will handle an HTTP request. The method must not be annotated with a request method designator. You must declare a subresource locator within a subresource class, and only subresource locators are used for runtime resource resolution.

The following code snippet shows a subresource locator:

```
// Root resource class
@Path("/employeeinfo")
public class EmployeeInfo {

    // Subresource locator: obtains the subresource Employee
    // from the path /employeeinfo/employees/{empid}
    @Path("/employees/{empid}")
    public Employee getEmployee(@PathParam("empid") String id) {
        // Find the Employee based on the id path parameter
        Employee emp = ...;
        ...
        return emp;
    }
}


// Subresource class
public class Employee {

    // Subresource method: returns the employee's last name
    @GET
    @Path("/lastname")
    public String getEmployeeLastName() {
        ...
        return lastName;
    }
}
```

In this code snippet, the getEmployee method is the subresource locator that provides the Employee object, which services requests for lastname.

If your HTTP request is GET /employeeinfo/employees/as209/, the getEmployee method returns an Employee object whose id is as209. At runtime, JAX-RS sends a GET /employeeinfo/employees/as209/lastname request to the getEmployeeLastName method. The getEmployeeLastName method retrieves and returns the last name of the employee whose id is as209.

31.4 Integrating JAX-RS with EJB Technology and CDI

JAX-RS works with Enterprise JavaBeans technology (enterprise beans) and Contexts and Dependency Injection for Java EE (CDI).

In general, for JAX-RS to work with enterprise beans, you need to annotate the class of a bean with @Path to convert it to a root resource class. You can use the @Path annotation with stateless session beans and singleton POJO beans.

The following code snippet shows a stateless session bean and a singleton bean that have been converted to JAX-RS root resource classes:

```
@Stateless
@Path("stateless-bean")
public class StatelessResource { ... }

@Singleton
@Path("singleton-bean")
public class SingletonResource { ... }
```

Session beans can also be used for subresources.

JAX-RS and CDI have slightly different component models. By default, JAX-RS root resource classes are managed in the request scope, and no annotations are required for specifying the scope. CDI managed beans annotated with @RequestScoped or @ApplicationScoped can be converted to JAX-RS resource classes.

The following code snippet shows a JAX-RS resource class:

```
@Path("/employee/{id}")
public class Employee {
    public Employee(@PathParam("id") String id) { ... }
}

@Path("{lastname}")
public final class EmpDetails { ... }
```

The following code snippet shows this JAX-RS resource class converted to a CDI bean. The beans must be proxyable, so the Employee class requires a nonprivate constructor with no parameters, and the EmpDetails class must not be final:

```
@Path("/employee/{id}")
@RequestScoped
public class Employee {
    public Employee() { ... }

    @Inject
    public Employee(@PathParam("id") String id) { ... }
}

@Path("{lastname}")
@RequestScoped
public class EmpDetails { ... }
```

31.5 Conditional HTTP Requests

JAX-RS provides support for conditional GET and PUT HTTP requests. Conditional GET requests help save bandwidth by improving the efficiency of client processing.

A GET request can return a Not Modified (304) response if the representation has not changed since the previous request. For example, a website can return 304 responses for all its static images that have not changed since the previous request.

A PUT request can return a Precondition Failed (412) response if the representation has been modified since the last request. The conditional PUT can help avoid the lost update problem.

Conditional HTTP requests can be used with the Last-Modified and ETag headers. The Last-Modified header can represent dates with granularity of one second.

In the following code snippet, the constructor of the Employee class computes the entity tag from the request URI and calls the request.evaluatePreconditions method with that tag. If a client request returns an If-none-match header with a value that has the same entity tag that was computed, evaluate.Preconditions returns a pre-filled-out response with a 304 status code and an entity tag set that may be built and returned:

```
@Path("/employee/{joiningdate}")
public class Employee {

    Date joiningdate;

    @GET
    @Produces("application/xml")
    public Employee(@PathParam("joiningdate") Date joiningdate,
                    @Context Request req,
                    @Context UriInfo ui) {

        this.joiningdate = joiningdate;
        ...
        this.tag = computeEntityTag(ui.getRequestUri());
        if (req.getMethod().equals("GET")) {
            Response.ResponseBuilder rb = req.evaluatePreconditions(tag);
            if (rb != null) {
                throw new WebApplicationException(rb.build());
            }
        }
    }
```

```
    }
}
```

31.6 Runtime Content Negotiation

The @Produces and @Consumes annotations handle static content negotiation in JAX-RS. These annotations specify the content preferences of the server. HTTP headers such as Accept, Content-Type, and Accept-Language define the content negotiation preferences of the client.

For more details on the HTTP headers for content negotiation, see HTTP /1.1 - Content Negotiation (http://www.w3.org/Protocols/rfc2616/rfc2616-sec12.html).

The following code snippet shows the server content preferences:

```
@Produces("text/plain")
@Path("/employee")
public class Employee {

    @GET
    public String getEmployeeAddressText(String address) { ... }

    @Produces("text/xml")
    @GET
    public String getEmployeeAddressXml(Address address) { ... }
```

The getEmployeeAddressText method is called for an HTTP request that looks like the following:

```
GET /employee
Accept: text/plain
```

This will produce the following response:

```
500 Oracle Parkway, Redwood Shores, CA
```

The getEmployeeAddressXml method is called for an HTTP request that looks like the following:

```
GET /employee
Accept: text/xml
```

This will produce the following response:

```
<address street="500 Oracle Parkway, Redwood Shores, CA" country="USA"/>
```

With static content negotiation, you can also define multiple content and media types for the client and server:

```
@Produces("text/plain", "text/xml")
```

In addition to supporting static content negotiation, JAX-RS also supports runtime content negotiation using the `javax.ws.rs.core.Variant` class and `Request` objects. The `Variant` class specifies the resource representation of content negotiation. Each instance of the `Variant` class may contain a media type, a language, and an encoding. The `Variant` object defines the resource representation that is supported by the server. The `Variant.VariantListBuilder` class is used to build a list of representation variants.

The following code snippet shows how to create a list of resource representation variants:

```
List<Variant> vs = Variant.mediatypes("application/xml", "application/json")
        .languages("en", "fr").build();
```

This code snippet calls the `build` method of the `VariantListBuilder` class. The `VariantListBuilder` class is invoked when you call the `mediatypes`, `languages`, or `encodings` methods. The `build` method builds a series of resource representations. The `Variant` list created by the `build` method has all possible combinations of items specified in the `mediatypes`, `languages`, and `encodings` methods.

In this example, the size of the `vs` object as defined in this code snippet is 4, and the contents are as follows:

```
[["application/xml","en"], ["application/json","en"],
    ["application/xml","fr"],["application/json","fr"]]
```

The `javax.ws.rs.core.Request.selectVariant` method accepts a list of `Variant` objects and chooses the `Variant` object that matches the HTTP request. This method compares its list of `Variant` objects with the `Accept`, `Accept-Encoding`, `Accept-Language`, and `Accept-Charset` headers of the HTTP request.

The following code snippet shows how to use the `selectVariant` method to select the most acceptable `Variant` from the values in the client request:

```
@GET
public Response get(@Context Request r) {
    List<Variant> vs = ...;
    Variant v = r.selectVariant(vs);
    if (v == null) {
        return Response.notAcceptable(vs).build();
    } else {
        Object rep = selectRepresentation(v);
```

```
        return Response.ok(rep, v);
    }
}
```

The selectVariant method returns the Variant object that matches the request or null if no matches are found. In this code snippet, if the method returns null, a Response object for a nonacceptable response is built. Otherwise, a Response object with an OK status and containing a representation in the form of an Object entity and a Variant is returned.

31.7 Using JAX-RS with JAXB

Java Architecture for XML Binding (JAXB) is an XML-to-Java binding technology that simplifies the development of web services by enabling transformations between schema and Java objects and between XML instance documents and Java object instances. An XML schema defines the data elements and structure of an XML document. You can use JAXB APIs and tools to establish mappings between Java classes and XML schema. JAXB technology provides the tools that enable you to convert your XML documents to and from Java objects.

By using JAXB, you can manipulate data objects in the following ways.

- You can start with an XML schema definition (XSD) and use xjc, the JAXB schema compiler tool, to create a set of JAXB-annotated Java classes that map to the elements and types defined in the XSD schema.

- You can start with a set of Java classes and use schemagen, the JAXB schema generator tool, to generate an XML schema.

- Once a mapping between the XML schema and the Java classes exists, you can use the JAXB binding runtime to marshal and unmarshal your XML documents to and from Java objects and use the resulting Java classes to assemble a web services application.

XML is a common media format that RESTful services consume and produce. To deserialize and serialize XML, you can represent requests and responses by JAXB annotated objects. Your JAX-RS application can use the JAXB objects to manipulate XML data. JAXB objects can be used as request entity parameters and response entities. The JAX-RS runtime environment includes standard MessageBodyReader and MessageBodyWriter provider interfaces for reading and writing JAXB objects as entities.

With JAX-RS, you enable access to your services by publishing resources. Resources are just simple Java classes with some additional JAX-RS annotations. These annotations express the following:

- The path of the resource (the URL you use to access it)

- The HTTP method you use to call a certain method (for example, the GET or POST method)

- The MIME type with which a method accepts or responds

As you define the resources for your application, consider the type of data you want to expose. You may already have a relational database that contains information you want to expose to users, or you may have static content that does not reside in a database but does need to be distributed as resources. Using JAX-RS, you can distribute content from multiple sources. RESTful web services can use various types of input/output formats for request and response. The customer example, described in Section 31.8, "The customer Example Application," uses XML.

Resources have representations. A resource representation is the content in the HTTP message that is sent to, or returned from, the resource using the URI. Each representation a resource supports has a corresponding media type. For example, if a resource is going to return content formatted as XML, you can use application/xml as the associated media type in the HTTP message.Depending on the requirements of your application, resources can return representations in a preferred single format or in multiple formats. JAX-RS provides @Consumes and @Produces annotations to declare the media types that are acceptable for a resource method to read and write.

JAX-RS also maps Java types to and from resource representations using entity providers. A MessageBodyReader entity provider reads a request entity and deserializes the request entity into a Java type. A MessageBodyWriter entity provider serializes from a Java type into a response entity. For example, if a String value is used as the request entity parameter, the MessageBodyReader entity provider deserializes the request body into a new String. If a JAXB type is used as the return type on a resource method, the MessageBodyWriter serializes the JAXB object into a response body.

By default, the JAX-RS runtime environment attempts to create and use a default JAXBContext class for JAXB classes.However, if the default JAXBContext class is not suitable, then you can supply a JAXBContext class for the application using a JAX-RS ContextResolver provider interface.

The following sections explain how to use JAXB with JAX-RS resource methods.

31.7.1 Using Java Objects to Model Your Data

If you do not have an XML schema definition for the data you want to expose, you can model your data as Java classes, add JAXB annotations to these classes, and use JAXB to generate an XML schema for your data. For example, if the data you want to expose is a collection of products and each product has an ID, a name, a description, and a price, you can model it as a Java class as follows:

```
@XmlRootElement(name="product")
@XmlAccessorType(XmlAccessType.FIELD)
public class Product {

    @XmlElement(required=true)
    protected int id;
    @XmlElement(required=true)
    protected String name;
    @XmlElement(required=true)
    protected String description;
    @XmlElement(required=true)
    protected int price;

    public Product() {}

    // Getter and setter methods
    // ...
}
```

Run the JAXB schema generator on the command line to generate the corresponding XML schema definition:

```
schemagen Product.java
```

This command produces the XML schema as an .xsd file:

```
<?xml version="1.0" encoding="UTF-8" standalone="yes"?>
<xs:schema version="1.0" xmlns:xs="http://www.w3.org/2001/XMLSchema">

    <xs:element name="product" type="product"/>

    <xs:complexType name="product">
      <xs:sequence>
        <xs:element name="id" type="xs:int"/>
        <xs:element name="name" type="xs:string"/>
        <xs:element name="description" type="xs:string"/>
        <xs:element name="price" type="xs:int"/>
      </xs:sequence>
    <xs:complexType>
</xs:schema>
```

Once you have this mapping, you can create `Product` objects in your application, return them, and use them as parameters in JAX-RS resource methods. The JAX-RS runtime uses JAXB to convert the XML data from the request into a `Product` object and to convert a `Product` object into XML data for the response. The following resource class provides a simple example:

```
@Path("/product")
public class ProductService {
    @GET
    @Path("/get")
    @Produces("application/xml")
    public Product getProduct() {
        Product prod = new Product();
        prod.setId(1);
        prod.setName("Mattress");
        prod.setDescription("Queen size mattress");
        prod.setPrice(500);
        return prod;
    }

    @POST
    @Path("/create")
    @Consumes("application/xml")
    public Response createProduct(Product prod) {
        // Process or store the product and return a response
        // ...
    }
}
```

Some IDEs, such as NetBeans IDE, will run the schema generator tool automatically during the build process if you add Java classes that have JAXB annotations to your project. For a detailed example, see Section 31.8, "The customer Example Application." The customer example contains a more complex relationship between the Java classes that model the data, which results in a more hierarchical XML representation.

31.7.2 Starting from an Existing XML Schema Definition

If you already have an XML schema definition in an `.xsd` file for the data you want to expose, use the JAXB schema compiler tool. Consider this simple example of an `.xsd` file:

```
<xs:schema targetNamespace="http://xml.product"
           xmlns:xs="http://www.w3.org/2001/XMLSchema"
           elementFormDefault="qualified"
           xmlns:myco="http://xml.product">
```

```
<xs:element name="product" type="myco:Product"/>
<xs:complexType name="Product">
  <xs:sequence>
    <xs:element name="id" type="xs:int"/>
    <xs:element name="name" type="xs:string"/>
    <xs:element name="description" type="xs:string"/>
    <xs:element name="price" type="xs:int"/>
  </xs:sequence>
</xs:complexType>
</xs:schema>
```

Run the schema compiler tool on the command line as follows:

```
xjc Product.xsd
```

This command generates the source code for Java classes that correspond to the types defined in the .xsd file. The schema compiler tool generates a Java class for each complexType defined in the .xsd file. The fields of each generated Java class are the same as the elements inside the corresponding complexType, and the class contains getter and setter methods for these fields.

In this case, the schema compiler tool generates the classes product.xml.Product and product.xml.ObjectFactory. The Product class contains JAXB annotations, and its fields correspond to those in the .xsd definition:

```
@XmlAccessorType(XmlAccessType.FIELD)
@XmlType(name = "Product", propOrder = {
    "id",
    "name",
    "description",
    "price"
})
public class Product {
    protected int id;
    @XmlElement(required = true)
    protected String name;
    @XmlElement(required = true)
    protected String description;
    protected int price;

    // Setter and getter methods
    // ...
}
```

You can create instances of the Product class from your application (for example, from a database). The generated class product.xml.ObjectFactory contains a method that allows you to convert these objects to JAXB elements that can be returned as XML inside JAX-RS resource methods:

```
@XmlElementDecl(namespace = "http://xml.product", name = "product")
public JAXBElement<Product> createProduct(Product value) {
  return new JAXBElement<Product>(_Product_QNAME, Product.class, null, value);
}
```

The following code shows how to use the generated classes to return a JAXB element as XML in a JAX-RS resource method:

```
@Path("/product")
public class ProductService {
    @GET
    @Path("/get")
    @Produces("application/xml")
    public JAXBElement<Product> getProduct() {
        Product prod = new Product();
        prod.setId(1);
        prod.setName("Mattress");
        prod.setDescription("Queen size mattress");
        prod.setPrice(500);
        return new ObjectFactory().createProduct(prod);
    }
}
```

For @POST and @PUT resource methods, you can use a Product object directly as a parameter. JAX-RS maps the XML data from the request into a Product object:

```
@Path("/product")
public class ProductService {
    @GET
    // ...

    @POST
    @Path("/create")
    @Consumes("application/xml")
    public Response createProduct(Product prod) {
        // Process or store the product and return a response
        // ...
    }
}
```

31.7.3 Using JSON with JAX-RS and JAXB

JAX-RS can automatically read and write XML using JAXB, but it can also work with JSON data. JSON is a simple text-based format for data exchange derived from JavaScript. For the preceding examples, the XML representation of a product is as follows:

```
<?xml version="1.0" encoding="UTF-8"?>
<product>
  <id>1</id>
  <name>Mattress</name>
  <description>Queen size mattress</description>
  <price>500</price>
</product>
```

The equivalent JSON representation is as follows:

```
{
    "id":"1",
    "name":"Mattress",
    "description":"Queen size mattress",
    "price":500
}
```

You can add the format `application/json` or `MediaType.APPLICATION_JSON` to the `@Produces` annotation in resource methods to produce responses with JSON data:

```
@GET
@Path("/get")
@Produces({"application/xml","application/json"})
public Product getProduct() { ... }
```

In this example, the default response is XML, but the response is a JSON object if the client makes a GET request that includes this header:

```
Accept: application/json
```

The resource methods can also accept JSON data for JAXB annotated classes:

```
@POST
@Path("/create")
@Consumes({"application/xml","application/json"})
public Response createProduct(Product prod) { ... }
```

The client should include the following header when submitting JSON data with a POST request:

```
Content-Type: application/json
```

31.8 The customer Example Application

This section describes how to build and run the `customer` example application. This application is a RESTful web service that uses JAXB to perform the create, read, update, delete (CRUD) operations for a specific entity.

The `customer` sample application is in the *tut-install*/`examples/jaxrs/customer/` directory. See Chapter 2, "Using the Tutorial Examples," for basic information on building and running sample applications.

31.8.1 Overview of the customer Example Application

The source files of this application are at *tut-install*/`examples/jaxrs/customer/` `src/main/java/`. The application has three parts.

- The `Customer` and `Address` entity classes. These classes model the data of the application and contain JAXB annotations.

- The `CustomerService` resource class. This class contains JAX-RS resource methods that perform operations on `Customer` instances represented as XML or JSON data using JAXB. See Section 31.8.3, "The CustomerService Class," for details.

- The `CustomerBean` session bean that acts as a backing bean for the web client. `CustomerBean` uses the JAX-RS client API to call the methods of `CustomerService`.

The `customer` example application shows you how to model your data entities as Java classes with JAXB annotations.

31.8.2 The Customer and Address Entity Classes

The following class represents a customer's address:

```
@Entity
@Table(name="CUSTOMER_ADDRESS")
@XmlRootElement(name="address")
@XmlAccessorType(XmlAccessType.FIELD)
public class Address {
    @Id
    @GeneratedValue(strategy = GenerationType.AUTO)
    private Long id;
    @XmlElement(required=true)
    protected int number;

    @XmlElement(required=true)
    protected String street;
```

```
@XmlElement(required=true)
protected String city;

@XmlElement(required=true)
protected String province;

@XmlElement(required=true)
protected String zip;

@XmlElement(required=true)
protected String country;

public Address() { }

// Getter and setter methods
// ...
}
```

The @XmlRootElement(name="address") annotation maps this class to the
address XML element. The @XmlAccessorType(XmlAccessType.FIELD)
annotation specifies that all the fields of this class are bound to XML by default.
The @XmlElement(required=true) annotation specifies that an element must be
present in the XML representation.

The following class represents a customer:

```
@Entity
@Table(name="CUSTOMER_CUSTOMER")
@NamedQuery(
    name="findAllCustomers",
    query="SELECT c FROM Customer c " +
          "ORDER BY c.id"
)
@XmlRootElement(name="customer")
@XmlAccessorType(XmlAccessType.FIELD)
public class Customer {
    @Id
    @GeneratedValue(strategy = GenerationType.AUTO)
    @XmlAttribute(required=true)
    protected int id;

    @XmlElement(required=true)
    protected String firstname;

    @XmlElement(required=true)
    protected String lastname;
```

```
@XmlElement(required=true)
@OneToOne
protected Address address;

@XmlElement(required=true)
protected String email;

@XmlElement (required=true)
protected String phone;

public Customer() { ... }

// Getter and setter methods
// ...
}
```

The Customer class contains the same JAXB annotations as the previous class, except for the @XmlAttribute(required=true) annotation, which maps a property to an attribute of the XML element representing the class.

The Customer class contains a property whose type is another entity, the Address class. This mechanism allows you to define in Java code the hierarchical relationships between entities without having to write an .xsd file yourself.

JAXB generates the following XML schema definition for the two preceding classes:

```
<?xml version="1.0" encoding="UTF-8" standalone="yes"?>
<xs:schema version="1.0" xmlns:xs="http://www.w3.org/2001/XMLSchema">

  <xs:element name="address" type="address"/>
  <xs:element name="customer" type="customer"/>

  <xs:complexType name="address">
    <xs:sequence>
      <xs:element name="id" type="xs:long" minOccurs="0"/>
      <xs:element name="number" type="xs:int"/>
      <xs:element name="street" type="xs:string"/>
      <xs:element name="city" type="xs:string"/>
      <xs:element name="province" type="xs:string"/>
      <xs:element name="zip" type="xs:string"/>
      <xs:element name="country" type="xs:string"/>
    </xs:sequence>
  </xs:complexType>

  <xs:complexType name="customer">
    <xs:sequence>
```

```
        <xs:element name="firstname" type="xs:string"/>
        <xs:element name="lastname" type="xs:string"/>
        <xs:element ref="address"/>
        <xs:element name="email" type="xs:string"/>
        <xs:element name="phone" type="xs:string"/>
    </xs:sequence>
    <xs:attribute name="id" type="xs:int" use="required"/>
  </xs:complexType>
</xs:schema>
```

31.8.3 The CustomerService Class

The CustomerService class has a createCustomer method that creates a customer resource based on the Customer class and returns a URI for the new resource:

```java
@Stateless
@Path("/Customer")
public class CustomerService {
    public static final Logger logger =
            Logger.getLogger(CustomerService.class.getCanonicalName());
    @PersistenceContext
    private EntityManager em;
    private CriteriaBuilder cb;

    @PostConstruct
    private void init() {
        cb = em.getCriteriaBuilder();
    }
    ...
    @POST
    @Consumes({MediaType.APPLICATION_XML, MediaType.APPLICATION_JSON})
    public Response createCustomer(Customer customer) {

        try {
            long customerId = persist(customer);
            return Response.created(URI.create("/" + customerId)).build();
        } catch (Exception e) {
            logger.log(Level.SEVERE,
                    "Error creating customer for customerId {0}. {1}",
                    new Object[]{customer.getId(), e.getMessage()});

            throw new WebApplicationException(e,
                    Response.Status.INTERNAL_SERVER_ERROR);
        }
    }
    ...
```

```
private long persist(Customer customer) {
    try {
        Address address = customer.getAddress();
        em.persist(address);
        em.persist(customer);
    } catch (Exception ex) {
      logger.warning("Something went wrong when persisting the customer");
    }
    return customer.getId();
}
```

The response returned to the client has a URI to the newly created resource. The return type is an entity body mapped from the property of the response with the status code specified by the status property of the response. The WebApplicationException is a RuntimeException that is used to wrap the appropriate HTTP error status code, such as 404, 406, 415, or 500.

The @Consumes({MediaType.APPLICATION_XML, MediaType.APPLICATION_JSON}) and @Produces({MediaType.APPLICATION_XML, MediaType.APPLICATION_JSON}) annotations set the request and response media types to use the appropriate MIME client. These annotations can be applied to a resource method, a resource class, or even an entity provider. If you do not use these annotations, JAX-RS allows the use of any media type ("*/*").

The following code snippet shows the implementation of the getCustomer and findbyId methods. The getCustomer method uses the @Produces annotation and returns a Customer object, which is converted to an XML or JSON representation depending on the Accept: header specified by the client:

```
@GET
@Path("{id}")
@Produces({MediaType.APPLICATION_XML, MediaType.APPLICATION_JSON})
public Customer getCustomer(@PathParam("id") String customerId) {
    Customer customer = null;

    try {
        customer = findById(customerId);
    } catch (Exception ex) {
        logger.log(Level.SEVERE,
                "Error calling findCustomer() for customerId {0}. {1}",
                new Object[]{customerId, ex.getMessage()});
    }
    return customer;
}
...
private Customer findById(String customerId) {
    Customer customer = null;
```

```
        try {
            customer = em.find(Customer.class, customerId);
            return customer;
        } catch (Exception ex) {
            logger.log(Level.WARNING,
                    "Couldn't find customer with ID of {0}", customerId);
        }
        return customer;
    }
```

31.8.4 Using the JAX-RS Client in the CustomerBean Classes

Use the JAX-RS Client API to write a client for the customer example application.

The CustomerBean enterprise bean class calls the JAX-RS Client API to test the CustomerService web service:

```
@Named
@Stateless
public class CustomerBean {
    protected Client client;
    private static final Logger logger =
            Logger.getLogger(CustomerBean.class.getName());

    @PostConstruct
    private void init() {
        client = ClientBuilder.newClient();
    }

    @PreDestroy
    private void clean() {
        client.close();
    }

    public String createCustomer(Customer customer) {
        if (customer == null) {
            logger.log(Level.WARNING, "customer is null.");
            return "customerError";
        }
        String navigation;
        Response response =
                client.target("http://localhost:8080/customer/webapi/Customer")
                .request(MediaType.APPLICATION_XML)
                .post(Entity.entity(customer, MediaType.APPLICATION_XML),
                        Response.class);
        if (response.getStatus() == Status.CREATED.getStatusCode()) {
            navigation = "customerCreated";
```

```
        } else {
            logger.log(Level.WARNING, "couldn''t create customer with " +
                    "id {0}. Status returned was {1}",
                    new Object[]{customer.getId(), response.getStatus()});
            navigation = "customerError";
        }
        return navigation;
    }

    public String retrieveCustomer(String id) {
        String navigation;
        Customer customer =
                client.target("http://localhost:8080/customer/webapi/Customer")
                .path(id)
                .request(MediaType.APPLICATION_XML)
                .get(Customer.class);
        if (customer == null) {
            navigation = "customerError";
        } else {
            navigation = "customerRetrieved";
        }
        return navigation;
    }

    public List<Customer> retrieveAllCustomers() {
        List<Customer> customers =
                client.target("http://localhost:8080/customer/webapi/Customer")
                .path("all")
                .request(MediaType.APPLICATION_XML)
                .get(new GenericType<List<Customer>>() {});
        return customers;
    }
}
```

This client uses the POST and GET methods.

All of these HTTP status codes indicate success: 201 for POST, 200 for GET, and 204 for DELETE. For details about the meanings of HTTP status codes, see http://www.w3.org/Protocols/rfc2616/rfc2616-sec10.html.

31.8.5 Running the customer Example

You can use either NetBeans IDE or Maven to build, package, deploy, and run the customer application.

31.8.5.1 To Build, Package, and Deploy the customer Example Using NetBeans IDE

1. Make sure that GlassFish Server has been started (see Section 2.2, "Starting and Stopping GlassFish Server").

2. From the **File** menu, choose **Open Project**.

3. In the Open Project dialog box, navigate to:

   tut-install/examples/jaxrs

4. Select the `customer` folder.

5. Click **Open Project**.

6. In the **Projects** tab, right-click the `customer` project and select **Build**.

   This command builds and packages the application into a WAR file, `customer.war`, located in the `target` directory. Then, the WAR file is deployed to GlassFish Server.

7. Open the web client in a browser at the following URL:

   `http://localhost:8080/customer/`

   The web client allows you to create and view customers.

31.8.5.2 To Build, Package, and Deploy the customer Example Using Maven

1. Make sure that GlassFish Server has been started (see Section 2.2, "Starting and Stopping GlassFish Server").

2. In a terminal window, go to:

   tut-install/examples/jaxrs/customer/

3. Enter the following command:

   `mvn install`

   This command builds and packages the application into a WAR file, `customer.war`, located in the `target` directory. Then, the WAR file is deployed to GlassFish Server.

4. Open the web client in a browser at the following URL:

   `http://localhost:8080/customer/`

   The web client allows you to create and view customers.

Index

sessions, 365
  associating attributes, 366
  associating with user, 367
  invalidating, 366
  notifying objects associated with, 366
SingleThreadModel interface, 355
SOAP, 541, 545, 558
SOAP messages, 16, 33
SOAP with Attachments API for Java (SAAJ), 33
specialization, CDI, 496
SQL, 30
standard converters, 97
  converter tags, 200
  NumberConverter class, 199
  using, 198
standard validators, 99
  using, 207
stereotypes, CDI, 507
subresources, JAX-RS, 604
substitution parameters, defining. *See* messages, param tag

T

templating
  Facelets, 121

U

UI component behavioral interfaces, 94
  ActionSource interface, 94, 98, 269, 281
  ActionSource2 interface, 94, 269
  ClientBehaviorHolder interface, 95
  ConvertibleValueHolder interface, 95
  EditableValueHolder interface, 95, 269
  NamingContainer interface, 95, 269
  StateHolder interface, 95, 270, 277
  SystemEventListenerHolder interface, 95
  ValueHolder interface, 95, 270
UI component classes, 93, 95, 259
  javax.faces.component package, 269
  UIColumn class, 93
  UICommand class, 93, 96
  UIComponent class, 93, 96
  UIComponentBase class, 93, 269, 272
  UIData class, 93, 219
  UIForm class, 93

UIGraphic class, 94
UIInput and UIOutput classes, 218
UIInput class, 94, 98
UIMessage class, 94
UIMessages class, 94
UIOutcomeTarget class, 94
UIOutput class, 94, 97
UIPanel class, 94
UIParameter class, 94
UISelectBoolean class, 94, 220
UISelectItem class, 94, 223
UISelectItems class, 94, 223
UISelectMany class, 94, 221
UISelectOne class, 94, 96, 222
UIViewRoot class, 94
  See also custom UI components
UnavailableException class, 356
undeploying modules and applications, 77
Unicode character set, 442
unified expression language. *See* EL
Uniform Resource Identifiers (URIs), 559
URI path parameters, JAX-RS, 575
URI path templates, JAX-RS, 564
URL paths, 77
URLs, mapping, 577
US-ASCII character set, 442
using pages, 126
UTF-8 character encoding, 442

V

validating input. *See* Bean Validation, validation model
validation, 447
  customizing, 455
  groups, 457
  localization, 457
  messages, 457
  ordering, 458
validation model, 93, 99
  referencing a method that performs validation, 211
  validator attribute, 168, 210, 211, 229
  Validator implementation, 99, 297
  Validator interface, 99, 226, 229
    custom validator tags, 296
    implementing, 294

X

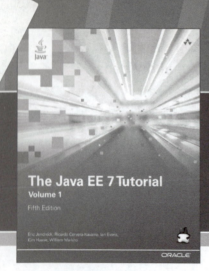

FREE Online Edition

Your purchase of *The Java EE 7 Tutorial, Volume 1*, includes access to a free online edition for 45 days through the **Safari Books Online** subscription service. Nearly every Addison-Wesley Professional book is available online through **Safari Books Online**, along with thousands of books and videos from publishers such as Cisco Press, Exam Cram, IBM Press, O'Reilly Media, Prentice Hall, Que, Sams, and VMware Press.

Safari Books Online is a digital library providing searchable, on-demand access to thousands of technology, digital media, and professional development books and videos from leading publishers. With one monthly or yearly subscription price, you get unlimited access to learning tools and information on topics including mobile app and software development, tips and tricks on using your favorite gadgets, networking, project management, graphic design, and much more.

Activate your FREE Online Edition at
informit.com/safarifree

STEP 1:   Enter the coupon code: QUVZGAA.

STEP 2:   New Safari users, complete the brief registration form.
            Safari subscribers, just log in.

If you have difficulty registering on Safari or accessing the online edition,
please e-mail customer-service@safaribooksonline.com